THE NEW WEBSTER'S THESAURUS

THE NEW WEBSTER'S
THESAURUS
VEST POCKET
EDITION

Prepared by

Donald O. Bolander, M.A., Litt. D.
Jean A. McCormick Vreeland, M. Ed.

LEXICON PUBLICATIONS, INC.

ISBN: 0-7172-4504-7

A

abandon, abdicate, discontinue, relinquish, resign, surrender, vacate, desert, forsake, leave, quit. ANT.—defend, maintain, occupy, stay, support.

abase, degrade, disgrace, mock, shame. ANT.—dignify, elevate, honor, praise.

abate, assuage, decrease, diminish, lessen, lower, mitigate, moderate, reduce, suppress. ANT.—enlarge, increase, intensify, prolong, revive.

abbreviate, abridge, condense, contract, curtail, lessen, limit, reduce, shorten. ANT.—enlarge, expand, extend, lengthen.

abbreviation, abridgement, contraction, curtailment, reduction, shortening. ANT.—enlargement, expansion, extension.

abdicate, abandon, relinquish, renounce, resign, surrender, vacate; desert, forsake, leave, quit. ANT.—defend, maintain, retain, stay.

aberrant, abnormal, deviate, eccentric, peculiar, unnatural, unusual, variable. ANT.—normal, ordinary, regular, usual.

abet, aid, assist, encourage, help, incite, stimulate. ANT.—deter, discourage, hinder, oppose, resist.

abeyance, adjournment, inaction, reservation, suspension. ANT.—action, enforcement, renewal, revival.

abhor, despise, detest, dislike, execrate, hate, loathe. ANT.—admire, desire, esteem, like, relish.

ability, aptitude, aptness, capability, capacity, dexterity, efficiency, faculty, knowledge, power, skill, talent. ANT.—incapacity, incompetency, stupidity.

abnormal, aberrant, erratic, irregular, odd, unnatural, unusual. ANT.—normal, usual, standard.

abode, domicile, dwelling, habitation, house, home, quarters, residence.

abolish, end, eradicate, throw out; abrogate, annul, cancel, invalidate, nullify, revoke. ANT.—confirm, continue, establish, institute, legalize, restore.

abominable, detestable, foul, hateful, horrible, loathsome, odious, repugnant, revolting, vile. ANT.—agreeable, enjoyable, delightful, pleasant.

abominate, abhor, despise, detest, dislike, hate, loathe. ANT.—admire, approve, cherish, like, love.

abrupt, hasty, impetuous, precipitate, quick, sudden; blunt, brusque, curt, rude, short; craggy, precipitous, rugged, sharp, steep. ANT.—anticipated, expected; courteous, gradual, smooth.

absent, away, departed, missing; absent-minded, abstracted, distracted, preoccupied. ANT.—attending, here, present; attentive.

absolute, complete, entire, infinite, perfect, pure, total, ultimate, unconditional; arbitrary, autocratic, despotic, supreme, tyrannous, unrestricted. ANT.— accountable, conditional, contingent, dependent, limited.

absolve, acquit, clear, discharge, exonerate, pardon, release. ANT.—accuse, bind, blame, charge, convict, incriminate.

absorb, assimilate, consume, engulf, imbibe, incorporate, merge, swallow; engage, engross. ANT.—discharge, dispense, eject, emit, exude.

abstinence, abstention, continence, fasting, moderation, self-denia
self-restraint, sobriety, temperance. ANT.—excess, gluttonny, greed, intemperance, self-indulgence.**abstract,** detach, excerpt, remove, select, separate; appropriate, steal; abridge, summarize. ANT.—add, combine, insert, replace, return, unite.

abstracted, appropriated, drawn from, parted, removed, separated, stolen; abridged, summarized. ANT.—added, combined, replaced, returned, united.

absurd, foolish, inconsistent, irrational, ludicrous, nonsensical, preposterous, ridiculous, self-contradictory, senseless, unreasonable. ANT.—logical, rational, reasonable, sensible, sound.

abundant, bountiful, copious, lavish, opulent, plentiful, profuse, rich. ANT.—insufficient, rare, scant, scarce.

abuse, damage, desecrate, dishonor, disparage, insult, mal-treat, molest, oppress, persecute, revile, upbraid. ANT.—approve, commend, laud, protect, respect, shield.

abuse, asperse, defame, disparage, harm, ill-use, malign, persecute, vilify; misuse. ANT.—cherish, favor, honor, praise, protect, respect, sustain.

academic, bookish, erudite, formal, learned, literary, pedantic, scholarly, theoretical. ANT.—common-sense, ignorant, practical, simple.

accede, agree, assent, consent. ANT.—dissent, protest, refuse.

accelerate, dispatch, expedite, facilitate, forward, hasten, hurry, push, quicken, rush, speed up. ANT.—block, hinder, impede, obstruct, resist, retard, slow.

accident, calamity, casualty, chance, diaster, happening, misfortune, mishap. ANT.—calculation, design, intention, plan, purpose.

accentuate, emphasize, exaggerate, heighten, intensify, stress, underline. ANT.—minimize, moderate, subdue.

acclaim, applaud, cheer, extol. honor, glorify, laud. ANT.—berate, dishonor, jear, revile.

accommodate, adapt, adjust, arrange, conform, harmonize, oblige, serve, supply. ANT.—embarass, disarrange, obstruct, prevent.

accompany, attend, chaperon, conduct, convoy, escort, follow, join. ANT.—desert, leave.

accomplice, abettor, accessory, ally, assistant, associate, confederate. ANT.—adversary, enemy, opponent, rival.

accomplish, achieve, attain, complete, consummate, do, effect, execute, finish, fulfill, manage, perform. ANT.—block, defeat, fail, frustrate, spoil.

accord, agree, allow, assent, concede, grant, permit; agreement, acquiesment, harmony, reconciliation, unison. ANT.—contend, disallow, dispute, question; dissension, opposition, strife.

accost, address, approach, greet, solicit, speak to. ANT.—avoid, evade, pass by.

account, chronicle, description, detail, history, narrative, recital, computation, reckoning, record, statement.

accrue, accumulate, amass, collect, gather, grow, increase, store. ANT.—diminish, disperse, dissipate.

accumulate, accrue, amass, assemble, collect, gather, hoard, increase, pile, store. ANT.—diminish, disperse, dissipate, spend, waste.

accuse, blame, censure, charge, denounce, incriminate, indict. ANT.—absolve, acquit, exonerate, vindicate.

achieve, accomplish, do, effect, execute, fulfill, gain, realize, win. ANT.—abandon, fail, lose, miss.

achievement, deed, exploit, feat, performance; accomplishment, attainment, execution, realiza-

tion, ANT.—neglect, omission: defeat, failure, misfortune.

acquaintance, cognizance, companionship, experience, familiarity, friendship, intimacy, knowledge. ANT.—ignorance, inexperience, unfamiliarity.

acquire, attain, collect, earn, get, obtain, procure, reach, secure, win. ANT.—fail, forego, lose, miss, surrender.

act, accomplishment, action, deed, do, doing, enact, execute. feat, operation, perform, transaction; decree, edict, law, statute. ANT.—abstain, cease, discontinue, stop.

action, achievement, activity, battle, deed, exploit, motion, movement, performance. ANT.—idleness, inactivity, inertia, repose.

active, operative, working; busy, industrious; agile, alert, brisk, energetic, lively, mobile, nimble, quick, sprightly. ANT.—dormant, inactive; idle, indolent, passive.

activity, action, agility, alertness, briskness, energy, enterprise, exercise, intensity, liveliness, motion, progress, quickness, rapidity. ANT.—dullness, idleness, inactivity, inertia.

actuality, certainty, fact, reality, truth; act, circumstance, deed, event, factual, incident, occurrence, sure. ANT.—delusion, fiction, supposition, theory, unreal.

adapt, accommodate, adjust, conform, modify, fit. ANT.—derange, misapply, misfit.

add, adjoin, affix, annex, append, attach, augment, increase. ANT.—deduct, detach, reduce, remove, subtract, withdraw.

address, accost, approach, greet, hail, salute, speak to. ANT.—avoid, ignore, pass by.

adequate, ample, capable, commensurate, enough, fitting, qualified, satisfactory, sufficient, suitable. ANT.—deficient, insufficient, lacking, scant.

adhere, attach, clasp, cleave, cling, fasten, grasp, grip; have, hold, keep, maintain, occupy, possess, retain, support; check, confine, accommodate, carry, contain. ANT.—leave, loosen, unfasten.

adjacent, abuting, adjoining, beside, bordering, close, near, next, neighboring. ANT.—away from, beyond, distant, disconnected, separate.

admire, appreciate, approve, esteem, praise, respect, venerate. ANT.—abhor, despise, detest, dislike, hate.

admissible, acceptable, allowable, justifiable, permissible, tolerable, suitable, warranted. ANT.—inadmissible, irrelevant, unacceptable, unsuitable.

admit, accept, acknowledge, agree, allow, assent, concede, confess, grant, open, permit, sanction. ANT.—debar, deny, dismiss, refuse, reject.

advance, accelerate, elevate, forward, further, improve, move, proceed, promote; allege, bring forward, offer, propose, propound; proceed, suggest. ANT.—halt, oppose, retard, return, retreat, withdraw.

advantage, gain, mastery, superiority, victory; benefit, help, profit. ANT.—detriment, handicap, harm, hindrance, restriction.

adverse, antagonistic, contrary, hostile, opposed, opposite; unfavorable. ANT.—favor, cooperate, assist, approve.

advice, admonish, counsel, instruct, recommend, suggest; inform, notify. ANT.—deceive, misdirect, misinform.

affect, alter, change, influence, modify, concern, interest, regard; impress, melt, move, soften, subdue, touch; adopt, assume, feign, pretend.

affection, attachment, friendliness, fondness, goodwill, kindness, love, tenderness. ANT.—animosity, antipathy, aversion, dislike, indifference, repugnance.

affirm, assert, aver, declare, maintain, state, swear, warrent. ANT.—contradict, demur, deny, dispute, oppose, nullify.

afraid, alarmed, cowardly, fearful, frightened, scared, timid, timorous. ANT.—assured, bold, brave, composed, courageous, valorous.

aggravate, heighten, increase, intensify, magnify, worsen; annoy, embitter, exasperate, irritate, provoke. ANT.—appease, improve, mitigate, soften, soothe.

aggregate, amount, collection, conglomeration, entirety, mass, sum, total, whole. ANT.—element, part, particular, unit.

agility, activity, briskness, energy, enterprise, intensity, liveliness, movement, quickness, rapidity, vigor. ANT.—dullness, idleness, inactivity, inertia.

agitate, arouse, disturb, excite, perturb, provoke, rouse, ruffle, shake, stir, trouble. ANT.—calm, ease, placate, soothe, quiet.

agony, ache, anguish, distress, misery, pain, suffering, trial, torment, torture, woe. ANT.—comfort, ease, happiness, health, mitigation, relief.

agree, accede, acquiesce, approve, assent, comply, concur, conform, consent. ANT.—contradict, differ, disagree, dispute, dissent.

agreeable, acceptable, amiable, gratifying, pleasant, pleasing, suitable, welcome, willing. ANT.—disagreeable, obnoxious, offensive, unpleasant.

aim, aspiration, design, end, endeavor, goal, intention, purpose. ANT.—aimlessness, carelessness, lack of purpose.

alarm, affright, apprehension, consternation, dismay, fear, signal, terror, warning. ANT.—assurance, calm, composure, peace, quiet, security, tranquility.

alien, adverse, contrasted, foreign, hostile, irrelevant, remote, strange, unlike. ANT.—akin, germane, relevant.

allege, affirm, aver, cite, claim, declare, maintain. ANT.—contradict, deny, dissent, refute, repudiate.

alleviate, abate, allay, diminish, extenuate, lighten, mitigate, relieve, soften, soothe. ANT.—aggravate, agitate, augment, increase, intensify, irritate.

alliance, association, coalition, combination, confederacy, federation, partnership, union; compact, marriage, treaty. ANT.—divorce, schism, secession, separation.

allot, apportion, dispense, distribute, divide, mete; allocate, assign, give, grant, measure. ANT.—confiscate, deny, keep, refuse, retain, withhold.

allow, empower, permit, sanction, tolerate; authorize, give, grant, yield; acknowledge, admit, concede. ANT.—deny, forbid, protest, refuse, resist.

allude, hint, imply, insinuate, intimate, refer, suggest. ANT.—declare, specify, state.

allure, attract, bewitch, captivate, charm, coax, entice, invite, seduce, tempt. ANT.—dissuade, discourage, repel, threaten.

ally, accessory, accomplice, assistant, associate, confederate. ANT.—adversary, enemy, opponent.

alone, deserted, desolate, isolated, lonely, secluded; unaccompanied, unaided; lone, only, single, solitary. ANT.—accompanied, attended, together.

also, besides, furthermore, in addition, likewise, moreover.

alternative, choice, elective, option, preference. ANT.—no choice, obligation, required.

always, ceaselessly, constantly, continually, eternally, ever, forever, perpetually. ANT.—never, occasionally, rarely, sometimes.

amalgamate, blend, coalesce, combine, consolidate, fuse, mingle, merge, unite. ANT.—separate, divide.

amateur, apprentice, beginner, learner, neophyte, nonprofessional, novice. ANT.—authority, expert, master, professional.

ambiguous, dubious, equivocal, indefinite, obscure, vague. ANT.—clear, explicit, lucid, unequivocal.

ambition, aspiration, desire, eagerness, end, goal, incentive. ANT.—contentment, indifference, laziness, resignation, satisfaction.

amend, better, change, correct, improve, reform, repair. ANT.—blemish, corrupt, debase, spoil.

amiable, agreeable, engaging, friendly, good-natured, gracious, pleasant. ANT.—disagreeable, hateful, ill-natured.

among, amid, amidst, between, interspersed, mingle, mixed. ANT.—apart, alone, separate.

amount, aggregate, collection, mass, number, quantity, sum, total, whole. ANT.—individual, part, particular.

ample, broad, extensive, great, large, spacious, wide; abundant, bountiful, complete, copious, full, generous, plentiful, profuse, rich, sufficient. ANT.—limited, small; insufficient, lacking, meager, sparse.

amplification, accrual, augmentation, dilation, enhancement, enlargement, expansion, extension, growth, heighten, increase, intensification, magnification, multiplication, raising. ANT.—contraction, condensation, curtailment, decrease, diminishing, reduction.

analogous, akin, alike, allied, comparable, correlative, correspondent, like, parallel, resemblance, similar. ANT.—different, dissimilar, divergent, incongruous.

anger, animosity, displeasure, exasperation, fury, indignation, ire, irritation, passion, petulance, rage, resentment, temper, vexation, wrath. ANT.—calmness, conciliation, forbearance, patience, peace, pleasantnes self-control.**angry,** enraged, exasperated, furious, incensed, indignant, irate, irritated, maddened, provoked, wrathful. ANT.—calm, happy, placid, pleased, satisfied.

anguish, agony, affliction, distress, grief, misery, pain, sorrow, suffering, torment, torture. ANT.—comfort, joy, relief, solace.

animate, activate, encourage, enliven, inspire, rouse, quicken, vitalize. ANT.—deactivate, discourage, kill.

animosity, bitterness, dislike, enmity, grudge, hatred, hostility, malevolence, malice, rancor, spite. ANT.—esteem, friendliness, goodwill, love.

annihilate, abolish, annul, destroy, eliminate, eradicate, extinguish, nullify, obliterate. ANT.—activate, preserve, save.

announce, advertise, broadcast, declare, expound, make known, notify, proclaim, promulgate, publish, report, reveal, tell. ANT.—bury, conceal, refrain, stifle, suppress, withhold.

annoy, bother, chafe, disturb, harass, harry, irk, irritate, molest, pester, plague, tease, trouble, vex. ANT.—accommodate, aid, console, gratify, please, soothe.

answer, acknowledge, confute, defend, rebut, rejoin, reply, respond, retort. ANT.—argue, ask, inquire, question.

anticipation, apprehension, contemplation, expectation, foresight, foretaste, forethought, hope, preconception, presentiment. ANT.—doubt, dread, fear, surprise, wonder, worry.

antipathy, abhorrence, antagonism, aversion, detest, dislike, hatred, opposition, repugnance, repulsion. ANT.—admiration, approval, liking, regard, respect.

anxiety, anguish, apprehension, care, concern, disquiet, dread, fear, misgiving, solicitude, trouble, worry. ANT.—assurance,

confidence, contentment, equanimity, nonchalance, peace.

apology, alibi, acknowledgement, confession, defense, excuse, explanation, justification, plea. ANT.—accusation, censure, complaint, denial, dissimulation.

appalling, alarming, awful, dire, dreadful, frightful, ghastly, hideous, horrible, horrid, repulsive, terrible. ANT.—assuring, beautiful, calming, enchanting, enjoyable, fascinating.

apparent, clear, evident, manifest, obvious, plain, self-evident, transport, unambiguous, unmistakable, visible. ANT.—ambiguous, dubious, hidden, indistinct, uncertain, unclear.

appeal, apply, ask, beg, beseech, call, entreat, plead, pray, request, supplicate. ANT.—deny, disclaim, refuse, recall, renounce.

appear, arise, arrive, emanate, emerge, issue, look, seem. ANT.—be, exist; disappear, vanish, withdraw.

appearance, advent, arrival, coming, air, aspect, demeanor, form, look, manner, mien; fashion, guise, pretense, semblance. ANT.—absence, departure, disappearance, leaving.

appease, allay, alleviate, assuage, calm, compose, conciliate, lull, mollify, pacify, placate, quell, quiet, relieve, satisfy, soothe. ANT.—aggravate, arouse, excite, incense, inflame, provoke.

appetite, hunger, relish, stomach, thirst, zest; craving, desire, inclination, liking, longing, passion, zest. ANT.—aversion, dislike, distaste, renunciation, repugnance, satiety.

appoint, assign, choose, command, designate, direct, name, ordain, select. ANT.—cancel, dismiss, remove, withdraw.

appreciate, admire, cherish, enjoy, esteem, prize, regard, value; apprehend, comprehend, realize, understand; improve, rise. ANT.—belittle, depreciate, disparage, misapprehend, misunderstand.

approach, accost, address, arrive, come near, greet, hail, speak to. ANT.—avoid, leave, depart.

appropriate, applicable, apt, becoming, fitting, particular, proper, suitable; assume, embezzle, loot, pilfer, plagiarize, plunder, purloin, steal. ANT.—contrary, improper, inappropriate; bestow. give, restore, return.

approval, approbation, assent, commendation, consent, endorsement, praise, sanction, support. ANT.—censure, reprimand, rejection, reproach.

approve, accept, appreicate, commend, like, praise; authorize, confirm, countenance, endorse, ratify, sanction, validate. ANT.—criticize, disapprove, disparage; condemn, nullify, reject.

aptness, ability, aptitude, capability, capacity, dexterity, knowledge, power, qualification, skill, talent. ANT.—inability, incapacity, incompetencey.

ardent, eager, enthusiastic, earnest, enthusiastic, fervent, fervid, glowing, impassioned, intense, keen, passionate, vehement, warm, zealous. ANT.—apathetic, indifferent.

ardor, devotion, eagerness, enthusiasm, fervor, passion, rapture, spirit. ANT.—apathy, disinterest, indifference, unconcern.

argue, debate, differ, discuss, dispute, plead, reason, wrangle; imply, indicate, prove, show. ANT.—agree, ignore, overlook, reject.

arraign, accuse, censure, charge, cite, incriminate, indict. ANT.—absolve, acquit, discharge, exonerate, release.

arraignment, accusation, charge, incrimination, indictment. ANT.—exculpation, exoneration, pardon.

arrange, adjust, array, assort, classify, dispose, group, organize, place; devise, organize, plan, prepare. ANT.—confuse, disarrange, disorder, disturb, scatter.

arrest, apprehend, check, delay, detain, halt, hinder, interrupt, obsruct, restrain, seize, stop, withhold. ANT.—activate, discharge, free, liberate, release.

arrive, appear, attain, come, emerge, land, reach, visit. ANT.—disappear, depart, exit, go, leave.

arrogant, disdainful, haughty, insolent, overbearing, proud. ANT.—humble, meek, servile.

artificial, affected, assumed, bogus, counterfeit, ersatz, fake, fictitious, sham, spurious, synthetic, unreal. ANT.—genuine, natural, real, true.

ascend, advance, climb, mount, progress, rise, scale, soar, tower. ANT.—decline, descend, fall, sink.

ask, appeal, beg, claim, entreat, invite, petition, request, solicit; inquire, interrogate, query, question. ANT.—answer, command, demand, dictate, insist, order, refuse, reply.

aspersion, abuse, defamation, desecration, dishonor, disparagement, insult, invective, outrage, profanation, reproach, reviling, upbraiding. ANT.—approval, commendation, plaudit, respect.

aspiration, aim, ambition, craving, desire, goal, hope, longing, objective. ANT.—contentment, indifference, laziness.

assault, assail, attack, bombard, charge, invade, onslaught, pound, rape, storm, strike. ANT.—defend, oppose, protect, surrender.

assemble, collect, combine, congregate, convene, gather, join, meet, muster, unite. ANT.—disperse, scatter.

assent, accept, acquiesce, agree, allow, approve, concede, concur, consent, ratify, recognize. ANT.—disapprove, reject.

assert, affirm, allege, claim, declare, express, insist, maintain, state. ANT.—contradict, deny, refute, reject.

assist, abet, aid, further, help, promote, serve, support, sustain.

ANT.—hamper, hinder, impede, prevent.

assistant, abettor, accessory, accomplice, accessory, accomplice, ally, associate, confederate. ANT.—adversary, opponent, rival.

associate, affiliate, ally, attach, combine, confederate, conjoin, connect, couple, join, link, unite. ANT.—disrupt, divide, disassociate, estrange, part, separate.

assume, appropriate, arrogate, take, usurp; adopt, affect, pretend, simulate, wear; presume, suppose. ANT.—relinquish, concede, grant, surrender; doff, remove; demonstrate, prove.

assurance, arrogance, assuredness, boldness, certainty, confidence, conviction, courage, firmness, security, self-reliance; pledge promise; assertion, declaration, statement. ANT.—humility, modesty, shyness, timidity, trepedation.

astonish, amaze, astound, frighten, perplex, startle, surprise. ANT.—bore, calm.

attach, adjoin, affix, annex, append, connect, fasten, join, stick, unite. ANT.—detach, disengage, remove, separate, sever, unfasten.

attachment, adherence, affection, affinity, bond, devotion, esteem, friendship, liking, regard. ANT.—alienation, aversion, enmity, estrangement, separation.

attack, aggression, assail, assault, criticism, denunciation, invade, offense, onslaught; convulsion, fit, paroxysm. ANT.—aid, defend, oppose, protect, resistance, surrender.

attain, accomplish, achieve, acquire, arrive, earn, effect, gain, get, master, obtain, procure, reach, secure, win. ANT.—abandon, desert, discard, fail, relinquish.

attempt, attack, effort, endeavor, essay, experiment, trial, undertaking. ANT.—inaction, laziness, neglect.

attend, accompany, care for, escort, follow, guard, protect, serve, tend, watch; be present, frequent. ANT.—abandon, absent, desert.

attention, alertness, circumspection, concentration, consideration, diligence, mindfulness, notice, observation, watchfulness; application, contemplation, reflection, study. ANT.—disregard, indifference, negligence.

attraction, affinity, allure, captivation, charm, fascination magnation, pull. ANT.—rejection, repulsion.

attitude, disposition, standpoint, viewpoint; aspect, pose, position, posture, stance; stand.

attractive, alluring, captivating, charming, enchanting, engaging, enticing, inviting, magnetic, pleasing, seductive, winning. ANT.—forbidding, obnoxious, repellent, repulsive.

audacity, arrogance, boldness, effrontery, fearlessness, impudence, rashness, temerity. ANT.—circumspection, humility.

austere, cruel, harsh, exacting, rigid, severe, sharp, stern, unrelenting. ANT.—gentle, kind, meek, mild, gentility, humility, meekness, restraint.

authentic, genuine, pure, legitimate, true, verifiable; accurate, authortative, certain, correct, reliable, trustworthy. ANT.—counterfeit, disputed, erroneous, false, spurious.

authority, command, control, domination, dominion, force, justification, power, right, supremacy; authorization, license, permission, rule, sanction; importance, influence, prestige, weight. ANT.—impotence, incapacity, weakness; denial, prohibition.

auxiliary, aid, ally, ancillary, assisting, conducive, confederate, furthering, helping, instrumental, subsidiary. ANT.—competitive, obstructive, opposing, retarding.

available, accessible, obtainable, on hand, prepared, present, ready, usable. ANT.—inaccessible, unavailable.

average, fair, intermediate, mean, median, mediocre, medium moderate, normal, ordinary, usual. ANT.—exceptional, extraordinary, outstanding, unusual.

aversion, abhorrence, antipathy, disgust, disinclination, dislike, distaste, dread, hatred, loathing, opposition, repugnance, repulsion, reluctance. ANT.—affection, attachment, devotion, enthusiasm, liking.

avoid, avert, dodge, escape, eschew, elude, evade, forbear, forestall, shun. ANT.—confront, encounter, meet, oppose, seek.

award, adjudge, allot, allow, bestow, honor, recognize, reward. ANT.—ignore, reject, withhold, withdraw.

aware, alert, apprised, cognizant, conscious, informed, mindful, observant, perceptive, ANT.—ignorant, oblivious, unaware.

away, abroad, absent, aside, departed, gone, distant. ANT.—close, here, present.

awful, appalling, dire, dreadful, frightful, gruesome, horrible, terrible; awe-inspiring, imposing, impressive, majestic, solemn. ANT.—attractive, pleasant, commonplace, lowly, vulgar.

awkward, bungling, clumsy, gauche, inept, maladroit, rough, ungraceful, unskillful. ANT.—adroit, graceful, skillful.

axiom, adage, aphorism, apothegn, byword, fundamental, maxim, principle, proposition, proverb, rule, saying, theorem, truism. ANT.—absurdity, paradox, sophism.

B

backward, regressive, retrogressive, retrograde, revisionary; dull,

sluggish, stupid; disinclined, indisposed, loath, reluctant. ANT.—advanced, civilized, intelligent, progressive.

bad, base, deleterious, evil, immoral, noxious, pernicious, rotten, sinful, unsound, spurious, vile, villainous, wicked. ANT.—excellent, good, honorable, moral, right, virtuous.

balance, composure, equilibrium, harmony, poise, stability, steadiness, proportion, symmetry; excess, remainder, remains, residue. ANT.—fall, imbalance, instability, unsteadiness.

baleful, bad, base, deleterious, evil, harmful, immoral, noxious, pernicious, wicked. ANT.—excellent, good, honorable, moral.

banal, commonplace, fatuous, hackneyed, inane, insipid, ordinary, trite, vapid. ANT.—exciting, fresh, novel, original, striking.

banish, debar, deport, dismiss, eject, exclude, exile, expatriate, expel, ostracize, oust. ANT.—accept, admit, forgive, receive, repatriate.

barbarous, atrocious, barbaric, brutal, crude, cruel, inhuman, merciless, ruthless, savage, uncivilized, uncultured, uncouth. ANT.—civilized, cultured, humane, kind, polite, refined.

barren, desolate, empty, sterile, unproductive. ANT.—fecund, fertile, productive.

barrier, bar, blockade, bulwark, obstacle, obstruction, rampart.

ANT.—admittance, entrance, opening, passage.

base, abject, contemptible, degraded, despicable, ignominious, inferior, low, mean, shameful, sordid, vile, vulgar. ANT.—esteemed, exalted, lofty, moral, noble, righteous, superior.

bashful, abashed, coy, diffident, embarrassed, modest, sheepish, shy, timid, timorous. ANT.—adventurous, daring, fearless, gregarious.

basic, essential, fundamental, indispensable, primary, principal, vital. ANT.—additional, extra, secondary.

batter, beat, belabor, bruise, demolish, dent, disfigure, mar, pound, pummel, smash, thrash. ANT.—cover, protect, secure, treat gently.

battle, combat, conflict, contest, fight, fray, skirmish, strife, struggle. ANT.—accord, agree, peace, truce.

bear, support, sustain, uphold; allow, endure, maintain, permit, suffer, tolerate; carry, convey, transport; produce, spawn, yield. ANT.—avoid, cast aside, dodge, evade, refuse, shun.

beat, batter, belabor, buffet, castigate, flog, hit, knock, pound, pummel, punch, strike, thrash; conquer, defeat, overpower, overthrow, rout, subdue, vanquish, whip; palpitate, pulsate, pulse, throb. ANT.—assist, help, defend, shield; fail, relinquish, surrender.

beautiful, attractive, beauteous, charming, comely, elegant, graceful, handsome, lovely, pretty. ANT.—foul, hideous, homely, repulsive, unsightly.

becoming, befitting, comely, decorous, decent, fitting, pleasing, proper, seemly, suitable, worthy. ANT.—unbecoming, displeasing, unseemly, unsuitable.

before, ahead, earlier, forward, prior, sooner. ANT.—after, afterward, behind, later.

beg, adjure, ask, beseech, crave, entreat, implore, importune, petition, pray, request, solicit, supplicate. ANT.—assist, bestow, cede, favor, give, grant.

begin, commence, enter, inaugurate, initiate, institute, open, originate, start. ANT.—complete, conclude, end, finish, terminate.

beginning, commencement, inauguration, inception, opening, origin, outset, source, start. ANT.—close, completion, conclusion, consummation, end, finish, termination.

behavior, action, attitude, bearing, breeding, carriage, conduct, deed, demeanor, deportment, disposition, manner, strategy, tactics.

belief, certitude, confidence, conviction, credence, faith, opinion, persuasion, reliance, trust. ANT.—denial, doubt, heresy, incredulity.

beloved, dear, esteemed, precious, valued; costly, expensive, valuable. ANT.—despised, unwanted; cheap.

below, beneath, lower, under, underneath. ANT.—above, aloft, over, overhead.

bend, bow, contract, crook, curve, deflect, divert, flex, incline, lean, stoop, turn, twist; influence, mold; submit, yield. ANT.—break, resist, stiffen, straighten.

beneficial, advantageous, good, helpful, profitable, salutary, useful, wholesome. ANT.—destructive, detrimental, harmful, injurious.

benefit, advantage, avail, behalf, blessing, favor, gain, good, interest, profit, service. ANT.—distress, handicap, injury, trouble.

benevolence, altruism, beneficence, charity, generosity, goodwill, humanity, kindness, liberality, magnanimity, munificence, philanthropy. ANT.—cruelty, ill-will, malevolence, selfishness, unkindness.

beyond, above, distant, far, farther, more, over, superior, yonder. ANT.—close by, here, near.

bias, bent, disposition, inclination, leaning, partiality, penchant, predilection, predisposition, prejudice, proneness, propensity, slant, tendency. ANT.—equity, fairness, impartiality, justice.

big, bulky, colossal, enormous, extensive, giant, great, huge, hulking, immense, large, majestic, massive, monstrous, vast.

ANT.—little, petite, slight, small, tiny.

bigoted, dogmatic, fanatical, hidebound, illiberal, intolerant narrow-minded, opinionated, prejudiced. ANT.—liberal, open-minded, progressive, tolerant.

bind, attach, connect, engage, fasten, fetter, join, link, obligate, restrain, restrict, secure, tie. ANT.—free, loose, release, unfasten, untie.

bitter, acrid, biting, distasteful, pungent, sharp, sour, tart; galling, grievous, painful, poignant; cruel, fierce; acrimonious, caustic, harsh, sardonic, severe. ANT.—agreeable, pleasant, sweet.

blame, accuse, censure, condemn, implicate, rebuke, reprehend, reproach, reprove, upbraid. ANT.—absolve, acquit, exonerate; praise.

blank, bare, barren, empty, vacant, void. ANT.—filled, occupied.

bleak, bare, chilly, cold, desolate, dreamy, dismal, dull, gloomy. ANT.—cheerful, pleasant, warm, serene.

blemish, blot, mark, speck, stain; defect, disfigurement, disgrace, dishonor, fault, flaw, imperfection. ANT.—adornment, decoration, embellishment, perfection, purity.

blend, adjoin, amalgamate, coalesce, combine, commingle, conjoin, consolidate, fuse, merge, mingle, mix, unite. ANT.—decompose, disintegrate, separate.

blind, ignorant, oblivious, sightless, undiscerning, unmindful, unseeing; careless, headlong, heedless, obtuse, rash; stupid. ANT.—aware, calculated, discerning, farsighted, perceiving, sensible.

bliss, blessedness, blissfulness, ecstasy, gladness, happiness, joy, rapture. ANT.—grief, misery, pain, sadness, wretchedness.

block, bar, barricade, clog, close, stop; impede, hinder, obstruct. ANT.—clear, open; aid, assist, further, promote.

bluff, abrupt, blunt, bold, brusque, brazen, coarse, discourteous, frank, outspoken, uncivil. ANT.—civil, courteous, pleasant.

blunt, dull, edgeless, obtuse, pointless, stolid, thick-witted, unsharpened; abrupt, bluff, brusque, direct, impolite, outspoken, harsh, forthright, rough, unceremonious. ANT.—polished, polite, suave, subtle, tactful.

boast, bluster, brag, crow, exult, flaunt, flourish, glory, vaunt. ANT.—apologize, deprecate, minimize.

body, carcass, corpse, remains; form, frame, torso; bulk, mass; aggregate, association, company, group, society.

bold, adventurous, audacious, brave, courageous, daring, determined, fearless, intrepid; brazen, forward, impudent, insolent, rude; abrupt, conspicuous, prominent, striking. ANT.—bashful, cowardly, timid, retiring, shy.

bondage, captivity, confinement, imprisonment, serfdom, servitude, slavery. ANT.—freedom, liberation.

book, booklet, brochure, compendium, handbook, manual, pamphlet, textbook, tract, treatise, volume, work.

border, boundry, brink, edge, extremity, fringe, frontier, limit, margin, outskirts, rim, termination, trimming, verge. ANT.—center, core, inside, interior, mainland, region.

boredom, doldrums, dullness, ennui, lack of interest, tedium, weariness. ANT.—activity, excitement, motive, stimulus.

bother, annoy, disturb, harass, haunt, inconvenience, molest, perplex, pester, plague, tease, trouble, upset, worry. ANT.—gratify, please, relieve, soothe.

bottom, base, basis, foot, foundation, groundwork, lowest part. ANT.—apex, peak, summit, top, upper part.

bound, hop, jump, leap, ski; spring, vault; circumscribe, confine, curb, define, limit. ANT.—crawl, walk; enlarge extend.

bountiful, abundant, ample, copious, opulent, overflowing, plenteous, plentiful, profuse, rich. ANT.—deficient, insufficient, scant, scarce.

brag, bluster, boast, flaunt, flourish, vaunt. ANT.—debase, degrade, demean, denigrate.

brave, adventurous, bold, courageous, daring, fearless, hardy, heroic, intrepid, undaunted, valiant, valorous, venturesome. ANT.—cowardly, cringing, fearful, timid, weak.

break, burst, crack, crush, demolish, destroy, fracture, infringe, pound, rack, rend, rupture, sever, shatter, shiver, smash, split, squeeze; disobey, infringe, transgress, violate. ANT.—join, mend, repair, restore, unite.

breed, bear, beget, conceive, engender, generate, procreate, propagate, start; foster, nurture, raise, rear. ANT.—abort, kill, murder.

brief, concise, curt, laconic, pithy, short, succinct, terse; fleeting, momentary, passing, short-lived, transient. ANT.—extended, lengthy, long, prolonged, protracted.

bright, brilliant, clear, gleaming, lucid, luminous, lustrous, radiant, scintillating, shining, sunny, translucent; clever, intelligent, smart, witty. ANT.—dark, dull, gloomy, stupid.

bring, adduce, attract, bear, carry, cause, conduct, convey, draw, fetch, impart, induce, produce, transfer, transport, transmit. ANT.—abandon, leave, relinquish.

brisk, cool, fresh, refreshing, stimulating.

briskness, action, activity, agility, energy, enterprise, intensity, liveliness, quickness, rapidity, vigor. ANT.—dullness, idleness, inactivity.

brittle, breakable, crisp, crumbling, delicate, fragile, frail, tenuous. ANT.—durable, enduring, tough, strong, unbreakable.

broad, ample, comprehensive, extensive, large, sweeping, vast, wide; liberal, tolerant. ANT.—confined, conservative, narrow, restricted.

broken, crushed, destroyed, fractured, interrupted, reduced, ruptured, separated, shattered, smashed, wrecked. ANT.—repaired, united, whole.

brotherhood, brotherliness, fellowship, kindness, solidarity, unity; association, clan, fraternity, society. ANT.—acrimony, discord, opposition, strife.

brusque, hasty, precipitate, sudden, unannounced, unexpected; abrupt, blunt, curt, rude; harsh, precipitous, rough, rugged, steep. ANT.—anticipated, expected; courteous, gradual.

brutal, barbarous, bestial, brutish, carnal, coarse, cruel, ferocious, gross, inhuman, merciless, rough, rude, ruthless, savage. ANT.—civilized, courteous gentle, humane, kind.

build, construct, erect, establish, found, make, manufacture, put up, raise, rear. ANT.—demolish, destroy.

buoyant, effervescent, light, resilient; animated, blithe, cheerful, elated, lively, spirited, vivacious. ANT.—dejected, depressed, despondent, sullen.

burden, afflict, encumber, load, oppress, overload, trouble.

burn, blaze, char, consume, cremate, incinerate, ignite, scald, scorch, sear, singe. ANT.—extinguish, stifle, subdue, quench.

bury, conceal, cover, entomb, hide, immure, inhume, inter. ANT.—display, exhume, expose, reveal.

business, art, commerce, concern, duty, employment, engagement, enterprise, job, occupation, profession, pursuit, trade, vocation, work. ANT.—avocation, hobby.

busy, active, assiduous, diligent, hard-working, industrious, perseverant. ANT.—apathetic, indifferent, lethargic.

but, and, barely, besides, except, further, furthermore, however, just, moreover, nevertheless, notwithstanding, provided, save, still, though, unless, yet.

buy, acquire, bribe, get, negotiate, obtain, procure, purchase, secure. ANT.—market, sell, transfer, vend.

by, beside, near, next to; by means of, through, with; according to; from.

C

calamity, adversity, casualty, catastrophe, disaster, misfortune, mishap, ruin. ANT.—advantage, benefit, blessing, fortune.

calculate, calculation, compute, consider, count, enumerate, estimate, figure, reckon, value, weigh. ANT.—assume, conjecture, guess, miscalculate.

call, address, assemble, clamour, command, convoke, cry, demand, designate, exclaim, ejaculate, invite, name, phone, proclaim, rally, roar, scream, shout, shriek, summon, utter, yell.

callous, hard, impenitent, indifferent, indurate, insensible, insensitive, obdurate, tough, unfeeling, unsusceptible. ANT.—compassionate, sensitive, soft, tender.

calm, alleviate, appease, assuage, lull, pacify, placate, quell, quiet, relieve, satisy, soothe, tranquilize. ANT.—agitate, anger, arouse, incite, incense, inflame.

calm, collected, composed, cool, dispassionate, peaceful, placid, quiet, sedate, self-possessed, serene, still, tranquil, undisturbed, unperturbed. ANT.—agitated, angry, excited, violent.

calumny, aspersion, detraction, defamation, libel, lying, scandal, slander, vilification. ANT.—charity, commendation, defense, flattery, kindness, praise.

cancel, abolish, annul, delete, eliminate, erase, expunge, invalidate, nullify, obliterate, quash, repeal, rescind, revoke. ANT.—approve, confirm, enforce, ratify.

candid, frank, free, honest, ingenous, open, sincere, straightforward, truthful; fair, impartial, just, unbiased. ANT.—artful, insincere, scheming, sly.

ANT.—alleviate, console, ease, mitigate.

candor, fairness, frankness, impartiality, openness, rectitude, responsibility, sincerity, truthfulness, uprightness. ANT.—artifice, cheating, deceit, dishonesty, fraud, guile, stratagem.

capability, ability, aptitude, aptness, capacity, dexterity, efficiency, faculty, qualification, skill, talent. ANT.—incapacity, incompetency, unreadiness.

capable, able, clever, competent, efficient, fitted, qualified, skillful, suitable. ANT.—inadequate, incapable, incompetent, unable, unfit.

capacity, ability, aptness, capability, power, skill, talent; content, expanse, magnitude, size, volume. ANT.—impotence, inability, incapacity.

capital, chief, excellent, essential, fine, first, important, leading, major, principal, paramount; assets, collateral, money, property. ANT.—secondary, unimportant; impecunious, poor, poverty.

capitulate, abandon, acquiesce, relinquish, renounce, submit, surrender, yield. ANT.—conquer, overcome, rout.

capricious, changeable, fickle, idiosyncratic, inconstant, unstable, variable, vacillating. ANT.—constant, dependable, stable, steady.

captivity, bondage, confinement, imprisonment, servitude, slavery, subjection. ANT.—freedom, independence, liberty.

capture, apprehend, arrest, catch, grasp, take, seize, snare, take, trap. ANT.—free, liberate, lose, release.

care, concern, trouble, solicitude, worry; attention, caution, regard, precaution, vigilance, wariness, watchfulness; charge, custody, guardianship, ward. ANT.—disregard, indifference, neglect.

career, avocation, business, calling, course, experience, line, occupation, profession, pursuit, sphere, vocation. ANT.—idleness, retirement.

careful, attentive, meticulous, prudent, scrupulous, thoughtful; cautious, circumspect, discreet, guarded, vigilant, wary, watchful. ANT.—careless, improvident, indifferent, lax, negligent.

careless, inattentive, indiscrete, reckless, thoughtless, unconcerned. ANT.—accurate, careful, meticulous.

caress, cuddle, embrace, fondle, hug, kiss, pamper, pet. ANT.—annoy, buffet, neglect, spurn, tease, vex.

caricature, burlesque, exaggeration, farce, imitation, mimicry, parody, ridicule. ANT.—accuracy, exactitude, reality, truth.

carnal, base, concupisent, corporeal, lascivious, lustful, sensual, voluptuous, worldly. ANT.—chaste, ethereal, intellectual, spiritual.

carping, captious, caviling, disparaging, fault-finding, hypercritical, pedantic. ANT.—

appreciative, approving, commendatory, encouraging.

carriage, bearing, behavior, demeanor, deportment, disposition, manner, mien.

carry, bring, convey, move, remove, support, sustain, transmit, transport. ANT.—abandon, drop, leave.

cartel, combination, monopoly, pool, trust.

case, circumstance, condition, contingency, event, example, occurrance, situation.

caste, ancestry, blood, category, class, descent, grade, kind, lineage, order, race, rank.

casual, careless, chance, cursoary, haphazard, incidental, informal, nonchalant, offhand, random, relaxed, unconcerned, unpremediated. ANT.—expected, formal, intended, planned.

casualty, accident, adversity, calamity, disaster, misfortune, mishap. ANT.—design, intention, prosperity, purpose.

catastrophe, adversity, affliction, blow, calamity, casualty, cataclysm, disaster, mishap, misery, ruin. ANT.—benefit, blessing, happiness.

catch, apprehend, arrest, capture, clasp, grasp, grip, overtake, seize, snare, trap. ANT.—cast aside, liberate, lose, release, miss.

catching, communicable, contagious, infectious, pestilential, virulent. ANT.—healthful, hygienic, noncommunicable.

category, caste, class, denomination, division, genre, heading, kind; grade, order, rank, set.

catharsis, cleansing, purge, purification.

cause, agent, antecedent, determinant, inducement, motive, origin, originator, principle, reason, source; create, effect, evoke, incite, induce, occasion, originate, prompt. ANT.—consequence, development, effect, end, result.

caustic, acrid, bitter, biting, distasteful, pungent, sour, tart; acrimonious, harsh, sardonic, severe. ANT.—mellow, pleasant, sweet.

caution, care, heed, prudence, vigilance, wariness, watchfulness; admonish, counsel, injunction, warning. ANT.—abandon, carelessness, recklessness.

cautious, attentive, heedful, prudent, scrupulous, thoughtful; careful, circumspect, discreet, careless, vigilant, wary. ANT.—hasty, heedless, impetuous.

cease, abandon, desist, conclude, desist, discontinue, stop, terminate; relinquish, resign, surrender. ANT.—continue, initiate, persist, stay.

cede, assign, convey, delivery, grant, relinquish, surrender, transfer, yield. ANT.—gain, receive, win.

celebrate, commemorate, honor, keep, observe, solemnize; commend, extol, honor, laud, praise. ANT.—disregard, ignore, neglect, disgrace, dishonor, profane.

celebrated, distinguished, eminent, famous, glorious, illustrious, noted, renowned. ANT.—ignominious, unknown.

celebration, commemoration, festivity, glorification, observance.

celerity, alacrity, haste, quickness, rapidity, speed, swiftness. ANT.—slowness, sluggishness.

celestial, divine, ethereal, godlike, heavenly, holy, supernatural, transcendant. ANT.—earthly, infernal, mortal.

censure, blame, condemn, criticize, denounce, reproach, reprimand, rebuke, reproach, reprove, upbraid. ANT.—approve, commend, endorse, praise.

center, core, focus, heart, hug, middle, midpoint, midst, nucleus. ANT.—border, periphery, rim.

ceremony, form, formality, observance, parade, pomp, protocol, rite, ritual, solemnity.

certain, assured, definite, fixed, incontrovertible, indubitable, inevitable, positive, reliable, secure, sure, true, undeniable, unquestionable. ANT.—doubtful, false, probable, questionable.

certainty, assuredness, confidence, conviction, firmness, self-reliance, surety, statement.

certify, assure, attest, aver, declare, demonstrate, inform, prove, state, testify. ANT.—deny, disown, repudiate.

chagrin, confusion, dismay, humiliation, mortification, shame, vexation.

chain, course, progression, sequence, series, set, string, succession.

challenge, defiance, demand, invitation, question; obstacle, opportunity, trial.

chance, accident, calamity, casualty, contingency, disaster, fate, fortune, happen, luck, misfortune, mishap, occur, random, transpire. ANT.—aim, design, intention, purpose.

change, alteration, alternation, innovation, modification, mutation, revolution, substitution, transition, variation. ANT.—permanence, stability, uniformity.

change, exchange, substitute; alter, convert, modify, shift, transform, vary, veer. ANT.—retain; continue, preserve, stabilize.

changeable, fickle, inconstant, shifting, unstable, vacillating, variable, wavering. ANT.—constant, stable, steady.

chaos, anarchy, confusion, disorder, disorganization, jumble, muddle, shambles, snarl. ANT.—order, organization, system.

character, class, description, disposition, individuality, kind, nature, personality, reputation, repute, standing, temperament; mark, sign, symbol, type.

characteristic, attribute, feature, idiosyncracy, individuality, mark, peculiarity, property, singularity, quality, trait.

charge, accuse, arraign, ascribe, assess, attack, censure, exhort, incriminate, indict; tax. ANT.—absolve, acquit, exonerate.

charity, alms, altruism, benefaction, benevolence, bounty, generosity, humanity, kindness, liberality, magnanimity, philanthropy, tenderness. ANT.—inhumanity, malevolence, selfishness.

charlatan, cheat, faker, fraud, humbug, impostor, mountebank, pretender, quack.

charming, alluring, attractive, bewitching, captivating, delightful, enchanting, engaging, fascinating, irresistable, ravishing, winning. ANT.—offensive, repulsive, revolting.

chase, follow, hunt, persist, pursue, seek, stalk, track, trail. ANT.—avoid, elude, escape, flee, lose.

chaste, clean, clear, genuine, immaculate, pure, unadulterated, uncontaminated; guiltless, innocent, sincere, uncorrupted, undefiled, virgin, virtuous. ANT.—foul, polluted, tainted; corrupt, defiled, lewd, wanton.

chasten, afflict, correct, discipline, humble, humiliate, subdue. ANT.—assist, cheer, comfort, encourage.

chastise, castigate, correct, discipline, punish, reprove, reprimand, strike, whip. ANT.—comfort, forgive, pardon.

cheap, inexpensive, low-priced, poor; beggarly, common, inferior, mean, petty, shabby, contemptible, despicable. ANT.—costly, dear, expensive, valuable, dignified, noble, worthy.

cheat, beguile, bilk, deceive, defraud, dupe, fool, hoax, hoodwink, outwit, swindle, trick, victimize.

check, analyze, audit, curb, examine, hinder, impede, inquire, interrogate, question, quiz, repress, restrain, review, scan, scrutinize, survey, view, watch. ANT.—disregard, hasten, neglect, omit.

cheer, comfort, console, encourage, gladden, solace, soothe, sympathize. ANT.—antagonize, depress, dishearten.

cheerful, buoyant, gay, happy, joyous, lighthearted, merry, sprightly. ANT.—dejected, gloomy, morose, sad, sullen.

cherish, appreciate, hold dear, prize, treasure, value; foster, nurture, protect, shelter. ANT.—abandon, dislike, disregard, neglect.

chicanery, deception, duplicity, fraud, intrigue, machination, subterfuge, trickery, ANT.—fair dealing, honesty.

chief, captain, chieftain, commander, head, leader, master, principal, ruler. ANT.—attendant, servant, subordinate.

chief, cardinal, essential, first, leading, main, paramount, predominant, pre-eminent, prime, supreme. ANT.—minor, secondary.

chivalrous, brave, courageous, courteous, gallant, generous, heroic, knightly, spirited, valiant, valorous. ANT.—cowardly, rude, unmannerly, timerous.

choice, alternative, determination, election, option, preference, selection, volition; excellent.

choose, cull, elect, opt, pick, select. ANT.—refuse, reject.

chronic, confirmed, constant, established, inveterate, rooted, settled. ANT.—occasional, temporary.

chronicle, account, description, history, narration, narrative, recital, record.

circuitous, crooked, devious, distorted, erratic, indirect, roundabout, swerving tortuous, wandering, winding. ANT.—direct, straight.

circular, bulbous, chubby, curved, cylindrical, globular, plump, rotund, round, spherical.

circumspection, anxiety, care, concern, solicitude, worry; attention, caution, discreetness, heed, regard, vigilance, wariness. ANT.—audaciousness, disregard, indifference, negligence.

circumstance, condition, detail, event, fact, happening, incident, item, occurrence, particular, point, position, situation.

circumvent, balk, check, foil, forestall, frustrate, outwit, prevent, thwart. ANT.—aid, help.

cite, advance, affirm, allege, assign, claim, declare, maintain, mention, name, quote, summon. ANT.—deny, disprove, neglect, refute.

civil, affable, considerate, courteous, cultivated, gracious, polite, refined, urbane, well-mannered. ANT.—boorish, ill mannered, rude.

civilization, breeding, cultivation, culture, education, enlightenment, illumination, polish, refinement. ANT.—ignorance, illiteracy, vulgarity.

claim, advance, affirm, allege, assert, aver, contend, declare, demand, express, maintain, state; defend, support, uphold. ANT.—contradict, deny, refute.

clamor, blare, cry, din, hubbub, hullabaloo, noise, outcry, racket, row, sound, tumult, uproar. ANT.—quiet, silence, stillness.

clandestine, concealed, covert, furtive, hidden, private, secret, stealthy, surreptitious. ANT.—conspicuous, exposed, known, open.

clarify, decipher, educate, explain, illustrate, interpret, make clear, purify, refine, resolve, unravel. ANT.—confuse, muddy, obscure.

clasp, adhere, clutch, grasp, grip, hold, have, keep, maintain, occupy, possess, retain, support.

class, caste, category, denomination, division, genus, group, kind; degree, grade, order, rank, set, standing; elegance, excellence.

classic, antique, clean-cut, elegant, first-rate, model, neat, pure, refined, simple, trim; Greek or Roman. ANT.—barbaric, baroque, mixed, modern.

clean, unadulterated, cleanse, mop, purify, scrub, spotless, stainless, sweep, wash. ANT.—dirty, soiled, stained.

clear, cloudless, fair, sunny; limpid, transparent; apparent, distinct, evident, intelligible, lucid, manifest, obvious, plain, perspicuous, unmistakable, vivid; open, unobstructed. ANT.—cloudy, overcast; ambiguous, obscure, vague.

clemency, charity, compassion, forgiveness, leniency, mercy, mildness, pity. ANT.—punishment, vengeance.

clever, able, adroit, dexterous, keen, quick, quickwitted, skillfull, talented, witty; bright, expert, ingenious, intelligent, sharp, smart. ANT.—awkward, clumsy, slow, unskilled; foolish, ignorant, stupid.

cleverness, comprehension, intellect, intelligence, perspicacity, sagacity, sense, understanding; fun, humor, irony, pleasantry, satire, wit.

climax, acme, apex, cosummation, culmination, height, peak, summit, vertex, zenith. ANT.—anticlimax, depth, floor.

climb, ascend, mount, rise, scale, soar. ANT.—descend, fall.

cloak, clothe, conceal, cover, disguise, hide, mask, protect, screen, shield, shroud, veil. ANT.—bare, expose, reveal, unveil.

clog, see close.

cloister, abbey, convent, hermitage, monastery, nunnery, priory; isolation, meditation, retirement, seclusion, solitude.

close, abutting, adjacent, adjoining, contiguous, immediate, impending, near, nearby, neighboring; confidential, devoted, intimate. ANT.—away, distant, faraway, removed.

close, bar, enclose, fence in, occlude, seal, shut; clog, obstruct, plug, stop; cease, complete, conclude, end, finish, terminate. ANT.—open, unlock; begin, commence, start.

clothes, apparel, array, attire, clothing, dress, garb, garments, raiment. ANT.—nakedness, nudity.

cloudy, dark, dim, indistinct, murky, obscure, shadowy. ANT.—bright, clear, distinct, sunny.

clumsy, awkward, cumbersome, inept, maladroit, ponderous, unwieldly. ANT.—adroit, dexterous, skillful.

clutch; cling to, embrace, grapple, grasp, grip, seize. ANT.—free, release. **coalition,** alliance, association, combination, confederacy, federation, league, partnership, union.

coarse, crude, harsh, impure, rough, unrefined; bawdy, gross, immodest, indelicate, inelegant, rude, unpolished, vulgar. ANT.—fine, refined, smooth; cultivated, cultured, dainty.

coax, cajole, entice, inveigle, invite, persuade, wheedle.

coerce, compel, constrain, drive, enforce, force, impel, oblige.

ANT.—allure, convince, induce, persuade, prevent.

coercion, compulsion, constraint, force, pressure, violence. ANT.—persuasion.

cogent, convincing, effective, forcible, persuasive, potent, powerful, sound, strong, urgent. ANT.—ineffective, unconvincing, weak.

cognizance, acquaintance, awareness, information, knowing, knowledge, learning, perception, scholarship, understanding, wisdom. ANT.—ignorance.

cohesion, cementing, coagulation, coherence, concretion, consolidation, integration.

coincide, accord, agree, collude, concur, correspond, equal, harmonize, match, square, syncronize, tally. ANT.—differ, disagree, diverge.

cold, arctic, bleak, chilly, cool, freezing, frigid, frosty, frozen, icy, wintry; indifferent, passionless, reserved, stoical, unconcerned, unfeeling. ANT.—heated, hot, torrid; affectionate, passionate.

collapse, cave in, decline, decrease, diminish, drop, fail, faint, fall, fall down, sink, subside; stumble, topple, tumble.

colleague, ally, associate, collaborator, companion, comrade, confederate, consort, friend, mate, partner. ANT.—adversary, opponent, stranger.

collect, accumulate, amass, assemble, concentrate, congregate, consolidate, gather, gain, hoard, obtain, pile; reap, receive. ANT.—disperse, distribute, scatter.

collected, calm, composed, cool, placid, quiet, sedate, tranquil; unperturbed. ANT.—agitated, excited, perturbed.

collision, clash, conflict, encounter, fight, impact, meeting, shock, struggle; contention, controversy, discord, clashing, interference, opposition, variance. ANT.—agreement, concord, harmony.

colloquial, conversational, dialectal, familiar, informal.

collusion, cabal, combination, complicity, conspiracy, deceit, intrigue, machination, plot treachery, treason.

color, complexion, dye, hue, paint, pigment, shade, stain, tincture, tinge, tint; blush, flush, redden.

colossal, elephantine, enormous, gargantuan, gigantic, huge, immense, large, mammoth, prodigious, tremendous. ANT.—little, small, tiny.

comatose, drowsy, faint, lethargic, stuporous, torpid, unconscious.

combat, battle, brawl, conflict, contest, duel, encounter, fight, skirmish, struggle; controversy, discord, opposition. ANT.—accord, peace, truce.

combination, alliance, association, coalition; confederacy, entente, federation, league, partnership, union; blend, mixture.

combine, accompany, adjoin, associate, attach, conjoin, connect, couple, join, link, unite; mix, blend.

combustion, burning, oxidation; disturbance, rioting, violence.

comely, beautiful, charming, elegant, fair, fine, graceful, handsome, lovely, pleasing, pretty. ANT.—homely, unattractive, unsightly.

comfort, aid, allay, alleviate, assist, cheer, console, encourage, gladden, relieve, solace, soothe, support, succor, sympathize. ANT.—antagonize, depress, dishearten, trouble.

comfortable, acceptable, agreeable, commodious, contented, cozy, gratifying, warm, pleasurable, protected, relaxed, restful, well-off. ANT.—miserable, wretched.

comical, amusing, diverting, droll, farcical, funny, humorous, laughable, ludicrous, ridiculous, witty. ANT.—serious, sober, solemn.

command, bidding, decree, dictate, direct, direction, injunction, instruction, mandate, order, requirement. ANT.—requisition; authority, control, govern, power, rule.

command, point, train; conduct, govern, guide, manage, regulate, rule; bid, direct, instruct, order. ANT.—countermand, distract, misdirect, misguide.

commemorate, celebrate, honor, memorialize, observe; solemnize. ANT.—disdain, dishonor, neglect.

commensurate, celebrate, honor, solemnize; commend, extol, glorify, praise. ANT.—overlook; disgrace, dishonor, profane.

commence, arise, begin, enter, establish, found, inaugurate, initiate, institute, introduce, open, originate, start. ANT.—cease, complete, finish, terminate.

commencement, beginning, inception, opening, outset, start. ANT.—completion, consummation, end, termination.

commend, appreciate, approve, praise; authorize, confirm, endorse, praise, ratify, sanction. ANT.—censure, criticize, condemn, rebuke.

comment, annotation, note, observation, remark, statement.

commerce, business, enterprise, industry, intercourse, trade, work.

commiseration, compassion, condolence, empathy. ANT.—coldness, indifference.

commission, appointment, authority, board, committee, delegation, duty, errand, function, power, warrant.

commit, perform, perpetrate; commend, consign, entrust, trust; bind, obligate, pledge. ANT.—fail, neglect, release, renounce; free, loose.

commodious, accommodating, appropriate, comfortable, convenient, expedient, favorable, roomy, timely, useful, suitable.

ANT.—confined, inconvenient, troublesome, uncomfortable.

commodity, articles, assets, goods, materials, possessions, property, stock, wares.

common, habitual, frequent, mutual, ordinary, prevalent, public, usual; low, mean, vulgar. ANT.—aristocratic, extraordinary, scarce; noble, refined.

commotion, agitation, chaos, confusion, disarray, disorder, disturbance, ferment, tumult, turmoil. ANT.—calmness, order, peace, tranquility.

communicate, convey, disclose, divulge, impart, inform, promulgate, reveal, tell, transmit. ANT.—conceal, suppress, withhold.

communion, association, concord, fellowship, intercourse, sacrament, union. ANT.—alienation; contention, discord.

community, area, district, locality, neighborhood, region, section.

commute, exchange, interchange, reduce, substitute, travel.

compact, close, condensed, constricted, contracted, dense, firm, narrow, pressed, snug, stretched, tense, tight. ANT.—diffuse, loose, relaxed, slack.

compact, accordance, concord, concurrence, understanding, unison; agreement, bargain, contract, covenant, pact. ANT.—disagreement, dissension, variance.

companion, associate, colleague, comrade, consort, crony, fellow, friend, mate, partner. ANT.—adversary, enemy, stranger.

company, assembly, band, conclave, convention, party, throng, troop; association, fellowship, society, corporation. ANT.—dispersion, loneliness, seclusion, solitude.

comparable, akin, alike, allied, analogous, correlative, corresponding, like, parallel, similar. ANT.—dissimilar, divergent, incongruous, opposed.

compare, contrast, differentiate, discriminate, distinguish.

compassion, commiseration, kindness, mercy, pity, sympathy. ANT.—cruelty, inhumanity, ruthlessness, severity, tyranny.

compatible, accordant, agreeable, congruous, consonant, correspondent, harmonious. ANT.—contradictory, incompatible, incongruous, inconsistent.

compel, coerce, constrain, drive, enforce, force, impel, oblige. ANT.—deter, hamper, impede, obstruct.

compensation, earnings, payment, recompense, return, reward, salary, stipend, wages. ANT.—forfeiture, loss, penalty.

competent, capable, efficient, fitted, proficient, qualified, skillful. ANT.—inadequate, incapable, incompetent, inept.

complain, deplore, grouch, grumble, lament, protest, remonstrate, repine, whine. ANT.—applaud, approve, praise, sanction.

complete, accomplish, achieve, conclude, consummate, end, finish, perfect, terminate; thorough, total, unbroken, undivided. ANT.—abandon, neglect, withdraw; deficient, lacking, unfinished.

complex, complicated, compound, intricate, involved, obscure. ANT.—apparent, plain, simple.

complexion, color, hue, pigment, shade, tincture, tinge, tint. ANT.—paleness, transparency.

compliant, humble, meek, modest, submissive, unassuming, unpretentious. ANT.—arrogant, boastful, haughty, ostentatious, proud, vain.

compliment, adulation, commendation, endorse, flattery, praise, tribute. ANT.—censure, criticism, denounce, reprehend.

comply, accede, acquiesce, agree, assent, consent; coincide, concur, conform, submit. ANT.—disagree, dissent, disobey, oppose.

comport, act, bear, behave, carry, conduct, operate.

compose, construct, create, fashion, formulate, forge, produce, shape; constitute, form; arrange, combine, organize; devise, frame, invent. ANT.—agitate, destroy, disfigure, dismantle.

composed, calm, collected, comfortable, imperturbable, peaceful, placid, quiet, sedate, tranquil. ANT.—agitated, excited, perturbed.

composer, author, creator, inventor, maker, originator.

composure, balance, calmness, equilibrium, poise, self-possession. ANT.—agitation, excitement, rage, turbulence.

compound, alloy, amalgamate, blend, combine, complex, complicated, composite, fraternize, join. ANT.—elemental, simple, single, unmixed.

comprehend, apprehend, conceive, discern, embrace, grasp, know, learn, perceive, realize, see, understand. ANT.—exclude, misapprehend, misinterpret, mistake, misunderstand.

comprehension, cognizance, discernment, insight, understanding. ANT.—ignorance, insensibility, misconception.

compress, condense, consolidate, constrict, crowd, reduce, squeeze. ANT.—expand, extend, increase, rarify, stretch, swell.

comprise, consist, contain, embody, embrace, encompass, hold, include, involve. ANT.—except, fall short, lack, reject.

compromise, accommodation, adjustment, agreement, arbitration, concession, conciliation. ANT.—controversy, disagreement, dispute, dissention.

compulsion, might, potency, power, strength, vigor; coercion, constraint, force, urgency. ANT.—feebleness, frailty, impotence, weakness; persuasion.

compute, calculate, count, enumerate, estimate, figure, reckon. ANT.—conjecture, guess, surmise.

comrade, associate, colleague, companion, consort, friend, partner. ANT.—adversary, stranger.

conceal, bury, camouflage, cover, disguise, hide, mask, screen, secrete, veil. ANT.—disclose, divulge, expose, lay bare, reveal, uncover.

concede, assent, acquiesce, permit, sanction, surrender; authorize, give, grant, relinquish yield; acknowledge, admit, allow. ANT.—object, protest, refuse, reject.

conceit, egotism, pride, self-glorification, vanity. ANT.—diffidence, humility, meekness, modesty.

conceive, become pregnant, concoct, design, devise, frame, imagine, visualize.

concentrated, close, compact, compressed, condensed, crowded, dense, thick. ANT.—diluted, dispersed, dissipated, sparse.

concept, conception, idea, notion, thought. ANT.—entity, matter, substance.

concern, affair, business; anxiety, care, solicitude, worry. ANT.—apathy, inconsequence, indifference, unconcern.

concise, brief, compact, condensed, crisp, incisive, pithy, succinct, terse. ANT.—lengthy, redundant, repetitive, verbose, wordy.

conclusion, close, completion, consummation, determination, termination; decision, deduction, inference, resolution, result. ANT.—beginning, commencement, inception, introduction, preamble, prelude, start.

concord, accordance, agreement, harmony, peace. ANT.—difference, disagreement, discord, dissension, variance.

concrete, actual, definite, firm, hard, material, particular, specific, solidified, tangible. ANT.—abstract, immaterial, intangible.

concur, agree, approve, assent, certify, comply, consent; coincide, conform, endorse. ANT.—argue, contradict, differ, disapprove, dispute, dissent, oppose, reject.

condemn, blame, censure, denounce, doom, reprehend, reproach, reprobate, reprove, upbraid; convict, sentence. ANT.—approve, commend, condone, forgive, praise; absolve, acquit, exonerate, pardon, set free.

condition, case, circumstance, situation, state: provision, requirement, specification, stipulation, term; make ready for work or use.

conditional, contingent, dependent, relying, subject, subordinate. ANT.—absolute, autonomous, independent.

condone, absolve, allow, disregard, excuse, forgive, overlook, pardon, remit. ANT.—condemn, forbid, punish.

conduct, action, attitude, bearing, behavior, carriage, demeanor, deportment, disposition, manner.

conduct, direct, govern, guide, lead, steer; manage, regulate, supervise.

confederate, abettor, accessory, accomplice, ally, assistant, associate, colleague, supporter. ANT.—adversary, enemy, opponent, opposition.

confederation, alliance, coalition, confederacy, entente, federation, league, union; compact, treaty. ANT.—schism, separation.

confer, converse, consult, deliberate, discuss, talk; bestow, donate, give, grant.

confess, acknowledge, admit, allow, avow, concede, disclose, divulge, own, reveal. ANT.—conceal, deny, disclaim, disguise, disown, repudiate, veil.

confidence, assurance, assuredness, boldness, certitude, conviction, self, possession, surety. ANT.—apprehension, diffidence.

confine, bind, bound, circumscribe, enclose, encompass, envelop, fence, imprison, limit, restrict. ANT.—develop, enlarge, expand, free, release, unfetter.

confirm, corroborate, substantiate, verify; assure, establish, settle; approve, fix, ratify, sanction; strengthen, validate. ANT.—annul, abrogate, cancel, destroy, shatter, void.

confiscate, appropriate, capture, commandeer, take; grip, seize.

ANT.—give back, restore, return.

conflict, battle, combat, duel, encounter, fight, struggle; contention, discord, dissention, opposition, strife, variance, war. ANT.—concord, harmony, peace, repose, tranquility.

conform, adapt, adjust; assent, comply, submit. ANT.—dissent.

confront, combat, encounter, meet squarely, oppose. ANT.—agree, submit, support.

confuse, bewilder, complicate, confound, derange, disconcert, obscure, perplex, puzzle. ANT.—clarify, illumine, organize.

confusion, agitation, chaos, clutter, commotion, disarrangement, disarray, discomposure, disorder, ferment, jumble, pendemonium, stir, tumult, turmoil. ANT.—method, order, sense, system.

confute, confound, confuse, defect, dismay, disprove, refute. ANT.—affirm, confirm, endorse, prove, verify.

congruous, accordant, agreeing, compatible, consonant, correspondent, in harmony. ANT.—contradictory, discrepant, incongruous.

conjecture, guess, hypothesis, presumption, speculation, supposition, theory. ANT.—certainty, fact, proof, truth.

connect, adjoin, affiliate, affix, annex, append, attach, join, link, unite. ANT.—detach, disconnect, disengage, separate.

conquer, beat, checkmate, crush, defeat, humble, master, overcome, overthrow, prevail, quell, rout, subdue, subjugate, surmount, vanquish. ANT.—cede, forfeit, lose, retreat, succumb, surrender.

conquest, subjugation, triumph, victory. ANT.—defeat, failure.

conscientious, careful, exacting, honest, incorruptible, just, scrupulous, trusty, upright. ANT.—corrupt, dishonest, unjust.

conscious, apprised, aware, certain, cognizant, informed, mindful, percipient, sensible. ANT.—ignorant, insensible, oblivious, senseless, unaware.

consecrate, dedicate, exalt, extol, glorify, hallow, honor, revere, sanctify, venerate. ANT.—debase, degrade, dishonor.

consent, accede, acquiesce, agree, allow, assent, comply, concede, concur, conform, yield. ANT.—demur, disagree, dissent, prevent, protest, refuse.

consequence, effect, end, fruit, issue, outcome, product, sequel. ANT.—beginning, cause, commencement, origin, start.

conserve, maintain, preserve, save; retain; keep, guard, protect. ANT.—discard, reject; relinquish; neglect.

consider, contemplate, deliberate, examine, meditate, ponder, reflect, weigh; regard. ANT.—abandon, dismiss, forget, ignore, neglect, overlook.

considerate, cautious, charitable, kind, prudent; meditative, solicitous, sympathetic, unselfish. ANT.—harsh, impervious, inconsiderate, rash, repressive, scornful, thoughtless.

consideration, attention, care, mindfulness, watchfulness, reflection; pay, recompense, value. ANT.—disregard, failure, indifference, negligence, omission, oversight.

consign, commit, condemn, delegate, deliver, devote, send, ship. ANT.—hold, receive, retain.

consistent, accordant, agreeing, compatible, conforming, consonant, constant, equable, harmonious, regular, undeviating, uniform. ANT.—contradictory, discrepant, incongruous, inconsistent, varying.

console, cheer, comfort, ease, freshen, gladden, invigorate, soothe, support. ANT.—depress, grieve, wound.

consolidate, affiliate, amalgamate, blend, coalesce, combine, compact, compress, condense, conjoin, fuse, merge, solidify, unite. ANT.—disjoin, disperse, separate, sever, thin(out).

conspicuous, celebrated, clear, commanding, distinguished, manifest, noticeable, obvious, outstanding, plain, prominent, visible. ANT.—concealed, covered, hidden, obscure, unknown, unseen, secret.

conspiracy, cabal, collusion, combination, intrigue, plot, treachery.

constancy, faithfulness, fealty, fidelity, firmness, fixedness, loyalty, permanence, reliability, resolution, stability, steadiness. ANT.—capriciousness, disloyalty, faithlessness, fickleness, fluctuation, instability, vacillation.

constantly, always, continually, eternally, ever, evermore, forever, incessantly, perpetually, unceasingly. ANT.—fitfully, never, occasionally, rarely, sometimes.

consternation, alarm, amazement, astonishment, dismay, fear, horror, panic, surprise, terror, wander. ANT.—calm, peacefulness, quietness, repose, tranquility.

constrain, compel, confine, drive, force, oblige, press, prevent, repress, restrain, urge. ANT.—ask, implore, plead, supplicate.

constrict, bind, compress, cramp, hamper, limit, shrink, squeeze, tighten. ANT.—expand, free, loosen, release, untie.

construct, build, compose, erect, fabricate, form, frame, make, produce. ANT.—demolish, destroy, dismantle, raze.

consult, confer, discuss, seek advisement.

consume, absorb, annihilate, assimilate, destroy, devour, engulf, exhaust, imbibe, squander, swallow, waste. ANT.—accumulate, collect, gather, hoard, store.

consummate, accomplish, achieve, close, complete, conclude, end, execute, finish, fulfill, perfect, terminate; absolute, best, excellent, supreme. ANT.—incomplete, second rate, unfinished.

contagious, catching, communicable, pestilential, spreading, virulent. ANT.—incommunicable.

contaminate, befoul, corrupt, debase, defile, deprave, infect, poison, pollute, soil, stain, taint, vitiate. ANT.—disinfect, purify.

contemplate, conceive, picture, meditate, muse, ponder, reflect, consider, study; intend, view. ANT.—discard, disregard, neglect, reject.

contemporary, coequal, coeval, coincident, contemporaneous, current, modern, new, simultaneous. ANT.—ancient, antiquated, bygone, old.

contempt, derision, detestation, disdain, disregard, disrespect, disparagement, mockery, scorn, slight, slur. ANT.—approbation, awe, endorsement, esteem, regard, respect.

contemptible, depraved, degenerate, despicable, low, mean, scurrilous, sordid, vile. ANT.—admirable, dignified, exalted, gracious, pleasing, respectable, worthy.

contend, battle, combat, compete, contest, cope, dispute, engage, fight, grapple, maintain, oppose, strain, struggle, vie. ANT.—cease, cede, desert, halt, stop, quit.

contention, altercation, animosity, battle, combat, conflict, duel, enmity, feud, fight, struggle; controversy, discord, opposition, quarrel, strife; variance. ANT.—amity, benevolence, concord, goodwill, harmony, kindness, regard, respect, sympathy.

contentment, acceptance, delight, ease, gladness, happiness, joy, satisfaction, serenity. ANT.—despair, discomfort, dissent, grief, misery, regret, sadness, sorrow.

contest, argue, contend, debate, dispute, fight, object, oppose; altercation, battle, conflict, engagement, feud, match, race. ANT.—agree, assent, relinquish; calm, repose, tranquility.

contingent, conditional, dependent, depending, relying, subject, subordinate. ANT.—autonomous, independent.

continual, ceaseless, constant, continuous, endless, incessant, invariable, perpetual, persistent, steady, unbroken, unceasing, uninterrupted, unremitting, unvarying. ANT.—checked, concluded, intermittent, interrupted, stopped.

continuance, continuation, duration, existence, extension, production, prolongation. ANT.—arrest, finish, hindrance, impediment, stoppage.

continue, advance, extend, maintain, proceed, persevere, persist, sustain. ANT.—arrest, check, complete, desist, end, finish, interrupt.

contract, abbreviate, abridge, condense, diminish, lessen, narrow, reduce, restrict, shorten, shrink; agreement, cartel, covenant, pledge, promise. ANT.—elongate, enlarge, expand, extend, lengthen.

contradict, correct, contravene, demur, disclaim, dispute, oppose, recall, recant, rectify, refute. ANT.—acquiesce, accept, approve, agree, confirm, sanction, seal, sign, verify, vouch.

contrary, adverse, antagonistic, opposed, opposite, conflicting, contradictory, counteractive, dissimilar, unlike. ANT.—agreeing, alike, correspondent, homogeneous, similar.

contrast, differentiate, discriminate, distinguish; antithesis, disparity, dissimilarity, divergence, incongruity, variation.

contravene, annul, contradict, defeat, hinder, interpose, nullify, obstruct, oppose, thwart, void. ANT.—agree, approve, assent, assist, concur, consent.

contribute, add(to), aid, assist, befriend, benefit, cooperate, donate, favor, furnish, help, share, subscribe, supply. ANT.—counteract, disapprove, harm, ignore, neglect, oppose, shun, withhold.

contrite, penitent, regretful, remorseful, repentant, sorrowful. ANT.—impenitent, obdurate, remorseless.

contrivance, apparatus, appliance, construction, design, device, invention, mechanism; plan, plot, ruse, scheme, trick.

contrive, arrange, design, devise, execute, form, frame, invent, make, plan, plot, project, scheme. ANT.—abolish demolish, disrupt, ruin, smash.

control, coerce, command, direct, dominate, guide, govern, hold, manage, regulate, rule, superintend; check, curb, prevent, repress, restrain. ANT—abandon, forsake, ignore, relinquish, renounce, resign.

controversy, altercation, argument, bickering, contention, debate, disagreement, dispute, quarrel, squabble, wrangling. ANT.—agreement, concord, forbearance, harmony, peace, restraint.

convalesce, improve, rally, recover, recuperate, revive. ANT.—die, fail, falter, regress.

convene, assemble, collect, congregate, convoke gather, meet, muster. ANT.—adjourn, disperse, scatter.

convenient, accessible, adapted, appropriate, available, commodious, favorable, fitting, handy, opportune, suitable. ANT.—inaccessible, inconvenient, inexpedient, troublesome, unsuitable.

conventional, accepted, customary, formal, ordinary, orthodox, prevalent, social, stipulated, usual. ANT.—extraordinary, foreign, informal, irregular, strange, unconventional, unusual.

convergence, approach, assemblage, concourse, confluence, conjunction, focal point, meeting. ANT.—disjunction, divergence, division.

conversation, chat, colloquy, communication, communion, conference, dialogue, discourse, discussion, intercourse, interview, palaver, parley, talk.

converse, chat, communicate with, discuss, speak with; communion, conversation, discussion, intercourse, parley.

convert, adapt, alter, change, metamorphose, modify, resolve, shift, transfigure, transform, transmute, turn(from), veer. ANT.—retain; continue, keep, maintain, persist, preserve.

convey, bring, carry, communicate, impart, inform, transmit, transport. ANT.—hold, keep, preserve, retain.

convict, criminal, culprit, felon, malefactor, offender, transgressor; censure, condemn, doom, sentence. ANT.—absolve, acquit, exonerate, pardon.

convince, affect, clarify, coax, exhort, induce, influence, persuade, prevail upon, satisfy, sway, touch, win over. ANT.—deprecate, dissuade, warn.

convivial, cordial, festive, hospitable, jolly, merry, sociable. ANT.—dismal, severe, solemn, staid.

convoke, assemble, call, collect, convene, gather, muster, summon. ANT.—adjourn, disband, discharge, dismiss, disperse, dissolve, separate.

convolution, circumvolution, coil, curl, involution, sinuosity, twist, wave, winding line. ANT.—level surface, straight line, uncurved.

convoy, accompany, attend, chaperone, escort, go with, protect, support, watch over. ANT.— abandon, avoid, desert, ignore, leave, neglect, quit.

cool, apathetic, calm, distant, fresh, frigid, frosty, gelid, indifferent, shivery, unfeeling, unresponsive, wintry; freeze, harden, refrigerate. ANT.—feeling, glowing, responsive, sultry, sunny, warm-hearted.

cooperate, aid, approve, assist, combine, connive, encourage, endorse, forward, fraternize, help, perform, plan, promote, relieve, second, support. ANT.— delay, disturb, encumber, handicap, hinder, impede, prevent.

copious, abundant, ample, bountiful, exuberant, overflowing, plenteous, plentiful, profuse, rich, teeming. ANT.—deficient, meager, scant, scarce, sparse.

cordial, amicable, earnest, friendly, genial, gracious, hearty, kindly, pleasant, sincere, sociable, warm. ANT.—aloof, cool, hostile, indifferent, inhospitable, taciturn, unfriendly.

corporal, bodily, carnal, corporeal, in the flesh, physical, somatic; material. ANT.— immaterial, incorporeal, spirtual.

corpulent, beefy, fat, fleshy, obese, paunchy, plump, portly, rotund, stocky, stout, thickset. ANT.— gaunt, lean, slender, thin.

correct, accurate, exact, faultless, impeccable, precise, proper, right, true. ANT.—erroneous, inaccurate, incorrect, false, faulty, untrue, wrong.

correct, amend, mend, improve, rectify, reform, remedy, repair; chastise, discipline, punish, reprove. ANT.—aggravate, ignore, spoil; coddle, condone, pamper.

correlation, correspondence, likeness, reciprocation, similarity. ANT.—difference, disparagement, divergence, unlikeness.

corroborate, affirm, approve, assure, back, certify, confirm, endorse, sanction, support. ANT.— contradict, deny, disallow, disclaim, disprove, oppose, refute.

corrupt, base, contaminated, contemptible, corrupted, crooked, debased, demoralized, depraved, dishonest, impure, infected, lewd, low, perverted, profligate, putrid, rotten, spoiled, tainted, unprincipled, unscrupulous, unsound, venal, vitiated. ANT.— clean, decent, honorable, noble, pure, wholesome.

corruption, baseness, criminality, decay, degradation, depravity, graft, guiltiness, infamy, perversion, putrefaction, rottenness, swindling, vice, wickedness. ANT.—honesty, integrity, morality, soundness, uprightness.

counsel, acquaint, admonish, advise, apprise, guide, inform, instruct, recommend, suggest, warn. ANT.—conceal, misinform, mislead, withhold.

count, calculate, compute, enumerate, figure, number, reckon, score, total. ANT.—conjecture, estimate, guess, miscalculate.

counterfeit, artificial, bogus, dishonest, ersatz, fake, false, feigned, fictitious, forged, fraudulent, phony, sham, spurious, synthetic, unreal. ANT.—genuine, honest, natural, real, true.

couple, adjoin, attach, combine, conjoin, connect, copulate, join, link, unite; brace, pair, two. ANT.—detach, disconnect, disjoin, separate.

courage, boldness, bravery, chivalry, daring; dauntlessness, fearlessness, fortitude, gallantry, hardihood, heroism, intrepidity, mettle, prowess, spirit, valor. ANT.—cowardice, fear, pusillanimity, timidity, weakness.

courteous, affable, agreeable, civil, considerate, cultivated, genteel, mannerly, obliging, polished, polite, refined, suave, urbane, well-bred, well-mannered. ANT.—boorish, dictatorial, discourteous, impertinent, rude, uncivil, uncouth.

covenant, agreement, alliance, concord, understanding; bargain, compact, concordat, contract, pact, stipulation. ANT.—difference, disagreement, variance.

cover, cloak, clothe, conceal, curtain, disguise, envelop, guard, hide, mask, overlay, overspread,

protect, screen, shield, veil; comprise, embody, embrace. ANT.—bare, divulge, expose, reveal, uncover, unveil.

covert, clandestine, concealed, disguised, furtive, hidden, secret, sly, underhand, unseen. ANT.—candid, conspicuous, evident, explicit, frank, open, overt, unconcealed, visible.

covetousness, avarice, craving, cupidity, desire, envy, greed, jealousy. ANT.—benevolence, generosity, liberality, munificence.

cowardly, afraid, chicken-hearted, effeminate, faint-hearted, not courageous, shy, sissy, spiritless, timid, timorous. ANT.—bold, brave, courageous, daring, dauntless.

crafty, calculating, cunning, deceitful, foxy, furtive, guileful, plotting, scheming, shrewd, stealthy, surreptitious, sly, tricky, underhand, wily. ANT.—candid, frank, ingenuous, open, sincere, undesigning.

crass, brutish, coarse, crude, insensitive, raw, rough, uncouth, unfinished, unpolished, unrefined. ANT.—finished, cultivated, polished, refined.

craving, appetite, desire, longing, passion, yearning. ANT.—disgust, distaste, repugnance.

crazy, crazed, delirious, demented, deranged, idiotic, imbecilic, insane, lunatic, mad, maniacal. ANT.—rational, reasonable, sane, sensible.

create, bring about, cause, design, engender, fashion, form, formulate, generate, invent, make, originate, produce; appoint, ordain. ANT.—annihilate, destroy; disband, terminate.

credible, believable, plausible, probable, reasonable, reliable, trustworthy. ANT.—improbable, incredible, unbelievable.

crest, acme, crown, head, peak, pinnacle, summit, top, plume, tuft; decoration, insignia. ANT.—base, bottom.

crime, atrocity, depravity, felony, immorality, infringement, injustice, misdeed, misdemeanor, offense, outrage, transgression, vice, wickedness, wrong. ANT.—benevolence, benignity, honor, innocence, morality, uprightness, virtue.

criminal, convict, culprit, delinquent, felon, malefactor, offender, transgressor; abominable, blamable, culpable, felonious, iniquitous, sinful, vicious, vile, wrong. ANT.—faultless, good, honest, innocent, just, legal, sinless, virtuous.

crisis, critical juncture, crucial point, emergency, exigency, strait, turning point. ANT.—calm, equilibrium, normality.

crisp, breakable, brittle, crumbling, fragile, frail, splintery; brisk, bracing, fresh, lively, sharp. ANT.—flexible, tough, unbreakable.

criterion, fact, gauge, law, measure, model, norm, opinion, principle, proof, rule, standard, test, touchstone. ANT.—chance, conjecture, guess, possibility, probability, supposition.

critical, discerning, discriminating, exact, fastidious, particular; captious, carping, caviling, censorious, disapproving, faultfinding; acute, crucial, decisive, momentous, pressing, urgent. ANT.—cursory, superficial; approving, commendatory, encouraging; insignificant, unimportant.

crooked, abased, adulterated, corrupt, criminal, deceitful, defiled, degraded, depraved, dishonest, fraudulent, lawbreaking, vitated; angular, bent, bowed, curved, deformed, winding, wry, zig-zag. ANT.—honest, law-abiding, mortal, respectable, direct, regular, straight.

crowd, assembly, horde, masses, mob, multitude, populace, throng; compress, cramp, jostle, press, shove, squeeze, swarm.

crown, apex, chief, crest, head, peak, pinnacle, ridge, summit, top, vertex, vortex, zenith; coronet, tiara; decorate, glorify, honor. ANT.—base, bottom, foot, foundation.

cruel, barbarous, brutal, cold-blooded, ferocious, harsh, inhuman, merciless, pitiless, ruthless, savage, sadistic. ANT.—benevolent, charitable, passionate, considerate, gentle, humane, kind, merciful.

cull, choose, pick out, select, separate. ANT.—refuse, reject.

culmination, acme, apex, climax, conclusion, consummation, crown, end, height, peak, summit, termination, zenith. ANT.—base, beginning, inception.

culprit, criminal, delinquent, felon, malefactor, offender, sinner, transgressor, wrongdoer.

cultivate, civilize, develop, educate, farm, foster, grow, promote, pursue, raise, refine, tend, train, work. ANT.—depress, deteriorate.

culture, breeding, civilization, cultivation, development, education, enlightenment, knowledge, learning, propagation, refinement, scholarship. ANT.—boorishness, ignorance, illiteracy, pretension, stupidity, vulgarity.

cultured, cultivated, educated, enlightened, polished, refined, well-bred. ANT.—crude, ignorant, simple, uncouth.

cunning, calculating, crafty, devious, plotting, scheming, sly; artful, clever, skillful, tricky. ANT.—direct, honest; clumsy, dull, inept, stupid.

curb, bridle, check, constrain, control, hinder, hold back, inhibit, limit, repress, restrain, stop, suppress. ANT.—aid, encourage.

cure, antidote, healing, remedy, restorative.

curious, examining, inquiring, inquisitive, interesting, interrogative, meddling, prying, searching; odd, peculiar, queer, strange, unusual ANT.—disinterested, dull, incurious, indifferent, unconcerned; common, ordinary.

cursory, careless, desultory, flimsy, frivolous, imperfect, shallow, slight, superficial. ANT.—complete, deep, meticulous, painstaking, perfect, profound, thorough.

curt, abrupt, unexpected, hasty, precipitate, sudden; blunt, brusque, rude; harsh, rough, sharp. ANT.—gradual, smooth; courteous.

curtail, abbreviate, abridge, condense, contract, diminish, lessen, limit, reduce, restrict, retrench, shorten. ANT.—elongate, enlarge, extend, lengthen, prolong.

custom, convention, fashion, habit, manner, mores, practice, precedent, rule, usage, wont. ANT.—departure, deviation, difference, divergence, irregularity.

cynical, contemptuous, distrustful, doubtful, pessimistic, petulant, satirical, testy. ANT.—believing, calm, good-natured, pleasant.

D

dainty, choice, delicate, elegant, exquisite, fastidious, fine, particular, pleasant, pleasing, pretty, pure, rare, refined, soft, sweet, tender. ANT.—coarse, harsh, inferior, repellent, unpleasant, vulgar.

dally, caress, coquet, dawdle, delay, flirt, fondle, idle, linger, philander, prolong, toy. ANT.—be attentive, hurry.

dam, bar, block, choke, clog, hamper, hinder, impede, obstruct, stop, suppress. ANT.—open, release, unblock.

damage, deface, harm, hurt, impair, injure, mar, spoil, wound; detriment, disadvantage, evil, injury, loss, misfortune, spoilation, wrong. ANT.—enhance, improve, mend, perfect, repair; advantage, award, benefit, favor, recompense, reward.

damn, anathematize, ban, banish, condemn, denounce, execrate, punish. ANT.—benefit, bless, exalt, favor, praise, promote.

danger, defenseless, exposure, hazard, insecurity, jeopardy, menace, peril, precariousness, risk. ANT.—carefulness, certainty, confidence, preservation, security, sureness.

daring, adventurous, audacious, bold, brave, chivalrous, courageous, defiant, enterprising, fearless, impudent, intrepid, obtrusive, stout-hearted. ANT.—cautious, chicken-hearted, cowardly, diffident, hesitating, modest, retiring, shy, timid.

dark, black, clouded, dim, gloomy, murky, obscure, opaque, overcast, shadowy; dusky; dismal, gloomy, mournful, somber, sorrowful; evil, sinister, sullen, wicked; hidden, mysterious mystic, occult, secret. ANT.—bright, clear, distinct, illumined, brilliant, pleasant; apparent, transparent, visible.

daunt, appall, discourage, dishearten, dismay, frighten, intimidate, scare, terrify. ANT.—aid, animate, assist, embolden, encourage, help, stimulate, succor.

dazzle, amaze, astonish, astound, bewilder, blind, confound, daze, impress, overpower. ANT.—befog, dampen, darken.

dead, deceased, defunct, departed, extinct, gone, inanimate, lifeless, obsolete, perished, spiritless. ANT.—alive, animate, being, continuing, enduring, existent, existing, living.

deadly, destructful, destructive, mortal, noxious, poisonous, virulent. ANT.—animating, energizing, invigorating, preservative, stimulating, strengthening, wholesome.

deal, affair, agreement, conspiracy, racket, transaction; allocate, allot, aportion, barter, distribute, give, mete, share. ANT.—hold, keep, receive, retain.

dear, beloved, esteemed, precious, valued; costly, exorbitant, expensive, high-priced, scarce, valuable. ANT.—despised, unwanted, valueless, worthless; cheap, common, inexpensive, low priced.

debase, abase, adulterate, contaminate, corrupt, defile, degrade, deprave, dishonor, humiliate, impair, lower, pervert, shame, taint, vitiate. ANT.—elevate, enhance, improve, lift, raise, vitalize.

debate, argue, contend, discuss; dispute, reason.

debauch, adulterate, contaminate, corrupt, debase, defile, degrade, pervert, pollute, seduce.

debris, detritus, litter, remains, rubbish, rubble, ruins, sediment, trash, wreckage.

debt, arrears, charge, debit, deficit, liability, obligation. ANT.—asset, excess, overage.

decay, decline, decompose, degenerate, dwindle, ebb, molder, putrefy, rot, spoil, wane, waste. ANT.—bloom, flourish, grow, increase, luxuriate, rise.

deceit, artifice, beguilement, cheat, chicanery, cunning, deceitfulness, deception, delusion, duplicity, falseness, fraud, guile, sham, treachery, trickery, wiliness. ANT.—authenticity, candor, honesty, openness, sincerity, truthfulness, uprightness.

deceive, be dishonest with, beguile, cheat, circumvent, defraud, delude, dupe, entrap, lie to, mislead, outwit, trick. ANT.—advise, aid, assure, be candid, be frank, be truthful, counsel, help, succor.

decent, adequate, becoming, befitting, decorous, fit, proper, respectable, seemly, suitable; chaste, modest. ANT.—inadequate, reprehensible, unsuitable; coarse, improper, indecent, lewd, obscene, vulgar.

deception, beguilement, chicanery, craft, cunning, deceit, deceitfulness, delusion, dishonesty, duplicity, equivocation, fabrication, falsehood, fraud, guile,

prevarication, trickery, sham, wiliness. ANT.—candor, frankness, honesty, openness, simplicity, square-dealing, sincerity, truthfulness, veracity.

decide, adjudicate, conclude, determine, end, judge, resolve, settle, terminate. ANT.—defer, delay, postpone, procrastinate, suspend, vacillate, wait, waver.

decision, conclusion, determination, finding, judgment, outcome, resolution, result, verdict. ANT.—deferment, delay, indefiniteness, indetermination, postponement, procrastination.

declaration, affirmation, allegation, announcement, avowal, assertion, proclamation, profession, statement, utterance. ANT.—denial, retraction, silence.

decline, descent, slant, slope; decay, decrease, degenerate, depreciate, deteriorate, diminish, dwindle, ebb, fail, lessen, retrogress, sink, wane, weaken; refuse, reject. ANT.—incline; improve, increase; accept.

decompose, crumble, decay, disintegrate, disperse, grow, improve, increase, multiply.

decorate, adorn, beautify, bedeck, embellish, enrich, garnish, ornament, trim. ANT.—strip, uncover.

decorum, dignity, etiquette, form, propriety, sedateness, seemliness. ANT.—impropriety, indecency, license.

decoy, beguile, entice, entrap, lure, mislead, tempt. ANT.—guide, lead, reveal, show.

decrease, abate, contract, curtail, decline, deduct, diminish, dwindle, lessen, minimize, narrow, reduce, shorten, shrink, subtract, wane. ANT.—add, develop, dilate, enlarge, expand, extend, grow, increase, widen.

decree, adjudicate, arbitrate, command, decide, determine, dictate, direct, judge, ordain, prescribe, sentence; edict, judgment, law, order, ordinance, statute.

decry, belittle, censure, condemn, criticize, depreciate, derogate, discredit, disparage, lower, minimize. ANT.—acclaim, aggrandize, approve, commend, exalt, extol, magnify, praise.

dedicate, apportion, bless, consecrate, devote, enshrine, give, hallow, offer, set apart. ANT.—alienate, desecrate, misapply, misconvert, misuse.

deduce, assume, believe, conclude, deem, derive, infer, judge, presume, reason, suppose, think.

deed, accomplishment, achievement, act, action, commission, exploit, feat, performance, perpetration, transaction. ANT.—failure, omission.

deface, blemish, damage, deform, disfigure, harm, hurt, impair, mar, spoil. ANT.—enhance, mend, repair.

defeat, beat, checkmate, conquer, crush, foil, frustrate, humble, master, overcome, quell, rout, subdue, subjugate, surmount, triumph, vanquish, whip, win.

ANT.—capitulate, cede, lose, retreat, surrender, yield.

defect, blemish, deficiency, drawback, error, failure, fault, flaw, impediment, imperfection, incompleteness. ANT.—advantage, completeness, excellence, faultlessness, perfection.

defend, cover, fortify, guard, insure, plead, protect, safeguard, save, screen, secure, shelter, shield; advocate, espouse, justify, maintain, uphold, vindicate. ANT.—abandon, abdicate, attack, desert, forsake, oppose, relinquish, renounce, resign, surrender.

defense, apology, bulwark, excuse, fortress, guard, justification, protection, refuge, safeguard, shelter, shield, vindication. ANT.—abandonment, betrayal, capitulation, desertion, surrender.

defer, adjourn, break up, dissolve, hinder, postphone, procrasinate, prolong, protract, put off, restrain, retard, suspend. ANT.—accelerate, advance, expedite, forward, further, hasten, quicken, stimulated.

deficient, defective, imperfect, inadequate, incomplete, insufficient, lacking, scanty, scarce, short, wanting. ANT.—adequate, ample, perfect, satisfactory, sufficient.

defile, befoul, contaminate, corrupt, debauch, infect, seduce, soil, spoil, stain, sully, taint. ANT.—clean, cleanse, disinfect, glorify, purify, sanctify, wash.

define, ascertain, decide, describe, determine, elucidate, explain, fix, interpret, limit. ANT.—confuse, derange, distort, mix, tangle, twist.

definite, bounded, certain, circumscribed, clear, definitive, determined, exact, explicit, fixed, limited, positive, precise, specific. ANT.—confused, equivocal, indefinite, indistinct, unbounded, vague.

definition, commentary, description, determination, elucidation, explanation, exposition, interpretation, meaning, rendering, restriction, significance, specification, translation. ANT.—absurdity, confusion, nonsense, vagueness.

deflate, empty, exhaust, reduce; humble. ANT.—blow up, fill, inflate, raise; flatter, praise.

deflect, avert, deviate, diverge, divert, swerve, turn, twist. ANT.—hit, strike.

deform, contort, cripple, deface, disfigure, distort, impair, injure, spoil. ANT.—beautify, improve, perfect, repair.

deformed, crippled, disfigured, disjointed, distorted, malformed, misshapen, twisted, unseemly, unsightly. ANT.—graceful, shapely, symmetrical, regular, well-built, well-formed.

defraud, beguile, cheat, deceive, delude, deprive, dupe, fool, gull, hoodwink, inveigle, overreach, rob, swindle, trick. ANT.—assist, befriend, contribute, help, remunerate, requite, support.

defray, adjust, bear, clear, discharge, liquidate, meet, pay, satisfy, settle. ANT.—abjure, deny, disclaim, disown, embezzle, refuse, repudiate.

deft, adept, adroit, agile, assured, clever, dexterous, expert, handy, nimble, skillful. ANT.—awkward, clumsy, inept, maladroit, ungainly.

defy, attack, brave, challenge, dare, disobey, flout, obstruct, oppose, provoke, resist, slight, spurn, thwart. ANT.—accept, cooperate, obey, relent, yield.

degenerate, corrupt, debase, debauch, decay, decline, demoralize, depreciate, deteriorate, diminish, dwindle, sink, weaken, worsen. ANT.—ameliorate, ascend, improve, increase.

degradation, abasement, baseness, debasement, decline, degeneracy, disgrace, dishonor, dismissal, humiliation, meanness, removal, vice. ANT.—admiration, ascendancy, elevation, exaltation, honor, reward, superiority.

degrade, abase, abash, break, corrupt, crush, debase, demote, discredit, humble, humiliate, mortify, shame, subdue, vitiate. ANT.—elevate, exalt, honor, praise.

degree, class, distinction, division, extent, grade, honor, interval, mark, measure, order, qualification, quality, rank, space, stage, station, step, testimony. ANT.—size, space, mass, numbers.

dejection, depression, despair, despondency, discontent, gloom, heaviness, melancholy, pensiveness, sadness, sorrow. ANT.—cheer, delight, exhilaration, gaiety, hilarity, joy, merriment.

delay, defer, postpone, procrastinate; arrest, detain, hinder, impede, prolong, protract, retard, stay; dally, dawdle, linger, loiter, tarry. ANT.—dispatch, expedite, facilitate, hasten, precipitate, quicken.

delectable, agreeable, delightful, delicious, gratifying, luscious, palatable, pleasant, savory, sweet, tasty, toothsome. ANT.—acrid, distasteful, loathsome, nauseating, repulsive, unpalatable, unsavory.

deleterious, bad, baleful, base, damaging, deadly, destructive, evil, harmful, hurtful, immoral, iniquitous, noxious, pernicious, poisonous, sinful, unsound, unwholesome, villainous, wicked. ANT.—advantageous, healthful, helpful, honorable, moral, reputable, salutary.

deliberate, careful, cautious, considered, contemplated, designed, intentional, judged, pondered, prudent, reasoned, slow, studied, thoughtful, unhurried, weighed; consider, consult, contemplate, estimate, examine, heed, meditate, ponder, regard, reflect, study, weigh. ANT.—careless, hasty, imprudent, unintentional; discard, neglect, reject, spurn.

delicate, compassionate, dainty, fastidious, feeble, fine, fragile, frail, gentle, nice, refined, sensitive, sickly, slender, slight, soft, tender, weak. ANT.—boisterous, coarse, depraved, indelicate, robust, rude, vulgar.

delicious, appetizing, choice, dainty, delectable, delightful, exquisite, gratifying, luscious, luxurious, palatable, pleasing, savory, sweet, tasteful. ANT.—acrid, coarse, disagreeable, distasteful, nauseous, unpalatable, unsavory.

delightful, agreeable, alluring, charming, enjoyable, glad, gratifying, inspiring, merry, pleasant, pleasing, pleasurable, satisfactory. ANT.—depressing, mournful, offensive, painful, wearisome.

delirium, aberration, dementia, frenzy, hallucination, insanity, lunacy, madness, mania, raving, wandering. ANT.—normality, reason, saneness, sanity, steadiness.

deliver, convey, give, hand over, impart, surrender, transfer, yield; announce, communicate, impart, proclaim, pronounce; discharge, emancipate, free, liberate, redeem, release, rescue, save. ANT.—confine, withhold; betray, capture, imprison, restrain, restrict.

delusion, chimera, deception, error, fallacy, fantasy, hallucination, illusion, mirage, misconception, phantom. ANT.—actuality, certainty, fact, materiality, reality, substance, truth.

demand, ask, beg, beseech, charge, crave, exact, implore, inquire, levy, order, request, require, seek, solicit, supplicate. ANT.—give, offer, present, reply, tender.

demeanor, air, appearance, attitude, bearing, behavior, conduct, manner. ANT.—misbehavior, unmannerliness.

demented, crazy, frenzied, insane, irrational, lunatic, maniacal. ANT.—lucid, normal, rational, reasonable, sane.

demise, alienation, conveyance, death, decease, end, transfer. ANT.—birth, non-alienation.

demolish, annihilate, destroy, devastate, dismantle, eradicate, exterminate, extinguish, level, obliterate, overturn, ravage, raze, ruin, wreck. ANT.—construct, embellish, improve, mend, restore, uphold.

demonstration, certainty, conclusion, consequence, corroboration, deduction, evidence, exhibition, explanation, exposition, induction, manifestation, presentation, proof, show, substantiation, verification. ANT.—concealment, confusion, distortion, falsification, misrepresentation.

demoralize, confuse, corrupt, disconcert, discourage, disorganize, incapacitate, pervert, undermine. ANT.—encourage, exalt, hearten, inspire, invigorate, organize.

demur, balk, delay, disapprove, dissent, falter, hesitate, object, pause, scruple, vacillate, waver. ANT.—accept, agree, assent, consent, decide, persevere, proceed.

demure, coy, decorous, diffident, modest, prim, prudish, sedate, shy, sober, staid. ANT.—impudent, indecorous, shameless, wanton.

denote, connote, express, imply, indicate, intend, mark, mean, signify, specify.

denounce, accuse, arraign, blame, censure, charge, condemn, curse, decry, indict, reprehend, reprimand, reproach, reprove, scold, upbraid. ANT.—applaud, commend, praise.

dense, close, compact, compressed, concentrated, crowded, impenetrable, thick; dull, obtuse, slow, solid, stupid, substantial. ANT.—dispersed, open, rare, scattered, sparse, thin; clever, quick.

deny, contradict, contravene, gainsay, oppose, refute; abjure, disavow, disclaim, disown, forbid, renounce; refuse, repudiate, withhold. ANT.—admit, affirm, agree, assert, concede, confirm.

depart, abandon, decamp, decease, desert, deviate, die, forsake, go, leave, quit, retire, set out, vanish, vary, withdraw.

ANT.—abide, dwell, linger, remain, stay, tarry.

dependable, certain, reliable, sure, trustworthy, trusty. ANT.—questionable, uncertain, unreliable, untrustworthy.

dependent, collateral, conditional, consequent, contingent, relative, reliant, relying, subject. ANT.—absolute, autonomous, categorical, independent, unconditional.

depict, characterize, delineate, describe, draw, illustrate, paint, picture, portray, sketch. ANT.—caricature, confound, confuse, distort.

deplete, diminish, drain, empty, exhaust, lessen, weaken. ANT.—augment, enlarge, fill, increase, strengthen.

deplore, be sorry (for), complain, cry (for), deprecate, fret, grieve, lament, mourn, wail, weep. ANT.—boast, cheer, delight, rejoice, revel.

deportment, air, bearing, behavior, carriage, comportment, conduct, demeanor, form, manner, mien, style.

deposit, hoard, lay down, leave, pledge, place, save, store; precipitate; sediment.

depravity, corruption, degeneracy, depravation, deterioration, immorality, sinfulness, wickedness. ANT.—honor, integrity, justice, morality, purity, virtue.

deprecate, condemn, deplore, disapprove, protest, regret. ANT.—approve, commend, endorse.

depreciate, decline, decrease, degenerate, deteriorate, diminish, dwindle, weaken; decry, denounce, despise, detract, disparage, underrate, undervalue. ANT.—increase, magnify, raise; approve, commend, extol, praise.

depress, abase, debase, degrade, deject, discourage, disgrace, dispirit, humble, humiliate, lower, sink. ANT.—cheer, comfort, encourage, praise, stimulate.

depression, despair, despondency, gloom, hopelessness, melancholy, misery, pessimism. ANT.—business boom; contentment, elation, hope, lightheartedness, optimism.

deprive, abridge, bereave, debar, depose, despoil, dispossess, divest, rob, separate, strip, take. ANT.—assist, confer, endow, enrich, repay, restore.

derelict, abandoned, neglected, wrecked; delinquent, negligent; bum, outcast, tramp, vagrant.

derision, contempt, disdain, disregard, disrespect, insult, irony, jeering, mockery, raillery, ridicule, sarcasm, scorn, slight, slur, sneering. ANT.—adulation, flattery, regard, respect, reference.

derivation, beginning, birth, cause, commencement, cradle, foundation, fountain, inception, nucleus, origin, rise, root, source, spring. ANT.—consequence, end, harvest, issue, outgrowth, termination.

derogatory, belittling, defamatory, deprecatory, disparaging, lessening. ANT.—favoring, helping, lauding, praising.

descent, debasement, degradation, decline; declivity, fall, slant, slope; ancestry, genesis, lineage, origin, pedigree. ANT.—ascension, ascent, climb, elevation, mountain, rise.

describe, characterize, define, delineate, depict, explain, express, illustrate, narrate, picture, portray, recite, recount, relate, represent. ANT.—caricature, confuse, deceive, distort, exaggerate, misrepresent.

desecrate, abuse, debase, defile, misuse, pervert, pollute, profane, secularize. ANT.—cleanse, consecrate, hallow, purify, sanctify.

desert, abandon, abdicate, abjure, forsake, leave, quit, relinquish, secede; surrender, vacate; wasteland, wilderness; due, merit, reward. ANT.—continue, remain; garden, oasis, pasture; penalty, retribution.

deserve, be worthy of, earn, have right to, merit, win. ANT.—undeserving, unworthy of.

design, decoration, delineation, diagram, draft, drawing, object, outline, pattern, picture, plan, project, sketch; artfulness, contrivance, cunning, end, intention, purpose, scheme. ANT.—accident, chance; candor, sincerity.

designate, appoint, characterize, choose, denominate, denote, indicate, manifest, name, reveal, select, show, signify, specify. ANT.—conceal, divert, falsify.

designing, astute, crafty, cunning, scheming, sly, tricky, underhanded, unscrupulous. ANT.—candid, frank, honest, naive, open.

desire, affection, ambition, appetite, ardor, aspiration, concupiscence, coveting, craving, eagerness, hungering, inclination, longing, wish, yearning, zeal. ANT.—abhorrence, aversion, detestation, distaste, repulsion.

desirable, acceptable, advisable, beneficial, delightful, enviable, judicious, pleasing, profitable, proper, valuable, wanted, worthy. ANT.—baneful, detrimental, harmful, injurious, noxious.

desist, abstain, arrest, bar, cease, check, discontinue, drop, end, halt, impede, obstruct, quit, relinquish, seal, stop, terminate. ANT.—continue, endure, proceed, retain, wait.

desolate, abandoned, alone, bare, bereaved, bleak, dejected, deserted, dismal, dreary, forgotten, forlorn, forsaken, inhospitable, lonely, miserable, secluded, solitary, uninhabited, unpeopled, waste, wild. ANT.—cultivated, enjoyable, fertile, inhabited, pleasant, teeming.

despair, dejection, depression, desperation, despondency, discouragement, gloom, hopelessness, pessimism, sadness. ANT.—anticipation, confidence, elation, faith, optimism.

desperate, audacious, bold, careless, critical, despondent, determined, extreme, foolhardy, frantic, furious, hopeless, irretrievable, mad, reckless, wild. ANT.—cautious, composed, confident, hopeful, peaceful, satisfied.

despicable, abject, base, contemptible, corrupt, cowardly, depraved, low, lying, malicious, nasty, pitiful, mean, scurrilous, shameless, sordid, vile, vulgar, worthless. ANT.—exalted, honorable, noble, praiseworthy, respectable.

despise, abhor, abominate, condemn, denounce, deride, detest, disdain, dislike, hold in contempt, loathe, scorn, spurn. ANT.—admire, applaud, cherish, commend, love.

despondent, dejected, depressed, despairing, disconsolate, disheartened, dispirited, doleful, low, melancholy, sad. ANT.—buoyant, ebullient, elated, happy, joyous.

despotic, absolute, arbitrary, arrogant, autocratic, cruel, tyrannical, tyrannous. ANT.—conditional, constitutional, limited.

destination, bourn, design, doom, end, fate, goal, intention, location, objective, point, port, purpose, terminus.

destiny, chance, conclusion, condition, decree, doom, end, fate, finality, fortune, judgment, lot, necessity, outcome, portion, predestination, predetermination. ANT.—choice, freedom, volition, will.

destitution, beggary, distress, indigence, lack, need, pauperism, penury, poverty, privation, want. ANT.—abundance, affluence, opulence, prosperity, security.

destroy, annihilate, consume, demolish, devastate, dismantle, dispel, eradicate, exterminate, extirpate, kill, obliterate, overthrow, ravage, raze, ruin, slaughter, terminate. ANT.—construct, fabricate, invigorate, renew, strengthen.

destruction, abolishment, annihilation, cataclysm, demolition, desolation, devastation, downfall, eradication, extermination, extinction, extirpation, fall, havoc, obliteration, overthrow, subversion. ANT.—recovery, renewal, restitution, restoration, revival.

desultory, abnormal, cursory, discursive, erratic, flighty, irregular, loose, rambling, superficial, unsettled, wandering. ANT.—constant, firm, methodical, stable, unalterable.

detach, disconnect, disengage, disjoin, disunite, loosen, part, remove, separate, sever, unfasten, untie, withdraw. ANT.—adhere, bind, coalesce, link, merge.

detail, appoint, assign, describe, itemize, narrate, particularize, relate, report, tell; account, article, description, item, minutia, narrative, particular, portion, recital, specification, trifle. ANT.—conceal, reserve, stifle, suppress; entirety, whole.

detain, arrest, bar, check, confine, curb, delay, hinder, impede, keep, limit, prevent, repress, restrain, retain, retard, stay, stop, withhold. ANT.—free, hasten, liberate, release, precipitate.

detect, apprehend, ascertain, catch, determine, disclose, discover, espy, expose, ferret out, find, identify, perceive, uncover, unearth, unmask. ANT.—blunder, miss, omit, overlook, pass by.

deter, discourage, disincline, dissuade, frighten, hinder, prevent, stop, warn. ANT.—encourage, foster, promote, stimulate, urge.

deteriorate, atrophy, collapse, corrode, decay, decline, decompose, discolor, disintegrate, ebb, erode, mold, oxidize, recede, retrogress, rot, rust, wane, wear. ANT.—improve, refurbish, renew.

determine, affect, ascertain, bound, conclude, decide, define, end, find out, fix, influence, limit, resolve, restrict, settle, specify. ANT.—doubt, falter, hesitate, vacillate, waver.

determined, decided, firm, fixed, immovable, resolute, stable, stubborn, unalterable, unwavering, willful. ANT.—irresolute, fluctuating, uncertain, undecided, wavering.

detest, abhor, abominate, despise, dislike, execrate, hate, loathe. ANT.—admire, appreciate, cherish, love, respect.

detour, by-pass, deviation, digression, side road. ANT.—direct route, highway.

detraction, aspersion, backbiting, calumny, defamation, depreciation, derogation, diminution, disparagement, libel, slander, vilification. ANT.—admiration, commendation, praise, recommendation, respect.

detriment, bane, damage, deterioration, disadvantage, evil, harm, hurt, impairment, inconvenience, infliction, injury, loss, misfortune, wrong. ANT.—advantage, assistance, benefit, favor, gain, profit.

devastate, demolish, desolate, despoil, pillage, ruin, sack, strip, waste, wreck. ANT.—benefit, cultivate, enrich, preserve, restore.

develop, amplify, cultivate, disclose, disentangle, enlarge, evolve, exhibit, expand, extend, grow, mature, uncover, unfold, unravel. ANT.—compress, conceal, contract, hide, restrict.

development, disclosure, expansion, evolution, growth, improvement, maturing, progress, project, subdivision, unfolding. ANT.—compression, curtailment, decline, degeneration.

deviate, bend, deflect, depart from, digress, diverge, divert, shift, shunt, sidetrack, stray, swerve, wander. ANT.—continue, direct, persevere, persist, remain.

device, agent, channel, instrument, means, medium, vehicle; apparatus, artifice, contrivance, design, gadget, invention, machine; plan, ruse, scheme, stratagem.

ANT.—hindrance, impediment, obstruction.

devious, circuitous, crooked, indirect, mazy, roundabout, swerving, tortuous, wandering, winding; crooked, cunning, tricky. ANT.—direct, straight; honest, straightforward.

devise, arrange, bequeath, concoct, contrive, invent, make, plan, prepare, will. ANT.—disarrange, fumble, muddle.

devoid, bare, destitute, empty, lacking, unendowed, unprovided, void, wanting, without. ANT.—abundant, complete, full, possessing, replete.

devolve, alienate, authorize, be handed down, commission, consign, depute, deliver, fall (upon).

devote, allot, apply, apportion, appropriate, assign, attend, consign, dedicate, study. ANT.—misappropriate, misuse, pervert, squander, waste.

devotion, adherence, ardor, consecration, dedication, devoutness, earnestness, fidelity, intensity, observance, piety, religiousness, sincerity, zeal. ANT.—alienation, apathy, aversion, indifference, neglect, unfaithfulness.

devour, bolt, consume, destroy, eat greedily, gobble, gorge, prey upon, swallow (up), waste. ANT.—disgorge, vomit.

devout, devotional, earnest, fervent, godly, holy, moral, pietistic, pious, religious, reverent, righteous, sacred, sincere, spir-

itual. ANT.—atheistic, impious, profane, secular, worldly.

dexterity, ability, adroitness, aptitude, aptness, art, capability, cleverness, deftness, facility, handiness, skill. ANT.—awkwardness, blundering, clumsiness, ineptitude.

diagram, blueprint, chart, drawing, map, outline, plan, sketch.

dialect, accent, idiom, jargon, patois, provincialism, vernacular. ANT.—official language, standard speech.

dictate, command, decree, direct, order, prescribe. ANT.—ask, beg, follow, obey, plead.

dictatorial, arbitrary, arrogant, dogmatic, domineering, haughty, imperious, overbearing, tyrannical. ANT.—acquiescent, docile, obsequious, submissive, subservient, passive.

diction, choice of words, enunciation, phraseology, pronunciation, vocal expression.

die, cease, decay, decease, decline, depart, expire, fade, languish, pass away, perish, recede, sink, vanish, wane, wither; mold, stamp. ANT.—begin, endure, flourish, grow, live, survive.

difference, deviation, discrepancy, disparity, dissimilarity, distinction, divergence, inequality, separation, variation, variety; disagreement, discord, dissension, estrangement. ANT.—congruity, similarity, uniformity; agreement, harmony.

different, contrary, differing, discordant, dissimilar, distinct, distinctive, divers, diverse, heterogeneous, incongruous, unlike, variant, various. ANT.—alike, congruous, harmonious, homogeneous, same.

differentiate, contrast, discriminate, distinguish, isolate, particularize, separate. ANT.—confound, confuse, group, mingle.

difficult, arduous, complex, complicated, demanding, enigmatical, hard, intricate, involved, laborious, obscure, perplexing, puzzling, rigid, toilsome, troublesome, trying, unmanageable, unyielding. ANT.—easy, facile, pleasant, simple, tranquil.

difficulty, annoyance, anxiety, argument, complication, contention, dilemma, discouragement, dispute, distress, embarrassment, entanglement, impediment, intricacy, obstacle, obstruction, oppression, perplexity, problem, trouble, worry. ANT.—comfort, facility, felicity, flexibility, pleasure, satisfaction.

diffident, bashful, hesitant, modest, shrinking, shy, timid. ANT.—bold, brash, brazen.

diffuse, copious, discursive, repetitive, tedious, tiresome, wordy. ANT.—abbreviated, brief, restricted.

diffusion, broadcasting, circulation, distribution, dispersion, spreading. ANT.—collection, restriction, suppression.

dignify, adorn, advance, award, decorate, elevate, ennoble, exalt, extol, glorify, honor, magnify, prefer, proclaim, promote, revere. ANT.—belittle, degrade, demean, humiliate, slander.

dignity, decency, decorum, eminence, grace, greatness, propriety, stateliness, station, worth. ANT.—degradation, lowliness.

digress, bend, deflect, depart, deviate, diverge, divert, ramble, sidetrack, stray, turn aside, wander. ANT.—continue, persevere, persist, preserve.

dilapidated, crumbling, decayed, depreciating, deteriorating, sagging. ANT.—rebuilt, renewed, restored.

dilate, broaden, distend, enlarge, expand, extend, increase, magnify, open, spread, stretch, swell, widen. ANT.—abridge, compress, contract, diminish, reduce.

dilemma, difficulty, fix, perplexity, plight, predicament, problem, quandary. ANT.—advantage, freedom, solution.

diligence, alertness, application, assiduity, attention, care, carefulness, earnestness, heed, industry, intensity, keenness, perseverance, quickness. ANT.—ennui, indolence, laziness, lethargy, slowness.

dilute, reduced, thin, watery, weak. ANT.—concentrated, rich, strong, thick.

dim, blurred, clouded, dull, faint, gloomy, indefinite, indistinct, misty, mysterious, obscure, shaded, shadowy. ANT.—bright, brilliant, clear, distinct.

dimension, amplitude, area, bulk, capacity, extent, magnitude, measurement, size.

diminish, abate, abridge, assuage, compress, contract, curtail, decrease, degrade, dwindle, impair, lessen, lower, minimize, moderate, reduce, shorten, shrink. ANT.—amplify, enlarge, increase, intensify, magnify.

din, clamor, clangor, clash, clatter, hubbub, noise, racket, row, tumult, uproar. ANT.—quiet, silence, stillness.

diplomatic, adroit, artful, courteous, discreet, judicious, politic, tactful. ANT.—blunt, gruff, rude, tactless.

direct, aim, point, train; conduct, control, demonstrate, explain, govern, guide, head, inform, instruct, lead, manage, order, regulate, supervise, teach, usher. ANT.—deceive, delude, misdirect, misguide.

direction, address, aim, course, end, goal, inclination, line, tendency, way; administration, government, leadership, management, superintendence; command, control, guidance, instruction, order.

dirty, dingy, discolored, filthy, foul, grimy, muddy, soiled, squalid; indecent, obscene, sordid; base, contemptible, despicable, low, mean, shabby.

ANT.—clean, immaculate, spotless; pure, wholesome.

disability, decrepitude, defect, disqualification, feebleness, forfeiture, handicap, impotence, inability, inadequacy, incompetence, infirmity, powerlessness, unfitness, weakness. ANT.—ability, capability, capacity, power, strength.

disadvantage, block, check, detriment, difficulty, drawback, evil, harm, hindrance, hurt, prejudice, stumbling, block. ANT.—advantage, assistance, benefit, profit, utility.

disaffect, alienate, disdain, dislike, disorder, estrange.

disagree, argue, clash, combat, contend, differ, dispute, dissent, fight, oppose, quarrel, vary. ANT.—agree, coincide, concur, harmonize.

disappear, cease, depart, dissolve, evaporate, fade, melt, vanish, withdraw. ANT.—appear, materialize.

disappoint, baffle, betray, deceive, delude, fail, foil, frustrate, thwart, vex. ANT.—assist, befriend, please, support, relieve.

disapproval, blame, censure, condemnation, depreciation, disapprobation, dislike, disparagement, odium. ANT.—approval, sanction.

disaster, adversity, calamity, casualty, cataclysm, catastrophe, evil, misadventure, mischance, misfortune, mishap, tragedy.

ANT.—advantage, fortune, privilege, prosperity.

disband, break up, demobilize, disperse, dissolve. ANT.—assemble, mobilize, unite.

disburse, expend, distribute, pay, settle, spend. ANT.—collect, deposit, receive, retain, save.

discard, abandon, cancel, discharge, dismiss, divorce, eliminate, reject, repudiate, scrap, shed. ANT.—adopt, embrace, keep, retain.

discern, descry, detect, discover, discriminate, distinguish, espy, know, observe, perceive, recognize, see, understand. ANT.—disregard, neglect, omit, overlook, slight.

discerning, acute, critical, discriminating, exacting, fastidious, particular, sharp-sighted, shrewd. ANT.—cursory, shallow, superficial, uncritical.

discernment, acumen, discrimination, insight, judgment, penetration, perspicuity. ANT.—obtuseness.

discharge, acquit, clear, dismiss, eject, emit, exile, expel, fire, free, oust, pay, perform, project, release, retire, settle, shoot. ANT.—load, hire, imprison, retain.

disciple, adherent, devotee, follower, votary.

discipline, control, order, regulation, restraint; drill, instruction, method, rule, training; chastisement, correction, punishment. ANT.—chaos, confusion, disorder, mutiny, turbulence.

disclaim, abandon, deny, disallow, disavow, disown, reject, renounce, repudiate, retract. ANT.—acknowledge, claim, own, recognize.

disclose, acknowledge, betray, concede, declare, discover, divulge, expose, grant, inform, reveal, show, tell, uncover, unfold, unmask, unveil, utter. ANT.—cloak, conceal, cover, deceive, withhold.

disconsolate, broken-hearted, cheerless, dejected, depressed, despondent, dismal, doleful, gloomy, inconsolable, lugubrious, melancholy, mournful, sad, sorrowful. ANT.—cheerful, glad, happy, joyous, merry.

discontent, disappointment, disillusionment, dissatisfaction, frustration, uneasiness, vexation. ANT.—content, peace, satisfaction.

discord, animosity, clash, confusion, contention, difference, disagreement, disharmony, dissension, dissonance, disturbance, harshness, quarreling, variance, wrangling. ANT.—agreement, amity, concord, harmony, peace.

discount, allowance, deduction, drawback, loss, rebate, reduction, refund. ANT.—increase, increment, premium, rise.

discourage, block, check, dampen, depress, deter, dishearten, dispirit, dissuade, hamper, hinder, impede, obstruct, oppose, prevent, resist, restrain, retard, thwart. ANT.—assist, encourage, expedite, facilitate, promote.

discourteous, abusive, blunt, boorish, disrespectful, forward, gruff, ill-mannered, impolite, impudent, insolent, rough, rude, surly, uncivil, ungracious, unmannerly, unpolished, vulgar. ANT.—civil, courteous, genteel, polished, polite.

discover, ascertain, contrive, descry, detect, discern, disclose, elicit, expose, find, find out, invent, learn, manifest, realize, reveal, uncover, unearth. ANT.—cover, hide, mask, screen, suppress.

discreet, attentive, careful, cautious, circumspect, considerate, discerning, discriminating, judicious, prudent, sensible, serious, thoughtful, watchful, wise. ANT.—indiscreet, injudicious, rash, thoughtless.

discrepancy, contrariety, difference, disagreement, inconsistency, variance. ANT.—accordance, agreement, concurrence, harmony.

discretion, carefulness, caution, circumspection, finesse, foresight, judgment, prudence, sagacity, thoughtfulness. ANT.—foolishness, imprudence, rashness, recklessness, thoughtlessness.

discrimination, acumen, acuteness, care, caution, circumspection, differentiation, discernment, distinction, foresight, forethought, heed, perception, perspicacity, prudence, sagacity, vigilance, wisdom. ANT.—carelessness, imprudence, negligence, rashness, senselessness.

discuss, analyze, argue, confer, consult, controvert, converse, debate, deliberate, dispute, examine, explain.

disdain, arrogance, contempt, contumely, derision, detestation, haughtiness, pride, scorn, scornfulness, superciliousness. ANT.—admiration, esteem, regard, respect, reverence.

disease, affliction, ailment, complaint, disorder, distemper, illness, infirmity, malady, plague, pestilence, sickness, unhealthiness, unsoundness. ANT.—health, healthiness, soundness, sturdiness, vigor.

disengage, clear, detach, disentangle, extricate, free, liberate, loose, loosen, release, separate, unravel, withdraw. ANT.—attach, bind, fasten, tighten, unite.

disfigure, blemish, damage, deface, deform, distort, injure, mar, mutilate, spoil. ANT.—adorn, decorate, repair, restore.

disgrace, abasement, baseness, disfavor, dishonor, disrepute, humiliation, infamy, ignominy, mortification, odium, opprobrium, reproach, scandal, shame. ANT.—dignity, exaltation, glory, honor, renown, respect.

disguise, camouflage, change, cloak, conceal, cover, dissemble, feign, hide, mask, masquerade, pretend, screen, secrete, shroud, suppress, veil, withhold. ANT.—bare, disclose, divulge, expose, reveal, uncover.

disgust, abhorrence, abomination, aversion, detestation, dislike, distaste, hatred, loathing, nausea, repugnance, resentment, revulsion. ANT.—admiration, approbation, esteem, respect, reverence.

dishonest, cheating, corrupt, corruptible, crooked, debased, deceitful, false, fraudulent, lying, perfidious, unsound, unscrupulous, untrue, untrustworthy, venal, vitiated. ANT.—honest, scrupulous, trustworthy.

dislike, abhorrence, antipathy, aversion, disaffection, disapproval, disinclination, distaste, hatred, loathing, repugnance, repulsion. ANT.—affection, attachment, devotion.

disloyal, apostate, disaffected, faithless, false, perfidious, subversive, traitorous, treacherous, treasonable, unfaithful, unpatriotic. ANT.—faithful, loyal, true, worthy.

dismal, bleak, cheerless, dark, depressing, dingy, direful, doleful, dolorous, dreadful, dreary, dull, funereal, gloomy, horrible, horrid, melancholy, sad, somber, sorrowful, unhappy. ANT.—bright, cheerful, joyous, pleasant.

dismantle, demolish, raze, strip, take apart, take down. ANT.—assemble, build, construct, raise.

dismay, alarm, anxiety, apprehension, awe, consternation, discouragement, dread, fear, fright, horror, misgiving, trepidation. ANT.—assurance, confidence, courage, intrepidity.

dismiss, banish, bounce, decline, depose, discard, discharge, exile, expel, fire, oust, remove, repel, repudiate, suspend. ANT.—accept, recall, retain.

disobey, defy, disregard, ignore, infringe, invade, rebel, resist, transgress, violate. ANT.—accept, obey, submit.

disorder, anarchy, bustle, chaos, confusion, disarrangement, disorganization, disturbance, illness, indisposition, irregularity, jumble, muddle, riot, sickness, tumult. ANT.—order, organization, system, vigor.

disorderly, chaotic, confused, disheveled, irregular, lawless, tumultuous, unrestrained, unruly. ANT.—calm, disciplined, law-abiding, neat, orderly.

disparage, asperse, belittle, decry, defame, deprecate, depreciate, derogate, discredit, dishonor, lower, minimize, traduce, underestimate, underrate, undervalue. ANT.—aggrandize, commend, exalt, magnify, praise, sanction.

dispatch, accelerate, conclude, expedite, hasten, kill, perform, send, speed, transmit. ANT.—hold, retain, slow.

dispel, banish, diffuse, dismiss, disperse, disseminate, dissipate, dissolve, rout, scatter, spread, strew. ANT.—accumulate, amass, assemble, collect, gather, increase.

dispense, administer, allocate, allot, apply, apportion, appropriate, assign, carry out, distribute, dole out, execute, mete, sell; excuse, exempt, release. ANT.—absorb, keep, retain, withhold.

disperse, diffuse, dispel, disseminate, dissipate, dissolve, distribute, fade, scatter, separate, sow, strew. ANT.—amass, assemble, collect, concentrate, gather.

displace, confuse, crowd out, depose, derange, disarrange, discharge, dislodge, dismiss, displant, dispossess, disturb, eject, jumble, mislay, misplace, mix, remove, shift, unseat, unsettle, uproot. ANT.—arrange, classify, group, sort.

display, exhibit expose, flaunt, open, parade, reveal, show, unfold; evince, manifest; array, demonstration, exhibition, flourish, layout, manifestation, ostentation, show. ANT.—conceal, cover, disguise, hide, suppress.

displease, anger, annoy, antagonize, bother, chagrin, disappoint, disgruntle, disgust, dissatisfy, disturb, exasperate, gall, harass, irritate, mortify, pester, pique, plague, provoke, tantalize, taunt, tease, trouble, vex, worry. ANT.—delight, gratify, pacify, propitiate, satisfy.

dispose, adapt, adjust, arrange, bestow, classify, conform, give, locate, order, place, regulate, settle. ANT.—conceal, disarrange, disorder, displace, retain.

disposition, bent, bias, character, inclination, leaning, make-up, nature, personality, proclivity, temper, temperament, tendency; adjustment, arrangement, control, disposal.

dispute, altercation, argument, contention, contest, controversy, debate, denial, difference, disagreement, discord, discussion, dissension, estrangement, feud, quarrel, questioning, squabble, variance. ANT.—agreement, concord, harmony, unison.

disqualify, bar, disable, disenfranchise, incapacitate, prohibit, remove from contention. ANT.—accept, fit, quality.

disregard, contemn, disobey, ignore, neglect, omit, overlook, skip, slight. ANT.—include, notice, regard.

disrespectful, contemptuous, derisive, discourteous, disparaging, flippant, impertinent, impious, impolite, insolent, insulting, irreverent, uncivil. ANT.—courteous, respectful.

dissatisfaction, disappointment, disapproval, discomfort, discontent, disgruntlement, dislike, displeasure, distaste, malcontentment, uneasiness. ANT.—contentment, gratification, happiness, recompense, satisfaction.

dissect, analyze, anatomize, cut up, examine. ANT.—assemble, synthesize.

dissent, censure, condemn, conflict, contend, differ, disagree, disapprove, disclaim, dispute, except, oppose, vary. ANT.—agree, commend, concur, endorse, sanction.

dissertation, commentary, composition, discourse, essay, homily, lecture, sermon, study, theme, thesis, tract.

dissipate, debauch, diffuse, disperse, lavish, scatter, spread, squander, waste. ANT.—absorb, accumulate, conserve, preserve, save.

dissolve, destroy, disappear, disintegrate, disorganize, divide, evanesce, evaporate, fade, render, thaw, vanish. ANT.—assemble, concentrate, unite.

distant, afar, apart, faint, far, indistinct, remove, removed, separated; aloof, cold, cool, haughty, indifferent, reserved, shy, stiff, unfriendly. ANT.—close, near, nigh, cordial, friendly, sympathetic, warm.

distasteful, disagreeable, disgusting, displeasing, loathsome, nauseating, objectionable, obnoxious, offensive, repellent, repugnant, repulsive, unpalatable, unsavory. ANT.—agreeable, delectable, pleasing, savory, welcome.

distend, blow up, dilate, expand, grow, inflate, stretch, swell, tumefy. ANT.—constrict, contract, narrow, shrink.

distinct, apparent, clear, definite, evident, exact, lucid, manifest, obvious, plain, precise, unmistakable, visible. ANT.—ambiguous, indefinite, obscure, unclear, vague.

distinction, attribute, characteristic, feature, peculiarity, property, quality, trait; acumen, acuteness, clearness, discernment, discrimination, elevation, eminence, judgment, note, rank, superiority. ANT.—amalgamation, combination; inferiority, mediocrity, sameness.

distinguished, brilliant, celebrated, conspicuous, eminent, extraordinary, famous, glorious, great, illustrious, noble, noted, prominent, renowned, well-known. ANT.—common, obscure, ordinary, unknown, unobtrusive.

distort, bend, contort, deface, deform, disfigure, falsify, gnarl, impair, mangle, misconstrue, misshape, pervert, slant. ANT.—align, balance, explain, straighten.

distract, bewilder, confound, confuse, daze, derange, disorder, embarrass, mislead, mystify, perplex. ANT.—allay, assure, mitigate, pacify, reassure.

distress, adversity, agony, anguish, calamity, catastrophe, danger, grief, hardship, misadventure, misery, misfortune, need, pain, perplexity, sorrow, suffering, torment, trouble, unhappiness, wretchedness. ANT.—comfort, joy, relief, satisfaction.

distribution, allotment, apportionment, arrangement, classification, deal, dispensation, disposal, division, dole, partition. ANT.—collection, hoard, maintenance, retention, storage.

distrust, disbelief, doubt, misgiving, mistrust, skepticism, suspicion, uncertainty. ANT.—belief, certainty, conviction, faith, trust.

disturb, agitate, annoy, arouse, bother, confuse, derange, disarrange, discompose, disconcert, disorder, displace, distress, interrupt, perplex, perturb, rouse, trouble, unbalance, unsettle, vex, worry. ANT.—compose, pacify, quiet, settle, soothe.

divergent, branching, contrary, deviating, differing, disagreeing, diverse, separating, varying. ANT.—convergent, identical, parallel, similar.

divest, bare, denude, deprive, disrobe, peel, strip, unclothe, uncover, undress. ANT.—clothe, cover, invest, restore (property).

diverse, contrary, different, dissimilar, distinct, divergent, diversified, heterogeneous, unlike, variant; divers, miscellaneous, numerous, several, sundry, various. ANT.—alike, identical, same, selfsame, similar.

divide, detach, disconnect, disengage, disjoin, dissolve, disunite, partition, separate, sever, split, sunder; allot, apportion, assign, dispense, distribute. ANT.—combine, convene, fasten, join, unite.

divine, celestial, consecrated, godlike, heavenly, holy, sacred, sanctified, spiritual, superhuman, supernatural, transcendent, venerable. ANT.—blasphemous, diabolical, impious, profane, wicked.

division, allotment, compartment, department, detachment, difference, discord, disunion, partition, portion, share. ANT.—concord, indivisibility, oneness, union, unity.

divulge, betray, communicate, describe, disclose, discover, expose, impart, inform, relate, reveal, show, tell, uncover, unveil. ANT.—cloak, conceal, disguise, hide, obscure.

do, accomplish, achieve, complete, conclude, consummate, effect, enact, execute, finish, fulfill, perform, terminate; carry on, conduct, discharge, transact; make, produce, work; commit, perpetrate. ANT.—evade, shirk.

docile, amenable, compliant, gentle, manageable, meek, mild, obedient, pliable, pliant, submissive, tame, tractable, yielding. ANT.—determined, mulish, obstinate, stubborn, unyielding.

doctrine, belief, conviction, creed, cult, dogma, faith, gospel, opinion, persuasion, precept, principle, propaganda, proposition, religion, rule, teaching, tenet, theory.

document, account, archive, certificate, chronicle, deed, manuscript, notation, paper, record, script, statement, writing.

dodge, avoid, elude, equivocate, escape, evade, quibble, side-step. ANT.—approach, confront, encounter, face, meet.

dogmatic, arrogant, authoritarian, dictatorial, doctrinaire, domineering, imperious, immovable, magisterial, opinionated, overbearing, peremptory, positive, unchangeable; authoritative, doctrinal. ANT.—fluctuating, indecisive, questioning, skeptical, vacillating.

dole, allot, apportion, dispense, distribute; allotment, alms, apportionment, benefit, distribution, division, gratuity, pittance, portion, share.

domestic, domesticated, gentle, household, internal, native, tame. ANT.—foreign, savage, untamed, wild.

domicile, abode, accommodations, apartment, dwelling, habitation, home, lodging, residence, quarters.

dominant, aggressive, authoritative, commanding, controlling, domineering, governing, imperative, imperious, lordly, predominant, prevailing, ruling. ANT.—humble, non-aggressive, obscure, retiring, subordinate.

dominion, ascendancy, authority, control, government, jurisdiction, sway; commonwealth, country, district, empire, region, territory. ANT.—bondage, dependency, inferiority, subjection, submission.

donation, benefaction, benefit, bequest, boon, bounty, charity, contribution, endowment, favor, gift, grant, gratuity, largess, present, provision, subscription. ANT.—deprivation, loss.

done, achieved, completed, concluded, consummated, ended, executed, finished, over, performed, solved. ANT.—inchoate, incomplete, partial, raw, unfinished.

dormant, inactive, inert, quiescent, sleeping, unconscious, unoccupied. ANT.—active, awake, industrious, occupied, working.

double, counterpart, duplicate, stand-in, twin, understudy; duplicate, enlarge, repeat; bipartite, coupled, dual, duplex, paired, twin, twofold. ANT.—lone, single, unique.

doubt, agnosticism, concern, disbelief, distrust, dubiousness, hesitancy, hesitation, incredulity, indecision, irresolution, misgiving, mistrust, perplexity, qualm, quandary, question, scruple, skepticism, suspense, suspicion, unbelief, uncertainty. ANT.—assurance, belief, certainty, conviction, faith.

doubt, hesitate, question, waver; distrust, mistrust, suspect. ANT.—believe, confide, rely upon, trust.

draft, delineate, draw, sketch; call up, conscript, impress; bill of exchange, check, letter of credit, money order; breeze, wind.

draw, drag, haul, pull, tow, tug; extract, remove, take out; unsheathe; allure, attract, entice, induce, lure; delineate, depict, sketch, trace; compose, draft, formulate, write; conclude, deduce, derive, infer; extend, lengthen, prolong, protract, stretch. ANT.—alienate, rebuff, reject, repel, repulse.

drawback, allowance, defect, detriment, discount, flaw, hindrance, injury, rebate. ANT.—advantage, benefit, extra, premium.

dread, alarm, anxiety, apprehension, awe, consternation, dismay, fear, fright, horror, misgiving, panic, terror, trepidation. ANT.—boldness, bravery, confidence, courage.

dreadful, appalling, awful, dire, fearful, formidable, frightful, ghastly, horrible, terrible. ANT.—beautiful, enchanting, enjoyable, lovely.

dream, chimera, conceit, deception, delusion, fallacy, fancy, fantasy, hallucination, illusion, imagination, nightmare, reverie. ANT.—actuality, materiality, reality, solidity, verity.

dreary, bleak, cheerless, dark, depressing, discouraging, disheartening, dismal, doleful, dull, funereal, gloomy, lonesome, melancholy, sad, somber, wearisome. ANT.—cheerful, joyous, lively, pleasant.

dress, apparel, appearance, array, attire, clothing, costume, drapery, frock, garb, garments, gown, habiliments, habit, rai-

ment, robes, uniform, vestments, vesture. ANT.—bareness, disarray, nakedness, nudity.

drift, end, inference, intent, meaning, objective, purpose, result, scope, tendency, tenor; bearing, course, direction; advance, be carried, deviate (from course), float, heap up, move, wander.

drill, condition, discipline, exercise, instruction, lesson, practice, repetition, study, training; boring tool; bore, perforate, puncture. ANT.—idleness, repose, rest.

drive, coerce, compel, force, hammer, hurl, impel, incite, propel, push, thrust; actuate, conduct, control, direct, guide, move, steer, ride. ANT.—drag, tow, tug; discourage, hinder, repress.

drop, collapse, decline, decrease, descend, diminish, fall, plunge, sink, subside; stumble, topple, tumble, droop, extend downward, faint, hang; dribble, drip, trickle, percolate; abandon, dismiss, give up, relinquish; cease, stop, terminate. ANT.—rise, soar; flow, splash; continue, pursue.

drown, deluge, engulf, immerse, inundate, muffle, overflow, overpower, overwhelm, perish, plunge, sink, submerge, suffocate, swamp. ANT.—extricate, preserve, recover.

drug, anesthetic, biological compound, dope, extract, medicine, narcotic, pharmaceutical; anesthetize, desensitize, knock out, narcotize, sedate.

dry, arid, dehydrated, desiccated, drained, juiceless, moistless, parched, thirsty, watertight; barren, dull, jejune, prosy, stale, tedious, tiresome, uninteresting, vapid. ANT.—damp, moist; fresh, interesting, lively.

dubious, doubtful, equivocal, hesitant, problematical, questionable, reluctant, uncertain, unclear, unreliable, unsettled, unsure. ANT.—certain, definite, positive, sure.

dull, dense, doltish, half-witted, insipid, obtuse, senseless, slow, stolid, stupid, vapid, witless; blunt, obtuse; boring, commonplace, dismal, dreary, gloomy, monotonous, prosy, sad, tedious, uninteresting; insensate, unfeeling; dry, lifeless; dark, dim. ANT.—animated, intelligent, sharp; clear, interesting.

dumb, brainless, dense, dull, foolish, obtuse, senseless, stupid, witless; aphonic, mute, speechless, voiceless. ANT.—alert, bright, clever, discerning, intelligent; articulate, fluent, talkative, voluble.

duplicate, copy, counterpart, exemplar, facsimile, likeness, replica, reproduction, tracing, transcript, twin; copy, redo, repeat, reproduce, trace. ANT.—original, prototype.

duplicity, artifice, deceit, dishonesty, fraud, guile, hypocrisy, perfidy. ANT.—guilelessness, honesty, openness, simplicity.

durable, abiding, changeless, constant, continuing, enduring, fixed, hard, indestructible, lasting, permanent, remaining, strong, unchangeable. ANT.—ephemeral, temporary, transient, transitory, unstable.

duress, captivity, coercion, compulsion, confinement, constraint.

duty, accountability, allegiance, business, calling, charge, employment, function, obligation, office, province, responsibility, service, task. ANT.—betrayal, disloyalty, falsehood, inconstancy, irresponsibility.

dwelling, abode, accommodations, apartment, domicile, flat, habitat, habitation, hearth, home, house, quarters, residence, seat.

dwindle, abridge, contract, curtail, decline, decrease, diminish, drop, fade, fall, lessen, melt, narrow, reduce, shorten, shrink, wane. ANT.—augment, enlarge, expand, multiply, widen.

dye, color, imbue, infuse, pigment, stain, tinge, tint. ANT.—bleach, fade.

E

eager, ablaze, ambitious, anxious, ardent, athirst, avid, burning, desirous, earnest, enthusiastic, fervent, glowing, hot, impassioned, impatient, impetuous, importunate, intense, intent, keen, longing, solicitous, vehement, yearning, zealous. ANT.—apathetic, indifferent, phlegmatic, uninterested.

earn, achieve, acquire, attain, deserve, gain, get, make, merit, obtain, secure, win. ANT.—forfeit, lose.

earnest, ardent, candid, eager, fervent, frank, genuine, heartfelt, honest, open, resolute, serious, sincere, straightforward, true, truthful, unfeigned, upright, warm, zealous. ANT.—affected, capricious, dishonest, insincere, untruthful.

earnings, allowance, commission, emolument, income, interest, profits, remuneration, reward, salary, stipend, wages. ANT.—costs, expenses, losses.

earthly, base, carnal, earthy, global, material, mundane, profane, sordid, temporal, worldly. ANT.—heavenly, immaterial, incorporeal, spiritual.

ease, allay, alleviate, assuage, comfort, facilitate, lighten, mitigate, pacify, relieve, soothe; comfort, contentment, peace, quietude, repose, security, solace, tranquility; easiness, expertise, facility. ANT.—annoyance, discomfort, disquiet, turmoil, vexation; difficulty.

easy, comfortable, effortless, elementary, facile, light, relaxed, simple, unanxious, uncomplicated; flexible, manageable, pliant, smooth. ANT.—arduous, demanding, difficult, hard, laborious.

ebb, abate, decay, decline, dwindle, fall, lessen, recede, retire, retreat, sink, wane. ANT.—flow, improve, increase, revive, wax.

eccentric, aberrant, bizarre, curious, deviating, erratic, odd, outlandish, peculiar, quaint, queer, singular, strange, unusual, wayward. ANT.—common, conventional, familiar, normal, regular.

economical, circumspect, frugal, moderate, penurious, provident, reasonable, saving, sparing, thrifty, watchful. ANT.—extravagant, improvident, lavish, munificent, wasteful.

ecstasy, bliss, delight, ebullience, elation, exaltation, glee, glorification, joy, rapture, ravishment, transport. ANT.—depression, despair, doldrums, melancholy, pessimism.

eddy, reverse, spin, swirl, whirl; maelstrom, vortex, whirlpool. ANT.—calm, still.

edge, border, boundary, brim, brink, butt, circumference, extremity, fringe, margin, periphery, rim, ring, side, tip, verge; intensity, keenness, sharpness, sting. ANT.—center, extension, interior; bluntness, dullness.

edict, announcement, command, decree, law, mandate, manifesto, order, ordinance, proclamation, public notice, statute, writ.

edifice, building, establishment, house, skyscraper, structure.

edit, adapt, arrange, change, compile, compose, correct, rectify, reduce, revise, select, trim.

education, background, cultivation, culture, development, discipline, edification, enlightenment, instruction, knowledge, learning, scholarship, schooling, study, training. ANT.—ignorance, illiteracy.

eerie, curious, fantastic, grotesque, odd, peculiar, strange, supernatural, uncanny, weird. ANT.—natural, normal, usual.

efface, annul, blot, cancel, destroy, erase, expunge, obliterate, wipe. ANT.—confirm, keep, renew, retain, strengthen.

effect, achieve, accomplish, attain, complete, conclude, consummate, do, execute, finish, fulfill, perform, realize; completion, conclusion, consequence, consummation, issue, outcome, result. ANT.—abandon, defeat, fail, neglect, omit; beginning, cause, commencement, origin, source.

effective, adept, capable, competent, conducive, effectual, efficacious, efficient, fruitful, potent, productive, proficient, serviceable, talented, trenchant, useful. ANT.—fruitless, incompetent, ineffectual, inefficient, nonproductive.

effeminate, feminine, unmanly, unvirile, womanish. ANT.—manly, masculine, robust, virile.

effervescent, bubbling, buoyant, frothy, gay, gleeful, volatile. ANT.—flat, sedate, sober, staid.

efficiency, ability, adaptability, capability, capacity, competency, effectiveness, fitness, power, proficiency, suitability, thoroughness. ANT.—impotence, inability, inadequacy, incompetency, weakness.

effort, application, attempt, endeavor, energy, essay, exertion, trial, work; labor, pains, strain, strife, struggle, toil, trouble. ANT.—ease, failure, neglect.

egotistic, boastful, bombastic, conceited, egocentric, inflated, narcissistic, ostentatious, pretentious, pompous, self-centered, self-important, showy, vain. ANT.—deferent, humble, modest, reserved, unobtrusive.

eject, banish, cast out, discard, discharge, dislodge, dismiss, exile, expel, evict, oust, propel, remove. ANT.—accept, appoint, establish, settle, retain.

elaborate, gaudy, ostentatious, showy; complex, complicated, detailed, intricate, perfected, polished, refined. ANT.—common, ordinary, simple, unrefined, usual.

elapse, expire, glide, go away, intervene, lapse, pass, vanish. ANT.—remain, stand still, stay.

elastic, adaptable, compliant, ductile, extensible, flexible, limber, lithe, pliable, pliant, resilient, rubbery, springy, stretchable, supple, tractable. ANT.—brittle, rigid, stiff, tense, unbending.

elated, animated, delighted, ecstatic, exhilarated, exultant, gleeful, high-spirited. ANT.—depressed, downhearted, gloomy, low.

elect, call, choose, cull, decide on, judge, opt, ordain, pick, prefer, select. ANT.—cancel, recall, refuse, reject.

elegant, beautiful, courtly, elaborate, fair, fine, handsome, lovely, luxurious, opulent, polished, pretty, refined, rich, sophisticated, sumptuous. ANT.—common, repulsive, rustic, unrefined, vulgar.

elementary, basic, constituent, easy, elemental, fundamental, initial, primary, rudimentary; pure, simple, uncompounded, unmixed. ANT.—abstruse, advanced, complex, intricate; compounded, mixed.

elevate, advance, buoy, dignify, erect, exalt, glorify, heighten, hoist, honor, improve, lift, promote, raise, revere, uplift. ANT.—abase, condemn, deprecate, depreciate, depress.

elicit, bring forth, draw, educe, evoke, extort, extract, prompt, wrest. ANT.—repress, suppress.

eliminate, abolish, abrogate, banish, cancel, delete, discharge, dislodge, efface, eject, eradicate, erase, excise, exclude, expel, expunge, expurgate, exterminate, extirpate, liquidate, obliterate, oust, proscribe, pluck, remove. ANT.—accept, admit, include, maintain, preserve.

elongate, extend, lengthen, prolong, protract, stretch. ANT.—contract, shrink, slacken, shorten.

elucidate, clarify, decipher, explain, expound, illuminate, illustrate, interpret. ANT.—becloud, confuse, darken, distract, obscure.

elude, avert, avoid, baffle, dodge, escape, eschew, evade, foil, frustrate, parry. ANT.—attract, confront, encounter, meet, solicit.

emanate, arise, come, emerge, flow, issue, originate, proceed, radiate, stem. ANT.—return, sink, withdraw.

emancipate, free, let go, liberate, release, set free. ANT.—confine, imprison, subjugate.

embarrass, abash, annoy, bewilder, bother, complicate, confound, confuse, discomfit, disconcert, distress, encumber, entangle, fluster, hamper, hinder, mortify, obstruct, perplex, plague, rattle, trouble, vex. ANT.—cheer, encourage, help, inspire, relieve.

embellish, adorn, beautify, deck, decorate, enrich, garnish, ornament, trim; exaggerate. ANT.—debase, defame, strip, obliterate; simplify.

embezzle, appropriate, cheat, defalcate, defraud, falsify, filch, forge, misapply, misappropriate, misuse, pilfer, plunder, purloin, rob, swindle. ANT.—balance, recompense, reimburse, return, satisfy.

emblem, brand, figure, image, representation, sign, symbol, token, trademark.

embody, codify, comprise, concentrate, contain, embrace, hold, include, incorporate, integrate, systematize. ANT.—discharge, disperse, disintegrate, exclude.

embrace, caress, clasp, encircle, hug; accept, adopt, espouse, receive, subscribe to, welcome; comprehend, comprise, contain, embody, include, incorporate. ANT.—exclude, reject, renounce, scorn, spurn.

emergency, casualty, crisis, dilemma, distress, exigency, juncture, pressure, quandary, strait, urgency. ANT.—conventionality, regularity, routine, stability, solution.

emigrate, abandon, depart, egress, escape, leave, migrate, move, part, quit. ANT.—dwell, remain, reside, stay.

eminent, celebrated, conspicuous, distinguished, elevated, exalted, famous, foremost, glorious, illustrious, noted, prominent, renowned, superior, supreme, well-known. ANT.—common, humble, insignificant, obscure, ordinary.

emit, breathe forth, discharge, eject, emanate, exhale, expel, express, hurl, issue, open, publish, report, shoot, spurt, utter, vent. ANT.—contain, retain, stop, suppress.

emotion, affection, feeling, impression, inspiration, mood, passion, presentiment, sensation, sensibility, sentiment. ANT.—apathy, dispassion, impassivity, indifference, insensibility.

empathy, affinity, appreciation, commiseration, compassion, insight, sensitivity, understanding.

ANT.—insensitivity, unfeelingness.

emphatic, affecting, determined, effective, energetic, forceful, forcible, insistent, pointed, potent. ANT.—bashful, bland, modest, reserved, weak.

employment, business, calling, career, craft, engagement, job, occupation, profession, pursuit, service, vocation, work. ANT.—ennui, idleness, inactivity, laziness, leisure.

empty, bare, barren, destitute, devoid, foolish, hollow, hungry, meaningless, senseless, stupid, unfilled, unfurnished, unoccupied, vacant, vacuous, void, worthless. ANT.—erudite, full, inhabited, occupied, replete.

enable, allow, authorize, empower, let, permit, sanction. ANT.—disallow, oppose, prevent.

enchant, bewitch, captivate, charm, enrapture, enthrall, entice, fascinate, ravish. ANT.—disenchant, disgust, offend, repel.

encompass, beset, circumscribe, encircle, enclose, enfold, envelop, environ, gird, hem in, invest, span, surround. ANT.—free, release, unwrap.

encounter, assailment, assault, attack, battle, clash, collision, combat, conflict, engagement, fight, invasion, meeting, onslaught, skirmish, struggle. ANT.—amity, avoidance, concord, consonance, harmony, retreat, union.

encourage, advise, animate, cheer, comfort, embolden, enliven, exhilarate, favor, hearten, impel, incite, inspire, inspirit, urge; foster, promote, sanction, stimulate, spur, support. ANT.—deject, deter, discourage, dispirit, dissuade.

encroach, attack, infract, infringe, intrude, invade, poach, transgress, trespass, violate. ANT.—abandon, avoid, evacuate, relinquish, shun.

encumbrance, burden, clog, drag, difficulty, drawback, hindrance, impediment, lien, load, mortgage, obstacle, weight. ANT.—advantage, assistance, incentive, stimulant.

end, aim, ambition, cessation, close, completion, conclusion, consequence, expiration, extremity, finish, goal, issue, limit, object, purpose, result, termination, terminus; cease, close, conclude, stop, terminate. ANT.—beginning, commencement, inception, introduction; inaugurate, institute, establish, start.

endanger, expose, hazard, imperil, jeopardize, peril, risk. ANT.—guard, protect, secure.

endeavor, aim, aspire, attempt, contend, contest, essay, exert, strive, try, undertake; labor, pains, strain, strife, struggle, toil.

endless, boundless, ceaseless, constant, continuous, eternal, everlasting, illimitable, immeasurable, imperishable, incessant, infinite, interminable, perpetual, unbounded, uninterrupted, unlimited. ANT.—bounded, finite, limited, transient, transitory.

endorse (also spelled indorse), assist, attest, authorize, back, confirm, corroborate, guarantee, ratify, recommend, sanction, secure, sign, subscribe, support, warrant. ANT.—admonish, censure, denounce, oppose, reject.

endowment, ability, attainment, benefaction, benefit, bequest, bounty, capacity, donation, empowerment, genius, gift, grant, gratuity, mentality, natural gift, provision, qualification, talent. ANT.—drawback, harm, injury, loss.

endurance, allowance, continuance, courage, diligence, firmness, forbearance, fortitude, longsuffering, patience, perseverance, persistence, resignation, resistance, stamina, strength, submission, tolerance. ANT.—faltering, succumbing, surrender, weakness.

enemy, adversary, antagonist, attacker, calumniator, competitor, defamer, defiler, falsifier, foe, opponent, predator, rival, slanderer, traducer, vilifier. ANT.—accomplice, ally, comrade, confederate, friend.

energetic, active, aggressive, animated, brisk, cogent, determined, diligent, dynamic, enterprising, forcible, industrious, lively, mighty, potent, powerful, spirited, strong, vigorous. ANT.—idle, lazy, listless, spiritless, vacillating.

energy, effectiveness, efficiency, force, might, potency, power, puissance, robustness, strength, vigor, vim, vitality, zeal. ANT.—apathy, frailty, impotence, indolence, weakness.

enervate, attenuate, daze, debilitate, enfeeble, impair, injure, paralyze, reduce, sap, soften, weaken, weary. ANT.—animate, buoy, energize, invigorate, strengthen.

enforce, coerce, compel, constrain, drive, exact, execute, exert, force, impel, necessitate, oblige, persuade, press, require, strain, urge. ANT.—dismiss, disregard, give up, leave, omit.

enfranchise, emancipate, empower, enable, free, license, release, right, qualify. ANT.—disenfranchise, disqualify, revoke (license).

engage, busy, employ, engross, enlist, hire; bind, commit, pledge; mesh (with gears). ANT.—dismiss, release; decline, refuse; disengage.

engagement, appointment; battle, combat, encounter; betrothal, bond, commitment, compact, consenting, espousal, pledge, plighting.

engender, breed, cause, create, excite, fashion, form, formulate, generate, incite, make, originate, procreate, produce, reproduce. ANT.—annihilate, demolish, destroy.

engross, absorb, assimilate, bewitch, captivate, consume, engulf, fascinate, monopolize, swallow up; busy, engage, occupy. ANT.—dissatisfy, neglect, repel.

engulf, absorb, assimilate, bury, consume, deluge, drown, entomb, fill up, inundate, overcome, overflow, overwhelm, sink, swallow up. ANT.—discharge, dispense, emit, expel.

enhance, advance, augment, elevate, heighten, increase, intensify, magnify, raise, swell. ANT.—assuage, degrade, diminish, reduce.

enigmatic, baffling, cryptic, inscrutable, mysterious, puzzling, vague. ANT.—clear, explicit, obvious, open, plain.

enjoyment, bliss, comfort, delight, ecstasy, exultation, gladness, gratification, happiness, hedonism, indulgence, joy, liking, pleasure, rapture, satisfaction. ANT.—dejection, discomfort, misery, sorrow, unhappiness.

enlarge, add, amplify, augment, broaden, dilate, distend, expand, extend, grow, heighten, increase, lengthen, magnify, protuberate, spread, swell, widen. ANT.—abbreviate, abridge, condense, contract, diminish.

enlighten, brighten, clarify, communicate, disclose, edify, educate, elucidate, illuminate, illumine, illustrate, inculcate, indoctrinate, irradiate. ANT.—

confound, confuse, darken, obfuscate, obscure.

enlist, attract, engage, employ, enroll, enter, get, hire, incorporate, induce, interest, join, obtain, procure, register, reserve, retain. ANT.—check, constrain, demobilize, deter, hold back.

enliven, animate, arouse, brighten, cheer, encourage, excite, exhilarate, gladden, quicken, refresh, rouse, stimulate, vivify. ANT.—dampen, debilitate, exhaust, sadden, stultify.

enmity, abhorrence, acrimony, animosity, antagonism, antipathy, aversion, detestation, disgust, hatred, hostility, illwill, invidiousness, malevolence, malice, malignity, rancor, repugnance, spitefulness. ANT.—affection, cordiality, friendliness, good will, love.

ennui, boredom, languor, listlessness, surfeit, tedium. ANT.—buoyancy, enthusiasm, energy, vigor.

enough, adequate, ample, full, plenty, satisfactory, sufficient. ANT.—deficient, inadequate, lacking, scant.

enrage, anger, chafe, craze, exasperate, goad, incense, inflame, infuriate, irk, madden. ANT.—appease, conciliate, soften, soothe, pacify.

enrich, adorn, beautify, embellish; cultivate, fertilize, improve; endow. ANT.—deplete, impoverish, reduce, rob, take from.

enroll, enlist, enter, inscribe, join, list, record, register, subscribe.

ANT.—cancel, deactivate, discard, reject.

ensue, follow; succeed, come next; result. ANT.—forsake; precede; cause.

enter, penetrate, pierce, perforate; enlist in, enroll, join, register; encroach, intrude; begin, introduce, start. ANT.—depart, exit, vacate, withdraw.

enterprise, achievement, activity, adventure, business, commerce, endeavor, engagement, project, undertaking, venture, work. ANT.—inaction, indolence, passivity, sloth.

entertainment, amusement, diversion, enjoyment, fun, game, merriment, party, pastime, play, pleasure, recreation, social event, sport. ANT.—boredom, ennui, labor, toil, work.

enthusiasm, ardor, devotion, eagerness, earnestness, excitement, fervency, fervor, inspiration, intensity, optimism, passion, vehemence, vigor, warmth, zeal. ANT.—apathy, calmness, ennui, indifference, lethargy, pessimism.

entice, allure, attract, beguile, captivate, charm, draw, enchant, ensnare, fascinate, inveigle, lure, prevail upon, seduce, tempt, wheedle. ANT.—alienate, disgust, reject, repel, repulse.

entire, all, complete, intact, integral, perfect, total, unabridged, unbroken, undivided, unimpaired, unscathed, whole. ANT.—defective, deficient, incomplete, partial.

entrance, door, doorway, entry, gate, gateway, ingress, inlet, opening, portal; admission, beginning, commencement, initiation. ANT.—egress, exit, outlet; departure, exclusion, rejection, withdrawal.

entreat, ask, beg, beseech, implore, importune, petition, plead, request, solicit, supplicate. ANT.—command, compel, demand, force, take.

envelop, blanket, conceal, cover, embrace, enclose, encompass, enfold, hide, surround, wrap. ANT.—open, reveal, uncover, unwrap.

envious, cautious, covetous, displeased, invidious, jealous, malicious, odious, resentful, suspicious. ANT.—benevolent, charitable, helpful, laudatory, pleased, well-disposed.

environment, background, conditions, location, neighborhood, setting, surroundings, vicinity.

envoy, agent, ambassador, commissioner, delegate, diplomat, messenger, nuncio, plenipotentiary, representative.

epicurean, fastidious, gastronomic, luxurious, particular, sensual, sybaritic, voluptuous. ANT.—ascetic, austere, puritanical, self-denying.

episode, affair, circumstance, event, happening, incident, issue, occurrence.

epistle, communication, dispatch, lesson, letter, message, missive, note, writing.

epitome, abridgment, abstract, compendium, condensation, digest, summary, syllabus, synopsis, synthesis; embodiment, essence, ideal example of. ANT.—augmentation, development, expansion, extension, increment.

equable, calm, constant, equal, even, regular, serene, steady, unchanging, uniform, unruffled. ANT.—changeable, fluctuating, spasmodic, variable.

equal, adequate, alike, commensurate, equable, equitable, equivalent, even, fair, identical, invariable, just, like, same, uniform, unvarying; compeer, match, parallel, peer, rival, tie. ANT.—different, disparate, disproportionate, dissimilar, unjust; inferior, subordinate.

equanimity, balance, calmness, composure, evenness, poise, serenity, self-control. ANT.—agitation, anxiety, disturbance, excitation, perturbation.

equipment, accouterments, apparatus, array, furnishings, gear, material, outfit, paraphernalia.

equitable, fair, honest, impartial, just, objective, reasonable, unbiased, unprejudiced. ANT.—biased, dishonorable, fraudulent, inequitable, partial.

equivalent, alike, commensurate, equal, identical, indistinguishable, interchangeable, like, reciprocal, same, synonomous, tantamount. ANT.—contrary, disparate, dissimilar, opposed, unequal.

eradicate, abolish, annihilate, destroy, eliminate, erase, expel, exterminate, extinguish, extirpate, kill, nullify, oust, remove, uproot. ANT.—establish, fortify, foster, propagate, secure.

erase, cancel, cross out, delete, efface, eliminate, expunge, obliterate, rub out; abolish, abrogate, annul, invalidate, nullify, quash, repeal, rescind, revoke. ANT.—confirm, enact, perpetuate.

erect, unbent, upright, straight, vertical; build, construct, raise. ANT.—bent, cringing, crooked, horizontal, recumbent; raze.

erode, abrade, corrode, destroy, deteriorate, eat, gnaw, rub, wear, weather.

erotic, carnal, concupiscent, erogenous, libidinous, lustful, passionate, sensual, sexual. ANT.—celibate, passionless, spiritual.

erratic, aberrant, capricious, changeable, desultory, flighty, fluctuating, odd, peculiar, strange, uncertain, unreliable, unruly, wandering. ANT.—dependable, methodical, regular, reliable, steady.

erroneous, fallacious, false, faulty, inaccurate, incorrect, mistaken, unprecise, untrue, wrong. ANT.—correct, right, true.

error, blunder, deviation, fall, fallacy, fault, inaccuracy, indiscretion, misapprehension, misconception, omission, oversight, slip, transgression. ANT.—accuracy, certitude, correction, precision, truth.

erudite, cultured, educated, enlightened, knowing, learned, scholarly. ANT.—ignorant, illiterate, uneducated, unlettered.

eruption, commotion, discharge, efflorescence, explosion, outbreak, outburst; rash.

escape, abscond, break, decamp, defect, flee, fly; avert, avoid, elude, evade, shun. ANT.—confront, face, invite, meet.

escort, accompany, attend, chaperon, conduct, convoy, guard, guide, lead, protect, safeguard, serve, tend, squire, usher, watch.

especially, chiefly, definitely, mainly, particularly, primarily, principally, specially, specifically.

essay, article, composition, disquisition, dissertation, thesis; attempt, effort, trial.

essential, basic, characteristic, fundamental, indispensable, inherent, intrinsic, key, necessary, requisite, vital. ANT.—auxiliary, expendable, extrinsic, optional, peripheral.

establish, authorize, form, found, institute, organize, raise, set up; confirm, fix, ordain, sanction, settle, strengthen; confirm, demonstrate, prove, substantiate, verify. ANT.—abolish, demolish, overthrow, unsettle, upset; controvert, disprove, scorn.

estate, belongings, commodities, domain, effects, goods, holdings, inheritance, land, merchandise, possessions, property, stock, wares, wealth. ANT.—

destitution, poverty, privation, want.

esteem, admiration, appreciation, approbation, approval, commendation, deference, favor, honor, praise, regard, reverence, sanction, value, veneration; estimate, rate, reckon.

estimate, appraise, assess, assign, calculate, compute, count, evaluate, measure, rate, reckon, value, weigh. ANT.—disregard, guess.

estrangement, alienation, disaffection, removal, separation, withdrawal. ANT.—affinity, alliance, bond, coalition, union.

eternal, boundless, ceaseless, deathless, endless, enduring, immortal, imperishable, infinite, never-ending, perpetual, timeless, undying, unending. ANT.—ephemeral, finite, mortal, mutable, temporal, transient.

ethical, decent, good, honest, honorable, just, moral, principled, righteous, scrupulous, virtuous. ANT.—amoral, corrupt, dishonest, licentious, unethical.

eulogize, applaud, celebrate, commend, compliment, extol, laud, praise. ANT.—condemn, degrade, demean, scorn.

evacuate, abandon, clear, desert, emit, empty, expel, leave, purge, quit, relinquish, retreat, vacate. ANT.—charge, enter, fill, occupy, take over.

evade, avoid, shun; dodge, equivocate, quibble; conceal, deceive, trick. ANT.—confront, face; confess, declare, verify.

evaporate, disappear, disperse, dissolve, dry, evanesce, fade, vanish, vaporize. ANT.—appear, consolidate, crystallize.

evaluate, appraise, assess, calculate, estimate, judge, rate, value, weigh. ANT.—guess, hazard.

even, flat, flush, level, plane, smooth; equal, unbroken, uniform, unvarying; calm, peaceful. ANT.—jagged, rough; broken, irregular; agitated, troubled.

event, affair, circumstance, episode, happening, incident, issue, milestone, occurrence; consequence, end, outcome, result. ANT.—antecedent, cause, origin, start.

everlasting, ceaseless, deathless, endless, eternal, immortal, imperishable, incessant, infinite, interminable, perpetual, timeless, unceasing, undying. ANT.—ephemeral, finite, mortal, temporal, transient.

evict, debar, deprive, discard, dispossess, eject, exclude, expel, oust. ANT.—accept, admit, receive, welcome.

evidence, confirmation, corroboration, data, demonstration, documentation, facts, grounds, indication, premises, proof, testimony, verification. ANT.—contradiction, disproof, fallacy, invalidity, refutation.

evident, apparent, clear, conspicuous, discernible, distinct, incontrovertible, indisputable, indubitable, manifest, obvious, open, overt, patent, perceptible,

plain, unmistakable, visible.
ANT.—concealed, covert, hidden, obscure, questionable.

evil, baseness, calamity, contamination, corruption, crime, depravity, disaster, harm, ill, immorality, iniquity, malignity, mischief, misfortune, offense, profligacy, sin, transgression, ungodliness, vice, viciousness, wickedness, wrong; base, deleterious, immoral, noxious, pernicious, sinful, vicious, wicked.
ANT.—goodness, innocence, purity, virtue; honorable, moral, reputable.

evince, demonstrate, disclose, display, evidence, exhibit, indicate, manifest, prove, show. ANT.—conceal, hide, repress, suppress.

evoke, arouse, educe, elicit, excite, provoke, rouse, stimulate, summon, waken. ANT.—quiet, repress, silence, squelch, stifle.

exact, accurate, correct, definite, distinct, literal, methodical, particular, precise, punctual, rigorous, scrupulous, specific, strict, true, undeviating, unequivocal; demand, extort, wrest. ANT.—approximate, careless, erroneous, inaccurate, vague, variable; request.

exaggerate, amplify, embellish, embroider, enlarge, expand, heighten, magnify, overdo, overstate, stretch. ANT.—depreciate, lessen, minimize, reduce, understate.

exalt, advance, aggrandize, applaud, commend, consecrate, dignify, elevate, ennoble, erect, extol, glorify, hallow, honor, laud, magnify, praise, raise. ANT.—degrade, dishonor, humble, humiliate, scorn.

examination, analysis, audit, check-up, exploration, inquiry, inquisition, inspection, interrogation, investigation, probing, query, quest, questioning, quiz, research, scrutiny, search, test, trial, review. ANT.—disregard, inattention, negligence.

example, archetype, exemplification, ideal, illustration, instance, model, pattern, precedent, prototype, representation, sample, specimen, symbol, typical case.

exasperate, aggravate, annoy, chafe, enrage, exacerbate, frustrate, incense, inflame, infuriate, irritate, nettle, provoke, vex. ANT.—appease, calm, mitigate, palliate, soften.

exceed, eclipse, excel, outdo, outstrip, surmount, surpass, top, transcend. ANT.—fail, fall behind, lag, tarry.

excellent, admirable, commendable, eminent, estimable, exemplary, expert, favorable, honorable, meritorious, peerless, prime, proficient, superior, surpassing, valuable, worthy. ANT.—inferior, lesser, negligible, poor.

except, barring, but, excepting, excluding, exempting, omitting, rejecting, saving. ANT.—admitting, embracing, including.

exceptional, infrequent, occasional, unusual; choice, extraordinary, incomparable, marvelous, novel, precious, rare, remarkable, scarce, singular, uncommon, unique, unparalleled, unprecedented, wonderful. ANT.—customary, frequent, ordinary, usual; abundant, commonplace, numerous, worthless.

excerpt, abbreviation, citing, clipping, culling, extract, quote, selection.

excess, extravagance, immoderation, intemperance, lavishness, luxuriance, plenty, profusion, redundance, redundancy, superabundance, superfluity, surplus, waste. ANT.—dearth, deficiency, lack, paucity, want.

exchange, barter, change, convert, reciprocate, substitute, swap, switch, trade, transfer. ANT.—preserve, retain.

excite, activate, aggravate, agitate, arouse, awaken, disconcert, disquiet, disturb, goad, incense, incite, induce, inflame, irritate, kindle, perturb, provoke, rouse, stimulate, stir up, taunt, unsettle. ANT.—allay, calm, pacify, quiet, tranquilize.

exclaim, call out, clamor, cry, cry out, ejaculate, proclaim, shout, vociferate. ANT.—murmur, mutter, whisper.

exclude, ban, bar, blackball, boycott, debar, except, expel, obviate, omit, ostracize, prevent, prohibit, reject, shut out, veto. ANT.—accept, admit, include, incorporate, welcome.

excruciating, acute, agonizing, extreme, grueling, intense, overwhelming, painful, racking, rending, severe, tormenting. ANT.—comforting, mild, pleasing, soothing.

excursion, digression, divergence, episode, expedition, jaunt, journey, outing, travel, trip, tour, voyage.

excuse, absolve, acquit, exculpate, exempt, exonerate, forgive, free, pardon, release, remit; alibi, apology, defense, explanation, plea, pretext, vindication. ANT.—convict, prosecute, punish; accusation.

execrate, abhor, berate, condemn, curse, damn, objurgate, reprehend, revile. ANT.—applaud, commend, extol, laud, praise.

execute, accomplish, achieve, administer, attain, carry out, complete, consummate, do, effect, finish, fulfill, obtain, perfect, perform, realize; behead, electrocute, guillotine, hang. ANT.—abandon, fail, neglect, omit, shelve.

exempt, absolved, clear, excluded, excused, free, freed, liberated, privileged, released, unbound, unchecked, uncontrolled, undrafted, unrestricted. ANT.—answerable, bound, compelled, nonexempt, obliged.

exercise, act, action, activity, application, drill, employment, exertion, lesson, operation, performance, practice, task, training, use; calisthenics, gymnastics. ANT.—idleness, indolence, relaxation, repose, rest.

exertion, attempt, effort, endeavor, grind, labor, strain, struggle, toil, travail, trial. ANT.—idleness, inaction, laziness, lethargy.

exhausted, consumed, depleted, drained, empty, faint, fatigued, jaded, spent, tired, wasted, wearied, weary, worn. ANT.—fresh, hearty, invigorated, rested, restored.

exhibit, demonstrate, disclose, display, evince, expose, flaunt, manifest, parade, present, reveal, show. ANT.—conceal, cover, disguise, hide.

exhilarate, elate, enliven, inspirit, invigorate, rejoice, stimulate, thrill. ANT.—deject, depress, discourage, repress, sadden.

exigency, crisis, demand, difficulty, distress, emergency, need, strait, urgency, want. ANT.—normality, regularity.

exile, banishment, deportation, expatriation, expulsion, extradition, ostracism, proscription. ANT.—admittance, welcome.

existence, animation, being, life, liveliness, reality, spirit, vigor, vitality, vivacity. ANT.—death, demise, languor, lethargy.

exonerate, absolve, acquit, clear, discharge, except, exempt, free, justify, release, relieve, restore, vindicate. ANT.—accuse, blame, censure, condemn, indict.

exorbitant, excessive, extravagant, extreme, inordinate, overpriced, unreasonable. ANT.—below cost, fair, inexpensive, moderate, reasonable.

expand, advance, amplify, augment, develop, dilate, distend, enlarge, extend, grow, increase, magnify, mature, spread, stretch, swell, widen. ANT.—abbreviate, atrophy, contract, diminish, shrink, wane.

expansion, development, dilation, distention, elaboration, enlargement, unfolding, unraveling; evolution, growth, maturing, progress. ANT.—abbreviation, compression, curtailment.

expect, anticipate, await, contemplate, envision, foresee, hope, look for. ANT.—despair of, doubt, fear.

expedite, accelerate, advance, dispatch, facilitate, forward, hasten, hurry, push, quicken, rush, speed, urge. ANT.—hinder, impede, obstruct, retard, slow.

expedition, campaign, cruise, excursion, journey, mission, passage, pilgrimage, quest, safari, tour, travel, trek, trip, undertaking, voyage; alacrity, speed.

expel, banish, discharge, dismiss, evict, excommunicate, exile, ostracize, oust, proscribe, remove; dislodge, eject, eliminate, excrete, void. ANT.—accept, admit, include, invite; absorb, take in.

expense, charge, cost, disbursement, expenditure, outgo, outlay, payment, price, upkeep, value. ANT.—gain, income, profits, receipts, revenue.

expensive, costly, dear, highpriced. ANT.—cheap, inexpensive, worthless.

experience, adventure, encounter, episode, happening, incident, meeting, occurrence; feeling, sensation; background, knowledge, practice, sagacity, seasoning, testing, wisdom. ANT.—ignorance, inexperience, lack of knowledge.

experiment, assay, attempt, endeavor, examination, exercise, practice, research, test, trial, undertaking.

expert, able, accomplished, adept, adroit, apt, clever, competent, ingenious, masterful, practiced, proficient, skilled, skillful. ANT.—awkward, bungling, incompetent, inexpert, maladroit, unskillful.

expire, cease, decease, depart, die, disappear, end, pass away, perish, sink, vanish. ANT.—commence, live, survive.

explain, clarify, decipher, elucidate, expound, illustrate, interpret, manifest, resolve, solve, teach, unfold, unravel. ANT.—baffle, cloud, confuse, mystify, obscure.

explanation, clarification, deduction, defense, elucidation, explication, exposition, excuse, interpretation, justification, key, solution.

explicit, clear, comprehensible, definitive, determinate, distinct, evident, exact, express, intelligible, lucid, manifest, obvious, plain, positive, precise, specific. ANT.—ambiguous, equivocal, hazy, obscure, vague.

exploit, adventure, bold act, deed, feat; accomplishment, achievement, attainment, performance, realization; manipulate, take advantage of, use unfairly. ANT.—neglect, omission; defeat, failure.

exposed, agape, ajar, open, unclosed, uncovered, unlocked, unmasked, unveiled; clear, passable, unobstructed; accessible, public, unrestricted. ANT.—concealed, hidden, suppressed.

expound, analyze, clarify, construe, elucidate, explain, express, illuminate, illustrate, interpret, lecture, present, state, teach. ANT.—baffle, confuse, darken, obscure.

express, clear, definitive, explicit, lucid, manifest, positive, specific, unmistakable; fast, quick, rapid, speedy; affirm, assert, avow, claim, communicate, declare, denote, designate, dispatch, explain, forward, propound, recite, represent, say, send, signify, specify, state, tell, utter. ANT.—ambiguous, equivocal, implied, obscure, vague; slow; conceal, restrain, retain, suppress, withhold.

exquisite, appealing, attractive, charming, choice, dainty, delicate, elegant, excellent, fine, matchless, perfect, precious, rare, refined, select, splendid, superb, vintage; beautiful, debonair, handsome, pretty; acute, intense, sharp. ANT.—common, ordinary, unrefined, worthless; ugly; dull, mild.

extant, contemporary, enduring, existent, existing, lasting, surviving, undestroyed. ANT.—departed, destroyed, extinct, gone.

extemporaneous, ad lib, extemporary, informal, impromptu, improvised, informal, offhand, unplanned, unpremeditated, unprepared, unstudied. ANT.—designed, planned, premeditated, prepared, studied.

extend, add, amplify, augment, dilate, distend, enlarge, elongate, expand, lengthen, protract, spread, stretch; give, grant. ANT.—contract, decrease, loosen, reduce, shrink, slacken; take.

extensive, broad, expanded, sweeping, vast, wide. ANT.—confined, narrow, restricted.

extent, amount, compass, degree, expanse, length, magnitude, measure, range, reach, scope, size, stretch, volume.

exterior, cover, face, front, outside, shell, skin, surface. ANT.—core, inside, interior, internal (part).

exterminate, abolish, annihilate, banish, decimate, destroy, eradicate, expel, extirpate, kill, overthrow, uproot. ANT.—cherish, guard, maintain, preserve, protect.

external, exterior, extrinsic, foreign, outer, outside, superficial. ANT.—domestic, inside, internal, intrinsic, within.

extinguish, abate, abolish, annihilate, choke, destroy, eradicate, exterminate, extirpate, obscure, quench, suppress. ANT.—animate, ignite, kindle, light.

extol, celebrate, commend, eulogize, exalt, glorify, honor, laud, praise. ANT.—decry, disgrace, dishonor, profane.

extract, derive, distill, draw, educe, elicit, eradicate, evoke, extirpate, extort, obtain, pull, remove. ANT.—insert, instill, introduce.

extraneous, foreign, irrelevant, remote, strange, unconnected. ANT.—akin, germane, relevant.

extraordinary, egregious, exceptional, inordinate, marvelous, peculiar, phenomenal, rare, remarkable, singular, special, uncommon, unusual, unwonted, wonderful. ANT.—common, customary, ordinary, standard, usual.

extravagant, abundant, copious, excessive, extreme, exuberant, immoderate, improvident, inordinate, lavish, liberal, luxuriant, overflowing, plentiful, prodigal, profuse, wasteful. ANT.—economical, meager, parsimonious, penurious, sparse.

extreme, farthest, greatest, maximum, outermost, utmost; final, last, terminal, ultimate; extravagant, immoderate, intensive; fanatical, radical. ANT.—adjacent, near; calm, dispassionate; moderate.

extricate, affranchise, deliver, disengage, disentangle, free, let go, liberate, loose, ransom, release, rescue, unbind, unchain, unfasten, untie. ANT.—bind, chain, confine, incarcerate, restrain.

exuberant, abundant, copious, energetic, lavish, luxuriant, overflowing, profuse, prolific, rank, vigorous, wanton. ANT.—austere, barren, depleted, needy, sterile.

F

fabric, cloth, dry goods, material, organization, structure, stuff, substance, textile.

fabricate, arrange, build, compose, construct, counterfeit, devise, erect, fake, feign, forge, form, frame, invent, plan, prevaricate, produce, put together. ANT.—demolish, disrupt, ruin, shatter, wreck.

fabulous, amazing, astounding, exaggerated, extraordinary, false, feigned, fictitious, incredible, legendary, mythical, ridiculous, untrue. ANT.—common, credible, proven, true, usual.

facade, affectation, appearance, cover-up, false front, front, ornamentation, veneer. ANT.—base, character, sincerity.

face, appearance, countenance, features, mien, physiognomy, visage; assurance, audacity, boldness, confidence, effrontery, impertinence, impudence; brave, challenge, confront, dare, defy, meet, oppose, resist, venture; cover, exterior, front, outside, surface. ANT.—humility,

timidity; shrink, retreat, withdraw; interior, rear.

facile, able, adroit, agreeable, apt, artful, clever, dexterous, easy, expert, flexible, proficient, skillful, smooth, tactful. ANT.—awkward, difficult, disagreeable, rude, tedious.

facilitate, allay, alleviate, assuage, ease, lighten, mitigate, relieve, soothe. ANT.—confound, distress, disturb.

facility, ability, adroitness, civility, cleverness, courtesy, dexterity, ease, expertness, proficiency, readiness, skillfulness. ANT.—awkwardness, difficulty, discourtesy, ineptitude.

facsimile, copy, duplicate, pattern, photograph, picture, replica, reproduction, transcript. ANT.—distinction, opposite, variation.

fact, actuality, certainty, evidence, reality, truth; act, circumstance, deed, detail, event, incident, item, occurrence, point. ANT.—fiction, supposition, theory, delusion, falsehood.

faction, block, cabal, circle, clique, combination, coterie, denomination, division, party, sect, wing. ANT.—conformity, entirety, homogeneity, unity.

factious, contentious, dissident, insubordinate, rebellious, recalcitrant, seditious. ANT.—cooperative, helpful, united.

factitious, artificial, bogus, counterfeit, fabricated, forced, phony, sham, spurious, synthetic, unnatural. ANT.—authentic, bona fide, genuine, natural, real.

factor, actor, agent, attorney, bailiff, commissioner, delegate, deputy, manager, proxy, representative, steward, vicar; constituent, element, part.

faculty, ability, aptitude, bent, capability, capacity, function, gift, knack, power, skill, talent. ANT.—impotence, inability, incapacity, incompetence, ineptness.

fade, bleach, blur, deteriorate, dim, disappear, dwindle, ebb, evanesce, pale, taper off, vanish, wane, wither. ANT.—darken, enhance, improve, recover, strengthen.

fail, abandon, abort, collapse, decline, default, defeat, desert, disappoint, drop, fade, flounder, leave, miscarry, neglect, omit, quit, wither. ANT.—accomplish, achieve, capture, deliver, recover.

faint, dim, faded, faltering, fatigued, feeble, inaudible, indistinct, irresolute, languid, listless, pale, powerless, thin, timid, weak, wearied, worn. ANT.—distinct, forceful, intrepid, strong, vigorous.

fair, bright, clear, dry, light, mild, pleasant, sunny; attractive, blond, comely, lovely; candid, decent, equitable, frank, honest, impartial, just, open, reasonable, unbiased; average, mediocre, passable. ANT.—foul, tempestuous, ugly, unattractive; devious, dishonorable, fraudulent, partial; excellent, first-rate, worst.

faith, assurance, conviction, credence, reliance, trust; belief, creed, doctrine, dogma, tenet; constancy, fidelity, loyalty, promise, word. ANT.—doubt, incredulity, mistrust, skepticism; infidelity.

faithful, attached, constant, dependable, devoted, firm, honorable, incorruptible, loyal, staunch, steadfast, true, unswerving, unwavering; accurate, reliable, trusty. ANT.—disloyal, false, fickle, treacherous, untrustworthy.

fall, abate, collapse, decline, decrease, descend, diminish, drop, ebb, lessen, plunge, sink, subside, weaken; stumble, topple, totter, tumble; droop, extend downward, hang. ANT.—arise, ascend, climb, reach, scale, soar.

fallacy, casuistry, delusion, equivocation, error, fantasy, illusion, misconception, mistake, sophistry, subterfuge, untruth. ANT.—certainty, fact, reality, truth, verity.

false, bogus, counterfeit, deceptive, dishonest, erroneous, fabricated, fallacious, illusory, incorrect, lying, mendacious, misleading, mock, pretended, sham, spurious, unreal, untrue. ANT.—accurate, confirmed, substantiated, true, valid.

falter, delay, demur, doubt, flinch, fluctuate, hesitate, hobble, pause, reel, shrink, slip, stammer, stutter, totter, tremble, vacillate, weaken. ANT.—continue, endure, persevere, persist.

familiar, acquainted, cognizant, conversant, informed, intimate, knowing, versed, well-known; accessible, affable, amicable, approachable, casual, close, comfortable, courteous, easy, friendly, informal, sociable, unconstrained, unreserved; common, customary, usual; impudent, disrespectful. ANT.—constrained, distant, formal, reserved, unfamiliar.

famous, celebrated, distinguished, eminent, glorious, honorable, illustrious, noted, renowned, well-known. ANT.—ignominious, infamous, obscure, undistinguished, unknown.

fanatical, biased, bigoted, dogmatic, extreme, illiberal, intolerant, narrow-minded, obsessed, prejudiced, rabid, radical, unreasonable, zealous. ANT.—dispassionate, liberal, reasonable, tolerant.

fancy, conceit, conception, idea, imagination, notion; caprice, fantasy, vagary, whim; fondness, inclination; elaborate, ornamental, ornate. ANT.—actuality, reality; precision, stability; aversion; plain, unadorned.

fantastic, capricious, fanciful, farfetched, imaginary, visionary, whimsical; bizarre, eccentric, odd, peculiar, quaint, strange, vague; amazing, wonderful. ANT.—fixed, precise, steady; common, ordinary, usual.

far, away, distant, remote, removed. ANT.—close, convenient, handy, near.

farcical, absurd, comic, droll, foolish, funny, hilarious, ludicrous, ridiculous. ANT.—sober, tragic.

far-sighted, clairvoyant, clear-sighted, foresighted, judicious, level-headed, prepared, prudent. ANT.—impractical, imprudent, injudicious, rash, unprepared.

fascinate, allure, beguile, bewitch, captivate, delight, enamor, enchant, enrapture, enthrall, entrance, ravish. ANT.—agitate, anger, disgust, repel, weary.

fashion, appearance, fashion, manner, mode, vague; cast, contrive, create, design, fabricate, form, make, manufacture, mold, sculpture, style.

fast, accelerated, brisk, expeditious, fleet, lively, quick, rapid, speedy, swift; constant, firm, inflexible, lasting, permanent, secure, solid, stable, steadfast, steady, tight, unswerving, unyielding; dissipated, dissolute, reckless, wild. ANT.—slow, sluggish; insecure, loose, unstable, unsteady; exemplary, upright, virtuous.

fasten, affix, anchor, attach, bind, connect, link, lock, secure, tie. ANT.—detach, loosen, open, release, untie.

fastidious, choosy, critical, finicky, fussy, meticulous, particular, squeamish. ANT.—gross, indifferent, tasteless, uncritical.

fat, beefy, corpulent, fleshy, obese, portly, rotund, stout, swollen, thickset, unctuous, unwieldy;

luxuriant, rich, wealthy, well-to-do. ANT.—gaunt, lean, slender, slim, thin; indigent, penniless, poor.

fatal, deadly, lethal, mortal, murderous, pernicious. ANT.—animating, enlivening, invigorating, nourishing, vital.

fate, chance, consequence, fortune; destiny, doom, issue, lot, outcome, result; predestination, predetermination.

fatigue, debilitation, enervation, exhaustion, languor, lassitude, tiredness, weakness, weariness. ANT.—liveliness, rejuvenation, restoration, vigor, vivacity.

fault, blemish, defect, detriment, drawback, error, failure, flaw, foible, imperfection, misdeed, misdemeanor, mistake, omission, shortcoming, slip, weakness. ANT.—correctness, merit, perfection.

favorable, advantageous, assisting, auspicious, beneficial, conducive, helpful, propitious, salutary, useful. ANT.—detrimental, disadvantageous, harmful, hindering, opposed.

fear, alarm, apprehension, anxiety, cowardice, dismay, disquietude, dread, fright, horror, panic, phobia, scare, terror, timidity, trepidation; awe, reverence. ANT.—assurance, boldness, bravery, courage, fearlessness; nonchalance, unconcern.

feasible, achievable, attainable, practicable, practical, workable. ANT.—impractical, inconceivable, unrealistic, visionary.

feat, accomplishment, achievement, act, action, attainment, deed, execution, exercise, exploit, maneuver, operation, performance. ANT.—failure, inactivity, laziness, passivity, stagnation.

fee, account, bill, charge, compensation, cost, emolument, pay, payment, remuneration.

feeble, debilitated, decrepit, delicate, enervated, exhausted, faint, forceless, frail, impaired, infirm, languid, puny, sickly, weak. ANT.—forceful, hearty, lusty, stout, strong, vigorous.

feeling, consciousness, sensation, sense, sensitivity; affection, emotion, passion, sensibility, sentiment, sympathy, tenderness; conviction, impression, opinion. ANT.—anesthesia, unconsciousness; coldness, imperturbability, insensibility, stoicism; fact.

felicitate, compliment, congratulate, greet. ANT.—discourage, dismay, reject.

felonious, corrupt, criminal, depraved, evil, heinous, injurious, malicious, noxious, perfidious, perverse, vicious. ANT.—commendable, decent, honorable, meritorious, praiseworthy.

feminine, female, ladylike, maidenly, womanish, womanlike, womanly; delicate, soft, tender. ANT.—male, manly, mannish, masculine; hardy, strong, virile.

ferment, agitate, boil, bubble, concoct, embroil, excite, fret, heat, leaven, raise, roil, seethe, stir. ANT.—calm, cool, dampen, quiet, soothe.

ferocious, barbarous, brutal, brutish, cruel, fearsome, fierce, murderous, ravenous, vehement, violent, wild. ANT.—docile, gentle. harmless, manageable, tame.

fertile, abundant, bountiful, copious, exuberant, fecund, fruitful, luxuriant, plenteous, plentiful, productive, prolific, rich, teeming. ANT.—barren, childless, fruitless, sterile, unproductive.

fervent, animated, ardent, eager, enthusiastic, intense, passionate, zealous. ANT.—cool, grudging, hesitant, impassive, phlegmatic.

fetid, foul-smelling, malodorous, noisome, putrid, rank, repulsive, stinking. ANT.—aromatic, fragrant, perfumed, sweet-smelling.

feudal, dependent, downtrodden, enslaved, peasant, servile, subject, vassal. ANT.—aristocratic, free, independent.

fever, ardor, delirium, excitement, frenzy, heat, mania, temperature. ANT.—calmness, coolness.

fiasco, catastrophe, debacle, failure, miscarriage. ANT.—achievement, success, triumph, victory.

fickle, capricious, changeable, fanciful, fitful, inconstant, irresolute, restless, shifting, unreliable, unstable, variable, volatile, wavering, wayward. ANT.—constant, reliable, stable, steady, trustworthy.

fiction, allegory, creation, epic, fable, fabrication, falsehood, fancy, figment, imagination, invention, legend, myth, narrative, novel, parable, romance, story, tale. ANT.—fact, history, reality, truth, verity.

fidelity, adherence, allegiance, constancy, devotion, faithfulness, fealty, integrity, loyalty, obedience, steadfastness, support, zeal; accuracy, exactness, precision, truth. ANT.—disloyalty, faithlessness, inconstancy, perfidy, treachery.

fiendish, atrocious, cruel, demoniac, devilish, diabolical, infernal, inhuman, malicious, malignant. ANT.—angelic, benign, kindly.

fierce, angry, barbarous, brutal, dangerous, enraged, ferocious, fiery, passionate, savage, truculent, violent, wild. ANT.—docile, kind, peaceful, placid, tender.

fight, battle, box, brawl, combat, conflict, contend, contest, dispute, quarrel, scuffle, skirmish, squabble, strive, struggle, wrangle.

figment, fabrication, falsehood, fantasy, fiction, imagination, invention. ANT.—fact, reality, truth.

figure, allegory, amount, appearance, character, construction, design, emblem, form, metaphor, numeral, outline, picture, representation, shape, sum, symbol, type.

fill, fill up, occupy, pack, pervade; distend, feed, glut, gorge, load, permeate, sate, satiate, satisfy, saturate, stuff, swell. ANT.—deplete, drain, empty, exhaust, void.

filter, clarify, infiltrate, purify, refine, screen, separate, settle, strain.

final, concluding, conclusive, decisive, definitive, ending, extreme, last, terminal, ultimate. ANT.—first, inaugural, original, rudimentary, unending.

fine, admirable, attractive, choice, clarified, dainty, delicate, elegant, excellent, exquisite, keen, minute, nice, polished, pure, refined, sensitive, smooth, splendid, small, thin; ground, pulverized; amercement, charge, cost, forfeiture, penalty. ANT.—blunt, coarse, rough, unpolished, thick; amends, compensation, reward.

finish, accomplish, achieve, close, complete, conclude, consummate, end, execute, fulfill, get done, perfect, terminate; close, completion, end, termination, terminus. ANT.—begin, initiate, start; initiation, origin, source.

finite, bounded, circumscribed, determinate, limited, measurable, restricted, terminate. ANT.—endless, eternal, infinite, unbounded.

firm, constant, enduring, fixed, resolute, rugged, solid, stable, steadfast, steady, strong, tenacious, unfaltering, unyielding. ANT.—defective, disjointed, irresolute, wavering, weak.

first, beginning, chief, earliest, initial, leading, original, premier, primary, prime, primeval, primitive, pristine; chief, foremost. ANT.—hindmost, last, latest, least, subordinate.

fit, accommodate, adapt, adjust, conform, equip, prepare, suit; adapted, appropriate, becoming, befitting, competent, congruous, pertinent, prepared, proper, qualified, seemly. ANT.—disturb, misapply, misfit; awkward, inadequate, incongruous, unfit.

fitful, capricious, changeable, convulsive, desultory, fickle, inconstant, intermittent, restless, spasmodic, unstable, variable, whimsical. ANT.—constant, reliable, stable, steady, trustworthy, uniform.

fix, affix, attach, bind, fasten, link, place, plant, root, secure, set, stick, tie; define, determine, establish, limit, locate, prepare, set, settle; adjust, correct, mend, rectify, regulate, repair, restore. ANT.—displace, remove, unfasten; alter, change, disturb, modify; damage, mistreat.

flaccid, drooping, flabby, lax, limber, loose, soft, weak, yielding. ANT.—firm, strong, sturdy, tenacious, unyielding.

flagrant, atrocious, glaring, gross, infamous, monstrous, outrageous, rank, wicked. ANT.—mild, unrestrained.

flame, blaze, burn, flare, ignite, light. ANT.—extinguish, quench.

flashy, flamboyant, gaudy, garish, jazzy, meretricious, pretentious, showy. ANT.—simple, sober, subdued.

flat, even, flush, horizontal, level, plane; dull, insipid, stale, tasteless, vapid; dejected, depressed, heavy, low, spiritless. ANT.—hilly, irregular, mountainous, sloping; bubbling, exciting, frothy, savory; keen, spirited.

flatter, blandish, blarney, cajole, coax, court, entice, exalt, extol, fawn, laud, praise, soften, wheedle. ANT.—denounce, insult, mock, ridicule, spurn.

flaunt, blazon, brandish, expose, flash, flourish, parade, vaunt. ANT.—cloak, conceal, disguise, hide, retire.

flavor, essence, gusto, quality, relish, savor, soul, spirit, tang, taste, zest.

flawless, exact, immaculate, impeccable, perfect, pure, spotless, unblemished, unmarred, whole. ANT.—damaged, defective, flawed, imperfect, tainted.

fleeting, brief, ephemeral, evanescent, flitting, fugitive, momentary, passing, short, temporary, transient, transitory, vanishing. ANT.—constant, enduring, eternal, long-lived, perpetual.

flexible, bending, compliant, docile, ductile, elastic, limber, lithe, plastic, pliable, pliant, supple, tractable, yielding. ANT.—brittle, obstinate, rigid, stiff, unbending.

flicker, flare, fluctuate, flutter, glint, quiver, shimmer, waver. ANT.—glow, shine steadily.

flinch, cower, cringe, falter, recoil, retreat, run, shrink, wince, withdraw. ANT.—confront, face, hold out, sustain.

fling, cast, chuck, heave, pitch, throw, toss. ANT.—catch.

float, drift, fly, glide, hover, sail, skim, wave.

flourish, brandish, conquer, grow, increase, prosper, thrive, triumph, vaunt, wave, win. ANT.—collapse, decay, diminish, fade, weaken.

flow, circulate, course, float, glide, gush, move, pass, roll, run, spout, spurt, stream; emanate, issue, originate, proceed, progress, result; abound, be copious. ANT.—cease, cork, retard, stagnate, stop.

fluctuate, change, deflect, detour, deviate, digress, hesitate, oscillate, sway, swerve, teeter, totter, undulate, vacillate, vary, veer, vibrate, wander, waver. ANT.—adhere, decide, persist, remain, stick.

fluent, copious, easy, expert, flowing, liquid, moving, smooth, voluble. ANT.—hesitant, motionless, slow, sluggish, stammering.

flux, activity, change, discharge, flow, fluctuation, motion, mutation, transition. ANT.—constancy, fixity, inactivity, stability.

fly, ascend, flit, float, flutter, glide, hover, mount, rise, sail, skim, soar, wing; dart, rush, shoot, spring; abscond, decamp, escape, flee, run away. ANT.—descend, fall, plummet, sink; remain, stay.

focus, center, centrum, concentration, cynosure, limelight.

foe, adversary, antagonist, enemy, opponent, rival, vilifier. ANT.—assistant, comrade, friend, helper.

follow, come next, succeed; comply, conform, heed, obey, observe, practice; adopt, copy, imitate, mimic; accompany, attend; chase, pursue, trace, track, trail; ensue, result. ANT.—precede; guide, lead; avoid, elude, flee; cause.

follower, adherent, attendant, devotee, disciple, henchman, partisan, pupil, protege, pursuer, servant, successor, supporter, votary. ANT.—chief, head, leader, master; adversary, antagonist, objector, oppressor, scorner.

folly, absurdity, fatuity, foolishness, imbecility, imprudence, indiscretion, madness, misconduct, shallowness, silliness, simplicity, weak-mindedness, weakness. ANT.—cunning, discernment, judgment, prudence, reasonableness, wisdom.

fondle, caress, cuddle, indulge, neck, nuzzle, pet, stroke, toy. ANT.—disdain, reject.

fool, cheat, con, deceive, delude, dupe, hoodwink, trick; buffoon, clown, harlequin, jester; blockhead, dolt, dunce, idiot, imbecile, nincompoop, numbskull, oaf, simpleton. ANT.—genius, philosopher, sage, scholar.

foolish, absurd, asinine, brainless, crazy, fatuous, idiotic, imbecile, irrational, nonsensical, preposterous, ridiculous, senseless, silly, simple, witless. ANT.—astute, judicious, prudent, sagacious, wise.

forbearance, abstention, abstinence, fortitude, leniency, patience, self-denial, tolerance. ANT.—excess, haste, impatience, intolerance, self-indulgence, strictness.

force, energy, intensity, might, potency, power, strength, vigor; coercion, compulsion, constraint, duress, violence; aggregation, armament, army, battalion, body, company, division, navy, number, organization, regiment, troops; coerce, compel, constrain, drive, impel, incite, instigate, push, rush. ANT.—feebleness, frailty, impotence, weakness; persuasion; hamper, retard, suppress, thwart.

forego, see FORGO

foreign, alien, distant, extraneous, far, remote, strange, unaccustomed, unknown, unnatural. ANT.—accustomed, familiar, indigenous, known.

forever, always, continually, endlessly, eternally, everlastingly, immortally, unremittingly. ANT.—briefly, fleetingly, shortly, temporarily.

forget, disregard, ignore, lose, neglect, omit, overlook, slight. ANT.—recall, recollect, remember, reminisce.

forgo (forego), abandon, abstain, desist, leave, quit, relinquish, renounce, resign, waive. ANT.—accomplish, execute, fulfill, perform, yield.

form, assemble, build, construct, create, design, erect, fashion, forge, make, mold, produce, shape; compose, constitute, make up; arrange, combine, organize, plan; devise, frame, invent; conformation, figure, formation, structure; ceremony, ritual, image, likeness. ANT.—destroy, disfigure, dismantle, misshape, wreck; amorphism, distortion, irregularity, shapelessness.

formal, ceremonial, ceremonious, decorous, exact, functional, methodical, orderly, precise, proper, punctilious, regular, ritualistic, solemn, stiff, systematic. ANT.—casual, easy, natural, unconstrained, unconventional.

former, antecedent, anterior, before, foregoing, preceding, previous, prior. ANT.—after, ensuing, latter, succeeding, subsequent.

formulate, devise, concoct, express, fabricate, frame. ANT.—fumble, guess, hazard.

forte, feature, genius, knack, skill, strong point, talent. ANT.—clumsiness, impotence, incompetence.

fortuitous, accidental, casual, chance, contingent, felicitous, fortunate, happy, incidental, lucky, propitious, random. ANT.—arranged, calculated, deliberate, plotted, unlucky.

fortunate, advantageous, auspicious, benign, encouraging, favored, felicitous, fortuitous, fortunate, happy, lucky, propitious, prosperous, satisfied, successful. ANT.—cheerless, condemned, crushed, ill-fated, persecuted.

fortune, accident, chance, destiny, end, fate, goal, luck; determination, judgment; inheritance, possession, property, riches, wealth. ANT.—catastrophe, downfall, hardship, misfortune, poverty.

forward, advance, aggrandize, bring forward, cultivate, elevate, encourage, expedite, favor, further, help, promote. ANT.—hinder, oppose, retard, retreat, withhold.

foul, dirty, fetid, filthy, grimy, muddy, polluted, putrid, soiled, squalid, tainted; indecent, nasty, obscene, offensive, vulgar; base, contemptible, corrupt, despicable, low, mean, pitiful, shabby. ANT.—clean, immaculate, neat, presentable; pure, unblemished, wholesome.

foundation, base, basis, bottom, endowment, establishment, footing, ground, groundwork, institution, origin, root, substructure, support, underpinning, understructure. ANT.—arch, crown, peak, superstructure, top.

fraction, bit, division, part, percentage, piece, portion, section, segment. ANT.—all, entirety, total, whole.

fracture, breach, break, crack, rent, rift, rupture, split. ANT.—conjugation, juncture, union.

fragile, breakable, brittle, delicate, feeble, frail, infirm, weak. ANT.—durable, enduring, hardy, strong, sturdy, tough.

frank, aboveboard, candid, direct, easy, familiar, free, honest, ingenuous, plain, sincere, straightforward. ANT.—cunning, deceptive, dishonest, hypocritical, insincere.

fraud, artifice, cheat, chicanery, deceit, deception, dishonesty, duplicity, forgery, guile, hoax, imposition, imposture, swindle, treachery, trick. ANT.—fairness, honesty, integrity, sincerity, truth.

free, autonomous, emancipated, exempt, freed, independent, liberated, unconfined, unconstrained, unencumbered, unfettered, unobstructed, unrestricted; clear, loose, open, unfastened, unobstructed; immune; careless, candid, easy, familiar, frank, open, unreserved; artless, bounteous, bountiful, generous, liberal, munificent; costless, gratis. ANT.—confined, restrained, restricted; blocked, clogged, impeded; subject; illiberal, parsimonious, stingy; costly, expensive, priceless.

freedom, deliverance, emancipation, exemption, familiarity, franchise, frankness, immunity, independence, liberation, liberty, license, openness, prerogative, privilege, right, unrestraint. ANT.—bondage, coercion, compulsion, constraint, servitude.

freight, burden, cargo, lading, load, shipment, transportation.

frenzy, agitation, delirium, derangement, excitement, fury, madness, mania, rage, wildness. ANT.—calmness, delight, sanity.

frequent, common, general, habitual, many, numerous, often, persistent, recurrent, recurring, regular, repeated, usual. ANT.—exceptional, infrequent, rare, scanty, sporadic.

fresh, modern, new, novel, recent, unused; additional, further; brisk, cool, hardy, healthy, natural, refreshing, vigorous, young; artless, green, inexperienced, natural, raw; bold, cheeky, flippant, impertinent. ANT.—decayed, faded, hackneyed, musty, stagnant; courteous, deferential, respectful.

fret, agitate, anger, annoy, chafe, corrode, disturb, fidget, gall, gnaw, worry. ANT.—calm, placate, please, soften, soothe.

friction, abrasion, attrition, erosion, frication, grating, rubbing, traction; conflict, disagreement, discord, disharmony. ANT.—lubrication, smoothness; accord, agreement, harmony, unity.

friend, companion, comrade, confidant, crony, intimate, pal; adherent, advocate, defender, patron, supporter; ally, associate, colleague. ANT.—adversary, enemy, stranger.

friendly, affable, affectionate, amicable, brotherly, companionable, cordial, genial, intimate, kindly, neighborly, propitious, sociable, solicitous, sympathetic. ANT.—antagonistic, cool, distant, hostile, reserved.

frighten, abash, affright, alarm, appall, astound, browbeat, daunt, discourage, dishearten, dismay, dispirit, hector, horrify, intimidate, scare, startle, terrify, terrorize, threaten. ANT.—embolden, gladden, inspire, reassure, soothe.

frigid, arctic, chilling, cool, ice-cold; dull, formal, inhibited, lifeless, passionless, reserved, rigid. ANT.—temperate, warm; amorous, fervid, responsive, uninhibited.

fringe, border, boundary, edge, edging, flounce, outskirts, perimeter, tassel, trimming. ANT.—center, core, heart, inside, interior.

front, anterior, facade, face, forepart, prow, van; bearing, brow, forehead, manner, mien. ANT.—astern, back, posterior, rear.

frown, disapprove, glare, glower, lower, scowl, sulk. ANT.—approve, beam, shine, smile.

frugal, conservative, economical, miserly, moderate, parsimonious, penurious, provident, saving, sparing, stingy, temperate, thrifty. ANT.—extravagant, intemperate, self-indulgent, wasteful.

fruitful, abundant, ample, bountiful, copious, exuberant, fecund, fertile, luxuriant, plenteous, productive, prolific, rich, teeming, yielding. ANT.—barren, fruitless, impotent, sterile, unproductive.

frustrate, baffle, balk, bar, circumvent, confound, counteract, defeat, disappoint, disconcert, foil, hinder, nullify, prevent, stop, thwart. ANT.—accomplish, facilitate, fulfill, further, promote.

fulfill, accomplish, complete, consummate, finish, realize, terminate; discharge, perform; comply, fill, meet, satisfy. ANT.—abandon, disappoint, fail, neglect, withdraw.

full, crammed, filled, glutted, gorged, packed, replete, sated, satiated, soaked, stocked, surfeited, swollen; ample, complete, copious, extensive, plentiful, sufficient, whole; baggy, flowing, loose, voluminous; circumstantial, detailed, exhaustive. ANT.—depleted, devoid, empty, vacant; insufficient, lacking, partial.

function, bailiwick, business, duty, job, office, position, role, task; do, moderate, officiate, operate, perform, preside, serve, work. ANT.—idleness, unemployment; ignore, malfunction, mismanage.

fundamental, basic, chief, elemental, essential, indispensable, intrinsic, primary, principal, radical. ANT.—auxiliary, dispensable, secondary, subordinate, superficial.

funny, absurd, amusing, bizarre, comical, diverting, droll, farcical, humorous, laughable, ludicrous, ridiculous, witty; curious, odd, queer. ANT.—melancholy, sad, serious, sober, solemn.

furious, angry, ferocious, fierce, frenzied, fuming, inflamed, infuriated, raging, turbulent, violent, wild. ANT.—calm, composed, peaceful, self-possessed, tranquil.

furnish, appoint, cater, endow, equip, fit, outfit, provide, purvey, supply; afford, give, produce, yield. ANT.—denude, despoil, divest, strip, withhold.

further, advance, aid, assist, expedite, promote, support. ANT.—check, delay, frustrate, hinder, impede.

furtive, clandestine, covert, secret, sly, stealthy, surreptitious. ANT.—aboveboard, forthright, open, overt.

futile, abortive, empty, fruitless, idle, ineffective, ineffectual, resultless, unsatisfying, useless, vain, valueless. ANT.—beneficial, conducive, efficient, profitable, useful.

G

gain, accretion, acquisition, advantage, behalf, benefit, emolument, favor, good, increase, increment, interest, net, profit; accomplish, achieve acquire, attain, benefit, consummate, earn, effect, get, obtain, procure, profit, reach, realize, reap, secure, win. ANT.—decrease, handicap, loss; forfeit, lose, surrender.

galaxy, array, assemblage, bevy, cluster, collection, company, constellation, group.

gamble, bet, chance, hazard, play, risk, speculate, stake, wager. ANT.—insure, invest, plan, safeguard.

game, adventure, amusement, contest, diversion, entertainment, festivity, frolic, fun, gaiety, gambol, lark, match, merriment, merrymaking, pastime, play, recreation, sport; courageous, daring, disposed, favorable, sporting, valiant, willing. ANT.—business.

gamut, compass, extent, range, register, scope.

gap, abyss, aperture, breach, cavity, chasm, chink, cleft, crack, crevice, fissure, gulf, hiatus, hole, hollow, interstice, lacuna, opening, orifice, passage, space, vacancy, vacuity, void.

garble, corrupt, deface, distort, falsify, misquote, misrepresent, misstate, mix, muddle, mutilate, pervert, scramble. ANT.—clarify, communicate, correct, edit, unscramble.

garment, apparel, array, attire, clothes, clothing, drapery, dress, garb, habiliment, raiment, robe, vestment, vesture, wrap. ANT.—nakedness, nudity.

garner, accumulate, collect, deposit, harvest, hoard, husband, reserve, save, store.

garnish, adorn, array, beautify, bedeck, deck, decorate, embellish, enhance, enrich, furnish, grace, ornament, strew, trim. ANT.—debase, defame, expose, strip, uncover.

garrulous, babbling, bumptious, chattering, chatty, loquacious, prattling, prolix, talkative, verbose, wordy. ANT.—laconic, reticent, silent, taciturn, uncommunicative.

gather, accumulate, acquire, amass, assemble, collect, congregate, convene, convoke, group, meet, muster; compress, contract; cull, garner, glean, harvest, heap, pick, pile, reap; conclude, deduce, infer, judge. ANT.—disband, disperse, distribute, scatter, separate.

gaudy, cheap, flamboyant, flashy, garish, glaring, tasteless, tawdry, vulgar. ANT.—pale, refined, solemn, somber, tasteful.

gauge, calculation, caliber, criterion, diameter, evaluation, measure, norm, standard, template, thickness. ANT.—estimate, guess, hazard.

gaunt, attenuated, bony, emaciated, empty, flimsy, haggard, hollow, hungry, lank, lean, meager, scanty, scraggy, scrawny, shriveled, shrunken, skinny, slender, slight, slim, spare, thin, withered. ANT.—broad, bulky, fat, obese, portly.

gay, blithe, buoyant, cheerful, colorful, convivial, festive, frolicsome, glad, happy, hilarious, jolly, jovial, joyful, lighthearted, lively, merry, sprightly, vivacious, waggish. ANT.—depressed, glum, mournful, sad, sullen.

gaze, behold, discern, eye, gape, gawk, glance, look, peer, stare, survey, view, watch; examine, inspect, observe, regard. ANT.—avert, ignore, miss, overlook.

genealogy, ancestry, descent, lineage, parentage, pedigree, progeniture, stock.

general, all-embracing, common, commonplace, comprehensive, conventional, customary, everyday, extensive, familiar, frequent, generic, habitual, inclusive, indefinite, normal, ordinary, popular, prevailing, prevalent, regular, universal, usual, whole, widespread; indefinite, inexact, vague. ANT.—exceptional, rare, singular; definite, particular, specific.

generally, chiefly, commonly, mainly, ordinarily, principally, usually. ANT.—especially, occasionally, particularly, rarely, seldom.

generation, age, breed, creation, engendering, family, formation, procreation, production, reproduction; epoch, era, period, span, time. ANT.—breakdown, dissolution, obliteration, wreckage.

generic, characteristic, comprehensive, general, ideal, representative, typical. ANT.—individual, particular, peculiar, special.

generosity, altruism, beneficence, benevolence, bounty, bountifulness, charity, humanity, kindness, lavishness, liberality, magnanimity, munificence, nobleness, philanthropy. ANT.—cruelty, inhumanity, malevolence, selfishness, unkindness.

generous, beneficent, bountiful, forgiving, giving, high-minded, honorable, liberal, magnanimous, munificent, openhanded, open-hearted, unselfish, whole-hearted. ANT.—covetous, greedy, miserly, selfish, stingy.

genial, affable, animated, brotherly, cheerful, congenial, convivial, cordial, fraternal, hospitable, pleasant, pleasing, warm-hearted, well-disposed. ANT.—doleful, inhospitable, moody, petulant, sullen.

genius, ability, acumen, aptitude, brains, brilliance, capacity, creativity, endowment, faculty, gift, inspiration, intellect, knack, leaning, perspicacity, propensity, sagacity, talent; intellectual, master, prodigy, wizard. ANT.—ineptitude, obtuseness, shallowness, stupidity; dolt, dullard, moron.

gentle, benign, calm, compliant, docile, genteel, meek, mild, moderate, pacific, peaceful, placid, relaxed, serene, soft, soothing, tame, temperate, tender, tractable. ANT.—fierce, harsh, rough, savage, violent.

genuine, actual, authentic, bona fide, exact, frank, honest, legitimate, natural, proven, real, sincere, tested, true, unadulterated, unaffected, unalloyed, unmixed, unquestionable, valid, veritable. ANT.—artificial, bogus, counterfeit, false, sham.

germ, beginning, first principal, origin, rudiment, source; bud, embryo, seed; spore; microbe, microorganism, pathogen. ANT.—conclusion, end, fruit, issue, outgrowth.

germane, allied, appropriate, apropos, cognate, fitting, pertinent, related, relevant. ANT.—inapplicable, irrelevant, unfitting, unrelated.

germinate, bud, develop, effloresce, evolve, grow, shoot, sprout, swell, vegetate. ANT.—die.

gesture, indication, motion, movement, portent, sign, signal, symbol.

get, achieve, acquire, arrive, attain, capture, comprehend, earn, gain, generate, grasp, learn, obtain, procure, propagate, reach, receive, secure, seize. ANT.—abnegate, forfeit, leave, renounce, surrender.

ghastly, ashen, cadaverous, dreadful, frightful, ghostly, grisly, hideous, horrible, pallid, revolting, shocking, terrifying. ANT.—attractive, captivating, healthy, pleasant, rosy.

ghost, apparition, banshee, fairy, goblin, haunt, image, phantom, shade, shadow, specter, spirit, sprite, spook, wraith. ANT.—essence, existence, fact, reality, substance.

giant, colossal, enormous, gigantic, huge, immense, monstrous, super, titanic, vast, whopping. ANT.—dwarf, infinitesimal, minute, stunted, tiny.

gift, alms, benefaction, bequest, bestowal, boon, bounty, charity, donation, endowment, favor, grant, gratuity, largess, legacy, munificence, present; provision, support; aptitude, faculty, genius, knack, talent. ANT.—deprivation, forfeiture, indemnity, loss; incapacity, ineptitude, stupidity.

gigantic, amazing, colossal, elephantine, enormous, extensive, gargantuan, great, huge, immense, mammoth, massive, monstrous, prodigious, stupendous, titanic, vast. ANT.—diminutive, insignificant, little, minute, tiny.

gimmick, adjunct, angle, contrivance, device, fraud, gadget, swindle, trick.

gird, arm, bind, clothe, encircle, endow, equip, fortify, furnish, girdle, invest, support, surround. ANT.—divest, loosen, release, strip, untie.

girth, boundary, cinch, circumference, corpulence, dimensions, measure, outline, perimeter.

gist, core, crux, drift, essence, import, meaning, pith, point, purpose, sense, significance, signification, substance, tenor, upshot.

give, bestow, bequeath, confer, contribute, convey, deliver, donate, furnish, grant, impart, present, provide, supply, yield. ANT.—deprive, keep, retain, seize, withdraw.

glad, blithesome, cheerful, cheering, content, delighted, exulting, gay, gratified, happy, jolly, joyful, joyous, lighthearted, merry, pleased, pleasing, vivacious. ANT.—dejected, depressed, dispirited, melancholy, sad.

glamour, allure, aura, bewitchment, charm, enchantment, fascination, magic, spell. ANT.—blandness, dullness, lackluster, obscurity.

glance, eye, gaze, look, scan, see; view, watch. ANT.—avert, hide, miss, overlook.

glare, beam, dazzle, flash, gleam, glimmer, glisten, glow, radiate, scintillate, sparkle, twinkle; frown, glower, scowl, stare.

glassy, bright, crystalline, glossy, lustrous, polished, silken, smooth, transparent, vitreous; dull-eyed, expressionless, limpid. ANT.—dim, lusterless, obscure, opaque, tarnished.

gleam, beam, blaze, flash, flicker, glare, glimmer, glance, glint, glisten, glitter, glow, radiate, ray, scintillate, shimmer, shine, sparkle, twinkle.

glib, articulate, diplomatic, facile, fluent, oily, polished, sleek; smooth, suave, urbane, vocal, voluble. ANT.—harsh, inarticulate, rough, rugged, stammering.

gloat, brag, boast, crow, exult, flaunt, rejoice, revel, triumph. ANT.—condole, commiserate, sympathize.

gloomy, cheerless, crestfallen, dejected, depressed, depressing, despondent, disconsolate, discontented, discouraged, dismal, dispirited, doleful, downcast, down-hearted, dull, funereal, glum, heavy, melancholy, miserable, moody, morose, oppressive, pessimistic, sad, somber, sorrowful, sullen, unhappy; clouded, dark, dim, dusky, shady. ANT.—cheerful, happy, joyous, merry, optimistic.

glorify, adore, applaud, bless, celebrate, consecrate, dignify, elevate, enshrine, enthrone, esteem, exaggerate, exalt, extol; hallow, honor, idolize, laud, magnify, prize, revere, sanctify, value, venerate. ANT.—abase, debase, degrade, dishonor, mock.

glorious, brilliant, celebrated, elevated, exalted, grand, high, lofty, magnificent, majestic, marvelous, noble, raised, resplendent, shining, splendid, sublime, supreme, wondrous. ANT.—atrocious, base, contemptible, ignoble, ridiculous.

glossy, elegant, glazed, lustrous, polished, refined, reflecting, shining, sleek, velvety; deceptive, showy, specious, superficial. ANT.—lusterless, rough, unpolished; genuine, honest, uncouth, unrefined.

glow, beam, blaze, burn, flame, flare, flash, flicker, glare, gleam, glimmer, glisten, glitter, light, radiate, scintillate, shimmer, shine, sparkle, twinkle. ANT.—die, fade.

glum, blue, dejected, dismal, dispirited, dour, gloomy, low, moody, morose, sulky, sullen. ANT.—amiable, buoyant, cheerful, joyous, merry.

glut, overfeed, overstock, oversupply; cloy, cram, deluge, flood, gorge, overeat, sate, satiate, satisfy, stuff, surfeit. ANT.—abstain, curb, deplete, empty, void.

glutinous, adhesive, cohesive, gluey, gummy, sticky, viscid, viscous. ANT.—clean, dry, glueless, powdery.

gnarled, contorted, knotted, knotty, rugged, twisted. ANT.—direct, plain, smooth, straight.

go, abandon, abscond, budge, decamp, depart, desert, disappear, exit, fade, flee, leave, move, pass, proceed, quit, recede, relinquish, retire, retreat, run, step, stir, travel, vanish, walk, withdraw. ANT.—arrive, come, enter, stay, stop.

goad, impel, pressure, prod, prompt, provoke, push, spur, urge. ANT.—deter, discourage, dissuade, restrain.

goal, aim, ambition, aspiration, desire, destination, end, hope, intention, object, objective; basket, end zone, finish line, target.

godly, consecrated, devotional, devout, divine, godlike, hallowed, immaculate, incorrupt, inviolate, pious, pure, religious, reverent, sacred, saintly, sinless, stainless. ANT.—corrupt, profane, sacrilegious, ungodly, wicked.

good, chaste, conscientious, exemplary, honest, incorrupt, moral, pure, reliable, reputable, righteous, sinless, upright, virtuous, worthy; admirable, commendable, excellent, genuine, precious, real, sound, valid; benevolent, gracious, humane, kind; agreeable, cheerful, friendly, genial, gratifying, health-giving, invigorating, pleasant; fair, honorable, immaculate, stainless, unspotted, untainted; auspicious, beneficial, favorable, profitable, propitious, serviceable, suitable, useful, valuable; able, capable, efficient, expert, proficient, skillful; adequate, ample, satisfactory, sufficient. ANT.—contemptible, evil, injurious, odious, vile.

goods, belongings, chattels, commodities, effects, freight, material, merchandise, property, stock, wares.

gorge, bolt, cram, fill, glut, gobble, sate, satiate, surfeit. ANT.—diet, fast, starve.

gorgeous, dazzling, glorious, grand, magnificent, majestic, resplendent, splendid, superb, surpassing. ANT.—common, homely, modest, plain, unpretentious.

govern, administer, command, conduct, control, curb, dictate, direct, dominate, guide, influence, lead, manage, mold, order, oversee, regulate, reign, restrain, rule, superintend, supervise. ANT.—acquiesce, assent, obey, submit, surrender.

graceful, beautiful, becoming, comely, congruous, dignified, easy, elegant, flowing, fluid, harmonious, lithe, nimble, pleasing, refined, smooth, supple, symmetrical, tasteful, trim, unaffected. ANT.—awkward, clumsy, gawky, ungainly, unrefined.

gracious, agreeable, amiable, beneficent, benevolent, compassionate, congenial, courteous, engaging, friendly, good-natured, hospitable, kind, merciful, mild, munificent, pleasing, tender. ANT.—acrimonious, churlish, disagreeable, ill-natured, surly.

grade, brand, category, denomination, genre, kind; order, rank, set, stage, step; hill, incline, slope. ANT.—sameness, uniformity; level, plane.

gradual, creeping, dawdling, delaying, deliberate, dull, inching, laggard, leisurely, progressive, sluggish, slow, step-by-step, tired, unintermittent. ANT.—abrupt, hasty, quick, rapid, swift.

graduate, end, finish, qualify; adapt, adjust, calibrate, measure, proportion, regulate.

graft, bud, scion, shoot, transplant; booty, bribe, corruption, favoritism, kickback, loot.

grandeur, augustness, dignity, greatness, loftiness, magnificence, majesty, pomp, splendor, stateliness. ANT.—humility, lowliness, simplicity.

grant, allocate, allot, apportion, appropriate, assign, bestow, confer, deal, dispense, distribute, divide, furnish, give, measure, mete, present, transfer; accede, agree, allow, comply, concede, concur, permit, yield; benefaction, endowment, gift, present, privilege, reward. ANT.—confiscate, damage, refuse, retain, withhold; oppose, reject, renounce; charge, decrement, deduction, forfeiture, loss.

graphic, clear, definite, detailed, distinct, explicit, forcible, illustrative, pictorial, powerful, striking, telling, vivid. ANT.—abstract, ambiguous, obscure, weak.

grapple, clasp, clinch, clutch, contend, hook, seize, struggle, wrestle; comprehend, understand, unite. ANT.—abandon, ignore, loose, release, surrender.

grasp, apprehend, arrest, capture, catch, clasp, clutch, grapple, grip, lay hold of, retain, seize, snare, trap; comprehend, discern, perceive, recognize, understand. ANT.—extricate, liberate, lose, release; misconstrue, misunderstand.

grate, abrade, creak, grind, pulverize, rasp, scrape, scratch; annoy, irritate, jar, vex. ANT.—comfort, placate, please, soothe.

grateful, appreciative, beholden, gratified, indebted, obliged, thankful; acceptable, agreeable, pleasing. ANT.—thankless, unappreciative; abusive, careless, rude.

gratification, comfort, consolation, contentment, delight, ease, enjoyment, fulfillment, happiness, indulgence, pleasure, relief, reward, satisfaction, self-indulgence, solace, succor. ANT.—affliction, discomfort, misery, sacrifice, submission, suffering.

gratis, free, freely, gratuitous. ANT.—costly.

gratuitous, free, groundless, spontaneous, unfounded, unprovoked, voluntary, wanton. ANT.—deserved, earned, merited, warranted.

grave, consequential, critical, heavy, important, momentous, serious, weighty; demure, dignified, earnest, intense, ponderous, sedate, sober, solemn, staid, thoughtful. ANT.—insignificant, trifling, trivial; airy, buoyant, frivolous, merry.

great, big, enormous, gigantic, huge, immense, large, vast; numerous, countless; celebrated, eminent, famed, famous, illustrious, prominent, renowned; critical, important, momentous, serious, vital, weighty; august, dignified, elevated, exalted, glorious, grand, honorable, majestic, noble; excellent, fine, magnificent, splendid; brave, chivalrous, courageous, daring, fearless, heroic, intrepid, valiant. ANT.—diminutive, little, minute, small; common, obscure, ordinary, unknown; menial, paltry, servile, shameful.

greedy, acquisitive, avaricious, covetous, grasping, grudging, illiberal, mercenary, miserly, parsimonious, rapacious, selfish; devouring, gluttonous, ravenous, stingy, voracious. ANT.—charitable, generous, munificent, philanthropic, sharing; full, satisfied.

greet, accost, address, approach, hail, receive, salute, speak to, welcome. ANT.—avoid, ignore, pass by.

gregarious, affable, amicable, companionable, convivial, friendly, hospitable, neighborly, outgoing, sociable. ANT.—antisocial, disagreeable, hermitic, inhospitable, unsociable.

grief, adversity, affliction, anguish, bereavement, calamity, catastrophe, distress, heartache, lamentation, misery, mourning, pain, sadness, sorrow, trial, tribulation, woe. ANT.—comfort, exhilaration, gladness, happiness, joy.

grievance, affliction, burden, complaint, damage, detriment, grief, hardship, harm, injury, injustice, sorrow, trial, tribulation, wrong. ANT.—benefit, happiness, justice, right, victory.

grieve, bemoan, bewail, deplore, lament, mourn, regret, rue, sorrow, suffer, weep; afflict, distress, pain, try, wound. ANT.—celebrate, rejoice, revel; console, heal.

grim, austere, dour, forbidding, gloomy, glum, inflexible, morose, severe, sinister, stern, sullen, terrifying, threatening. ANT.—blithe, enlivening, pleasant, serene, wining.

grip, capture, clasp, clutch, grab, grasp, hold, seize, snare, trap. ANT.—drop, loosen, relax, release.

grit, courage, decision, endurance, fortitude, mettle, nerve, pluck, spirit; abrasive, gravel, sand. ANT.—cowardice, fear, timidity.

groan, complain, cry, growl, grumble, lament, moan, sigh, sob, wail. ANT.—applaud, cheer, laugh, rejoice, sing.

grope, attempt, finger, fumble, grapple, hesitate, search, try. ANT.—comprehend, perceive.

gross, aggregate, entire, total, whole; brutal, enormous, glaring, grievous, manifest, plain; coarse, crass, earthy, indelicate, lewd, obscene, repulsive; rough, rude, vulgar; big, bulky, corpulent, fat, fleshy, great, large, monstrous, obese, thick. ANT.—proper, refined; moral, purified, spiritual; appealing, comely, delicate.

grotesque, absurd, bizarre, fantastic, incongruous, misshapen, monstrous, odd, strange, unnatural. ANT.—average, customary, normal, typical, usual.

grouch, complain, grumble, lament, murmur, mutter, mope, protest, remonstrate, repine, sulk, whine. ANT.—applaud, approve, praise, rejoice.

ground, base, basis, bottom, foundation, groundwork, support, underpinning; assumption, postulate, premise, presumption, presupposition, principle; land, locality, property, region, territory; base, establish, fix, set, settle; educate, instruct, train. ANT.—derivative, superstructure, trimming; demolish, unsettle.

group, aggregation, assemblage, assembly, audience, band, brood, bunch, class, clique, cluster, collection, company, crowd, flock, herd, horde, lot, meeting, mob, order, pack, party, set, swarm, throng, troupe.

groveling, abject, begging, contemptible, debased, crawling, cringing, cowering, crouching, despicable, dishonorable, fawning, ignoble, ignominious, low, lowly, mean, menial, servile, sneaking, snivelling, sordid, vile, vulgar. ANT.—commanding, controlling, esteemed, exalted, righteous.

grow, advance, accumulate, amplify, augment, bud, burgeon, develop, dilate, distend, enlarge, expand, extend, germinate, increase, inflate, mature, puff, stretch, swell, thicken, tumefy; breed, cultivate, farm, nurture, plant, raise, sow. ANT.—atrophy, contract, decay, diminish, shrink, stagnate; destroy, kill.

growl, bemoan, complain, groan, grumble, howl, mumble, murmur, mutter, snarl. ANT.—hum, purr, sing.

growth, accretion, advancement, development, elaboration, expansion, extension, increase, unfolding, unraveling; evolution, maturing, multiplication, progress, proliferation. ANT.—abbreviation, compression, curtailment, decline, failure.

grudge, animosity, aversion, detestation, enmity, grievance, hatred, hostility, ill will, malevolence, malice, malignity, rancor, resentment, resistance, spite. ANT.—affection, kindness, love, sympathy, toleration.

gruff, abrupt, acrimonious, blunt, brusque, churlish, coarse, cross, curt, harsh, morose, rough, rude, short, snappish, snarling, sour, stern, surly, unceremonious, uncivil, unpolished. ANT.—affable, complaisant, gracious, polished, serene.

guarantee, security, surety, warranty; affirm, allege, assert, attest, certify, declare, endorse, insure, guard, support, testify, verify, vouch, warrant. ANT.—deny, disown, ignore, reject, renounce.

guard, conceal, cover, curtain, defend, disguise, envelop, fortify, hide, mask, preserve, protect, safeguard, screen, secure, shelter, shield, shroud, treasure, veil. ANT.—disregard, divulge, expose, neglect, reveal.

guess, assume, believe, conjecture. estimate, fancy, imagine, opine, reckon, speculate, suppose, surmise. ANT.—ascertain, calculate, know, measure.

guide, conduct, control, direct, govern, lead, manage, pilot, regulate, shepherd, steer, supervise. ANT.—abandon, misguide, mislead, neglect.

guile, artifice, beguilement, cheat, chicanery, cunning, deceit, deception, dishonesty, doubledealing, duplicity, fraud, hypocrisy, imposture, sham, slyness, subtlety, trick, wiliness. ANT.—candor, honesty, integrity, openness, sincerity, truthfulness.

guilty, blameworthy, censurable, corrupt, criminal, culpable, faulty, immoral, liable, sinful, stained, tarnished, wicked. ANT.—blameless, faultless, innocent, innocuous, spotless.

guise, air, appearance, aspect, behavior, clothing, custom, demeanor, dress, garb, look, manner, mien, pose, posture, practice, role, semblance.

gush, burst, flood, flow, issue, pour, rave, spout, spurt. ANT.—fade, stop, trickle, wane.

H

habit, addiction, continuation, custom, fashion, manner, method, mode, observance, practice, prevalence, routine, style, use, way, wont; clothes, dress, garb, raiment.

habitual, accustomed, common, customary, established, frequent, general, often, perpetual, persistent, recurrent, regular, usual. ANT.—exceptional, infrequent, rare, uncommon, unique.

hack, botch, break, chip, chop, cut, drudge, lacerate, mangle, mutilate, split, tear, toil.

haggard, careworn, debilitated, emaciated, exhausted, fretted, gaunt, hollow-eyed, wasted, weak, weary. ANT.—exuberant, forcible, powerful, robust, vigorous.

haggle, bargain, cavil, deal, dicker, patter, quibble, stickle, wrangle.

hail, acclaim, accost, address, applaud, approach, cheer, greet, herald, honor, salute, summon, welcome. ANT.—avoid, disregard, ignore, scorn, shun.

hale, chipper, healthy, hearty, lusty, robust, salubrious, salutary, sound, strong, vigorous, well, wholesome. ANT.—delicate, diseased, feeble, frail, infirm.

half-hearted, cool, dull, indifferent, perfunctory, unenthusiastic, uninterested. ANT.—ardent, enthusiastic, warm, wholehearted, zealous.

hall, atrium, auditorium, building, corridor, dormitory, edifice, entrance, headquarters; house, manor, mansion, passage, residence, vestibule.

hallow, aggrandize, bless, consecrate, dignify, elevate, ennoble, erect, exalt, extol, glorify, raise, reverse, sanctify, venerate. ANT.—debase, degrade, curse, dishonor, humble.

hallucination, aberration, chimera, delusion, fantasy, illusion, mirage, phantasm, vision. ANT.—existence, reality, truth.

halt, arrest, bar, cease, check, close, cork, desist, discontinue, doubt, end, falter, hesitate, hinder, impede, intermit, interrupt, linger, obstruct, pause, stop, suspend, terminate. ANT.—advance, persevere, proceed, promote, speed.

hamper, encumber, hinder, impede, obstruct, perplex, prevent, restrain, restrict, retard, shackle, thwart. ANT.—assist, ease, facilitate, promote, relieve.

handicap, burden, defect, disadvantage, drag, encumbrance, impediment, limitation, obstruction, penalty; allowance, odds. ANT.—advantage, asset, benefit, remuneration, reward.

handle, direct, feel, finger, manage, manipulate, negotiate, operate, ply, wield; cope.

handsome, attractive, beauteous, beautiful, charming, comely, elegant, fair, fine, good-looking, graceful, lovely, pretty, shapely; ample, generous, large, liberal. ANT.—foul, hideous, homely, repulsive; insignificant, mean, poor, small.

handy, able, accessible, adapted, adept, adroit, advantageous, appropriate, available, clever, commodious, convenient, dexterous, favorable, fitting, helpful, ready, resourceful, skilled, skillful, suitable, timely, useful. ANT.—awkward, inconvenient, inopportune, troublesome, unskilled.

hang, attach, dangle, depend, drape, droop, hover, lean, suspend, swing; execute, gibbet, lynch.

happen, accrue, arrive, bechance, befall, betide, chance, come, ensue, eventuate, follow, occur, result, supervene, take place, transpire.

happiness, beatitude, blessedness, bliss, contentment, delight, ecstasy, exultation, felicity, gladness, merriment, mirth, peace, pleasure, rapture, satisfaction, wellbeing. ANT.—adversity, catastrophe, despair, grief, misery.

happy, blessed, blissful, blithe, bright, buoyant, cheerful, contented, delighted, delightful, ecstatic, elated, exhilarated, favorable, fortunate, gay, glad, gratified, jocund, jovial, joyful, joyous, merry, mirthful, opportune, pleasing, propitious, prosperous, rapturous, spirited, successful, thrilled, vivacious. ANT.—depressed, distressed, gloomy, heartsick, morose.

harass, aggravate, agitate, anger, annoy, badger, bother, calumniate, chafe, deride, disturb, enrage, exasperate, harry, incense, inflame, infuriate, irritate, molest, nag, nettle, pester, plague, provoke, rouse, ruffle, tantalize, taunt, tease, torment, traduce, twit, vex, vilify, worry. ANT.—comfort, delight, encourage, gratify, soothe.

harbor, cherish, contain, cover, foster, guard, house, nurture, protect, shield. ANT.—banish, eject, exile, expel.

hard, compact, concrete, durable, firm, impenetrable, impervious, rigid, solid, stable, steady, strong; arduous, burdensome, difficult, laborious, onerous, toilsome, tough, troublesome; intricate, perplexing, puzzling; austere, cruel, demanding, exacting, grinding, harsh, pitiless, rigorous, severe, stern, strict, unfeeling, unforgiving, unrelenting. ANT.—elastic, flabby, fluid, plastic, pliable, soft; easy, effortless, facile; compassionate, gentle, tender.

harden, anneal, cool, ossify, petrify, solidify, stiffen, toughen; accustom, brace, confirm, discipline, fortify, habituate, inure, season, steel, train. ANT.—melt, soften, warm; coddle, indulge, pamper, spoil.

hardship, adversity, affliction, burden, calamity, catastrophe, disaster, distress, injustice, misery, misfortune, oppression, ordeal, privation, suffering, trial, tribulation, trouble. ANT.—alleviation, assistance, blessing, consolation, profit.

hardy, brave, courageous, enduring, fearless, intrepid, resistant, robust, tenacious, undaunted, unyielding, vigorous. ANT.—delicate, feeble, infirm, puny, weak.

harm, abuse, damage, deprivation, deterioration, detriment, evil, hurt, ill, impairment, infliction, injury, loss, mischief, misfortune, mishap, wrong. ANT.—advancement, benefit, boon, favor.

harmful, baneful, damaging, deleterious, detrimental, hurtful, injurious, mischievous, noxious, pernicious, prejudicial, ruinous. ANT.—advantageous, beneficial, healing, helpful, profitable.

harmless, blameless, dependable, faultless, incorrupt, innocuous, inoffensive, protected, pure, reliable, safe, secure, trustworthy, undefiled. ANT.—dangerous, hazardous, injurious, perilous, unsafe.

harmony, agreement, alliance, coincidence, concord, concurrence, consonance, unanimity, understanding, unison; adaptation, concordance, congruity, consistency; amity, agreeableness, compatibility, suitableness. ANT.—conflict, disagreement, discord, dissension, variance.

harsh, abusive, acrimonious, austere, bitter, blunt, brutal, caustic, coarse, cutting, exacting, grating, gruff, hard, harsh, heartless, jarring, overbearing, rigorous, rough, rugged, severe, stern, strict, stringent, uncivil, unfeeling. ANT.—courteous, gentle, melodious, mild, soft.

harvest, crop, fruit, proceeds, produce, product, reaping, result, return, store, yield; consequence, effect, outcome, result; acquire, gain, garner, gather, glean, reap. ANT.—lose, plant, sow, squander.

hassle, argument, brawl, controversy, disagreement, dispute, fight, melee, quarrel, scrap, wrangle. ANT.—agreement, harmony.

haste, acceleration, briskness, celerity, dispatch, expedition, fleetness, flurry, hurry, quickness, rapidity, rush, speed, swiftness, urgency, velocity; accelerate, expedite, hurry, precipitate, press, quicken, urge. ANT.—delay, lingering, slowness, tarrying; decelerate, delay, procrastinate, retard.

hasten, accelerate, expedite, hurry, hustle, precipitate, quicken, race, run, rush, speed, spur. ANT.—delay, detain, prolong, retard, tarry.

hasty, brisk, cursory, fast, hurried, lively, precipitate, quick, rapid, rushing, speedy, swift; careless; excitable, foolhardy, impatient, imprudent, impulsive, indiscreet, irascible, rash, reckless, sharp, testy. ANT.—slow, sluggish; cautious, judicious, patient, thoughtful.

hate, abhor, abominate, despise, detest, dislike, execrate, loathe.

ANT.—admire, cherish, like, love, revere.

hatred, abhorrence, acrimony, animosity, antipathy, aversion, bitterness, detestation, dislike, enmity, grudge, hostility, ill will, loathing, malevolence, malice, malignity, odium, rancor, repugnance. ANT.—admiration, affection, friendship, love, reverence.

haughty, arrogant, cavalier, contemptuous, disdainful, egotistical, overbearing, proud, supercilious, swaggering, vain. ANT.—ashamed, humble, lowly, meek, unpretentious.

haul, deliver, drag, draw, lug, pull, tow, trail, tug. ANT.—drive, impel, shove, thrust.

haunt, attend, frequent, return (to), visit; disturb, frighten, obsess, persecute, terrorize; follow, importune, resort.

hauteur, arrogance, contempt, disdain, haughtiness, loftiness, pomp, pride, sauciness, scorn, superciliousness. ANT.—condescension, humility, lowliness, plainness.

have, carry, control, get, hold, obtain, occupy, maintain, own, possess, seize, take. ANT.—abandon, lack, lose, need, surrender.

haven, anchorage, asylum, harbor, port, refuge, retreat, shelter.

hazard, casualty, chance, contingency, danger, gamble, jeopardy, peril, risk, uncertainty, venture. ANT.—certainty, immunity, protection, safety, security.

hazardous, critical, dangerous, fearful, insecure, menacing, perilous, precarious, risky, threatening, uncertain, unsafe. ANT.—assured, firm, protected, safe, secure.

hazy, ambiguous, cloudy, dim, foggy, gauzy, indefinite, indistinct, murky, nebulous, obscure, uncertain, unclear, undetermined, unsettled, vague, wavering. ANT.—clear, explicit, lucid, precise, specific.

head, boss, chief, commander, director, foreman, leader, manager, master, principal, ruler; acme, apex, crest, crown, culmination, peak, pinnacle, summit, top; crisis, culmination; capacity, instinct, mind, understanding. ANT.—follower, subordinate; base, bottom, foot; incapacity, incompetence.

heal, cure, fix, harmonize, knit, mend, reconcile, remedy, repair, restore, soothe. ANT.—break, damage, harm, injure.

healthy, bracing, hale, hearty, invigorating, lusty, robust, sound, strong, vigorous, virile, well; beneficial, harmless, healing, hygienic, nutritious, salubrious, salutary, sanitary, wholesome. ANT.—delicate, frail, infirm; injurious, insalubrious, noxious.

heap, accrue, accumulate, add, aggregate, amass, augment, bank, collect, enlarge, expand, gather, hoard, increase, load, stock, store, swell; bestow, cast, give. ANT.—diminish, disperse, dissipate, minimize, scatter.

hear, attend, audit, consider, harken, heed, judge, learn, listen, monitor, note, regard.

heart, center, core, essence, focus, kernel, middle, midpoint, midst, nub, nucleus, pith. ANT.—border, exterior, outside, outskirts, periphery, rim.

heartache, affliction, anguish, distress, grief, heartbreak, lamentation, misery, misfortune, mourning, sadness, sorrow, trial, tribulation, woe. ANT.—blitheness, comfort, happiness, joy, solace.

heartbroken, abject, comfortless, desolate, disconsolate, discouraged, disheartened, distressed, forlorn, miserable, pitiable, wretched. ANT.—consoled, contented, fortunate, happy, joyful.

hearty, ardent, cheerful, cordial, enthusiastic, friendly, genial, glowing, gracious, sincere, sociable, warm; healthy, robust, sturdy, vigorous; earnest, genuine. ANT.—aloof, cool, reserved, taciturn; feeble, weak; deceptive, hypocritical, insincere.

heat, caloric, warmth, torridity; ardor, enthusiasm, excitement, fervency, fervor, fever, fire, impetuosity, intensity, passion, vehemence, zeal. ANT.—cold, frigidity, gelidity; apathy, lethargy, stoicism.

heathen, godless, heathenish, infidel, irreligious, pagan, paganic, unbelieving, unconverted. ANT.—believer, Christian, Jewish, Moslem.

heave, billow, bulge, elevate, hoist, lift, raise, rise, surge, swell, throw, toss, vomit. ANT.—ebb, lower, recede.

heavy, bulky, massive, ponderous, unwieldy, weighty; burdensome, cumbersome, grievous, onerous, oppressive, severe, troublesome, trying, vexatious; depressed, dull, gloomy, grave, sad, serious, sluggish. ANT.—inconsiderable, light; animated, brisk.

hectic, agitated, excited, feverish, flustered, nervous, restless, unsettling. ANT.—calm, cool, serene, unhurried.

heed, alertness, attachment, attention, care, caution, circumspection, consideration, devotion, mindfulness, notice, observance, vigilance, watchfulness; application, concentration, contemplation, reflection, study; attend, consider, contemplate, deliberate, examine, meditate, mind, notice, ponder, reflect, study, weigh; esteem, regard, respect. ANT.—apathy, indifference, omission; ignore, neglect, overlook.

height, acme, apex, culmination, peak, summit, zenith; altitude, loftiness; elevation; eminence, prominence, stature. ANT.—base, depth, floor, lowliness.

heighten, advance, amplify, augment, enhance, improve, increase, intensify, magnify, strengthen. ANT.—decrease, diminish, lessen, reduce, traduce.

heir, beneficiary, inheritor, legatee, scion, successor.

help, abet, aid, assist, benefit, cooperate, encourage, foster, nourish, succor, support, sustain, uphold; facilitate, further, improve, promote; alleviate, ameliorate, mitigate, relieve, remedy. ANT.—discourage, impede, thwart; arrest, counteract, hinder; afflict, injure.

herald, announce, declare, foretell, inform, introduce, precede, proclaim, publish. ANT.—silence, stifle, suppress.

herd, assemblage, drove, clock, gathering, group, horde, mob, multitude, school, throng.

hereditary, ancestral, congenital, constitutional, genetic, inherent, inherited, innate, patrimonial, transmitted. ANT.—acquired, bought, earned, won.

heretic, apostate, dissenter, nonconformist, nonjuror, renegade, schismatic, sectarian, sectary, secularist, separatist, traitor, unbeliever. ANT.—believer, loyalist.

hermetic, air-tight, sealed; cabalistic, emblematic, mysterious, occult. ANT.—clear, obvious, open, plain.

heroic, audacious, bold, brave, chivalrous, courageous, daring, dauntless, fearless, gallant, intrepid, majestic, noble, undaunted, valiant, valorous.

ANT.—cowardly, cringing, fearful, spiritless, timid.

hesitate, defer, delay, demur, doubt, falter, fear, fluctuate, pause, question, scruple, stall, stammer, stutter, vacillate, wait, waver. ANT.—continue, decide, persevere, proceed, resolve, tackle.

heterogeneous, conglomerate, contrary, contrasted, different, discordant, dissimilar, mingled, mixed, nonhomogeneous, unlike, variant. ANT.—homogeneous, identical, same, uniform, unvarying.

hidden, abstruse, concealed, covert, esoteric, latent, masked, quiescent, recondite, secret, undeveloped, unrevealed, unseen. ANT.—conspicuous, evident, explicit, exposed, manifest, visible.

hide, bury, camouflage, cloak, conceal, cover, curtain, disguise, dissemble, mask, screen, secrete, sequester, shade, shield, shroud, suppress, veil, withhold. ANT.—disclose, divulge, exhibit, expose, reveal.

hideous, abhorrent, abominable, awful, disgusting, dreadful, frightful, ghastly, grim, grisly, horrible, loathsome, monstrous, nauseating, putrid, repellent, repulsive, revolting, shocking, terrifying, ugly. ANT.—alluring, captivating, delightful, soothing, splendid.

high, elevated, lofty, raised, tall, towering; eminent, exalted, no-

ble; arrogant, boastful, bumptious, conceited, haughty, ostentatious, proud; costly, expensive; acute, intense, shrill, strident, strong; happy, intoxicated, merry. ANT.—short, stunted, tiny; base, low, mean; humble, meek; cheap, inexpensive; mild, weak; sober.

hilarious, blithe, gay, gleeful, jocund, jolly, joyful, lighthearted, merry, mirthful. ANT.—glum, morose, sad, somber.

hinder, block, check, encumber, hamper, impede, inhibit, interrupt, obstruct, postpone, prevent, resist, restrain, retard, stop, thwart. ANT.—assist, expedite, facilitate, hasten, promote.

hint, allusion, implication, intimation, inkling, innuendo, insinuation, reminder; allude (to), imply, insinuate, intimate, refer (to), suggest. ANT.—affirmation, declaration, statement; conceal, suppress, withhold.

hire, employ, engage, use; contract (for), lease, let, rent. ANT.—discard, discharge, reject; buy, purchase.

history, account, annals, archives, autobiography, biography, chronicle, description, detail, events, facts, log, lore, memoir, memorial, muniments, narration, narrative, recital, record, relation, report, saga, story; past. ANT.—fable, fiction, legend, myth, romance.

hit, batter, beat, knock, pound, pummel, punch, rap, slap, smite, strike; achieve, attain, contact, find, gain, reach, win.

hoard, accrue, accumulate, amass, collect, garner, gather, heap, increase, pile, save, stock, store, treasure. ANT.—diminish, disperse, dissipate, scatter, waste.

hoax, antic, artifice, canard, cheat, deception, delusion, device, fakery, fraud, guile, humbug, imposture, joke, ploy, ruse, spoof, stunt, subterfuge, swindle, trick, wile. ANT.—candor, honesty, openness, sincerity.

hobble, falter, limp, stagger, totter; bind, fetter, handicap, hold, impede, limit, restrain, shackle. ANT.—progress, speed, travel; aid, expedite, help, release.

hobby, amusement, avocation, diversion, enjoyment, fad, game, interest, pastime, recreation.

hold, adhere, clasp, clutch, grasp, grip; have, keep, maintain, occupy, own, possess, retain, support; check, confine, control, curb, detain, restrain; accommodate, carry, contain, receive, stow; affirm, attest, consider, judge, regard, think. ANT.—abandon, relinquish, renounce, surrender, vacate.

hole, abyss, aperture, cavity, chasm, excavation, fissure, gap, gulf, perforation, pit, rent; cave, den, holt, lair; opening, pore, void. ANT.—closure, imperforation.

hollow, empty, unfilled, vacant, void; artificial, faithless, false, hypocritical, insincere, superficial, transparent, vain; cavernous, concave, depressed, sunken. ANT.—full, solid, sound; genuine, sincere; convex, raised.

holy, angelic, blessed, consecrated, dedicated, devoted, devotional, devout, divine, godly, hallowed, immaculate, incorrupt, pious, pure, religious, reverent, righteous, sacred, saintly, spiritual, uncorrupt, virtuous. ANT.—diabolical, profane, sacrilegious, secular.

home, abode, domicile, dwelling, habitat, hearth, hearthstone, quarters, residence, seat; asylum, haven, refuge, retreat, sanctuary; birthplace, country, native land; heaven; family.

homely, common, ordinary, plain, unadorned, unattractive, uncomely; coarse, inelegant, rough, rude. ANT.—attractive, beautiful, fair, handsome, pretty; charming, dignified, polished, suave.

homogeneous, alike, consonant, harmonious, identical, same, similar, uniform. ANT.—heterogeneous, miscellaneous, mixed, unharmonious, variegated.

hone, file, grind, sharpen, strengthen, strop, whet. ANT.—make dull, roughen.

honest, candid, conscientious, fair, frank, genuine, honorable, ingenuous, just, principled, reliable, reputable, scrupulous, sincere, trustworthy, truthful, upright, unadulterated, unmixed. ANT.—deceitful, dishonest, fraudulent, lying, tricky; adulterated.

honesty, candor, fairness, faithfulness, frankness, honor, integrity, justice, openness, probity, rectitude, responsibility, self-respect, sincerity, trustworthiness, uprightness, veracity. ANT.—cheating, deceit, dishonesty, fraud, perfidy.

honor, admiration, adoration, adulation, commendation, deference, dignity, esteem, fame, glory, homage, praise, renown, respect, reverence, worship; confidence, faith, reliance, trust; admire, consider, esteem, heed, respect, revere, reverence, value, venerate; dignify, elevate, esteem. ANT.—contempt, derision, disgrace, reproach; abuse, despise, disdain, neglect, scorn.

honorary, commemorative, emeritus, gratuitous, titular. ANT.—complete, full, true.

hope, anticipation, aspiration, assurance, belief, desire, expectancy, expectation; confidence, faith, optimism, prospect, trust. ANT.—despair, despondency, fear, gloom, pessimism.

hopeless, abandoned, brokenhearted, condemned, dejected, despairing, futile, immitigable, inconsolable, incurable, irredeemable, irreparable, irretrievable, irrevocable, rash, reckless, ruined, useless. ANT.—cheering, encouraging, promising, reassuring, stimulating.

horde, army, assemblage, band, bevy, crew, crowd, crush, gang,

host, masses, mob, multitude, pack, populace, press, rabble, swarm, throng, troop.

horizontal, even, flat, level, linear, parallel, plane, straight; prone, supine. ANT.—hilly, inclined, sloping; erect, upright, vertical.

horrible, appalling, atrocious, awful, dire, dreadful, fearful, frightful, ghastly, grim, heinous, hideous, horrid, repulsive, shocking, terrible. ANT.—beautiful, enchanting, enjoyable, fascinating, lovely.

horror, alarm, antipathy, apprehension, aversion, awe, consternation, disgust, dismay, dread, fear, foreboding, loathing, terror. ANT.—assurance, comfort, confidence, consolation, delight.

hospitable, companionable, convivial, cordial, friendly, kind, neighborly, receptive, sociable. ANT.—grudging, inhospitable, reserved, solitary, unsociable.

host, entertainer; innkeeper, landlord; army, legion; horde, multitude, throng. ANT.—boarder, caller, guest, patron, visitor.

hostile, adverse, antagonistic, antipathetic, belligerent, bitter, contrary, inimical, malevolent, opposed, rancorous, repugnant, unfriendly, warlike. ANT.—amicable, cordial, favorable, neutral, uncommitted.

hot, blazing, burning, flaming, heated, scalding, scorching, searing, torrid, warm; ardent, eager, excited, fervent, fervid, fiery, hot-blooded, impetuous, intense, passionate; peppery, pungent, spicy. ANT.—cold, cool, freezing; apathetic, frigid, impassive, indifferent, passionless, phlegmatic; bland, sweet.

however, albeit, although, but, nevertheless, notwithstanding, still, though, yet; whatever, whatsoever.

hug, caress, clasp, coddle, cuddle, embrace, enfold, fondle, hold, press, squeeze. ANT.—annoy, buffet, spurn.

huge, capacious, colossal, enormous, extensive, giant, gigantic, great, immense, monstrous, tremendous, vast. ANT.—diminutive, little, miniature, small, tiny.

humane, benevolent, benign, benignant, charitable, civilized, clement, compassionate, forbearing, forgiving, gracious, human, kind, lenient, merciful, sympathetic, tender, tolerant. ANT.—brutal, cruel, merciless, pitiless, unfeeling.

humble, compliant, lowly, meek, modest, plain, poor, simple, submissive, unassuming, unobtrusive, unostentatious, unpretentious; abase, abash, break, crush, debase, degrade, humiliate, mortify, shame, subdue. ANT.—arrogant, boastful, haughty, proud, vain; dignify, elevate, exalt, honor, praise.

humbug, cheat, counterfeit, deception, dodge, fake, falseness, feint, fraud, hoax, hypocrisy, imposition, pretense, sham, trick. ANT.—honesty, reality, truth, validity.

humdrum, boring, commonplace, dull, everyday, monotonous, ordinary, prosaic, routine, tedious, tiresome, usual. ANT.—exciting, lively, stimulating.

humiliation, abashment, chagrin, mortification; abasement, disgrace, dishonor, disrepute, ignominy, odium, opprobrium, scandal, shame; humbleness, meekness. ANT.—dignity, glory, honor, praise, renown.

humor, caprice, chaff, comicality, drollery, facetiousness, fancy, jesting, jocosity, jocularity, joke, waggery, whimsicality, wit; disposition, mood, temper; favor, indulge, pamper, pet, placate, please, satisfy, spoil. ANT.—depression, gloom, gravity, melancholy, sorrow; affront, enrage, exasperate, irritate, provoke.

hunch, feeling, impression, intuition, omen, premonition, presentiment, suspicion; hump, protuberance; chunk, lump.

hunger, appetite, craving, desire, eagerness, inclination, longing, passion, relish; starvation. ANT.—disgust, distaste, renunciation, repugnance; satiety.

hungry, avid, covetous, famished, greedy, ravenous, starving, thirsting, voracious. ANT.—replete, sated, satisfied.

hunt, examination, exploration, inquiry, investigation, pursuit, quest, search; chase, ferret, investigate, probe, pursue, search,

hurl, seek, stalk. ANT.—abandonment, cession, resignation; desert, forsake, quit, relinquish, surrender.

hurl, cast, dart, expel, explode, fling, impel, pitch, project, propel, release, shoot, spring, throw, thrust, toss. ANT.—draw, haul, hold, pull, retain.

hurry, accelerate, drive, expedite, force, hasten, impel, precipitate, press, quicken, rush, scurry, speed. ANT.—delay, detain, hinder, retard, tarry. /dawdle, delay, impede, procrastinate; stall.

hurt, abuse, affront, damage, deteriorate, disfigure, harm, impair, injure, insult, maltreat, mar, outrage, pain, spoil, victimize, wound, wrong. ANT.—ameliorate, benefit, compliment, help, preserve.

hush, calm, muffle, quiet, relieve, silence, stifle, still. ANT.—amplify, encourage, excite, incite.

hustle, accelerate, bustle, dash, drive, expedite, hasten, hurry, jostle, push, run, rush, scurry, spur. ANT.—dawdle, delay, procrastinate, slow, stall.

hybrid, crossbred, half-blooded, half-bred, mixed, mongrel, mutant. ANT.—pedigreed, purebred, thoroughbred, unmixed.

hygienic, healthy, salubrious, salutary, sanitary, sterile, uncontaminated, wholesome. ANT.—contagious, contaminated, diseased, foul, infectious, noxious, unsanitary.

hypnotic, influential, impelling, irresistible, lethargic, magnetic, mesmeric, narcotic, quieting, soporific. ANT.—disturbing, exciting, reviving, stimulating.

hypocritical, canting, deceiving, deceptive, deluding, dishonest, dishonorable, dissembling, dissimulating, double-dealing, false, feigning, pharisaical, pretending, pretentious, sanctimonious, specious, unctuous, unprincipled. ANT.—candid, honest, ingenuous, principled, sincere.

hypothesis, assumption, conjecture, inference, postulate, presumption, proposal, supposition, theory, thesis. ANT.—certainty, confirmation, demonstration, fact, proof.

I

icy, chilled, chilling, cold, frigid, frosty, frozen, polar; cool, distant, forbidding, unemotional. ANT.—fiery, hot, torrid, tropical; ardent, fervent, passionate.

idea, abstraction, belief, concept, conception, fancy, image, impression, notion, opinion, principle, scheme, theory, thought. ANT.—actuality, entity, matter, reality, substance.

ideal, fancied, illusory, imaginary, impractical, intellectual, metaphysical, psychical, psychological, spiritual, unreal, utopian, visionary; complete, exemplary, faultless, perfect, supreme. ANT.—actual, material, real; faulty, imperfect.

identical, alike, coalescent, coincident, duplicate, equal, equivalent, indistinguishable, same, synonymous, uniform. ANT.—contrary, disparate, dissimilar, distinct, opposite.

identify, analyze, catalog, characterize, classify, determine, distinguish, name, note, point out, recognize; brand, label, mark, tag. ANT.—confuse, misinterpret, misname, mistake, mix up.

idiomatic, colloquial, dialectal, peculiar, regional, special, standard, stylized, vernacular. ANT.—classic, cultured, standard.

idle, aimless, barren, dormant, futile, inactive, indolent, inert, lazy, pointless, shiftless, slothful, unemployed, unimportant, unoccupied, unprofitable, unused, useless, vain. ANT.—active, employed, fruitful, industrious, occupied.

idolize, adore, deify, glorify, revere, venerate, worship. ANT.—abase, defile, desecrate, hate, profane.

ignoble, abject, base, coarse, contemptible, debased, degenerate, degraded, depraved, despicable, dishonorable, groveling, ignominious, low, lowly, mean, menial, scandalous, scurrilous, servile, shameful, sordid, vile, vulgar, worthless; humble, lowborn, plebeian, poor, untitled. ANT.—esteemed, exalted, honored, lofty, noble, righteous.

ignorant, dense, illiterate, obtuse shallow, superficial, unacquainted, uncultivated, uneducated, uninformed, uninstructed, unknowing, unlearned, unlettered, untaught. ANT.—cultured, educated, erudite, literate, wise.

ignore, disregard, forget, neglect, omit, overlook, reject, shun, skip, slight, snub. ANT.—acknowledge, heed, notice, recognize, regard.

ill, afflicted, ailing, diseased, distempered, feeble, impaired, indisposed, infirm, morbid, sick, sickly, unhealthy, unwell; calamity, danger, distress, evil, hardship, misery, pain, sorrow, trouble, vexation. ANT.—healthy, robust, vigorous, well; favor, fortune, prosperity, welfare.

illegal, banned, contraband, criminal, dishonest, illegitimate, illicit, interdicted, outlawed, prohibited, proscribed, unauthorized, unlawful, unlicensed. ANT.—authorized, honest, judicial, lawful, legal, permissible.

illogical, fallacious, incoherent, inconsistent, specious, spurious, unreasoned, unsound, untenable. ANT.—logical, reasoned, sensible, sound.

illuminate, brighten, clarify, demonstrate, elucidate, enlighten, explain, illumine, illustrate, irradiate, lighten, reveal. ANT.—complicate, confuse, darken, obfuscate, obscure, puzzle.

illusion, apparition, chimera, deception, delusion, dream, fallacy, fancy, fantasy, hallucination, mirage, phantom, vision; fairy, ghost, ghoul, poltergeist, specter, spirit, sprite. ANT.—actuality, certainty, happening, reality, substance.

illustration, drawing, engraving, etching, image, likeness, painting, panorama, photograph, picture, portrait, portrayal, print, representation, scene, sketch, view; case, comparison, example, instance, specimen.

illustrious, acclaimed, celebrated, distinguished, eminent, famed, famous, great, prominent, renowned; critical, important, momentous, serious, vital, weighty; august, dignified, elevated, grand, majestic, noble; brilliant, excellent, fine, magnificent, superior, superlative. ANT.—diminutive, little, minute, small; common, humble, obscure, ordinary, unknown; menial, paltry.

imagination, conceit, concept, conception, creation, fancy, fantasy, idea, impression, mental image, notion. ANT.—actuality, existence, materiality, realism, substance.

imaginative, artistic, clever, creative, fanciful, inventive, mystical, original, poetical, talented, visionary. ANT.—dull, factual, literal, methodical, prosaic.

imagine, conceive, dream, envision, fancy, picture, pretend, visualize; apprehend, assume, believe, conjecture, guess, opine, presume, suppose, surmise, think.

imbecile, blockhead, buffoon, cretin, dolt, dunce, fool, halfwit, idiot, ignoramus, moron, nincompoop, numbskull, oaf, simpleton, witling. ANT.—genius, intellectual, philosopher, sage, scholar.

imbue, animate, color, impregnate, infuse, inspire, instill, penetrate, permeate, pervade, saturate, suffuse.

imitate, ape, caricature, copy, counterfeit, duplicate, falsify, follow, impersonate, mimic, mirror, mock, personate, parody, represent, reproduce, simulate, transcribe. ANT.—alter, distort, diverge, oppose, vary.

immanent, inborn, inherent, innate, internal, intrinsic, natural, subjective; universal (as God). ANT.—acquired, external, extrinsic, objective.

immaterial, inessential, insignificant, irrelevant, trifling, trivial, unimportant; disembodied, impalpable, impertinent, incorporeal, spiritual, unsubstantial. ANT.—essential, important, relevant; corporeal, material, substantial.

immature, callow, childish, crude, embryonic, green, juvenile, premature, raw, undeveloped, unready, unripe, untimely. ANT.—adult, aged, grown, mature, ripe.

immeasurable, abysmal, boundless, endless, eternal, illimitable, immense, infinite, interminable, measureless, unbounded, unfathomable, unlimited, vast. ANT.—bounded, circumscribed, finite, limited, measurable.

immediately, abruptly, at once, directly, forthwith, instantaneously, instantly, now, presently, promptly, right away, speedily, straightaway. ANT.—after a while, by and by, distantly, hereafter, later.

immemorial, ancient, dateless, early, immemorable, old, prehistoric, timeless. ANT.—memorable, new, recent, young.

immense, colossal, elephantine, enormous, gargantuan, gigantic, great, huge, large, mighty, monstrous, prodigious, stupendous, titanic, tremendous, vast. ANT.—diminutive, dwarfish, microscopic, minute, tiny.

immerse, bathe, dip, douse, dunk, engulf, flood, inundate, plunge, sink, submerge; absorb, engage, engross, involve, overwhelm. ANT.—elevate, recover, retrieve, uncover, uplift.

imminent, abeyant, approaching, brewing, coming, destined, impending, inevitable, menacing, near, nigh, ominous, overhanging, pressing, threatening. ANT.—afar, distant, improbable, remote, retreating.

immoderation, excess, exorbitance, extravagance, extremism, inordinateness, intemperance, profusion, superabundance, superfluity, surplus. ANT.—dearth, deficiency, moderation, paucity, restraint.

immoral, bad, corrupt, depraved, dissolute, evil, indecent, lecherous, licentious, loose, profligate, unprincipled, vicious, wicked. ANT.—chaste, high-minded, noble, pure, virtuous.

immortal, abiding, ceaseless, deathless, endless, eternal, everlasting, imperishable, infinite, permanent, perpetual, timeless, undying. ANT.—ephemeral, finite, mortal, temporal, transitory.

immovable, anchored, cemented, constant, firm, fixed, fused, immobile, obdurate, rooted, stable, steadfast. ANT.—mobile, movable, plastic, wavering, yielding.

immune, excused, exempt, free, freed, hardened to, not liable, resistant, unaffected by, unsusceptible; clear, loose, open, unfastened, unobstructed. ANT.—subject.

immunity, acquittal, clearance, discharge, dispensation, exculpation, exemption, exoneration, freedom, license, privilege, protection, release, respite. ANT.—condemnation, conviction, indictment, interdiction, sequestration.

immutable, abiding, ceaseless, constant, continual, enduring, faithful, fixed, invariant, permanent, perpetual, persistent, stable, unalterable, unchanging, unwavering. ANT.—fluctuating, mutable, vacillating, variable, wavering.

impair, adulterate, blemish, blight, corrode, corrupt, cripple, damage, deface, degrade, deteriorate, harm, hurt, injure, mar, spoil, taint, weaken. ANT.— ameliorate, benefit, enhance, mend, repair.

impart, bestow, communicate, confer, convey, disclose, divulge, enlighten, give, grant, inform, instruct, notify, relate, reveal, tell, transmit. ANT.— conceal, hide, puzzle, suppress, withhold.

impartial, disinterested, equitable, fair, honest, indifferent, just, neutral, nonpartisan, nonsectarian, reasonable, unbiased, unconcerned, unprejudiced. ANT.—biased, dishonorable, fraudulent, involved, partial.

impasse, bar, deadlock, end, limit, obstacle. ANT.—clearance, gain, opening, solution.

impatient, abrupt, brusque, eager, fidgety, fretful, fussy, impetuous, nervous, restless. ANT.— calm, controlled, forbearing, patient, tolerant.

impeccable, faultless, immaculate, incorrupt, innocent, perfect, spotless. ANT.—defective, imperfect, messy, stained, sullied.

impede, arrest, bar, block, check, clog, counteract, delay, encumber, frustrate, hamper, hinder, interrupt, obstruct, offset, oppose, prevent, repress, restrain, retard, stop, thwart. ANT.—advance, assist, further, help, promote.

impediment, barrier, block, difficulty, disability, encumbrance, hindrance, inhibition, obstacle, obstruction, restriction, wall, weakness. ANT.—aid, assistance, collaboration, help, support.

impel, actuate, coerce, compel, constrain, drive, force, goad, induce, influence, instigate, move, oblige, prod, push, stimulate, urge. ANT.—delay, prevent, repress, repulse, suppress.

impenetrable, compact, dense, firm, hard, impervious, rigid, solid; arduous, burdensome, difficult, onerous, tough; abstruse, esoteric, intricate, perplexing, puzzling; adamant, cruel, harsh, obtuse, rigorous, severe, stern, stolid, strict, unfeeling. ANT.— brittle, elastic, flabby, fluid, penetrable, plastic, soft; easy, effortless, facile, simple; clear, comprehensible, intelligible; gentle, lenient, tender.

imperative, absolute, commanding, compelling, compulsory, critical, essential, exigent, impelling, important, importunate, inescapable, inexorable, insistent, mandatory, necessary, obligatory, peremptory, pressing, required, requisite, unavoidable, urgent, vital. ANT.— insignificant, optional, petty, trivial, unimportant.

imperceptible, inappreciable, inconspicuous, indistinct, indistinguishable, insignificant, invisible, negligible, undiscernible, unseen. ANT.—apparent, evident, perceptible, striking, visible.

imperfection, blemish, defect, deficiency, drawback, error, failure, fault, flaw, frailty, inadequacy, infirmity, mistake, shortcoming, stain, transgression, wrong. ANT.—completeness, correctness, faultlessness, perfection, purity.

imperil, endanger, expose, hazard, jeopardize, risk, threaten, uncover. ANT.—defend, guard, safeguard, secure, shield.

impersonate, ape, copy, duplicate, feign, imitate, mimic, mock, personify, portray, represent, simulate. ANT.—alter, distort, diverge, invent.

impertinent, abusive, arrogant, audacious, bold, brazen, contemptuous, impudent, insolent, insulting, intrusive, meddling, offensive, officious, rude; absurd, inane, inapplicable, irrelevant, trivial. ANT.—considerate, courteous, polite, respectful; important, momentous, pertinent, serious, significant.

impetuous, careless, fiery, hasty, heedless, impulsive, incautious, intractable, passionate, quick, rash, reckless, ungovernable, unruly. ANT.—cautious, composed, reasoning, retiring, tranquil.

impetus, force, impulse, incentive, momentum, motive, pressure, stimulus.

impinge, clash, collide, encroach, infringe, hit, strike, trespass,

touch, violate. ANT.—avoid, defer, miss, pass, respect.

implant, embed, engraft, fix, graft, inculcate, infuse, insert, instill, plant, set in, sow. ANT.—eliminate, excise, remove, uproot.

implement, accomplish, achieve, do, effect, effectuate, execute, expedite, fulfill, perform, realize. ANT.—cancel, defer, hinder, restrict.

implicate, accuse, blame, censure, challenge, charge, cite, embroil, enfold, entangle, imply, impute, incriminate, inculpate, involve, link, rebuke, reproach, trap, upbraid. ANT.—absolve, acquit, defend, exonerate, support.

implicit, accepted, implied, inferred, known, presupposed, recognized, tacit, understood, unspoken. ANT.—declared, explicit, expressed, specific.

imply, connote, hint, infer, insinuate, involve, mean, signify, suggest. ANT.—assert, define, describe, express, state.

import, emphasis, importance, influence, significance, stress, value, weight; bring in, convey, imply, introduce, purport, signify, transport. ANT.—insignificance, triviality; export, send out, ship out.

important, appreciable, authoritative, consequential, critical, decisive, essential, grave, great, imposing, influential, leading, material, momentous, paramount, powerful, pressing, principal, prominent, relevant, serious, significant, substantial, urgent, weighty. /insignificant, irrelevant, petty, picayune, trivial.

imposing, arresting, august, commanding, eminent, grand, grandiose, high, illustrious, imperial, impressive, lofty, magnificent, majestic, noble, stately, striking, sublime, towering. ANT.—common, humble, insignificant, ordinary, undignified.

impractical, impracticable, inexpedient, unachievable, unattainable, unfeasible, unrealistic, unworkable, visionary. ANT.—feasible, possible, practical, reasonable, workable.

impressive, absorbing, affecting, arresting, awesome, commanding, considerable, deep, exciting, forcible, imposing, majestic, momentous, moving, notable, penetrating, profound, prominent, remarkable, stirring, striking, thrilling, touching, vital. ANT.—commonplace, ordinary, shallow, trivial, unimpressive.

imprison, cage, confine, constrain, detain, enclose, hold, impound, incarcerate, limit, lock up, restrain. ANT.—acquit, discharge, extricate, free, release.

impromptu, ad lib, extemporaneous, improvised, impulsive, offhand, spontaneous, unplanned, unrehearsed. ANT.—deliberate, planned, premeditated, prepared, rehearsed.

improper, discourteous, immodest, incorrect, indecent, indelicate, lewd, offensive, unbecoming, unsuitable, wrong. ANT.—considerate, correct, fitting, proper, seemly.

improve, advance, ameliorate, amend, better, correct, help, mend, purify, rectify, refine, reform, revise; gain, get better, progress. ANT.—corrupt, damage, debase, impair, vitiate; decline, worsen.

imprudent, careless, heedless, incautious, indiscreet, reckless, thoughtless, unforeseeing, unwise. ANT.—careful, cautious, circumspect, meticulous, prudent.

impudence, arrogance, audacity, boldness, crudity, discourtesy, disrespect, effrontery, impertinence, incivility, insolence, presumption, rudeness, sauciness. ANT.—courtesy, diffidence, gentility, politeness, respect.

impulsive, careless, excitable, fiery, foolhardy, forcible, hasty, headstrong, heedless, impatient, impetuous, imprudent, incautious, indiscreet, quick, rash, reckless, uninhibited. ANT.—cautious, heedful, prudent, reasoning, restrained.

impure, adulterated, contaminated, corrupt, corrupted, debased, defiled, depraved, foul, indecent, mingled, mixed, obscene, polluted, profligate, putrid, spoiled, smutty, tainted, unsound, venal, vitiated. ANT.—clean, immaculate, impeccable, pure, spotless.

impute, allege, ascribe, assign, attribute, blame, brand, charge, implicate, inculpate, indict, trace (to). ANT.—defend, endorse, exculpate, exonerate, vindicate.

inactive, dormant, idle, inanimate, indolent, inert, latent, lazy, motionless, passive, quiescent, resting, sedentary, torpid, unemployed, unoccupied. ANT.—active, dynamic, industrious, occupied, working.

inadequate, defective, deficient, incompetent, incomplete, insufficient, lacking, partial, scanty, short, unfit, wanting. ANT.—adequate, ample, enough, satisfactory, sufficient.

inadvertent, accidental, careless, chance, heedless, negligent, thoughtless, unconscious, unintentional, unobservant. ANT.—attentive, careful, intentional, planned.

inane, absurd, banal, foolish, frivolous, insipid, pointless, silly, trite, vapid. ANT.—expressive, important, meaningful, salient, significant.

inappropriate, discordant, improper, inapt, incongruous, infelicitous, tasteless, unfitted, unsuitable. ANT.—appropriate, apt, becoming, fitting, proper.

inaugurate, arise, begin, commence, found, initiate, install, institute, introduce, open, originate, start. ANT.—adjourn, close, complete, finish, terminate.

incentive, enticement, incitement, inducement, lure, motive, provocation, spur, stimulus.

inception, beginning, birth, commencement, founding, inauguration, initiation, opening, origin, onset, source, start. ANT.—close, completion, consummation, end, termination.

incessant, ceaseless, constant, continual, continuous, endless, everlasting, interminable, perennial, perpetual, persistent, unceasing, uninterrupted, unremitting. ANT.—interrupted, occasional, periodic, rare, sporadic.

incident, chance, episode, event, happening, occasion, occurrence, situation.

incidental, accidental, accessory, associated, casual, collateral, concomitant, contingent, fortuitous, minor, nonessential, occasional, secondary, subordinate, undesigned, unintended. ANT.—cardinal, elementary, essential, fundamental, vital.

incisive, brief, compact, concise, condensed, crisp, decisive, direct, pithy, succinct, summary, terse. ANT.—lengthy, prolix, verbose, wordy.

incite, actuate, animate, arouse, cause, encourage, enrage, excite, fire, foment, goad, impel, induce, inflame, instigate, prompt, provoke, rouse, stimulate, stir up, urge. ANT.—deter, pacify, quiet, restrain, soothe.

inclination, bending, gradient, incline, leaning, slope; affection, allurement, attachment, attraction, bent, bias, desire, disposition, fancy, liking, partiality, penchant, predilection, preference, prejudice, proneness, propensity, tendency. ANT.— apathy, aversion, distaste, nonchalance, repugnance.

include, accommodate, comprise, consist of, contain, embody, embrace, encompass, hold, incorporate, involve, surround, take in. ANT.—eliminate, exclude, omit, preclude, reject.

income, annuity, dividends, earnings, emolument, gain, interest, proceeds, profits, receipts, rents, revenue, salary, stipend, wages, winnings. ANT.—charge, cost, expense, loss, outgo.

incompetent, bungling, clumsy, floundering, heavy-handed, inadequate, incapable, ineffectual, inefficient, inept, inexpert, maladroit, stumbling, unable, unfit, unqualified, unskilled, unsuitable, untalented. ANT.—competent, deft, expert, proficient, skillful.

incongruous, conflicting, contradictory, contrary, disagreeing, discordant, discrepant, disparate, divergent, illogical, incompatible, inconsistent, inharmonious, irreconcilable, mismatched, paradoxical. ANT.—compatible, congruous, consistent, correspondent, harmonious, homologous.

inconsiderate, careless, selfish, tasteless, thoughtless, undiscerning, unfeeling, unsympathetic. ANT.—considerate, helpful, sensitive, sympathetic, thoughtful.

inconsistent, changeable, contrary, fluctuating, incompatible, inconsonant, inconstant, shifting, unstable, unsteady, unsuitable, vacillating, variable, varying, wavering. ANT.—constant, stable, steady, unchanging, uniform.

incorporate, amalgamate, blend, consolidate, embody, establish, form, merge, mix, unite. ANT.— disperse, dissolve, divide, remove, separate.

increase, accelerate, accrue, advance, amplify, augment, develop, dilate, distend, enhance, enlarge, expand, extend, grow, heighten, inflate, intensify, magnify, multiply, raise, spread, swell, wax. ANT.—atrophy, contract, decrease, diminish, reduce.

incredible, astonishing, fantastic, far-fetched, implausible, suspicious, unbelievable. ANT.—believable, credible, creditable, plausible, realistic.

increment, addition, enlargement, increase, raise. ANT.—decline, decrease, diminution, loss.

incriminate, accuse, arraign, blame, censure, charge, implicate, impute, indict, involve, link. ANT.—absolve, acquit, exonerate, release, vindicate.

inculcate, discipline, drill (into), imbue, impart, implant, impress, indoctrinate, instill, instruct, teach.

incumbent, binding, coercive, imperative, inescapable, necessary, peremptory, pressing, stringent, urgent; occupant, officeholder. ANT.—absolved, exempt, free, liberated, released.

indebted, appreciative, beholden, grateful, thankful; bound, liable, obligated, owing, unpaid. ANT.—thankless, unappreciative; cleared (up), settled (accounts), squared (with) paid.

indecent, coarse, dirty, disgusting, filthy, gross, immodest, immoral, improper, impure, indelicate, lewd, obscene, offensive, pornographic, shameless, smutty, unbecoming. ANT.—decent, modest, pure, refined, virtuous.

indefinite, ambiguous, confused, dim, equivocal, hazy, inconclusive, indeterminate, inexact, lax, loose, obscure, uncertain, unclear, undefined, unfixed, unlimited, unsettled. ANT.—absolute, certain, evident, positive, unquestionable.

independent, alone, autonomous, exempt, free, liberated, self-governing, self-reliant, self-sufficient, separate, single, sovereign, unallied, unconfined, uncontrolled, unrestrained, unrestricted; affluent, rich, wealthy; exclusive, irrespective. ANT.—contingent, dependent, enslaved, restricted, subordinate; poor; inclusive.

indicate, connote, denote, designate, differentiate, disclose, evidence, hint, imply, intimate, manifest, mark, point out, register, reveal, show, signal, signify, specify, testify. ANT.—conceal, distract, divert, falsify, mislead.

indication, designation, emblem, evidence, gesture, hint, implication, manifestation, mark, note, omen, portent, proof, sign, signal, suggestion, symbol, symptom, token.

indict, accuse, arraign, blame, censure, charge, impeach, incriminate. ANT.—absolve, acquit, exonerate, release, vindicate.

indifference, apathy, callousness, carelessness, coldness, detachment, disinterest, disinterestedness, impartiality, impassivity, inattention, insensibility, insouciance, insusceptibility, neutrality, nonchalance, supineness, unconcern. ANT.—affection, ardor, fervor, passion, vivacity.

indigence, dearth, destitution, distress, famine, hunger, insufficiency, misery, necessity, need, pauperism, penury, poverty, privation, starvation, tenuity, want. ANT.—abundance, affluence, plenty, riches, wealth.

indigenous, aboriginal, domestic, endemic, inborn, inherent, innate, native, natural. ANT.—alien, foreign, imported, introduced, naturalized.

indignation, acrimony, agitation, anger, animosity, annoyance, exasperation, fury, huff, irascibility, ire, passion, petulance, pique, rage, resentment, scorn, temper, virulence, wrath. ANT.—forbearance, equanimity, patience, self-control, tranquility.

indignity, abuse, affront, discourtesy, dishonor, disparagement, disrespect, embarrassment, humiliation, ignominy, insult, irreverence, mockery, offense, opprobrium, outrage, scurrility, slight, taunt, vituperation. ANT.—courtesy, dignity, homage, praise, reverence.

indirect, circuitous, crooked, distorted, erratic, implied, inferred, oblique, roundabout, swerving, tortuous, wandering, winding; crooked, cunning, devious, tricky. ANT.—direct, straight, unswerving; blunt, candid, explicit, straightforward.

indiscreet, foolhardy, foolish, heedless, imprudent, rash, reckless, thoughtless, unwise. ANT.—careful, discreet, prudent, sensible, wise.

indiscriminate, heterogeneous, mixed, promiscuous, uncritical, unwise. ANT.—chosen, critical, homogeneous, selective.

indispensable, basic, essential, expedient, fundamental, imperative, intrinsic, necessary, needed, prerequisite, required, requisite, vital. ANT.—dispensable, extrinsic, optional, peripheral, superfluous.

indistinct, abstruse, ambiguous, blurred, cloudy, confused, cryptic, darkened, dim, dusky, faint, hazy, indefinite, imperceptible, inaudible, indistinguishable, misty, mysterious, nebulous, obscure, shadowy, uncertain, unintelligible, vague. ANT.—clear, distinct, lucid, obvious, perceptible.

individual, characteristic, different, distinct, distinctive, idiosyncratic, marked, original, particular, peculiar, personal, separate, singular, special, specific, unique. ANT.—common, conventional, general, ordinary, universal.

indoctrinate, discipline, drill, imbue, initiate, instruct, teach, train. ANT.—confuse, misguide, mislead, neglect.

indolent, drowsy, dull, idle, inactive, ineffectual, inert, lackadaisical, languid, lazy, lethargic, listless, remiss, slack, slothful, sluggish, somnolent, soporific, supine, torpid. ANT.—active, alert, assiduous, diligent, industrious.

indomitable, firm, impregnable, insurmountable, invincible, invulnerable, unassailable, unconquerable, untameable, unyielding. ANT.—feeble, powerless, vulnerable, weak, yielding.

induce, actuate, bring about, cause, create, effect, encourage, evoke, impel, incite, influence, instigate, motivate, move, originate, persuade, prompt, spur, stimulate, urge. ANT.—discourage, dissuade, hamper, repel, repress.

induct, initiate, install, introduce, invest, lead into; conclude, generalized, infer. ANT.—expel, lead away, reject; end, withdraw.

industrious, active, assiduous, busy, diligent, hard-working, indefatigable, perseverant, persistent, sedulous, zealous. ANT.—inactive, indolent, lackadaisical, laggard, lethargic.

inebriated, drunk, drunken, high, intoxicated, tight, tipsy; exhilarated, heartened, refreshed, stimulated. ANT.—abstinent, sober, temperate; calm, unmoved.

ineffective, assailable, feeble, frail, futile, idle, impotent, inadequate, ineffectual, inefficacious, unavailing, unfruitful, unproductive, useless, vain, vulnerable, weak. ANT.—effective, efficacious, potent, powerful, successful.

inept, awkward, clumsy, foolish, fumbling, inappropriate, incapable, maladroit, unfit, unhandy, unproductive, unskillful. ANT.—able, adroit, apt, competent, skillful.

inert, dead, dilatory, dormant, idle, impassive, impotent, inactive, indolent, lazy, lifeless, phlegmatic, powerless, quiescent, slothful, sluggish, stolid, supine, torpid. ANT.—active, industrious, moving, operational, working.

inevitable, assured, avoidless, certain, definite, fated, imminent, indefeasible, indubitable, ineluctable, inescapable, necessary, positive, predestined, sure, unavoidable, undeniable, unquestionable. ANT.—avoidable, doubtful, indeterminate, questionable, uncertain.

inexhaustible, illimitable, indefatigable, infinite, limitless, never-ending, untiring, unwearied. ANT.—ending, finite, limited, short-lived, wearying.

inexpensive, cheap, low-priced, reasonable (in price); beggarly, common, inferior, mean, shabby. ANT.—costly, dear, expensive, high-priced; valuable.

infantile, babyish, childish, immature, juvenile, naïve, puerile, young. ANT.—adult, grown up, mature, of age.

infatuated, beguiled, captivated, charmed, deluded, enamored, enthralled, fascinated, foolish. ANT.—disgusted, disillusioned, fancy-free, prudent, sensible.

infection, communicability, contagion, contamination, disease, epidemic, germs, impurity, poison, pollution, vitiation.

infectious, catching, communicable, contagious, contaminating, defiling, epidemic, noxious, pestiferous, pestilential, polluting, sickening, virulent, vitiating. ANT.—antiseptic, harmless, healthful, hygienic, sanitary.

inference, answer, conclusion, consequence, corollary, deduction, derivation, illation, judgment, result, solution. ANT.—

assumption, foreboding, foresight, preconception, presupposition.

inferior, deficient, inadequate, lesser, lower, minor, poorer, secondary, shoddy, subordinate, substandard. ANT.—better, first-class, foremost, prime, superior.

infinte, boundless, continual, continuing, countless, endless, eternal, everlasting, illimitable, immeasurable, incalculable, incomprehensible, inexhaustible, innumerable, interminable, perpetual, termless, timeless, unbounded, unlimited. ANT.—bounded, circumscribed, finite, limited, restricted.

infirm, ailing, debilitated, decrepit, doddering, drooping, enervated, enfeebled, exhausted, faint, feeble, forceless, frail, impaired, invalid, languid, powerless, sickly, spent, unhealthy, weak, worn. ANT.—forceful, hale, robust, sturdy, vigorous.

inflate, bloat, blow up, dilate, distend, elate, enlarge, exaggerate, expand, fill, pad, stuff. ANT.—compress, condense, deflate, shrink, trim.

inflexible, determined, dogged, firm, headstrong, immovable, inexorable, intractable, obdurate, obstinate, rigid, stiff, strict, stubborn, tenacious, uncompromising, unyielding. ANT.—compliant, elastic, flexible, pliable, yielding.

influence, absolutism, ascendancy, attraction, authority, character, command, control, credit, despotism, domination, effect, importance, leadership, magnetism, mastery, patronage, power, predominance, prerogative, pressure, prominence, reputation, rule, superiority, supremacy, sway, weight; actuate, act upon, affect, bias, carry weight, compel, control, counteract, direct, dominate, draw, drive, modify, move, outweigh, predominate, prejudice, pull, regulate, restrain, rouse, rule, spur. ANT.—impotence, inferiority, subjection, subserviency, weakness.

inform, acquaint, advise, apprise, edify, educate, enlighten, explain, impart, instruct, notify, relate, teach, tell, warn. ANT.—conceal, delude, distract, mislead.

informal, conventional, customary, easy, familiar, natural, offhand, regular, simple, unceremonious, unconstrained, unconventional, unofficial. ANT.—ceremonious, formal, official, perfunctory, rigid.

information, data, fact, instruction, intelligence, knowledge, learning, lore, news. ANT.—conjecture, guesswork, ignorance, rumor.

infrequent, irregular, isolated, occasional, odd, rare, scarce, sporadic, strange, unusual. ANT.—customary, frequent, ordinary, scheduled, usual.

infuse, animate, imbue, implant, inoculate, inspire, instill, permeate, steep.

ingenious, able, adroit, apt, bright, brilliant, capable, clever, competent, creative, deft, dexterous, endowed, expert, fertile, fresh, gifted, handy, imaginative, inventive, novel, original, productive, proficient, qualified, quick-witted, ready, resourceful, sagacious, sharp, skillful, talented. ANT.—bungling, clumsiness, fumbling, ineptitude, unqualified.

ingenuous, aboveboard, artless, candid, direct, fair, frank, free, guileless, honest, literal, natural, open, outspoken, plain, simple, sincere, straightforward, truthful, unaffected, undisguised, unsophisticated, unworldly. ANT.—artificial, cunning, deceptive, designing, scheming.

ingratitude, lack of response, thanklessness, unappreciation, unconcern, ungratefulness. ANT.—appreciation, gratefulness, gratitude, responsiveness, thankfulness.

ingredient, component, constituent, element, factor, material, part, substance.

inhabit, abide, dwell, establish residence, fill, live in, lodge, make home at, nestle, occupy, remain, rent, reside, room, settle, sojourn, stay, tenant. ANT.—abandon, exit, retreat, vacate, withdraw.

inherent, congenital, connatal, genetic, inborn, inbred, ingrained, inherent, inherited, innate, intrinsic, native, natural, real. ANT.—acquired, external, extraneous, extrinsic, supplemental.

inheritance, bequest, birthright, heritage, legacy, patrimony.

inhibit, arrest, bar, block, bridle, check, constrain, cramp, curb, disallow, discourage, hinder, hold back, impede, interdict, limit, obstruct, obtrude, oppose, prevent, prohibit, proscribe, repress, restrain, restrict, stop, sublimate, suppress, suspend, thwart. ANT.—aid, encourage, free, incite, liberate.

inhuman, barbarous, bestial, bloodthirsty, brutal, cold-blooded, cruel, diabolical, ferocious, fiendish, harsh, hateful, hellish, infernal, malevolent, malignant, pitiless, rancorous, remorseless, ruthless, savage, truculent, unfeeling, venomous. ANT.—benevolent, charitable, compassionate, humane, merciful.

iniquitous, baleful, base, criminal, degrading, deleterious, diabolical, dissolute, evil, fiendish, foul, immoral, infamous, infernal, lawless, nefarious, noxious, profligate, reprobate, shameful, sinful, transgressing, unjust, unprincipled, unrighteous, unsound, villainous, wicked. ANT.—exemplary, good, honorable, moral, reputable.

initial, antecedent, basic, beginning, earliest, elementary, first, fundamental, original, primary, prime, primeval, primitive, pristine, rudimentary; chief, foremost. ANT.—hindmost, last, latest; least, subordinate.

initiate, arise, begin, commence, enter, establish, inaugurate, indoctrinate, institute, introduce, invest, open, originate, start. ANT.—close, complete, finish, raze, terminate.

initiative, acceleration, action, drive, energy, enterprise, leadership, responsibility. ANT.—cowardice, lethargy, shyness, timidity.

injunction, bidding, canon, command, directive, law, mandate, order (of a judge), ordinance, regulation, rule.

injurious, damaging, defamatory, deleterious, destructive, detrimental, disadvantageous, harmful, hurtful, libelous, mischievous, pernicious, prejudicial, wrongful. ANT.—advantageous, beneficial, helpful, profitable, salutory.

injury, blemish, damage, detriment, disadvantage, grievance, harm, hurt, impairment, injustice, loss, mischief, prejudice, wound, wrong. ANT.—benefit, blessing, emolument, relief, remedy.

injustice, bias, encroachment, favoritism, grievance, illegality, inequality, inequity, infringement, injury, unfairness, violation, wrong. ANT.—equity, fairness, justice, lawfulness, righteousness.

inkling, clue, hint, idea, impression, indication, inference, in-nuendo, notice, suggestion, suspicion, tip.

innocent, artless, blameless, clean, exemplary, faultless, harmless, guiltless, impeccable, innocuous, irreproachable, lawful, pure, righteous, sinless, spotless, stainless, uninvolved, upright, virginal, virtuous. ANT.—corrupt, culpable, guilty, lascivious, sinful.

innocuous, gentle, harmless, inoffensive, insipid, mild, pallid, safe, undetrimental, uninjurious. ANT.—blighting, destructive, detrimental, injurious, pestiential.

innovation, addition, alteration, change, introduction, invention, modification, newness, novelty, remodeling, variation. ANT.—custom, habit, old (way), rut, tradition.

inquest, audit, examination, inquiry, inquisition, inspection, interrogation, investigation, probe, research, scrutiny.

inquire, examine, explore, hunt, interrogate, meddle, probe, pry, pursue, query, question, reconnoiter, research, scan, scout, scrutinize, search, seek, sift; ask, beg, claim, demand, entreat, invite, request, solicit. ANT.—abandon, neglect, shelve; answer, contradict, reply.

inquisitive, curious, inquiring, interrogative, intruding, intrusive, meddlesome, meddling, nosy, peeping, peering, prying, scrutinizing, searching, sniffing, snoopy. ANT.—apathetic, indifferent, lackadaisical, negligent, unconcerned.

insane, aberrant, crazy, daft, delirious, demented, deranged, fanatical, foolish, frenetic, frenzied, idiotic, imbecilic, incoherent, irrational, lunatic, mad, maniacal, manic, mentally ill, paranoiac, psychopathic, psychotic, rabid, raging, unbalanced, unsound. ANT.—lucid, rational, reasonable, sane, stable.

insecure, dangerous, endangered, exposed, hazardous, ill-protected, imperiled, precarious, rickety, risky, shaky, unguarded, unsafe, unstable; anxious, apprehensive, concerned, fearful, troubled, uncertain, worried. ANT.—safe, secure, fortified, strong; assured, certain, confident, serene.

insensitive, callous, cold, dull, hard, impenitent, indurate, insensible, obdurate, obtuse, phlegmatic, remote, thick-skinned, tough, unaffected, unemotional, unfeeling, unimpressionable, unresponsive. ANT.—compassionate, empathetic, responsive, sensitive, tender.

insertion, implantation, infusion, injection, inlay, inoculation, installation, interpolation, introduction. ANT.—extraction, removal, transfer, withdrawal.

insolent, abusive, arrogant, blustering, brazen, bumptious, contemptuous, contumelious, defiant, disdainful, disrespect-ful, domineering, haughty, imperious, impertinent, impudent, insulting, offensive, overbearing, presumptuous, rude, supercilious, swaggering, threatening, unmannerly. ANT.—considerate, courteous, humble, polite, respectful; abased, cowardly, groveling, parasitic, sniveling.

inspection, audit, checking, comparison, critique, examination, inquest, inquiry, inquisition, investigation, measuring, observation, overseeing, probing, review, scanning, scrutiny, study, supervision, survey.

inspiration, animation, arousal, enthusiasm, exaltation, fire, incitement, predilection, revelation, stimulation; fancy, hunch, impulse, notion, whim; incentive, influence, spur, stimulus; inhalation. ANT.—apathy, habitude, lethargy; aversion; exhalation.

insight, acumen, comprehension, discernment, intuition, introspection, judgment, keenness, penetration, perception, perspicacity, perspicuity, shrewdness, understanding. ANT.—confusion, ignorance, obtuseness, perplexity, shallowness.

insignificant, cheap, frivolous, inconsequential, meaningless, minute, paltry, petty, small, trifling, trivial, unimportant, valueless, worthless. ANT.—important, momentous, significant, valuable, weighty.

insinuate, connote, hint, imply, indicate, infer, ingratiate, intimate, involve, mean, purport, signify, suggest. ANT.—assert, express, state; conceal, disguise, suppress, veil.

insipid, bland, characterless, dull, flat, flavorless, inanimate, lifeless, mawkish, stale, tasteless, unimaginative, uninteresting, unsavory, vapid. ANT.—appetizing, exhilarating, racy, savory, tasty.

insistent, aggressive, clamorous, demanding, exigent, imperative, importunate, pressing, urgent. ANT.—acquiescent, agreeable, indifferent, lenient, tolerant.

instance, application, case, elucidation, example, exemplification, illustration, lesson, object, occurrence, point, sample, specimen, type.

instantaneous, abrupt, at once, direct, hasty, immediate, prompt, rapid, sudden, unexpected. ANT.—anticipated, delayed, gradual, late, slow.

instantly, abruptly, directly, forthwith, immediately, instantaneously, now, presently, promptly, straightaway, suddenly, urgently, without delay. ANT.—distantly, hereafter, in a while, later, sometime.

instinctive, accustomed, automatic, congenital, constitutional, fundamental, habitual, impulsive, inborn, ingrained, inherent, innate, intrinsic, involuntary, mechanical, natural, offhand, reflexive, regular, spontaneous, typical, usual. ANT.—acquired, deliberate, learned, meditated, voluntary, willed.

institute, begin, build, enact, erect, establish, fix, form, found, initiate, introduce, invent, invest, ordain, order, organize, originate, plan, raise, sanction, settle, start. ANT.—abolish, demolish, raze, terminate, unsettle.

instruct, admonish, advise, coach, command, convey, counsel, direct, discipline, drill, edify, educate, enlighten, exhort, expound, guide, impart, inculcate, indoctrinate, inform, instill, prime, promulgate, school, teach, train, tutor. ANT.—delude, falsify, misguide, misinform, misinterpret.

instrumental, accessory, assisting, auxiliary, conducive, contributory, expeditious, helpful, promoting, serviceable, serving, subsidiary. ANT.—detrimental, hindering, impeding, injurious, obstructive.

insubordination, contrariness, contumacy, defiance, disobedience, intractability, mutiny, perversity, rebellion, refractoriness, revolt, stubbornness. ANT.—loyalty, obedience, submission, tractability.

insufficient, bare, deficient, drained, imperfect, inadequate, incompetent, incomplete, lacking, limited, meager, rare, scant, scarce, short, slack, sparse ANT.—abundant, ample, copious, rich, sufficient.

insulate, alienate, cover, detach, disconnect, disengage, isolate, part, protect, quarantine, retire, seclude, segregate, separate, sequester, sunder, withdraw, wrap. ANT.—associate, connect, integrate, mingle, unite.

insult, abuse, acerbity, affront, derision, discourtesy, disrespect, gall, impudence, incivility, indignity, insolence, libel, mockery, offense, rudeness, scurrility, slight, slur, snub; abuse, affront, dishonor, injure, mock, offend, outrage, wrong. ANT.—apology, courtesy, homage, salutation; defer, praise, respect, revere.

integral, centralized, complete, consummate, constituent, definite, entire, one, perfect, uncut, unitary, whole. ANT.—divisional, fractional, indefinite, partial, segmental.

integration, alliance, amalgamation, blending, combination, consolidation, fusion, joining, merger, mingling, mixture, unification, union. ANT.—isolation, seclusion, segregation, separation.

integrity, candor, constancy, fairness, faithfulness, fidelity, frankness, honesty, honor, incorruptness, justice, loyalty, morality, openness, probity, purity, rectitude, responsibility, righteousness, sincerity, trustworthiness, uprightness, virtue; completeness, entirety, soundness, value, wholeness, worth. ANT.—deceit, fraud, infidelity, treason, turpitude; fragmenta-

tion, imperfection, loss, worthlessness.

intelligence, acumen, aptitude, astuteness, comprehension, discernment, grasp, insight, intellect, knowledge, mental ability, mind, penetration, perspicacity, reason, sense, understanding, wit; inside facts, secret information, secret report. ANT.—emotion, feeling, passion.

intelligent, alert, apt, astute, bright, brilliant, capable, clever, discerning, exceptional, keen, knowing, perceptive, quick, sensible, sharp, smart; enlightened, intellectual, knowledgeable, well-informed. ANT.—dull, insipid, obtuse, shallow, stupid.

intend, aim, contemplate, delineate, design, desire, destine, devise, hope, mean, outline, plan, plot, prepare, project, propose, purpose, scheme, sketch, try, want, wish.

intensity, acuteness, ardor, concentration, depth, eagerness, earnestness, emphasis, fervor, force, magnitude, might, potency, power, pressure, strain, strength, tension, toughness, vehemence, vigor. ANT.—feebleness, lassitude, lethargy, passivity, weakness.

intentional, aimed at, calculated, contemplated, deliberate, designed, determined, intended, meant, planned, premeditated, projected, purposed, studied, voluntary, willful. ANT.—accidental, fortuitous, haphazard, random, unforeseen.

intercept, ambush, appropriate, arrest, avert, block, catch, check, cut off, hinder, interpose, interrupt, obstruct, prevent, stop, take away, waylay. ANT.—aid, boost, forward, succor, uphold.

interest, advantage, appeal, attention, behalf, benefit, charm, claim, concern, curiosity, fascination, gain, inquisitiveness, portion, premium, profit, right, share, stake, title; absorb, amuse, appeal to, beguile, cheer, concern, delight, divert, enliven, entertain, enthrall, fascinate, gratify, hold attention, intrigue, occupy, please. ANT.—apathy, indifference, insolvency, loss; bore, displease, stupefy, tire, vex.

interfere, bar, block, clash, collide, conflict, delay, frustrate, hamper, hinder, impede, inconvenience, interpose, interrupt, intrude, meddle, mediate, obstruct, obtrude, oppose, stall, tamper, thwart. ANT.—abet, aid, clear, help, stand aside.

interior, heart, inmost, inner, inside, internal, inward, middle; bowels, core, enclosure, hinterlands, inland. ANT.—boundary, coast, exterior, external, periphery.

interminable, boundless, continuous, endless, eternal, everlasting, illimitable, immeasurable, incessant, infinite, limitless, permanent, tedious, unbounded, unlimited, vast. ANT.—bounded, confined, finite, intermittent, periodic.

intermittent, alternate, broken, cyclic, discontinuous, fitful, flickering, fluttering, infrequent, interrupted, occasional, periodic, recurrent, remittent, spasmodic. ANT.—constant, continual, incessant, perpetual, regular.

internal, domestic, enclosed, esoteric, ingrained, inherent, innate, inner, inside, interior, intrinsic, inward. ANT.—alien, external, foreign, outer, superficial.

interpose, inject, insert, intercalate, interject, interpolate, introduce; arbitrate, intercede, intercept, interfere, interrupt, intersperse, intervene, intrude, meddle, mediate, negotiate, obtrude, sandwich, tamper. ANT.—extract, omit, withdraw; avoid, overlook, shun.

interpret, clarify, construe, decipher, decode, define, describe, disentangle, elucidate, explain, explicate, expound, illuminate, manifest, paraphrase, render, reveal, solve, translate, unfold, unravel. ANT.—confuse, distort, misconstrue, misinterpret, mystify.

interrogation, examination, inquiry, inquisition, interpellation, investigation, probe, query, test. ANT.—acknowledgement, answer, rejoinder, reply, response.

interrupt, arrest, adjourn, break, check, cut, defer, delay, disconnect, discontinue, disturb, divide, hinder, interfere, obstruct, postpone, sever, stay, stop, suspend. ANT.—continue, maintain, persist, prolong, sustain.

intervene, arbitrate, intercede, interpose, mediate, negotiate, step in; inject, insert, interfere, interject, interlope, introduce, intrude, meddle; divide, part, sever; befall, happen, occur. ANT.—ignore, stand aside; assist, help; assemble, convene.

intimate, affectionate, close, confidential, familiar, friendly, internal, loving, near, personal, private, secret, special, trusted. ANT.—ceremonious, cool, distant, formal, remote.

intimate, v. see insinuate.

intolerable, detestable, impossible, insufferable, insupportable, offensive, painful, unbearable, unendurable. ANT.—bearable, endurable, passable, satisfying, tolerable.

intolerant, biased, bigoted, discriminatory, dogmatic, fanatical, illiberal, narrow-minded, prejudiced, unfair, unyielding. ANT.—impartial, lenient, nondiscriminatory, open-minded, unbiased.

intrepid, adventurous, audacious, bold, brave, courageous, daring, dauntless, fearless, lionhearted, mighty, nervy, plucky, powerful, strong, unafraid, unflinching, unshrinking, valiant, valorous. ANT.—cowardly, cringing, faint-hearted, flinching, timid, trembling.

intricate, complex, complicated, compound, confused, convoluted, difficult, disarranged, inextricable, involved, irregular, knotted, labyrinthine, mixed, perplexing, raveled, tangled. ANT.—arranged, clear, plain, simple, uncompounded.

intrigue, cabal, chicanery, collusion, complication, connivance, conspiracy, craft, cunning, design, double-dealing, duplicity, machination, maneuvering, plan, plot, scheme, secret, stratagem, trickery, wire-pulling.

intrinsic, congenital, essential, fundamental, genuine, honest, inborn, inbred, indigenous, ingrained, inherent, innate, native, natural, real, subjective, true. ANT.—external, extraneous, extrinsic, incidental, objective.

introduction, beginning, commencement, foreword, inception, initiation, interjection, interpolation, meeting, overture, preamble, preface, prelude, presentation, prologue, start. ANT.—conclusion, end, epilogue, finale, postlude.

intrusive, encroaching, infringing, inquisitive, interfering, invading, meddlesome, obtrusive, snooping, trespassing. ANT.—unintrusive, unobtrusive, retiring.

intuitive, emotional, guessing, heedless, impulsive, instinctive, involuntary, unreasoning, unreflective; discerning, insightful, knowing, perceptive. /calculated, meditated, planned, reasoned; obtuse.

invalidate, abolish, abrogate, annul, cancel, counteract, negate, neutralize, null, nullify, quash, recall, revoke, stop, void. ANT.—endorse, establish, promote, sustain, validate.

invaluable, dear, expensive, inestimable, precious, priceless, valuable. ANT.—cheap, nugatory, useless, worthless.

invasion, aggression, assault, attack, entrance, foray, incursion, ingress, ingression, inroad, intrusion, irruption, onslaught, outbreak, raid, take-over. ANT.—defense, evacuation, fortification, protection, safeguard.

invective, abuse, aspersion, blasphemy, censure, condemnation, contumely, defamation, denouncement, denunciation, deprecation, disapprobation, disapproval, disparagement, insult, obloquy, opprobrium, raillery, reprimand, reprehension, reproach, sarcasm, scurrility, upbraiding, vituperation. ANT.—approval, commendation, laudation, plaudit, sanction.

invent, coin, conceive, concoct, conjure, contrive, design, devise, draft, fabricate, fashion, form, frame, imagine, improvise, manufacture, originate, outline, plan, project, sketch, visualize; deceive, equivocate, fake, falsify, lie, misrepresent, misstate. ANT.—copy, imitate,

reproduce; disabuse, disillusionize.

inventory, catalog, itemization, list, record, register, roll, roster, schedule, table; contents, stock, store, supply; examination, inspection, investigation.

investigation, catechism, discussion, examination, exploitation, exploration, inquiry, inquisition, interrogation, pursuit, query, quest, question, research, review, search, scrutiny. ANT.—disregard, inactivity, inattention, neglect, overlooking.

invincible, formidable, impregnable, incontestable, indomitable, inseparable, insuperable, insurmountable, invulnerable, irresistible, mighty, overpowering, resistless, sovereign, unassailable, unconquerable, unvanquishable, unyielding. ANT.—impotent, powerless, puny, vulnerable, weak.

invisible, evanescent, gaseous, imperceptible, indistinguishable, intangible, microscopic, occult, undiscernible, undisclosed, unreal, unseen, vaporous. ANT.—evident, perceptible, real, substantial, visible.

involve, comprehend, compromise, contain, cover, denote, embarrass, embroil, entail, entangle, envelop, enwrap, implicate, imply, include, incriminate, overwhelm, signify. ANT.—disconnect, disengage, extricate, separate, unravel.

irate, angry, enraged, ferocious, fierce, fuming, furious, incensed, infuriated, irritated, mad, nettled, piqued, provoked, rabid, raging, stormy, wrathful. ANT.—appeased, calm, pleased, quiet, restrained.

irk, annoy, bother, chafe, discompose, disturb, fret, inconvenience, irritate, perturb, pester, tease, trouble, upset, vex ANT.—console, delight, gladden, please, soothe.

irony, banter, criticism, derision, mockery, paradox, quip, raillery, reproach, ridicule, sarcasm, satire, twist. ANT.—approval, courtesy, deference, esteem, respect.

irrational, absurd, crazed, crazy, daft, demented, fatuous, feeble-minded, foolish, inconsistent, injudicious, illogical, nonsensical, odd, preposterous, queer, ridiculous, self-contradictory, silly, strange, stupid, unreasonable, unsound, vacuous, weak-minded. ANT.—logical, lucid, rational, reasonable, sound.

irreconcilable, divergent, implacable, incompatible, incongruous, inconsequent, inexorable, quarrelsome, unappeasable. ANT.—appeasable, compatible, congruous, reconcilable, solvable.

irregularity, aberration, abnormality, anomaly, asymmetry, caprice, deviation, disorderliness, eccentricity, fitfulness, inordinateness, inconstancy, intermittency, tardiness, unruliness, variation. ANT.—method, order, regularity, stability, system.

irrelevant, alien, extraneous, foreign, immaterial, inapplicable, inapposite, inappropriate, inconsequent, remote, strange, unconnected, unessential, unrelated. ANT.—apt, fitting, germane, pertinent, relevant.

irremediable, beyond help, hopeless, incurable, irrecoverable, irreparable, irretrievable, irrevocable, useless. ANT.—curable, recoverable, reparable.

irresolute, doubting, drifting, fickle, fluctuating, half-hearted, hesitant, hesitating, ineffective, irresponsible, lukewarm, pliable, shaky, uncertain, undecided, undetermined, unsettled, unstable, unsteady, vacillating, volatile, wavering, wobbling; bending, fragile, frail, yielding. ANT.—enduring, potent, powerful, relentless, tenacious.

irresponsible, arbitrary, capricious, careless, faltering, flighty, fluctuating, foolish, giddy, heedless, immature, irresolute, purposeless, rash, reckless, thoughtless, unaccountable, unanswerable, unreliable, unstable, unsteady, wobbly. ANT.—accountable, dependable, reliable, steady, trustworthy.

irritable, cantankerous, captious, choleric, excitable, fidgety, fiery, fractious, fretful, hasty, hot, ill-tempered, irascible, peevish, petulant, querulous, sensitive, snappy, susceptible, testy, thin-skinned, touchy. ANT.—agreeable, calm, composed, serene, tranquil.

irritate, aggravate, agitate, anger, annoy, bother, chafe, disturb, enrage, exacerbate, exasperate, fluster, foment, harass, inconvenience, inflame, infuriate, irk, madden, pester, pique, provoke, ruffle, sting, taunt, tease, trouble, vex. ANT.—accommodate, console, gratify, moderate, pacify.

isolate, alienate, disconnect, dissociate, exclude, insulate, quarantine, retire, seclude, segregate, separate, sequester, withdraw. ANT.—associate, integrate, join, mingle, unite.

issue, aftermath, conclusion, consequence, culmination, denouement, effect, emanation, eventuality, finish, fruits, offspring, product, progeny, result, termination; event, incident; point, question, subject, topic; arise, emanate, emerge, emit, ensue, eventuate, exude, flow, originate, proceed, result, spew, spread, spring, start; publish; circulate money; abound, be copious. ANT.—contain, repress, retain, suppress.

itinerary, circuit, course, flight, guidebook, log, map, path, plan, record, route, travel plans, trip.

Jjam, block, bruise, cram, crowd, crush, force, impede, improvise (music), interfere, mass, pack, press, push, squeeze, tamp, wedge. ANT.—expand, free, diffuse, disperse, separate.

jargon, argot, babble, bosh, cant, dialect, gibberish, idiom, jive, lingo, patois, phraseology, shop talk, slang, trade talk, vernacular.

jealous, covetous, distrustful, doubtful, doubting, dubious, envious, invidious, jaundiced, mistrustful, resentful, suspicious; solicitous, vigilant, watchful. ANT.—content, indifferent, lenient, serene, trusting.

jeer, deride, fleer, flout, gibe, hoot, mock, ridicule, scoff, sneer, taunt. ANT.—compliment, flatter, honor, laud, praise.

jeopardize, chance, compromise, conjecture, dare, endanger, expose, hazard, imperil, menace, peril, risk, threaten, venture. ANT.—determine, guard, insure, protect, shield.

jest, banter, humor, joke, prank, quip, wisecrack, witticism.

jocular, comical, droll, facetious, funny, humorous, joking, merry, pleasant, sportive, waggish, witty. ANT.—dull, grave, morose, serious.

join, accompany, add, adjoin, affiliate, associate, attach, bind, cement, combine, conjoin, connect, consolidate, couple, enter, knit, link, marry, tie, unify, unite. ANT.—detach, disconnect, leave, sever, sunder.

joint, articulation, collaboration, combination, connection, cooperation, junction, juncture, link, meeting, union; dove-tail, dowel, hinge, mitre, mortise, pivot, seam, welding; associated, combined, shared, united. ANT.—separate, single.

jolly, blithe, cheerful, congenial, convivial, frolicsome, gay, happy, humorous, jocose, jocular, jocund, jovial, joyous, merry, playful, sprightly, vivacious, witty. ANT.—depressed, glum, melancholy, mournful, sullen.

journal, account, chart, daily register, daybook, diary, gazette, log, magazine, newspaper, periodical, publication, record, register.

journey, course, cruise, excursion, expedition, jaunt, passage, peregrination, pilgrimage, safari, tour, travel, trek, trip, voyage. ANT.—stay, stop.

joy, bliss, cheer, delight, ecstasy, elation, exultation, felicity, gaiety, gladness, glee, happiness, merriment, mirth, pleasure, rapture, transport. ANT.—affliction, depression, despair, grief, wretchedness.

judge, adjudicator, arbiter, arbitrator, censor, connoisseur, critic, custodian, guardian, interpreter, judiciary, magistrate, protector, referee, reviewer, umpire; decide, decree, determine; adjudicate, arbitrate, condemn, try, umpire; appreciate, consider, estimate, evaluate, measure, think.

judgment, award, decision, discernment, decree, discrimination, injunction, intellectuality, perspicacity, ruling, sagacity, sentence, understanding, wisdom. ANT.—arbitrariness, senselessness, stupidity, thoughtlessness, vacuity.

jumble, confuse, disarrange, mess, mingle, mix up, muddle, shuffle; agitation, chaos, commotion, confusion, disarrangement, disarray, disorder, ferment, stir, tumult, turmoil. ANT.—arrange, classify, file, rectify, systematize; certainty, order, peace, tranquility.

jump, bounce, bound, caper, hop, jerk, leap, pounce, skip, spring, start, twitch, vault.

just, blameless, candid, conscientious, earned, equitable, fair, honest, honorable, impartial, innocent, judicious, lawful, legal, legitimate, merited, precise, rightful, scrupulous, sincere, true, unbiased, upright. ANT.—corrupt, deceitful, dishonest, fraudulent, lying, villainous.

justice, equity, fairness, fair play, impartiality, justness, lawfulness, legality, propriety, reasonableness, rectitude, right, righteousness, uprightness. ANT.—corruption, dishonor, favoritism, inequity, unlawfulness.

justify, absolve, acquit, advocate, clear, defend, excuse, exonerate, extenuate, forgive, free, maintain, support, uphold, vindicate. ANT.—accuse, blame, convict, indict, stigmatize.

K

keen, acrid, acute, ardent, bitter, caustic, clever, cunning, cutting, discerning, fervid, incisive, intense, lively, penetrating, perspicacious, piercing, pointed, quick, sagacious, severe, sharp, shrewd, stinging, vivid, wily, witty, zealous. ANT.—apathetic, blunt, dull, lethargic, sluggish.

keep, conserve, continue, defend, guard, maintain, preserve, protect, save, secure, support, sustain, tend, uphold; confine, detail, hold, imprison, reserve, restrain, retain, suppress, withhold; adhere, execute, obey; celebrate, commemorate, honor, observe. ANT.—destroy, discard, reject; dismiss, release, relinquish; disobey, ignore; abandon, forsake.

kill, assassinate, annul, butcher, choke, decimate, delete, destroy, extinguish, immolate, massacre, murder, obliterate, slaughter, slay, smother, strangle, veto. ANT.—animate, protect, resuscitate, safeguard, vivify.

kin, clan, family, kindred, kinsfolk, kinsmen, kith, relatives, siblings, tribe.

kind, accommodating, affable, affectionate, amiable, beneficent, benevolent, benign, caring, charitable, compassionate, considerate, cordial, forbearing, gentle, good, gracious, humane, indulgent, kind-hearted, kindly, loving, merciful, obliging, sympathetic, tender, thoughtful; brand, breed, category, character, class, family, genus, ilk, offspring, order, progeny, race, relation, sort, species, stock, strain, type, variety. ANT.—

cruel, inhuman, merciless, ruthless, vicious.

kindred, affinity, consanguinity, family, kin, kinsfolk, kinsmen, relations, relationship, relatives; allied, analogous, congenial, corresponding, empathetic, like, parallel, related, similar, sympathetic. ANT.—disconnection, foreigners, strangers; dissimilar, foreign, heterogeneous, unlike, unrelated.

kingdom, country, domain, dominion, empire, monarchy, nation, realm, rule, sovereignty.

kiss, buss, caress, cuddle, embrace, fondle, osculation, pax (kiss of peace), touch of the lips.

knack, ability, adeptness, adroitness, aptitude, cleverness, deftness, dexterity, expertness, facility, faculty, ingenuity, proficiency, readiness, skill, skillfulness, talent; device, trick. ANT.—awkwardness, clumsiness, incompetence, ineptitude.

knit, affiliate, bind, connect, crochet, interlace, intermingle, intertwine, join, link, loop, net, spin, tie, unite, weave, web. ANT.—divide, separate, unravel, untie.

knot, assemblage, bond, bunch, cluster, collection, complication, connection, difficulty, entanglement, gathering, intricacy, ligature, perplexity, protuberance, snarl, tangle, tie, tuft.

know, appreciate, apprehend, ascertain, cognize, comprehend, conceive, discern, distinguish, fathom, hold, interpret, perceive, recognize, remember, think, understand. ANT.—dispute, doubt, forget, misapprehend, misconstrue.

knowledge, acquaintance, apperception, apprehension, cognition, cognizance, comprehension, education, enlightenment, erudition, experience, familiarity, information, learning, light, lore, perception, recognition, scholarship, science, understanding, wisdom. ANT.—blindness, enigma, ignorance, illiteracy, stupidity.

L

labor, drudgery, effort, endeavor, exertion, industry, pains, painstaking, plodding, striving, struggle, task, toil, travail, work; childbirth. ANT.—idleness, inertia, lethargy, relaxation, sloth.

lack, dearth, deficiency, demerit, depletion, distress, failing, fault, inadequacy, insufficiency, neediness, privation, poverty, scantiness, scarcity, shortage; need, want. ANT.—abundance, excess, profusion, sufficiency, surplus.

lag, dally, dawdle, delay, fall behind, falter, idle, linger, loiter, plod, retard, saunter, slacken, stagger, tarry, trudge. ANT.—accelerate, bound, dash, hasten, hustle.

lame, crippled, defective, deformed, disabled, faltering, halt, hesitating, hobbling, impotent,

limping, maimed; feeble, ineffective, unconvincing, unsatisfactory, weak. ANT.—agile, robust, vigorous; convincing, effective, forceful.

lament, anguish, bemoan, bewail, commiserate, cry, deplore, fret, grieve, mourn, regret, repine, rue, wail, weep, worry. ANT.—celebrate, cheer, delight in, exult, rejoice.

language, brogue, cant, dialect, diction, expression, idiom, jargon, lingo, linguistics, literature, patois, philology, phraseology, slang, speech, terminology, tongue, utterance, vernacular, vocabulary, voice, words.

languid, apathetic, debilitated, drooping, drowsy, dull, faint, feeble, flagging, heartless, irresolute, laggard, languorous, leisurely, lethargic, listless, pensive, pining, sickly, slack, slow, sluggish, torpid, weak, wearied. ANT.—animated, brisk, enthusiastic, spirited, vigorous.

lanky, bony, gangling, gaunt, lank, lean, narrow, overgrown, rawboned, slim, spare, wiry. ANT.—brawny, burly, husky, portly, sturdy.

lapse, backsliding, blunder, boner, delay, error, fault, flaw, fumble, gap, indiscretion, misstep, mistake, omission, oversight, passing, sin, slip.

larceny, appropriation, burglary, embezzlement, peculation, pilfering, pillage, plunder, purloinment, robbery, shoplifting, theft.

ANT.—compensation, recoupment, repayment, restoration, return.

large, abundant, ample, big, broad, bulky, capacious, colossal, commodious, copious, corpulent, enormous, extensive, gigantic, grand, great, huge, immense, magnificent, massive, mighty, monstrous, long, obese, plentiful, roomy, sizeable, towering, vast, wide. ANT.—infinitesimal, microscopic, minute, paltry, puny.

lash, abuse, beat, castigate, drive, flagellate, flail, goad, impel, press, pummel, scourge, spank, spur, strike, urge, whip; satirize, scold, rate.

last, closing, concluding, conclusive, crowning, extreme, final, finishing, hindmost, latest, least, supreme, terminal, ultimate, utmost. ANT.—commencing, first, foremost, leading, primary.

late, delayed, dilatory, lagging, overdue, slow, tardy; deceased, demised, departed; bygone, defunct, extinct, gone, lapsed; advanced, new, recent. ANT.—early, prompt, punctual, ready; alive, animated, living; aged, ancient, antique, old.

latent, allusive, concealed, dormant, hidden, implicit, implied, inactive, inherent, invisible, involved, lurking, passive, potential, quiescent, recondite, secret, undeveloped, unknown, unobserved, unperceived, unseen, vestigial. ANT.—apparent, conspicuous, known, prominent, unmistakable, visible.

latitude, breadth, compass, distance, extent, freedom, leeway, length, range, reach, room, scope, space, sweep, width; laxity.

laudable, admirable, commendable, creditable, deserving, dutiful, estimable, excellent, exemplary, honorable, ideal; meritorious, model, praiseworthy, righteous, worthy. ANT.—corrupt, damnable, degraded, iniquitous, odious.

laughable, absurd, amusing, asinine, bizarre, comic, comical, droll, eccentric, facetious, farcical, foolish, funny, jocose, ludicrous, quaint, ridiculous, waggish, whimsical. ANT.—depressive, funereal, melancholy, morbid, painful.

launch, begin, cast, commence, dart, dispatch, enlarge, expatiate, float, hurl, inaugurate, initiate, open, project, start, throw. ANT.—close, end, finish, land, splash down.

lavish, abundant, costly, dear, excessive, exhaustive, exorbitant, exuberant, generous, inordinate, liberal, luxuriant, prodigal, profligate, profuse, replete, superabundant, unrestrained, unstinted, wasteful; bestow, deluge, dissipate, expend, flood, glut, gorge, indulge, inundate, load, misuse, overload, overrun, scatter, spend, squander, waste, wear out. ANT.—deficient, inadequate, jejune, meager, scanty; conserve, curtail, economize, skimp, treasure.

law, act, canon, code, command, commandment, constitution, covenant, decree, edict, enactment, equity, formula, jurisprudence, justice, legality, legislation, mandate, order, ordinance, precept, principle, regulation, rule, statute. ANT.—felony, illegality, lawlessness, outlawry, transgression.

lawful, admitted, allowable, approved, authorized, canonical, conceded, constitutional, granted, judicial, legal, legislative, legitimate, licit, official, permissible, recognized, right, rightful, sanctioned, warranted. ANT.—arbitrary, criminal, illegal, prohibited, unauthorized.

lax, careless, depraved, derelict, desultory, flaccid, immoral, inaccurate, lawless, limp, neglectful, negligent, relaxed, remiss, unconscientious, undutiful, unobservant, unprincipled, vague, weak. ANT.—determined, faithful, honorable, meticulous, rigid, rigorous.

lay, common, earthly, mundane, noncleric, nonecclesiastical, nonprofessional, popular, profane, secular, temporal, worldly; arrange, deposit, dispose, place, put, set. ANT.—professional, spiritual, unworldly; disarrange, disturb, misplace, remove.

lazy, idle, inactive, indolent, inert, lackadaisical, laggard, lethargic, negligent, shiftless, sleepy, slothful, sluggish, supine, torpid, weak, worn. ANT.—active, assiduous, diligent, industrious, persevering.

lead, conduct, direct, escort, guide, pilot, shepherd, steer; command, control, govern, manage, regulate, superintend, supervise; begin, open, pioneer, precede, start. ANT.—perform; acquiesce, comply, obey, submit; follow.

leader, captain, chief, chieftain, commander, conductor, director, guide, head, master, principal, ruler, superior, vanguard. ANT.—adherent, devotee, disciple, follower, henchman.

league, alliance, association, cartel, club, coalition, combination, confederacy, confederation, entente, federation, fraternity, partnership, pool, society, union.

leak, dribble, drip, escape, exude, filter, ooze, overflow, pass, percolate, seep, spill, trickle.

lean, bend, cant, careen, crook, decline, deflect, deviate, dip, hang, heel, incline, list, sag, shelve, sidle, slant, slope, tend, tip; depend, rely, trust. ANT.—erect, raise, rise, straighten.

leap, bound, caper, dance, frisk, frolic, gambol, hop, jerk, jump, romp, skip, spring, start, trip, vault.

learn, acquire, ascertain, determine, discern, discover, gain, gather, hear, imbibe, master, memorize, read, receive, study, unearth.

learned, academic, accomplished, deep, discerning, educated, enlightened, erudite, informed, intelligent, knowing, lettered, literate, pedantic, penetrating, philosophic, profound, sagacious, scholarly, solid, sound, well-informed, wise. ANT.—dull, ignorant, illiterate, shallow, uncultured.

leave, absence, allowance, concession, consent, freedom, furlough, holiday, liberty, license, permission, vacation, withdrawal; abandon, allow, decamp, depart, desert, forsake, give up, go, let, permit, quit, relinquish, renounce, retire, vacate, withdraw. ANT.—confinement, hindrance, prohibition, restriction, taboo; abide, endure, persist, remain, tarry.

lecture, address, discourse, dissertation, homily, lesson, prelection, sermon, speech, talk; scold, upbraid.

legal, admitted, allowable, allowed, authorized, constitutional, correct, equitable, fair, lawful, legitimate, permissible, rightful, sanctioned, valid, warranted. ANT.—criminal, illegal, illicit, prohibited, unconstitutional.

legendary, fabulous, fanciful, fictitious, mythical, romantic, traditional. ANT.—actual, factual, historical, real, true.

legitimate, correct, genuine, justifiable, lawful, legal, logical, real, sanctioned, true, valid, warranted. ANT.—illegal, illegitimate, invalid.

leisure, calm, ease, peace, quiet, relaxation, repose, rest, tranquility; cessation, freedom, idleness, intermission, leave, liberty, pause, retirement, respite, sparetime, vacation. ANT.—agitation, commotion, disturbance, tumult; drudgery, duty, toil, travail, work.

lengthen, dilate, draw out, elongate, extend, increase, prolong, protract, stretch. ANT.—abbreviate, curtail, cut, shorten, speed.

lenient, assuaging, charitable, clement, compassionate, easygoing, forbearing, forgiving, gentle, humane, indulgent, kind, merciful, moderate, reasonable, tender, tolerant. ANT.—brutal, cruel, pitiless, tyrannical, unfeeling.

lessen, abate, abridge, contract, curtail, decrease, deduct, diminish, narrow, pare, reduce, shrink, shorten, subtract, trim. ANT.—amplify, enlarge, expand, increase, strengthen.

let, allow, authorize, bear, concede, empower, grant, permit, sanction, suffer, tolerate, warrant, yield; lease, rent. ANT.—defeat, halt, inhibit, obstruct, prevent.

lethargy, apathy, drowsiness, insensibility, languor, lassitude, listlessness, numbness, passivity, stupefaction, stupor, torpor. ANT.—activity, alertness, energy, liveliness, vitality.

level, balanced, equal, even, flat, flush, horizontal, plane, smooth, uniform; genuine, honest. ANT.—hilly, irregular, learning, lumpy, rugged; dishonest.

lewd, coarse, dirty, disgusting, filthy, gross, impure, indecent, lecherous, lustful, obscene, offensive, pornographic, prurient, smutty. ANT.—chaste, decent, modest, pure, refined.

liable, accountable, amenable, answerable, apt, bound, chargeable, exposed to, likely, responsible, subject to, susceptible. ANT.—absolved, exempt, free, immune, unlikely.

libel, asperse, damage, defame, detract, injure, lampoon, satirize, slander, vilify; aspersion, backbiting, calumny, defamation, slander, vilification. ANT.—defend, elevate, help, justify; applause, commendation, defense, flattery, praise.

liberal, ample, bountiful, broad-minded, extensive, extravagant, free, generous, large, lavish, leftist, lenient, magnanimous, munificent, noble-minded, prodigal, profuse, tolerant, unselfish. ANT.—confined, conservative, greedy, penurious, narrow, restricted.

liberate, absolve, acquit, clear, deliver, discharge, dismiss, emancipate, extricate, free, loose, pardon, ransom, redeem, release, rescue, save, set free, unchain, unshackle, untie. ANT.—confine, imprison, oppress, prohibit, restrict.

liberty, autonomy, emancipation, freedom, independence, liberation, self-government; allowance, dismissal, exemption, furlough, immunity, leisure, license, opportunity, permission, privilege, right. ANT.—bondage, captivity, imprisonment, oppression, slavery; confinement, constraint, detention, duress, obligation.

license, allow, approve, authorize, commission, endorse, permit, sanction, warrant; exemption, familiarity, freedom, immunity, independence, liberty, privilege. ANT.—ban, check, forbid, limit, withhold; bondage, compulsion, necessity, servitude.

lie, deceive, deviate, distort, equivocate, evade, exaggerate, falsify, fib, misinform, misrepresent, stretch; lie (down), recline, remain, repose, rest, stay. ANT.—be honest, declare (truth); arise, be upright, rise, sit, stand.

life, animation, being, buoyancy, essence, existence, liveliness, principle, spirit, vigor, vitality, vivacity; origin, source; duration, longevity, survival. ANT.—cessation, death, demise, inaction, languor.

lifeless, dead, deceased, defunct, demised, departed, dull, extinct, flat, gone, inactive, inanimate, insensible, spiritless, stagnant, unconscious. ANT.—alive, animate, brisk, living, vigorous, vital.

lift, boost, elevate, erect, exalt, heave, heighten, hoist, intensify, lift, raise, uplift; purloin, steal, take. ANT.—abase, depreciate, depress, destroy, lower; repay, return.

light, beam, blaze, brightness, brilliancy, dawn, flame, gleam, glow, illumination, incandescence, lamp, luminosity, lustre, radiance, scintillation, shimmer, sparkle, shine; comprehension, enlightenment, insight, knowledge, understanding; airy, buoyant, effervescent; ethereal, resilient, volatile; animated, blithe, capricious, cheerful, elated, hopeful, jocund, lively, sparkling, spirited, vivacious. ANT.—darkness, gloom, ignorance, obscurity, shadow; burdensome, heavy, weighty; depressed, gloomy, morose, sullen, weary.

likable, agreeable, amiable, companionable, enjoyable, friendly, good-natured, pleasant. ANT.—disagreeable, offensive, unattractive, unlikable, unpleasant.

like, akin, allied, analogous, cognate, coincident, comparable, equal, equivalent, identical, indistinguishable, parallel, related, resembling, same, similar. ANT.—contrary, disparate, dissimilar, distinct, opposed.

likeness, analogy, correspondence, counterpart, equivalence, parity, resemblance, similarity, similitude; copy, facsimile, illustration, photograph, portrait, representation. ANT.—difference, distinction, variation.

limit, border, boundary, brink, confine, edge, end, extent, extreme, frontier, limitation, line, restraint, restriction, rim, terminus. ANT.—boundlessness, endlessness, extension, infinity.

limpid, bright, clear, crystal, crystalline, glassy, lucid, pellucid, pure, translucent, transparent. ANT.—cloudy, dark, muddy, opaque, turbid.

lineage, ancestry, birth, breed, children, clan, descent, extraction, family, folk, forefathers, genealogy, nation, people, progeny, race, stock, strain, succession, tribe.

linger, abide, bide, dawdle, delay, falter, hesitate, lag, loiter, lumber, remain, rest, stay, tarry, wait. ANT.—bustle, dash, dart, hurry, speed.

link, associate, attach, bind, bond, conjoin, connect, couple, fasten, go with, join, pin, tie, unite. ANT.—cut, detach, divide, separate, sever.

liquid, dissolved, flowing, fluent, fluid, juicy, liquefied, melted, molten, sappy, serous, solvent, succulent, watery. ANT.—congealed, dense, gaseous, solid, undissolved.

listen, attend to, audit, hear, hearken, heed, list, monitor, overhear; follow, grant, obey, observe. ANT.—disregard, ignore, reject, scorn.

little, condensed, diminutive, dwarfish, elfin, infinitesimal, insignificant, meager, miniature, minute, petite, petty, puny, scanty, slight, small, tiny, trifling, trivial, wee; mean, petty, selfish. ANT.—colossal, enormous, huge, immense, mighty, titanic.

lively, active, animated, blithe, brisk bustling, ebullient, energetic, exhilarated, frolicsome, intense, rapid, spirited, sprightly, supple, vigorous, vivacious; bright, clear, fresh, glowing, sparkling, vivid. ANT.—dull, insipid, listless, stale, vapid.

load, afflict, burden, encumber, oppress, overlook, pressure, tax, trouble, weigh. ANT.—alleviate, console, ease, lighten, mitigate.

loathe, abhor, abominate, condemn, denounce, despise, detest, dislike, hate, imprecate, oppose. ANT.—admire, approve, cherish, love, respect.

location, area, locale, locality, neighborhood, place, position, post, region, site, situation, spot, station, vicinity.

lock, attachment, bar, barrier, bolt, catch, clasp, connection, fastening, grapple, hasp, hook, latch, link, padlock; curl, ringlet, tress, tuft.

lofty, dignified, elevated, exalted, grand, grandiose, high, imposing, magnificent, majestic, noble, pompous, proud, stately, sublime; arrogant, conceited, haughty, pretentious, vain. ANT.—common, humble, lowly, modest, ordinary, plebian.

logical, cogent, coherent, convincing, dialectical, discriminating, effective, efficacious, rational, reasonable, sound, strong, telling, valid, weighty. ANT.—crazy, foolish, incoherent, incongruous, weak.

lone, deserted, desolate, isolated, lonely, lonesome, secluded, unaided, unattached; alone, only, single, sole, solitary, unique. ANT.—accompanied, attended, joined, surrounded, together.

lonely, alone, cheerless, desolate, dreary, forlorn, forsaken, isolated, lonesome, secluded, sequestered, solitary. ANT.—befriended, cheerful.

long, drawn out, elongated, enduring, extended, interminable, lasting, lengthy, lingering, prolix, prolonged, protracted, tedious, wordy; distant, far-away, far-off, remote. ANT.—abridged, brief, concise, short, terse; accessible, adjacent, close, neighboring.

look, behold, contemplate, discern, distinguish, eye, gaze, glance, glimpse, perceive, scan, see, stare, survey, view, watch, witness; appear, seem; examine, inspect, investigate, observe; air, appearance, aspect, bearing, behavior, carriage, conduct, condition, department, expression, face, front, manner, mien. ANT.—avert, hide, ignore, miss, overlook.

loose, disengaged, flowing, free, indefinite, lax, limp, relaxed, separate, slack, unbound, unconfined, unfastened, untied, vague; careless, dissolute, heedless, immoral, licentious, unrestrained, wanton. ANT.—fast, taut, tied, tight; inhibited, moral, restrained.

lose, blunder, botch, drop, fail, falter, flounder, flunk, fold, forfeit, fumble, miscarry, mislay, miss, squander, stumble, waste. ANT.—accomplish, improve, master, overcome, regain.

loss, casualty, damage, death, decline, deficiency, deprivation, deterioration, detriment, disadvantage, failure, impairment, lack, retardation, want. ANT.—achievement, acquisition, advancement, gain, improvement.

lot, doom, fate, fortune, portion; award, destiny, issue, outcome, result; chance, luck; assemblage, batch, gathering, group; land parcel.

loud, blaring, blatant, clamorous, crashing, deafening, noisy, piercing, resonant, resounding, shrill, sonorous, stentorian, vociferous; coarse, ill-bred, vulgar; bright, gaudy. ANT.—dulcet, faint, inaudible, quiet, soft, subdued; tasteful.

love, adoration, affection, ardor, attachment, charity, devotion, endearment, fervor, fondness, intimacy, liking, passion, regard, respect, sentiment, warmth, worship, yearning. ANT.—aversion, dislike, enmity, hatred, indifference, scorn.

lovely, adorable, attractive, beauteous, beautiful, captivating, charming, comely, delightful, elegant, enchanting, enticing, fair, fine, graceful, handsome, inviting, lovable, pretty, satisfying, sweet, winsome. ANT.—foul, hideous, homely, repulsive, repugnant.

low, abject, contemptible, debased, degraded, despicable, disgraceful, dishonorable, groveling, ignoble, ignominious, lowly, mean, menial, servile, shameless, sordid, vile, vulgar; feeble, ill, sick, weak; cheap, inexpensive, moderate; short, small; faint, hushed, muffled, soft; blue, dejected, moody; below, beneath, deep, depressed, flat, inferior, nether, prone, prostrate, squat, sunken, supine. ANT.—esteemed, exalted, honored, lofty, noble; healthy, strong, vigorous; costly, expensive; tall, towering; blatant, clamorous, deafening, loud, thunderous; elated, exhilarated; inflated, superior.

lower, inferior, minor, poorer, secondary, subordinate; abase, adulterate, corrupt, debase, defile, degrade, deprave, depress, humiliate, impair, pervert, vitiate. ANT.—better, greater, higher, superior; enhance, improve, raise, restore, vitalize.

loyal, constant, dedicated, devoted, earnest, faithful, patriotic, steadfast, true, trustworthy, unfailing, unswerving. ANT.—disloyal, faithless, false, seditious, treacherous.

lubricate, anoint, cream, grease, lather, oil, salve, wax.

lucid, bright, clear, diaphanous, glossy, limpid, luminous, radiant, serene, transparent; sane, sound, rational; distinct, evident, explicit, intelligible, manifest, obvious, plain, understandable, unmistakable, visible. ANT.—dark, gloomy, murky, nebulous, obscure; demented, deranged; confused, cryptic, enigmatic, puzzling, unintelligible.

lucky, advantageous, auspicious, benign, conquering, favored, felicitous, flourishing, fortuitous, fortunate, happy, propitious, prosperous, successful, thriving, triumphant, victorious. ANT.—cheerless, defeated, downtrodden, ill-fated, persecuted.

lucrative, advantageous, gainful, profitable, remunerative, self-sustaining, worthwhile. ANT.—costly, failing, losing, troublesome, wasteful. Spludicrous, absurd, bizarre, comical, farcical, funny, incongruous, laughable, outlandish, ridiculous, /logical, normal, reasonable, serious, solemn.

luminous, bright, brilliant, clear, gleaming, glowing, incandescent, lucid, lustrous, radiant, shining. ANT.—dim, dull, murky, obscure, unclear.

lunacy, aberration, craziness, delirium, delusion, dementia, derangement, frenzy, hallucination, imbalance, insanity, madness, mania, psychosis. ANT.—balance, normality, rationality, sanity, stability.

lure, allure, attract, bait, bewitch, charm, coax, decoy, ensnare, entangle, entice, entrap, fascinate, induce, inveigle, lead astray, mesmerize, persuade, seduce, tempt, trick, wheedle. ANT.—alienate, antagonize, discourage, repel, revolt.

lust, appetite, avarice, carnality, concupiscence, craving, cupidity, desire, greed, hankering, hungering, longing, urge, wantonness, yearning. ANT.—chastity, purity, restraint; abomination, aversion, distaste, loathing.

luster, brightness, brilliance, brilliancy, effulgence, glossiness, luminosity, radiance, sheen, shimmer, splendor; distinction, fame, renown, repute. ANT.—cloudiness, darkness, drabness, murkiness, shade; baseness, dishonor, disrepute, reproach, shame.

luxurious, epicurean, opulent, ornate, pampered, rich, self-indulgent, sensuous, splendid, sumptuous, voluptuous, wanton. ANT.—ascetic, bare, drab, monastic, spartan.

M

machine, apparatus, appliance, automatism, contrivance, engine, implement, instrument, mechanism, motor, tool, utensil; agent, cabal, organization, system.

mad, angry, enraged, exasperated, furious, incensed, provoked, raging, upset, wrathful; crazy, daft, delirious, demented, deranged, insane, lunatic, maniacal, paranoid, psychotic, scatterbrained, unbalanced, unhinged, unsettled. ANT.—calm, cool, serene; balanced, rational, reasonable, sane, sensible.

magic, black art, charm, conjuring, demonology, divination, enchantment, hexing, hocus-pocus, illusion, jugglery, legerdemain, necromancy, occultism, omen, prediction, rune, sorcery, trickery, voodoo, witchcraft, wizardry.

magnanimous, beneficent, bountiful, charitable, chivalrous, forgiving, generous, giving, greathearted, heroic, liberal, munificent, openhanded, unselfish. ANT.—covetous, egotistical, greedy, miserly, selfish.

magnificent, elegant, excellent, glorious, gorgeous, grand, kingly, majestic, overwhelming, radiant, rich, spectacular, splendid, stately, sublime, sumptuous, superb. ANT.—common, humble, modest, ordinary, plebeian.

magnify, aggrandize, amplify, augment, embroider, enhance, enlarge, exaggerate, expand, heighten, hyperbolize, increase, overstate, romanticize, stretch. ANT.—decrease, depreciate, diminish, minimize, understate.

magnitude, amplitude, bigness, brightness, bulk, dimensions, expanse, extension, extent, girth, greatness, highness, importance, intensity, largeness, loudness, mass, power, proportions, quantity, range, size, vastness, volume. ANT.—dimness, insignificance, paucity, mediocrity, quietness.

main, cardinal, central, chief, essential, first, foremost, highest, leading, necessary, paramount, predominant, prime, principal, supreme. ANT.—auxiliary, inessential, minor, secondary, subordinate.

maintain, continue, keep, preserve, retain, support, sustain, uphold; affirm, allege, assert, claim, confirm, contend, declare, defend, hold, justify, prove, vindicate. ANT.—abandon, discontinue, desert, forsake, quit; condemn, deny, oppose, reject, resist.

majestic, august, dignified, distinguished, eminent, exalted, grand, grandiose, high, illustrious, imperial, imposing, impressive, inspiring, lofty, magnificent, noble, pompous, prominent, splendid, stately, sublime, towering. ANT.—humble, insignificant, low, ordinary, shabby.

make, accomplish, achieve, assemble, build, carve, cause, compel, complete, compose, construct, create, do, drive, establish, execute, fabricate, fashion, force, forge, form, frame, gain, generate, invent, manufacture, mold, perfect, produce, shape. ANT.—annihilate, break, demolish, destroy, mutilate.

makeshift, alternative, expedient, momentary, provisional, short-term, stopgap, substitute, temporary. ANT.—abiding, fixed, permanent.

malady, affliction, ailment, disease, disorder, illness, indisposition, infirmity, sickness. ANT.—health, soundness, vigor, well-being.

malevolence, animosity, enmity, evil, grudge, hate, hostility, ill will, malice, malignancy, malignity, rancor, recrimination, spite, treachery. ANT.—affection, charity, love, sympathy, toleration.

malice, see **malevolence** .

malign, abuse, asperse, besmirch, calumniate, defame, detract, discredit, disparage, libel, revile, scandalize, slander, traduce, vilify; misapply, misemploy, misuse. ANT.—acclaim, celebrate, extol, praise, respect.

malignant, bitter, deadly, evil, fatal, hostile, malevolent, malign, mischievous, pernicious, spiteful, virulent. ANT.—benign, good, helpful, peaceful.

malleable, changeable, ductile, flexible, impressionable, moldable, plastic, pliant, shapeable, supple, yielding. ANT.—fixed, indomitable, resolute, rigid, unyielding.

manage, administer, command, conduct, control, direct, dominate, govern, guide, head, offi-

ciate, oversee, regulate, rule, run, steer, superintendent, supervise, watch; bridle, check, curb, repress, restrain. ANT.—abandon, bungle, mismanage, muff, spoil.

mandate, behest, charge, command, commission, decree, edict, fiat, injunction, law, order, ordinance, requirement, requisite, rule, statute, ukase.

maneuver, action, artifice, design, enterprise, execution, feint, movement, operation, performance, plan, plot, procedure, proceeding, ruse, scheme, stratagem, tactic, wile. ANT.—cessation, inaction, inactivity, rest.

mangle, cripple, crush, disfigure, dismember, fracture, hack, lacerate, maim, mutilate, rend, slash.

manifest, clear, cloudless, fair, sunny; limpid, transparent; apparent, conspicuous, defined, definite, distinct, evident, explicit, intelligible, lucid, obvious, patent, plain, unmistakable, unveiled, visible; open, unobstructed; disclose, exhibit, indicate, reveal, show. ANT.—cloudy, foul, overcast; ambiguous, complex, obscure, unclear, vague; buried, concealed, covered, hidden; conceal, distract, divert, falsify, mislead.

manipulate, bribe, compel, control, direct, feel, finger, guide, handle, lead, operate, rule, threaten.

manner, approach, custom, fashion, form, habit, method, mode, practice, style, way; air, bearing, behavior, carriage, conduct, demeanor, deportment, guise, mien.

many, countless, diverse, manifold, multifarious, multitudinous, myriad, numerous, several, sundry, various. ANT.—few, infrequent, meager, scanty, scarce, uniform.

mar, botch, bungle, damage, deface, deform, distort, harm, hurt, impair, injure, mutilate, scar, spoil, stain, twist, warp, waste. ANT.—adorn, beautify, benefit, enhance, vivify.

margin, bank, border, brim, brink, boundary, confines, fence, fringe, leeway, limit, lip, rim, shore, strand, wall. ANT.—center, extension, heart, interior, surface.

marine, aquatic, hydrographic, maritime, natatorial, nautical, naval, ocean, oceanic, oceanographic, pelagic, seafaring, seagoing. ANT.—alluvial, ashore, earthly, geodetic, terrestrial.

mark, brand, engraving, impression, imprint, scar, stamp, stigma, trace, vestige; badge, emblem, label, sign, symbol, token; characteristic, feature, indication, representation, symptom, trait; goal, target; attend to, behold, notice, observe, perceive, recognize, regard, see. ANT.—disregard, ignore, overlook, skip.

marriage, conjugality, espousal, matrimony, nuptials, oath, union, wedding, wedlock. ANT.—celibacy, divorce, separation, singleness, virginity.

marvelous, amazing, astonishing, awesome, exceptional, extraordinary, fabulous, incredible, indescribable, ineffable, miraculous, mysterious, peculiar, phenomenal, rare, remarkable, singular, superb, uncommon, unexpected, unusual, wonderful, wondrous. ANT.—commonplace, ordinary, plain, unremarkable, worthless.

masculine, aggressive, bold, brave, daring, hardy, husky, lusty, male, manly, mannish, robust, strong, vigorous, virile. ANT.—effeminate, emasculated, feminine, timorous, womanish.

mask, camouflage, cloak, conceal, cover, disguise, dissemble, falsify, hide, hoodwink, hush, muffle, mystify, screen, secrete, shield, suppress, veil, withhold. ANT.—bare, disclose, expose, reveal, unveil.

mass, body, carcass, corpse, remains; form, frame, torso; bigness, bulk, dimensions, magnitude, size; accumulation, aggregate, aggregation, assemblage, association, collection, company, heap, lump, society, sum, total, totality, whole; agglomeration, conglomeration. ANT.—mind, soul, spirit; individual, factor, part, portion.

massacre, annihilation, bloodshed, butchery, carnage, decimation, execution, extermination, genocide, killing, murder, pogrom, slaughter, slaying. ANT.—animation, preservation, protection, resuscitation.

massive, colossal, dense, heavy, huge, large, majestic, ponderous, weighty; burdensome, cumbersome, cumbrous, grievous, trying, unwieldy; gloomy, grave, serious, sluggish. ANT.—airy, delicate, light, small; flexible, pliant; animated, brisk, buoyant.

master, captain, champion, chief, commander, conqueror, director, employer, governor, head, leader, lord, manager, mentor, overseer, potentate, principal, ruler, superior, teacher, victor; holder, owner, proprietor; adept, expert. ANT.—apprentice, dependent, follower, pupil, servitor; amateur, beginner, greenhorn, neophyte, novice.

masterpiece, chef-d'oeuvre, forte, greatest accomplishment, magnum opus, masterstroke, masterwork, monument, paragon, peak.

mastery, advantage, ascendancy, command, conquest, control, domination, dominion, expertise, exultation, predominance, rule, skill, sovereignty, superiority, supremacy, sway, transcendence, triumph, victory. ANT.—defeat, failure, impotence, inferiority, subjugation.

mate, assistant, associate, attendant, chum, colleague, companion, comrade, consort, crony, friend, intimate, pal, partner, spouse; ship's officer; match, marry.

material, body, cloth, fabric, gear, matter, staple, stuff, substance; affair, cause, concern, occasion, subject, theme, thing, topic; consequence, essence, importance, moment; bodily, concrete, corporeal, palpable, physical, ponderable, sensible, solid, somatic, substantial, tangible, temporal. ANT.—nothingness; airy, bodiless, ethereal, intangible, spiritual.

matrimony, see **marriage**.

matter, see **material**.

mature, adult, aged, complete, consummate, developed, experienced, fertile, finished, full-grown, hardened, matronly, matured, mellow, prime, pubescent, ready, ripe, seasoned, virile; age, develop, perfect, ripen, season. ANT.—deficient, immature, juvenile, premature, raw, undeveloped.

mean, average, mediocre, medium, middle, model, normal; abject, base, contemptible, debased, degraded, despicable, ignoble, low, obscure, plebeian, sordid, vile, vulgar; bad-tempered, malicious, nasty, offensive; mercenary, miserly, parsimonious, penurious, selfish, stingy; contemplate, design, imply, indicate, intend, ordain, purpose, say, signify, state, suggest. ANT.—admirable, distinguished, extraordinary, high, superior; benevolent, charitable, kind; generous, indulgent, liberal, philanthropic, profuse.

meaning, acceptation, connotation, drift, explanation, gist, implication, import, intent, interpretation, purport, purpose, sense, significance, signification.

means, agent, apparatus, channel, device, expedient, factor, instrument, materials, measure, medium, method, tool, utensil, vehicle; capital, income, property, resources, riches, stock, wealth.

measure, criterion, gauge, law, principle, proof, rule, scale, standard, test, touchstone; amplitude, capacity, degree, extent, magnitude, limit, range, scope, size; amount, quantity; allotment, proportion, share; bill, design, draft, outline, plan, plot, project, proposal, proposition, scheme, sketch, suggestion.

mechanical, automated, automatic, autonomic, contrived, controlled, impulsive, instinctive, involuntary, machinelike, perfunctory, rote, routine, unreasoned.

meddle, annoy, impede, interfere, interpose, interrupt, intervene, intrude, mix, monkey, obtrude, pester, pry, tamper. ANT.—aid, avoid, encourage, shun, support.

mediocre, average, commonplace, fair, intermediate, mean, median, medium, middling, moderate, ordinary, passable. ANT.—exceptional, extraordinary, outstanding, superior, unusual.

meditate, cogitate, consider, contemplate, deliberate, muse, pon-

der, reason, reflect, speculate, study, think; conceive, imagine, picture, recall, recollect, remember; devise, intend, mean, plan, project, purpose, resolve. ANT.—dismiss, disregard, divert, neglect, overlook.

meek, calm, compliant, demure, docile, domestic, gentle, humble, mild, modest, obedient, pacific, patient, peaceable, subdued, submissive, tame, tolerant, unpretentious, yielding; dull, flat, insipid, tedious. ANT.—arrogant, fierce, obstinate, pompous, savage; animated, exciting, lively, spirited.

meet, collide, confront, connect, converge, cross, encounter, engage, find, greet, intersect, join, touch; answer, fulfill, gratify, satisfy; experience, suffer, undergo. ANT.—avoid, cleave, disperse, miss, separate.

melancholy, dejected, depressed, despondent, disconsolate, dismal, dispirited, doleful, forlorn, funereal, gloomy, glum, grim, joyless, moody, mournful, sad, sorrowful, sulky, wistful; grave, pensive, somber. ANT.—cheerful, happy, jubilant, spirited, vivacious.

mellow, aged, full-flavored, mature, perfected, ripe, sweet; delicate, pleasing, refined, relaxed, subdued, sweet-sounding. ANT.—dull, hard, immature, sour, stale; callous, crude, harsh, stubborn.

melody, air, aria, chant, concord, descant, euphony, harmony, lyric, mellifluence, monophony, strain, theme, tune.

member, allotment, apportionment, division, fragment, moiety, piece, portion, scrap, section, segment, share; component, constituent, element, ingredient; limb, organ, part.

memorial, commemoration, commemorative, inscription, memento, monument, remembrance, souvenir; chair, professorship, scholarship.

memory, mental trace, recollection, remembrance, reminiscence, retention, retrospection; fame, renown, reputation. ANT.—amnesia, effacement, forgetfulness, oblivion, unconsciousness.

mend, fix, patch, repair, restore, sew, touch up; ameliorate, better, correct, enhance, improve, rectify, refine, reform, refresh, remedy, renew, revive; get well, heal, recover. ANT.—damage, deform, impair, mar, wound; deteriorate, fall ill, wane, weaken.

mendicant, beggar, pauper, ragamuffin, scrub, solicitor, starveling, tatterdemalion, vagabond, wretch. ANT.—benefactor, contributor, donor, giver.

menial, abject, base, degrading, humble, ignoble, lowly, mean, servile, unimportant, unskilled. ANT.—elevated, expert, noble, professional, uplifting.

mentality, brain, capacity, comprehension, consciousness, faculties, intellect, intelligence, judgment, mind, perception, psyche, reason, reasoning, thought, understanding, wisdom; disposition, inclination, intention, purpose, will, wish. ANT.—corporeality, materiality, matter.

mentor, advisor, counselor, guide, instructor, leader, monitor, teacher. ANT.—disciple, follower, pupil, student.

mercenary, avaricious, corrupt, grasping, greedy, selfish, sordid, venal. ANT.—generous, honorable, liberal, unselfish.

merciful, beneficent, benignant, clement, compassionate, feeling, forbearing, forgiving, gracious, humane, kind, lenient, philanthropic, pitying, soft-hearted, sympathetic, tender, tolerant. ANT.—barbarous, cruel, pitiless, ruthless, tyrannical.

mercy, benevolence, benignity, charity, clemency, compassion, forbearance, forgiveness, grace, humanity, kindness, leniency, mildness, pardon, pity, tolerance. ANT.—banishment, inhumanity, oppression, punishment, vengeance.

merge, amalgamate, blend, coalesce, combine, commingle, conjoin, consolidate, fuse, integrate, join, mingle, mix, unify, unite. ANT.—decompose, divest, divide, separate.

merit, effectiveness, efficacy, force, power, strength; excellence, goodness, regard, value, virtue, worth, worthiness; reward; achieve, attain, deserve, earn, gain, obtain, win. ANT.—corruption, dishonor, evil, weakness, unworthiness; forfeit, lose, spend, waste.

merry, animated, blithe, buoyant, cheerful, ebullient, elated, exhilarated, exuberant, festive, gay, gleeful, hilarious, jocular, jolly, jovial, joyous, jubilant, light-hearted, lively, mirthful, rollicking, spirited, sprightly, vivacious. ANT.—gloomy, melancholy, morose, pessimistic, wretched.

mess, allowance, portion, ration; difficulty, dilemma, plight, predicament, problem; confusion, conglomeration, disorder, disorganization, hodgepodge, jumble, litter, medley, mélange, mixture, potpourri. ANT.—arrangement, method, order, system, tidiness.

message, indication, mark, sign, signal, symbol, token; annotation, comment, communication, dispatch, letter, memorandum, news, note, observation, remark, report, word.

method, arrangement, custom, design, fashion, form, manner, mode, order, plan, procedure, process, rule, scheme, style, system, technique, vogue, way. ANT.—chaos, confusion, disarrangement, disorder, irregularity, muddle.

meticulous, exacting, fastidious, finical, fussy, painstaking, particular, precise, punctilious, scrupulous, tidy. ANT.—careless, cursory, disheveled, sloppy, unkempt.

methodical, accurate, correct, definite, distinct, exact, formal, orderly, precise, regular, rigid, strict, systematic, unequivocal, well-regulated. ANT.—careless, informal, loose, rough, vague.

microscopic, diminutive, fine, infinitesimal, minimal, minute, tiny; detailed, exact, particular, precise. ANT.—enormous, huge, large; general.

middle, axis, center, core, focus, heart, marrow, mean, midpoint, midst, nucleus, pivot; average, axial, central, equidistant, halfway, interjacent, intermediate, mediocre, pivotal. ANT.—border, boundary, outskirts, periphery, rim; beginning, end; extreme, high, low.

might, ability, brawn, energy, force, potency, power, puissance, strength, sturdiness, sway, tenacity, vigor, vitality. ANT.—frailty, impotence, inability, vulnerability, weakness.

mighty, able, bold, concentrated, doughty, enduring, firm, forceful, great, hale, hardy, heavy, husky, immense, impregnable, indomitable, invincible, large, lusty, majestic, manful, momentous, muscular, overpowering, potent, powerful, puissant, resistless, robust, sinewy, stalwart, strapping, strong, stupendous, sturdy, tough, vigorous. ANT.—delicate, enervated, feeble, flaccid, weak.

mild, calm, genial, gentle, humane, kind, meek, mellow, moderate, pacific, patient, peaceful, placid, quiet, smooth, soft, soothing, temperate, tender, tepid, tranquil; bland, savory, sweet. ANT.—bitter, fierce, harsh, irritating, uncouth; acid, biting, bitter, sour, stringent.

militant, active, aggressive, armed, belligerent, combative, contentious, fighting, hostile, pugnacious, pushing, warring. ANT.—acquiescent, amenable, compliant, peaceful, submissive.

mimic, ape, burlesque, caricature, copy, counterfeit, duplicate, echo, feign, forge, imitate, impersonate, mock, parody, parrot, repeat, reproduce, simulate. ANT.—distort, diverge, invent.

mind, see **mentality**.

mingle, amalgamate, associate, blend, combine, commingle, compound, concoct, confound, conjoin, consort, fraternize, fuse, intermingle, intermix, join, jumble, merge, mix, participate, unite. ANT.—disjoin, distinguish, separate, sort.

miniature, abridged, bantam, diminutive, little, minuscule, minute, reduced, small, tiny. ANT.—full-size, large, normal, regular.

minimize, belittle, curtail, deduct, degrade, depreciate, derogate, detract, diminish, disparage, fault, lessen, reduce, shorten, subtract. ANT.—amplify, enlarge, exalt, expand, magnify, praise.

minister, ambassador, churchman, clergyman, cleric, consul, curate, delegate, diplomat, divine, ecclesiastic, envoy, official, padre, parson, pastor, preacher, priest, rector, representative, reverend, vicar; aid, assist, help, nourish, nurture, serve, support, sustain. ANT.—apostate, disciple, follower, layman, renegade; encumber, hinder, impede, obstruct, oppose.

minor, inconsiderable, inferior, junior, lesser, lower, petty, poorer, secondary, smaller, subordinate, unimportant, younger; adolescent, child. ANT.—first, greater, important, major; adult, of age.

minute, accurate, atomic, critical, detailed, diminutive, exact, exiguous, fine, inconsiderable, infinitesimal, insignificant, little, microscopic, miniature, minuscule, molecular, petty, precise, puny, small, tiny. ANT.—colossal, comprehensive, enormous, extensive, magnificent.

miraculous, astonishing, awesome, extraordinary, incredible, inexplicable, marvelous, metaphysical, preternatural, spectacular, spiritual, stupefying, superhuman, supernatural, unearthly. ANT.—commonplace, customary, insignificant, natural, ordinary.

mirage, apparition, delusion, dream, fantasy, figment, hallucination, illusion, phantasm, vision. ANT.—actuality, reality, substance.

miscarriage, defeat, failure, fiasco, frustration, malfunction; spontaneous abortion. ANT.—achievement, success, victory; pregnancy.

miscellaneous, assorted, dissimilar, diverse, diversified, heterogeneous, indiscriminate, mingled, mixed, motley, promiscuous, sundry, variant, varied, various. ANT.—classified, homogeneous, ordered, same, sorted.

mischief, affront, annoyance, damage, detriment, deviltry, disservice, evil, grievance, harm, hurt, ill, infliction, injury, misfortune, mishap, outrage, prank, roguery, wrong. ANT.—betterment, favor, kindness, support, vindication.

miserable, afflicted, ailing, comfortless, crushed, disconsolate, discontented, dismal, distressed, forlorn, heartbroken, pained, pitiable, sickly, sorrowful, suffering, wretched; abject, contemptible, despicable, lamentable, low, mean; insufficient, meager, paltry, poor, scanty, small, stingy. ANT.—contented, happy, lively, rejoicing; noble, respectable; fortunate, prosperous, significant.

miserly, avaricious, close, covetous, greedy, niggardly, parsimonious, penurious, rapacious, selfish, stingy, tight, tight-fisted. ANT.—altruistic, bountiful, extravagant, generous, liberal, munificent.

misery, agony, anguish, anxiety, desolation, despair, despondency, distress, grief, heartache, mortification, pain, sorrow, suffering, torment, trial, tribulation, woe, wretchedness; affliction, calamity, disaster, evil, misfortune, ordeal, trouble; illness, sickness. ANT.—bliss, delight, ecstasy, elation, joy; comfort, contentment, fortune, peace; health, salubrity, vigor.

misfortune, accident, adversity, affliction, bereavement, calamity, casualty, catastrophe, chastening, disaster, distress, hardship, harm, hurt, ill fortune, infliction, injury, loss, misadventure, mishap, privation, ruin, set-back, tribulation. ANT.—advantage, blessing, contentment, prosperity, success, well-being.

misgiving, distrust, doubt, hesitation, mistrust, suspicion, uncertainty. ANT.—certainty, security, sureness, trust.

mishap, accident, calamity, casualty, contretemps, disaster, misadventure, mischance, misfortune, reverse. ANT.—good fortune, luck.

misinterpret, distort, falsify, misconceive, misconstrue, misunderstand, pervert. ANT.—comprehend, perceive, understand.

misleading, deceitful, deceptive, delusive, delusory, fallacious, false, furtive, illusive, specious. ANT.—authentic, direct, forthright, genuine, straightforward, truthful.

misrepresent, belie, caricature, dissemble, distort, exaggerate, falsify, mislead, misstate, pervert, simulate. ANT.—delineate, depict, represent.

miss, fail, default, lack, lose, miscarry, omit, overlook, skip; crave, desire, want, yearn; drop, fumble, muff, snatch at; blunder, mishap, slip. ANT.—achieve, attain, have, succeed; detest, shun; catch, grab, hold; accomplishment, advancement, gain.

mission, activity, affair, attack, business, commission, delegation, errand, purpose; calling, duty, task, work.

mistake, aberration, blunder, downfall, error, failure, fallacy, fault, flaw, illusion, inaccuracy, lapse, misapprehension, misconception, mishap, omission, oversight, slip. ANT.—accuracy, correctness, perfection, precision, truth, veracity.

misunderstanding, confusion, difference, disagreement, discord, dissension, error, misapprehension, misconception, misinterpretation, mistake, quarrel, variance. ANT.—agreement, concord, understanding.

misuse, abuse, asperse, defame, desecrate, disparage, harm, illuse, injure, malign, maltreat, maul, mishandle, pervert, revile, scandalize, traduce, vilify, wrong; consume, dissipate, scatter, spend, squander, waste. ANT.—cherish, honor, protect, respect, succor; accumulate, conserve, economize, preserve, retain.

mitigate, abate, allay, alleviate, ameliorate, appease, assuage, calm, decrease, dilute, diminish, extenuate, lessen, lighten, moderate, modify, mollify, relieve, soften, solace, soothe, subdue, temper, weaken. ANT.—aggravate, deepen, increase, inflate, intensify, provoke.

mix, adulterate, alloy, blend, combine, commingle, commix, compound, concoct, crossbreed, homogenize, incorporate, intermingle, intermix, fuse, join, mingle, shuffle, stir; coalesce, integrate; confound, confuse, jumble, mix up, tangle; associate, consort, fraternize, join, unite. ANT.—detach, disperse, divide, separate, sort; segregate; clarify, enlighten, unravel, untangle; abandon, desert, dissociate, divide.

mixture, assortment, change, difference, dissimilarity, diversity, heterogeneity, hodgepodge, jumble, medley, mélange, miscellany, multifariousness, olio, potpourri, variety; alloy, amalgam, blend, composite, compound, fusion; breed, strain, subspecies. ANT.—homogeneity, likeness, sameness, uniformity; isolation, purity, separation; simplicity; pedigree, purebred.

mob, assemblage, bevy, crowd, crush, drove, flock, gang, gathering, herd, horde, host, masses, multitude, populace, press, rabble, riffraff, swarm, throng.

mobilize, adapt, assemble, call up, command, gather, increase, marshal, order, organize, prepare, transport, unify, unite. ANT.—demobilize, disperse, end, scatter, separate.

mock, ape, defy, deride, fleer, flout, gibe, insult, jeer, mimic, ridicule, satirize, scoff, sneer at, taunt. ANT.—compliment, flatter, honor, praise, support.

mode, condition, course, custom, design, fashion, habit, kind, manner, method, order, plan, practice, procedure, rule, scheme, state, system, usage, vogue, way. ANT.—confusion, disorder.

model, archetype, copy, criterion, design, duplicate, example, facsimile, form, gauge, image, mold, original, paragon, pattern, prototype, replica, representation, specimen, standard, tracing, type.

moderate, abate, allay, assuage, check, curb, deaden, decrease, diminish, lessen, lower, palliate, quell, reduce, subdue, suppress, temper, weaken; abstemious, cool, dispassionate, fair, judicious, measured, mild, regulated, sparing, steady, temperate, tolerant. ANT.—agitate, anger, excite, inflame, stimulate; excessive, extravagant, liberal, outrageous, radical.

modern, contemporary, current, fashionable, fresh, latest, new, novel, present, recent, renovated. ANT.—ancient, antiquated, bygone, primitive, obsolete, outmoded.

modest, bashful, constrained, demure, diffident, humble, meek, reserved, retiring, shy, timid, unassuming, unpretentious; inconsiderable, insignificant, minute, small; chaste, pure, undefiled, virtuous. ANT.—arrogant, bold, conceited, egotistical, ostentatious; excessive, grand, huge, magnificent; immodest, indelicate, obscene, prurient, unchaste.

modification, adaptation, alteration, alternation, change, limitation, modulation, mutation, qualification, substitution, transformation, variation, variety, vicissitude. ANT.—monotony, stability, uniformity.

modify, adapt, alter, change, convert, exchange, expand, limit, lower, moderate, qualify, shape, reform, restrict, shift, soften, substitute, temper, transfigure, transform, vary, veer. ANT.—preserve, retain, stabilize.

moist, aqueous, damp, dank, dewy, dripping, fresh, humid, infiltrated, juicy, muggy, saturated, sloppy, soaked, sodden, soppy, swampy, vaporous, watery. ANT.—arid, barren, dehydrated, dry, parched, waterless.

mold, alter, carve, cast, create, fashion, forge, form, frame, influence, make, model, modify, produce, sculpt, shape. ANT.—destroy, dismantle, mutilate, wreck.

molest, aggrieve, annoy, assail, attack, bother, chafe, damage, disturb, harass, hurt, inconvenience, injure, irk, irritate, maltreat, misuse, oppress, persecute, pester, plague, tease, trouble, vex, worry. ANT.—aid, comfort, defend, encourage, protect, soothe.

moment, flash, instant, jiffy, minute, second, twinkling, wink; consequence, gravity, importance, significance, weight.

momentous, consequential, critical, crucial, decisive, far-reaching, grave, important, influential, material, memorable, pressing, prominent, relevant, salient, serious, significant, solemn, vital, weighty. ANT.—boring, commonplace, immaterial, insignificant, trivial.

monastery, abbey, cloister, convent, hermitage, lamasery, nunnery, priory.

money, assets, bills, bullion, cash, change, checks, coin, currency, finances, gold, legal tender, lucre, notes, pelf, resources, revenue, silver, specie, sterling, wherewithal; capital, funds, opulence, property, riches, stock, wealth; payment, salary, wages.

monopolize, absorb, control, corner, direct, engross, own, possess.

monotonous, boring, burdensome, depressive, dilatory, dreary, dry, dull, flat, heavy, humdrum, irksome, prosy, repetitious, slow, sluggish, tardy, tedious, tiresome, undiversified, uninteresting, unvaried, wearisome. ANT.—appealing, entertaining, exciting, refreshing, varied, versatile.

monument, commemoration, memento, memorial, remembrance, souvenir, testimonial; gravestone, headstone, mausoleum, plaque, pyramid, shrine, statue, tomb, tombstone.

mood, behavior, conduct, disposition, frame of mind, humor, manner, nature, spirit, temper, temperament; inclination, propensity, tendency.

moral, chaste, decent, ethical, good, honest, honorable, just, noble, pure, right, righteous, scrupulous, upright, virtuous. ANT.—amoral, dishonorable, evil, immoral, unethical.

morose, acrimonious, cantankerous, churlish, crabbed, depressed, dour, fretful, gloomy, glum, grouchy, gruff, moody, morbid, petulant, splenetic, sulky, sullen, surly, unamiable. ANT.—buoyant, cheerful, exhilarated, good-natured, pleasant.

mortal, deadly, destructive, fatal, final, lethal, poisonous; extreme, serious; ephemeral, human, passing, temporal, transient. ANT.—curative, life-giving, reviving, strengthening, vivifying; trifling, trivial; external, everlasting, immortal, perpetual.

mortification, abasement, annoyance, chagrin, dissatisfaction, embarrassment, humiliation, shame, vexation; gangrene, necrosis. ANT.—elevation, happiness, praise, satisfaction, success.

motion, action, activity, change, gesture, mobility, move, movement, passage, revolution, transit, transition; proposal, proposition, recommendation, suggestion. ANT.—halt, immobility, inaction, repose, stillness.

motive, cause, determinant, encouragement, ground, impulse, incentive, incitement, inducement, influence, instigation, motivation, principle, prompting, purpose, reason, spur, stimulus, urge; mobile, motile, movable.

motley, assorted, composite, disparate, diverse, heterogeneous, incongruous, indiscriminate, miscellaneous, mixed, mottled, speckled, sundry, varied. ANT.—homogeneous, like, pure, similar, unvaried.

motto, adage, aphorism, apothegm, axiom, byword, epigram, maxim, proverb, saw, saying, sentiment, slogan.

mount, arise, ascend, aspire, climb, grow, increase, rise, scale, scramble, soar, surge, swell, tower. ANT.—collapse, decline, descend, diminish, drop, slump.

mourn, agonize, anguish, bemoan, bewail, cry, deplore, droop, fret, grieve, groan, languish, lament, miss, pray, regret, repine, rue, sigh, sing, sorrow, suffer, wail, weep (over), whimper, yearn. ANT.—celebrate, exult, laugh, rejoice, revel.

move, actuate, advance, agitate, arouse, convey, drive, excite, impel, incite, induce, influence, instigate, operate, persuade, proceed, propel, propose, push, rouse, run, shift, start, stimulate, stir, transfer, transport, travel, urge. ANT.—cease, deter, dissuade, halt, pacify, rest, suppress.

movement, see **motion**.

muddled, addled, befuddled, bewildered, chaotic, confounded, confused, deranged, disarrayed, disconcerted, disordered, disorganized, indistinct, jumbled, messy, mixed, obscured, perplexed, puzzled, snarled, stupid. ANT.—distinguished, lucid, obvious, ordered, organized.

multiply, augment, enlarge, generate, grow, increase, propagate, reproduce. ANT.—divide, lessen, reduce, shrink, waste.

multitude, aggregation, army, assemblage, congregation, crowd, galaxy, gathering, horde, host, legion, mob, populace, swarm, throng. ANT.—fraction, handful, nobody, paucity, scarcity.

mundane, carnal, earthly, laic, lay, mortal, profane, secular, temporal, terrestrial, worldly; everyday, normal, ordinary. ANT.—celestial, eternal, heavenly, paradisaic, spiritual, unearthly; extraordinary, special, unique.

munificent, altruistic, beneficent, benevolent, charitable, generous, hospitable, liberal, philanthropic, princely, unselfish.

ANT.—avaricious, covetous, grasping, miserly, selfish.

murder, annihilate, assassinate, butcher, choke, destroy, execute, exterminate, immolate, kill, massacre, poison, shoot, slaughter, slay, stab, victimize. ANT.—animate, propagate, nurse, refresh, restore, vitalize.

murmur, babble, complain, grouse, grumble, hum, mumble, mutter, protest, remonstrate, repine, ripple, rustle, whisper. ANT.—applaud, approve, honor, praise, recommend.

muscular, athletic, brawny, forceful, husky, powerful, sinewy, stalwart, strong, sturdy, vigorous. ANT.—feeble, flabby, infirm, puny, weak.

musical, agreeable, assonant, choral, euphonic, euphonious, harmonious, lyrical, mellow, melodic, melodious, pleasing, symphonic, tonal, tuneful, unisonant, vocal. ANT.—clashing, discordant, dissonant, grating, harsh.

muster, accumulate, amass, arrange, assemble, call, collect, congregate, convene, convoke, gather; marshal, organize, summon; cull, garner, harvest, pick, reap. ANT.—disjoin, disperse, divert, scatter, separate.

mute, calm, dumb, gagged, hushed, inarticulate, inaudible, noiseless, peaceful, quiet, silent, soundless, speechless, still, taciturn, tranquil, voiceless. ANT.—articulate, garrulous, loquacious, loud, raucous, talkative, vocal.

mutiny, anarchy, coup, insubordination, insurrection, outbreak, overthrow, rebellion, resistance, revolt, revolution, riot, upheaval, uprising.

mutter, complain, grouse, grumble, groan, grunt, maunder, moan, mumble, murmur, rumble, sputter, whisper.

mutual, analogous, common, convertible, correlative, correspondent, equivalent, identical, interchangeable, joint, like, reciprocal, self-same, shared, similar. ANT.—dissociated, divergent, separate, unlike, unshared.

mysterious, abstruse, ambiguous, baffling, cabalistic, covert, cryptic, dark, dim, enigmatical, hidden, impenetrable, incomprehensible, inconceivable, incredible, inexplicable, inscrutable, mystical, mystifying, obscure, occult, secret, surreptitious, unaccountable, unfathomable, unintelligible. ANT.—apparent, distinct, explicit, lucid, obvious.

mystery, conundrum, enigma, obscurity, perplexity, problem, puzzle, riddle, secret. ANT.—answer, key, solution.

mystical, see **mysterious**.

myth, allegory, chronicle, fable, fiction, folk ballad, folk tale, legend, lore, parable, saga, tale. ANT.—fact, history.

mythical, allegorical, apocryphal, fabricated, fabulous, fanciful, fantastic, fictitious, imaginary, invented, legendary, visionary. ANT.—actual, factual, historical, real, true.

N

nag, aggravate, annoy, badger, bother, browbeat, discompose, disturb, goad, harass, harry, heckle, irritate, molest, pester, plague, provoke, scold, tantalize, taunt, tease, torment, vex, worry. ANT.—comfort, delight, mollify, please, soothe.

naive, artless, guileless, inexperienced, ingenuous, innocent, natural, open, plain, provincial, simple, unaffected, unsophisticated. ANT.—crafty, cunning, experienced, sophisticated, wise.

naked, bare, exposed, nude, stripped, threadbare, unclad, unclothed, uncovered, undressed; bald, barren, unfurnished; definite, distinct, evident, exact, explicit, literal, mere, obvious, plain, simple, uncolored; defenseless, open, unprotected. ANT.—attired, clothed, dressed; furnished; artful, complex, concealed, secret; protected, shielded.

name, appellation, cognomen, denomination, designation, epithet, surname, title; character, reputation, repute; distinction, eminence, fame, renown; autograph, signature; nom de plume, pseudonym; appoint, call, characterize, christen, define, denominate, denote, designate, elect, entitle, identify, list, mark, mention, proclaim, signify, specify, term, title. ANT.—anonymity, namelessness.

narcotic, anaesthetic, anodyne, dope, drug, opiate, sedative, soporific, tranquilizer; anesthetizing, doping, drugging, nepenthic, stupefying, tranquilizing.

narrate, declaim, deliver, describe, detail, disclose, enumerate, mention, paint, picture, portray, proclaim, recite, recapitulate, recount, rehearse, relate, repeat, report, reveal, state, tell, unfold. ANT.—conceal, disguise, repress, stifle, withhold.

narrow, bigoted, dogmatic, fanatical, illiberal, intolerant, narrow-minded, prejudiced; miserly, parsimonious; close, confined, contracted, cramped, limited, restricted; scrawny, slender, spindling, thread-like. ANT.—liberal, progressive, radical, tolerant; bountiful, charitable, generous; broad, expanded, extended, wide; corpulent, fat, fleshy, stout.

nasty, dirty, foul, polluted, squalid; gross, indecent, lewd, obscene, smutty; disgusting, nauseating, offensive, repulsive, selfish; inclement, rainy, sleeting, stormy. ANT.—clean, spotless, unsullied; decent, pure; attractive, delightful, pleasant, sweet; clear, sunny.

nation, colony, commonwealth, community, country, empire, kingdom, nationality, people, principality, realm, republic, state, territory; clan, community, folk, people, populace, population, public, race, society.

native, aboriginal, congenital, domestic, endemic, inborn, indigenous, inherent, innate, local, natal, natural, original, pristine, regional, vernacular. ANT.—acquired, alien, artificial, extrinsic, foreign, imported, unnatural.

natural, characteristic, essential, fundamental, genetic, inherent, innate, intrinsic, native, original; normal, regular; artless, genuine, ingenuous, legitimate, real, simple, spontaneous, unaffected, unsophisticated. ANT.—contingent, external, extrinsic, objective; abnormal, artificial, irregular; beautified, embellished, forced, formal, unnatural.

nature, bent, character, constitution, disposition, essence, humor, individuality, kind, mood, reputation, repute, sort, temperament; creation, universe.

nauseous, abhorrent, abominable, despicable, detestable, disgusting, loathsome, nasty, offensive, repulsive, revolting, sickening, unpalatable. ANT.—ambrosial, delectable, delicious, desirable, savory.

naval, marine, maritime, nautical, navigating, ocean, oceanic, sailing, seafaring, seagoing, seaworthy.

near, abutting, adjacent, adjoining, bordering, close, contiguous, neighboring, proximate; approaching, coming, expected, imminent, impending, looming, next, prospective; dear, familiar, intimate. ANT.—far, remote; deferred, expired, postponed, stopped; distant, remote.

neat, adroit, clear, compact, correct, exact, finished, orderly, precise, proportioned, shapely, spotless, spruce, suitable, symmetrical, tidy, trim, well-done, well-ordered. ANT.—awkward, disordered, irregular, lax, slipshod, slovenly.

necessary, binding, compulsory, essential, expedient, imperative, indispensable, inevitable, inexorable, irrevocable, needed, obligatory, pressing, required, requisite, unavoidable, undeniable, urgent. ANT.—extravagant, optional, superfluous, unnecessary, worthless.

need, destitution, indigence, penury, pennilessness, poverty; distress, inadequacy, insufficiency, lack, misery, privation, shortage; emergency, necessity, obligation, requirement, urgency; lack, require, want, wish. ANT.—property, wealth; comfort, luxury, plenty; independence; competence, fullness.

neglect, apathy, carelessness, default, deferment, dereliction, disregard, disrespect, evasion, failure, heedlessness, indifference, negligence, nonchalance, omission, oversight, procrastination, recklessness, scorn, slight, thoughtlessness; defer, dismiss, disregard, fail, forget, ignore, omit, overlook, skip, slight, spurn, suspend, underestimate, undervalue. ANT.—attention, care, diligence, surveillance; accomplish, complete, perform, preserve, safeguard, work.

negotiate, accomplish, achieve, agree, arrange, bargain, compromise, confer, consult, contract, deal, debate, dicker, overcome, reflect, sell, transact.

neighborhood, community, district, environs, locality, region; adjacency, nearness, proximity, vicinity.

nerve, audacity, courage, determination, fortitude, hardihood, intrepidity, pluck, resolution, strength, vigor, vitality.

neutral, disinterested, impartial, indeterminate, indifferent, nonpartisan, unallied, unconcerned. ANT.—biased, decided, involved, positive, predisposed.

new, fresh, late, modern, novel, original, recent, strange, unaccustomed, unfamiliar, untried, up-to-date. ANT.—ancient, archaic, familiar, obsolete, outmoded.

news, advice, bulletin, communication, copy, information, intelligence, message, report, tidings.

nimble, active, agile, alert, brisk, bustling, coordinated, fast, flexible, lively, prompt, quick, rapid, speedy, sprightly, spry, supple, swift. ANT.—clumsy, dull, inert, lumbering, slow.

noble, aristocratic, august, dignified, distinguished, elevated, eminent, exalted, genteel, grand, honorable, illustrious, imperial, lofty, lordly, loyal, majestic, princely, regal, royal, stately, sublime, superior. ANT.—abject, base, ignoble, low, plebeian, servile.

noise, babel, blare, clamor, clangor, clatter, cry, din, hubbub, outcry, pandemonium, racket, row, sound, tumult, uproar. ANT.—calm, hush, quiet, silence, tranquility.

nonchalant, careless, inconsiderate, indifferent, negligent, unconcerned; casual, composed, cool, imperturbable, unruffled. ANT.—attentive, careful, considerate, concerned, vigilant; active, agitated, eager, enthusiastic, excitable, fervid, zealous.

nonsense, absurdity, babble, drivel, foolishness, gibberish, imbecility, inanity, inconsistency, jargon, jest, joke, rigamarole, senselessness, shallowness, silliness. ANT.—accuracy, clarify, common sense, substance, wisdom.

normal, average, common, conventional, customary, general, natural, ordinary, rational, reasonable, regular, sane, standard, steady, typical, uniform, unvaried, usual. ANT.—abnormal, exceptional, irregular, peculiar, strange.

nosy, curious, inquiring, inquisitive, interrogative, intrusive, meddling, peeping, prying, searching, snoopy. ANT.—decorous, incurious, indifferent, polite, restrained, unconcerned.

note, commentary, indication, explanation, mark, sign, symbol, token; acknowledgment, annotation, comment, dispatch, epistle, letter, memorandum, message, missive, notation, notice, observation, remark; distinction, fame, renown, reputation; contemplate, discern, notice, observe, perceive, remark, see, view.

noted, celebrated, distinguished, eminent, exalted, exceptional, extraordinary, famous, glorious, illustrious, imposing, memorable, outstanding, prominent, remarkable, renowned, significant, striking, uncommon, well-known. ANT.—common, insignificant, obscure, trivial, unknown.

notice, attend to, behold, detect, discern, discover, distinguish, examine, heed, mark, note, observe, perceive, recognize, regard, remark, see, warn; announcement, attention, bulletin, civility, cognizance, comment, consideration, heed, mention, note, observation, placard, poster, recognition, regard, respect, warning. ANT.—avoid, disregard, ignore, overlook, shun; evasion, forgetfulness, laxity, omission.

notify, acquaint, advise, alert, apprise, call, communicate, con-vey, disclose, divulge, enlighten, express, impart, indicate, inform, instruct, intimate, signify, specify, spread, teach, tell, warn. ANT.—conceal, deceive, delude, mystify, suppress.

notion, abstraction, belief, caprice, concept, conception, conviction, fancy, idea, image, imagination, impression, inclination, inkling, knowledge, opinion, perception, presumption, sentiment, theory, thought, understanding, view, viewpoint, whim.

novel, fiction, narrative, romance, story, tale; fresh, modern, new, original, unique, unprecedented, untried. ANT.—fact, history, reality, truth, verity; ancient, common, customary, familiar, primitive.

novice, amateur, apprentice, beginner, dabbler, dilettante, greenhorn, intern, learner, neophyte, newcomer, postulant, probationer, recruit, tenderfoot, tyro. ANT.—authority, expert, master, mentor, professional.

nude, see **naked**.

nullify, cancel, countermand, cross out, delete, destroy, discard, dispel, eliminate, erase, expunge, negate, obliterate, suppress, upset, void; abolish, abrogate, annul, invalidate, quash, repeal, rescind, revoke. ANT.—confirm, enact, enforce, execute, ratify, support.

number, aggregate, amount, quantity, sum, volume; calculate, compute, count, enumerate, figure, list, score. ANT.—nothing, nothingness, zero; estimate, guess.

numerous, see **many**.

nurture, cherish, hold dear, prize, treasure, uphold, value; feed, foster, nourish, nurse, rear, support, sustain, tend. ANT.—dislike, disregard, ignore, neglect; abandon, deprive, reject.

nutriment, aliment, diet, edibles, fare, feed, food, meal, nourishment, nutrition, provision, rations, repast, sustenance, viands, victuals. ANT.—hunger, starvation, want.

O

obdurate, adamant, callous, dogged, hard, headstrong, impenitent, indurate, inflexible, insensible, insensitive, mulish, obstinate, stubborn, tenacious, tough, unbending, unfeeling, unyielding. ANT.—amenable, compassionate, sensitive, submissive, tractable.

obedient, acquiescent, compliant, conformable, deferential, dutiful, faithful, law-abiding, loyal, submissive, surrendering, tractable, yielding. ANT.—defiant, insubordinate, intractable, lawless, obstinate, rebellious.

obese, adipose, corpulent, fat, fleshy, portly, rotund, stout, swollen, thickset, unwieldy. ANT.—emaciated, gaunt, lean, skeletal, slender, thin.

object, article, particular, thing; aim, design, end, goal, intention, mark, objective, purpose; balk, disapprove, oppose, protest, resist. ANT.—acquiesce, approve, comply, concur, sanction, welcome.

objection, argument, censure, criticism, disagreement, disapproval, dissent, opposition, protest, rejection, remonstrance, variance. ANT.—acceptance, accord, agreement, approval, compliance.

objective, aim, ambition, aspiration, design, desire, destination, end, goal, hope, intention, longing, mark, motive, object, purpose, scheme, target; dispassionate, equitable, fair, impartial, impersonal, unbiased. ANT.—biased, emotional, partial, personal, subjective.

obligation, accountability, bond, contract, duty, engagement, indebtedness, liability, pledge, promise, requirement, responsibility, stipulation. ANT.—choice, exemption, freedom.

oblige, bind, coerce, command, compel, constrain, drive, enforce, force, hinder, impel, insist, necessitate, restrain; accommodate, benefit, favor, gratify, help, please. ANT.—absolve, discharge, exempt, free, release, spare, unshackle.

obliterate, annihilate, cancel, delete, demolish, destroy, devastate, efface, eradicate, erase, exterminate, extinguish, nullify, ravage, raze, ruin, wreck.

obscene, coarse, corrupt, defiled, dirty, disgusting, filthy, foul, gross, impure, indecent, lascivious, lewd, licentious, offensive, polluted, pornographic, smutty, vulgar, wanton. ANT.— immaculate, innocent, modest, pure, virtuous.

obscure, abstruse, ambigious, blurred, cloudy, complex, complicated, concealed, cryptic, dark, dim, dusky, enigmatic, hazy, incomprehensible, indistinct, mysterious, nebulous, shadowy, unintelligible, unknown, vague, veiled. ANT.—apparent, clear, explicit, lucid, visible.

observant, alert, attentive, aware, careful, considerate, heedful, mindful, perceptive, wary, watchful; obedient, submissive. ANT.—careless, inattentive, indifferent, lax, nonobservant; disobedient, disrespectful.

observe, behold, comprehend, detect, discover, examine, eye, heed, inspect, mark, note, perceive, regard, see, view, watch; celebrate, commemorate, keep; express, mention, remark, utter. ANT.—avoid, disobey, disregard, ignore, neglect, overlook.

obsolete, ancient, antiquated, antique, archaic, disused, extinct, forgotten, obsolescent, old, old-fashioned, outdated, outmoded, out-of-date, outworn, primitive, rejected, timeworn. ANT.—current, modern, new, novel, recent, up-to-date.

obstacle, bar, barrier, block, check, difficulty, hindrance, impedi-

ment, interruption, obstruction, snag, stumbling block. ANT.— aid, blessing, boost, clearance, encouragement, help.

obstinate, contumacious, determined, dogged, firm, fixed, headstrong, immovable, indomitable, inflexible, intractable, mulish, obdurate, persistent, pertinacious, recalcitrant, resolute, stubborn, unaffected, uncompromising, unflinching, unyielding, willful. ANT.—amenable, compliant, docile, pliable, submissive.

obstruct, bar, barricade, block, choke, clog, close, cramp, cripple, curb, dam, frustrate, hamper, hinder, impede, inhibit, interfere, oppose, prevent, restrain, retard, stop, thwart. ANT.—assist, facilitate, forward, promote, support; clear, open.

obtain, acquire, assimilate, attain, collect, earn, gain, gather, get, procure, recover, secure, win. ANT.—forfeit, forsake, lose, miss, sacrifice.

obtuse, blunt, dense, dull, heavy, impassive, insensitive, phlegmatic, slow, stolid, stupid, unintelligent. ANT.—acute, brilliant, imaginative, keen, quick, sharp.

obvious, apparent, clear, comprehensible, conclusive, definite, distinct, evident, explicit, intelligible, lurid, manifest, palpable, patent, plain, precise, self-evident, unmistakable, visible.

ANT.—ambiguous, confused, esoteric, obscure, puzzling.

occupation, business, calling, commerce, craft, employment, enterprise, job, mission, position, profession, pursuit, trade, vocation, work.

occupy, absorb, busy, employ, engage, engross, entertain, fill, hold, keep, monopolize; capture, invade, seize; dwell, inhabit, own, possess, tenant, use. ANT.—relinquish, surrender; abandon, empty, leave, vacate.

occurrence, affair, circumstance, episode, event, eventuality, happening, incident, issue, occasion, proceeding, transaction.

odd, abnormal, bizarre, curious, eccentric, erratic, exceptional, extraordinary, mysterious, peculiar, quaint, queer, rare, singular, strange, unique, unnatural, unusual, weird; alone, lone, remaining, single, uneven, unmatched. ANT.—common, familiar, natural, normal, ordinary; even, matched.

odious, abhorrent, base, debased, depraved, detestable, disgusting, foul, hateful, hideous, horrible, loathsome, obnoxious, repellent, repugnant, repulsive, revolting, vicious, vile, wicked; abject, ignoble, low, mean, worthless, wretched. ANT.—delightful, inviting, lovable, pleasant, refreshing; honorable, upright, wholesome.

odor, aroma, essence, fetidness, fetor, fragrance, fume, incense, perfume, redolence, reek, scent, smell, stench, stink.

offense, affront, atrocity, indignity, injury, insult, outrage; aggression, assault, attack, crime, fault, felony, injustice, misdeed, misdemeanor, scandal, sin, transgression, trespass, vice, wrong. ANT.—compliment, defense, gentleness, support; justice, morality, right.

offer, overture, proposal, proposition, suggestion; advance, bid, exhibit, extend, move, present, proffer, propose, sacrifice, submit, suggest, tender, volunteer. ANT.—denial, rejection, withdrawal; refuse, reject, withdraw, withhold.

often, commonly, frequently, generally, ofttimes, recurrently, repeatedly. ANT.—infrequently, rarely, seldom, sporadically.

old, aged, ancient, antediluvian, antiquated, antique, archaic, elderly, experienced, faded, immemorial, obsolete, old-fashioned, patriarchal, prehistoric, remote, superannuated, venerable. ANT.—contemporary, current, fresh, inexperienced, modern.

omen, augury, auspice, emblem, foreboding, foreshadow, gesture, harbinger, indication, mark, note, portent, precursor, prediction, presage, proof, sign, signal, symbol, symptom, token, warning.

omit, bar, cancel, delete, discard, disregard, drop, eliminate, evade, except, exclude, forget, ignore, miss, neglect, overlook, preclude, reject, repudiate, skip, spare. ANT.—add, enroll, enter, include, insert, introduce, notice.

onerous, arduous, burdensome, difficult, hard, heavy, laborious, oppressive, tough; exacting, intricate, perplexing, ponderous, puzzling, troublesome. ANT.— easy, effortless, facile, trivial; clear, simple.

only, barely, but, entirely, exclusively, just, merely, particularly, simply, singly, solely, totally, uniquely, utterly, wholly.

opaque, cloudy, dark, dim, dull, dusky, filmy, gloomy, misty, murky, non-transparent, obfuscated, obscure, shadowy, shady, smoky, unilluminated. ANT.— crystalline, glassy, lustrous, pellucid, transparent.

open, agape, ajar, apart, gaping, unbarred, unclosed, uncovered, unlocked, unobstructed, unsealed; clear, passable, unobstructed; available, disengaged, free, unoccupied; accessible, exposed, public, undefended, unrestricted; artless, candid, explicit, frank, honest, overt, plain, sincere, unreserved; exhibit, expand, expose, rend, reveal, show, spread, start, unbar, unfasten, unfold, unlock, unseal. ANT.—blocked, closed, locked; impassable, obstructed; busy, engaged, occupied; concealed, hidden, private; covert, crafty,

cunning, designing, hypocritical; block, conceal, exclude, hinder, secrete.

operate, act, behave, comport, conduct, demean, deport, direct, execute, function, interact, manage, manipulate, perform, react, run, transact, work.

operation, act, action, agency, effort, enterprise, execution, instrumentality, maneuver, manipulation, performance, procedure, proceeding, process, transaction, working. ANT.— cessation, inaction, inactivity, inefficiency, uselessness.

operative, acting, active, busy, efficacious, efficient, effective, effectual, industrious, moving, performing, working. ANT.— dormant, inactive, inefficient, quiet, still.

opinion, belief, conclusion, consensus, conviction, determination, feeling, idea, impression, judgment, notion, persuasion, sentiment, theory, thought, verdict, view. ANT.—fact, knowledge.

opponent, adversary, antagonist, assailant, challenger, competitor, contestant, disputant, encroacher, enemy, foe, infringer, intruder, rival, violator. ANT.— ally, colleague, comrade, consort, partner.

opportunity, advantage, chance, contingency, occasion, occurrence, opening, possibility, situation, timeliness. ANT.— blockage, deterrent, disadvantage, hindrance, obstacle.

oppose, antagonize, bar, check, combat, confront, contradict, contrast, contravene, counteract, cross, defy, deny, hinder, impede, interfere, obstruct, protest, rebuff, resist, restrain, retaliate, snub, thwart, withstand. ANT.—approve, collude, endorse, fraternize, sanction, support.

opposite, antithesis, antonymous, contradictory, contrary, inverse, reverse. ANT.—compatible, counterpart, identical, like, same.

oppress, afflict, annoy, badger, burden, crush, harass, harry, hound, maltreat, overbear, overwhelm, persecute, pester, plague, torment, torture, tyrannize, vex, worry. ANT.—aid, assist, comfort, relieve, support.

optimistic, assured, confident, encouraging, enthusiastic, expectant, heartening, hopeful, inspiriting, promising, trusting. ANT.—despairing, doubtful, gloomy, hopeless, pessimistic.

option, alternative, choice, discretion, election, preference, prerogative, right, selection.

opulent, abundant, affluent, luxurious, moneyed, plentiful, profuse, rich, sumptuous, wealthy. ANT.—destitute, indigent, limited, poor, scarce, squalid.

oral, articulate, mouthed, said, spoken, uttered, verbal, vocal. ANT.—printed, recorded, written.

ordain, appoint, assign, command, commission, constitute, create, decree, delegate, destine, enact, install, institute, invest, order, prescribe, select. ANT.—abolish, abrogate, cancel, depose, dismiss, invalidate.

ordeal, affliction, agony, assay, cross, hardship, judgment, misery, misfortune, pain, strain, suffering, test, trial, tribulation. ANT.—alleviation, comfort, joy, pleasure.

order, arrangement, class, method, plan, rank, regularity, sequence, series, succession, symmetry, system; bidding, canon, command, decree, dictate, directive, injunction, instruction, law, mandate, precept, prescription, regulation, requirement, rule; appoint, arrange, bid, conduct, demand, direct, govern, exact, impose, methodize, ordain, proclaim, regulate, rule, systematize. ANT.—chaos, confusion, disorder, irregularity, muddle, perplexity; allowance, consent, liberty, permission; confuse, disorganize, misdirect, misguide.

ordinary, accustomed, average, common, consistent, conventional, customary, familiar, habitual, medium, natural, normal, regular, typical, usual; inferior, low, plain, trite, vulgar. ANT.—bizarre, eccentric, irregular, strange, unconventional; exceptional, exclusive, extraordinary, wonderful.

organic, constitutional, essential, fundamental, inherent, innate, natural, radical, structural, systematic, vital. ANT.—external, extraneous, inorganic, nonessential.

organization, arrangement, association, constitution, construction, establishment institution, method, mode, order, plan, process, regularity, rule, scheme, system. ANT.—chaos, disarray, disorganization, irregularity, labyrinth, maze.

organize, adjust, arrange, assort, classify, constitute, co-ordinate, devise, dispose, establish, form, found, frame, institute, plan, prepare, regulate, shape, systematize. ANT.—destroy, disband, disorganize, disperse, divide, scatter.

origin, beginning, birth, cause, commencement, cradle, derivation, foundation, inception, outset, rise, root, source, spring, start. ANT.—conclusion, consequence, finality, harvest, result, termination.

original, aboriginal, archetypal, causal, etiological, first, formative, inceptive, initial, primary, rudimentary; creative, fresh, inventive, model, new, novel, unique. ANT.—consequential, derivative, emanating, evolved, terminal; banal, copied, imitated, plagiarized.

ornamental, adorning, beautifying, decorative, embellishing, garnishing, gilt, ornate.

oscillate, change, fluctuate, hesitate, swing, undulate, vacillate, vary, vibrate, waver. ANT.—

halt, persist, remain, resolve, stay.

ostentation, boasting, bravado, display, exhibition, flourish, glitter, gloss, pageantry, parade, pomp, pomposity, pretension, show, tinsel, vanity, vaunting, veneer. ANT.—humility, modesty, reserve, restraint, timidity.

ostracize, banish, bar, blackball, deport, except, exclude, exile, expel, hinder, omit, prevent, prohibit, restrain. ANT.—accept, admit, embrace, include, welcome.

oust, banish, deport, depose, discharge, dislodge, dismiss, dispel, dispossess, eject, evict, exclude, exile, expatriate, expel, fire, ostracize, proscribe, reject, remove. ANT.—admit, appoint, empower, harbor, retain, shelter.

outcome, conclusion, consequence, destiny, effect, end, fate, fortune, issue, lot, outgrowth, portion, result, sequel, termination, upshot.

outline, alignment, boundary, brief, configuration, contour, delineation, draft, drawing, figure, form, framework, perimeter, plan, profile, representation, silhouette, skeleton, sketch, tracing.

outrage, abuse, affront, atrocity, grievance, indignity, injury, insult, maltreatment, mortification, offense, oppression, persecution, shock, transgression, trespass, vice, violation.

outrageous, abominable, abusive, atrocious, despicable, excessive, fierce, flagrant, furious, heinous, monstrous, nefarious, scandalous, villainous, violent, wanton, wicked. ANT.—calm, dispassionate, favorable, peaceable, soothing, tranquil.

outspoken, abrupt, bluff, blunt, brusque, candid, direct, forthright, frank, impolite, open, plain, rough, rude, unceremonious, unreserved. ANT.—cautious, circumspect, misleading, reserved, sincere, suave, taciturn.

outstanding, conspicuous, distinguished, dominant, eminent, exceptional, important, notable, noticeable, prominent, remarkable, salient, striking, superior; owing, unpaid, unsettled. ANT.—average, commonplace, inconspicuous, ordinary, usual; paid, settled.

overcome, beat, conquer, crush, defeat, humble, master, overpower, overthrow, quell, rout, subdue, subjugate, suppress, surmount, vanquish. ANT.—fail, lose, succumb, surrender, yield.

overflowing, abounding, abundant, ample, bountiful, copious, fruitful, plenteous, plentiful, profuse, sufficient, teeming, unlimited. ANT.—deficient, insufficient, poor, scanty, scarce.

overlook, disregard, drop, eliminate, exclude, forget, ignore, miss, neglect, omit, skip, slight; condone, excuse, forgive, pardon; dominate, examine, inspect, oversee, supervise.

ANT.—note, observe, regard, see, watch; charge, indict, punish; acquiesce, serve, surrender.

oversee, administer, command, direct, engineer, execute, guide, maintain, manage, order, preside, superintend, supervise. ANT.—obey, follow, take orders.

oversight, aberration, blunder, error, failure, fault, inadvertence, inattention, lapse, mistake, neglect, omission, slip; charge, control, direction, guidance, inspection, management, regulation, superintendence, supervision, surveillance, watchfulness. ANT.—attention, care, diligence.

overt, apparent, candid, frank, honest, manifest, obvious, open, patent, plain, public, unconcealed, undisguised. ANT.—concealed, covert, hidden, latent, private, secret.

overthrow, abolish, conquer, crush, defeat, demolish, destroy, extirpate, obliterate, overcome, overpower, overturn, rout, ruin, subjugate, subvert, supplant, upset, vanquish. ANT.—assist, develop, maintain, preserve, restore, support.

overwhelm, see **overthrow**.

own, admit, allow, avow, concede, confess, control, disclose, hold, possess, recognize, retain, reveal. ANT.—deny, disavow, lack, lose, need, reject.

P

pacific, calm, composed, conciliatory, dispassionate, gentle, imperturbable, nonviolent, peaceful, placid, quiet, restful, serene, smooth, tranquil, undisturbed, unruffled, untroubled. ANT.—belligerent, combative, rough, stormy, tempestuous, turbulent.

pacify, allay, alleviate, ameliorate, appease, assuage, calm, compose, lull, mollify, placate, quell, quiet, reconcile, relieve, satisfy, soothe, still, subdue, quell, settle, tranquilize. ANT.—anger, antagonize, excite, incense, rile, roil.

pack, assemblage, amount, bag, band, bundle, collection, company, concourse, gathering, group, load, luggage, number, package, parcel, trunk, valise; arrange, bind, brace, collect, compress, condense, cram, gather, prepare, press, squeeze, stuff, tie. ANT.—allocate, distribute, dispose, loosen, scatter.

pact, agreement, alliance, arrangement, bargain, bond, cartel, compact, concord, contract, covenant, deal, league, stipulation, treaty, understanding, union.

pain, affliction, agony, anguish, discomfort, distress, grief, misery, suffering, torment, torture, woe; ache, pang, paroxysm, throe, twinge. ANT.—happiness, pleasure, solace, wellbeing; comfort, ease, relief.

painful, agonizing, bitter, distressing, excruciating, galling, grievous, poignant, racking; arduous, difficult, toilsome. ANT.—delightful, enjoyable, pleasant, sweet; easy, effortless, facile.

paint, adorn, color, daub, decorate, delineate, describe, explain, express, ornament, picture, portray, reveal; pigment; cosmetic, rouge.

palpable, apparent, appreciable, clear, discernible, evident, explicit, manifest, obvious, patent, perceptible, plain, prominent, self-evident, sensible, unmistakable, visible; bodily, corporeal, material, physical, real, sensible, tangible. ANT.—concealed, doubtful, mysterious, obscure, questionable; incorporeal, mental, spiritual.

paltry, abject, contemptible, despicable, insignificant, low, mean, measly, miserable, petty, picayune, pitiful, poor, puny, worthless. ANT.—important, large, momentous, rich, significant.

panic, alarm, apprehension, consternation, dismay, dread, fear, fright, horror, perturbation, terror, trembling, tremor, trepidation. ANT.—calm, composure, placidity, repose, serenity.

parade, cavalcade, cortege, file, procession, retinue, sequence, succession, train; display, expose, flaunt, publish, show, vaunt; march, strut.

paradox, absurdity, ambiguity, contradiction, enigma, inconsistency, mystery, perplexity, puzzle.

parallel, akin, alike, allied, analogous, comparable, concentric, concurrent, congruent, congruous, correlative, correspondent, corresponding, like, regular, similar, uniform. ANT.—different, divergent, incongruous, opposed, unique.

paralyze, astound, benumb, cripple, daunt, daze, deaden, demoralize, disable, dumfound, incapacitate, petrify, prostrate, stun, unnerve. ANT.—excite, revive, stimulate, vitalize.

pardon, absolve, acquit, condone, efface, exculpate, excuse, exonerate, forgive, liberate, overlook, quash, release, remit; absolution, acquittal, amnesty, deliverance, discharge, forgiveness, freedom, parole, release, remission, respite. ANT.—banish, castigate, chastise, condemn, punish; chastisement, penalty, punishment, retaliation, vengeance.

parley, chat, colloquy, conference, conversation, dialogue, interview, talk; argue, confer, converse, debate, dispute, negotiate, palaver, talk.

parody, burlesque, caricature, imitation, joke, lampoon, mimicry, mockery, spoof, travesty.

parsimonious, acquisitive, avaricious, covetous, frugal, greedy, grudging, mercenary, miserly, penurious, scrimping, sparing, stingy, tight, ungenerous. ANT.—altruistic, generous, lavish, liberal, prodigal.

part, allotment, apportionment, bit, chip, chunk, division, fragment, lump, moiety, morsel, piece, portion, scrap, section, segment, share, slice, subdivision; component, element, ingredient, member; concern, constituent, faction, interest, party, side; character, lines, role; detach, disunite, dissever, dissociate, divide, separate, sever, sunder; allot, apportion, distribute, share. ANT.—aggregate, entirety, sum, whole; combine, gather, join, unite; keep, withhold.

partiality, bent, bias, bigotry, favoritism, fondness, inclination, leaning, liking, preconception, predisposition, preference, prejudice, tendency, unfairness. ANT.—equality, fairness, honor, impartiality, justice.

participate, associate, commune, cooperate, enjoy, join, mingle, partake, share, unite, use.

particle, atom, bit, corpuscle, crumb, element, grain, iota, jot, mite, molecule, scintilla, scrap, shred, smidgen, speck, whit. ANT.—aggregate, entirety, mass, total, whole.

particular, characteristic, distinctive, exclusive, individual, peculiar, singular, specific, unusual; detailed, exact, minute, precise; careful, discrete, fastidious, meticulous, painstaking, scrupulous, squeamish; circumstance, detail, item, minutia, part, portion, section. ANT.—comprehensive, general, universal, usual; fallacious, ordinary; negligent, nonchalant, slovenly, untidy; generality.

partisan, adherent, aide, ally, assistant, attendant, backer, champion, devotee, disciple, follower, henchman, successor, supporter, votary. ANT.—chief, director, leader, master.

partner, accomplice, ally, assistant, associate, colleague, companion, comrade, confederate, consort, co-worker, crony, mate, participant, spouse. ANT.—adversary, enemy, foe, opponent, stranger.

pass, course, crossing, opening, passageway, route; license, passport, permit, ticket; lunge, thrust; advance, approve, depart, die, disappear, disregard, expire, go, ignore, move, overcome, overlook, overstep, ratify, recede, sanction, skip, surpass, transcend, vanish.

passable, acceptable, adequate, admissible, allowable, average, endurable, fair, mediocre, middling, ordinary, so-so, tolerable; navigable, penetrable, traversable. ANT.—excellent, inferior, intolerable, superior; impassable.

passage, aisle, arcade, avenue, channel, corridor, course, gateway, hall, pass, path, road, way.

passion, ardor, craving, desire, ecstasy, eroticism, excitement, fascination, fervor, frenzy, hunger, infatuation, intensity, lust, yearning. ANT.—calm, dispassion, frigidity, indifference, restraint, tranquility.

passionate, ardent, burning, excitable, extreme, fervent, fervid, feverish, fiery, glowing, hot, impetuous, intense, irascible, quickened, vehement, violent. ANT.—apathetic, calm, cool, dull, impassive, phlegmatic.

passive, cold, dull, idle, inactive, indifferent, inert, quiet, receptive, relaxed, resigned, stoical, submissive, supine, unresisting. ANT.—active, assertive, dynamic, operative, resistant.

patch, fix, mend, rebuild, renew, repair, restore, revamp, sew; ameliorate, better, correct, improve, rectify, remedy. ANT.—damage, destroy, impair, injure, ravage.

patent, apparent, clear, conspicuous, evident, manifest, obvious, open, overt, plain, unconcealed, unmistakable. ANT.—concealed, covered, covert, hidden, obscure.

path, access, avenue, channel, course, lane, passage, pathway, read, route, runway, sidewalk, street, thoroughfare, track, trail, walk, way.

pathetic, affecting, distressing, heart-rending, moving, piteous, pitiable, pitiful, plaintive, poignant, sad, touching. ANT.—cheering, comical, funny, happy, joyful.

patience, composure, constancy, endurance, forbearance, fortitude, imperturbability, moderation, perseverance, persistence, resignation, submission, sufferance, tolerance. ANT.—disquietude, excitability, impatience, petulance, perturbation, rage.

patient, assiduous, calm, composed, enduring, forbearing, gentle, imperturbable, indulgent, lenient, long-suffering, passive, placid, resigned, serene, stoical, submissive, tolerant, uncomplaining. ANT.—clamorous, high-strung, hysterical, irritable, turbulent, ungovernable.

pattern, archetype, blueprint, conformation, copy, exemplar, guide, ideal, model, mold, norm, original, outline, paradigm, paragon, plan, prototype, sample, standard.

pause, delay, demur, desist, doubt, falter, halt, hesitate, intermit, stop, vacillate, waver, wait; break, cessation, discontinuance, hesitation, intermission, interruption, lull, recess, suspension. ANT.—continue, persevere, proceed, resolve; continuance, continuity, extension, persistence, progression.

pay, allowance, compensation, earnings, fee, indemnity, payment, recompense, remuneration, reparation, retribution, reward, salary, settlement, stipend, wages; compensate, defray, discharge, expend, liquidate, offer, recompense, refund, reimburse, remunerate, reward, settle. ANT.—default, expenditure, expense, forfeiture, nonpayment, outlay, penalty; bilk, cheat, defraud, swindle, victimize.

peace, accord, agreement, amity, armistice, calm, conciliation, concord, harmony, hush, order, pacifism, quiescence, quiet, repose, serenity, silence, stillness, tranquility. ANT.—conflict, discord, disruption, fracas, uproar, warfare.

peaceful, calm, complacent, composed, gentle, mellow, mild, pacific, placid, quiet, serene, still, tranquil, undisturbed, unruffled. ANT.—agitated, noisy, perturbed, turbulent, upset, violent.

peak, acme, apex, climax, consummation, crest, culmination, height, high point, pinnacle, spire, summit, top, zenith. ANT.—abyss, base, bottom, lowest point, nadir.

peculiar, abnormal, bizarre, eccentric, exceptional, extraordinary, idiosyncratic, odd, rare, singular, strange, striking, unusual; characteristic, distinctive, especial, individual, particular, special, specific. ANT.—common, normal, ordinary, regular, visual.

peculiarity, attribute, characteristic, eccentricity, feature, idiosyncrasy, irregularity, mark, oddity, property, quality, singularity, trait. ANT.—normality, regularity, uniformity.

pedantic, academic, bookish, erudite, formal, impractical, learned, precise, professorial, scholarly, scholastic, theoretical; affected, dry, dull, stilted, stuffy, tedious. ANT.—ignorant, practical, simple; interesting, lively, stimulating.

peer, colleague, companion, compeer, equal, fellow, match, mate; aristocrat, knight, lord, nobleman. ANT.—commoner, inferior, superior.

peevish, acrimonious, cantankerous, cross, faultfinding, fractious, fretful, grouchy, grumbling, ill-natured, ill-tempered, irritable, moody, petulant, snappish, sulky, testy, touchy, ungracious, waspish. ANT.—affable, genial, gracious, pleasant, soothing.

penalty, chastisement, damages, fine, forfeiture, punishment, retribution; disadvantage, handicap. ANT.—benefit, compensation, forgiveness, prize, remuneration, reward.

penetrating, abstruse, deep, profound, recondite, solemn; acute, astute, clever, discerning, discriminating, incisive, keen, piercing, sagacious, sharp, shrewd. ANT.—shallow, slight, superficial, trivial; dull, idiotic, muddled, obtuse, stupid.

penitent, contrite, regretful, remorseful, repentant, sorrowful, sorry. ANT.—impenitent, incontrite, obdurate, remorseless.

penniless, beggared, destitute, empty-handed, fortuneless, impecunious, indigent, needy, poor, poverty-stricken. ANT.—affluent, opulent, prosperous, rich, wealthy.

pensive, contemplative, dreamy, grave, introspective, meditative, musing, reflective, serious, solemn, speculative, thoughtful. ANT.—careless, extroverted, heedless, rash, thoughtless, unconcerned.

penurious, avaricious, cheap, covetous, grasping, greedy, mercenary, miserly, parsimonious, stingy, tight, ungenerous. ANT.—altruistic, bountiful, charitable, generous, liberal, philanthropic.

people, citizens, community, inhabitants, populace, population; family, kindred, relations, siblings; humanity, human race, mankind; nationality, race, tribe; crowd, folk, masses, mob, multitude, rabble.

perceive, conceive, discern, note, notice, observe, recognize, see, sense; apprehend, comprehend, realize, understand. ANT.—confuse, ignore, miss, overlook; misapprehend, misunderstand.

perceptible, apparent, appreciable, apprehensible, discernible, noticeable, palpable, sensible, tangible, visible. ANT.—absurd, impalpable, imperceptible, invisible, obscure.

perception, acumen, acuteness, apprehension, cognizance, comprehension, discernment, insight, keenness, recognition, sharpness, understanding.

perceptive, alert, apprised, aware, cognizant, incisive, keen, observant. ANT.—dense, ignorant, mindless, obtuse, unaware.

perfect, complete, consummate, entire, finished, whole; blameless, faultless, flawless, immaculate, impeccable, ideal, infallible, inviolate, irreproachable, supreme, unblemished, unqualified. ANT.—deficient, incomplete, lacking, unfinished; blemished, defective, flawed, imperfect, worthless.

perform, accomplish, achieve, act, conduct, do, effect, execute, fulfill, impersonate, play, pretend. ANT.—fail, loaf, neglect, refrain, rest.

performance, accomplishment, achievement, action, deed, demonstration, entertainment, exploit, feat, production, show, spectacle, stunt.

perhaps, conceivably, haply, maybe, mayhap, peradventure, perchance, possibly, reasonably. ANT.—certainly, definitely, impossibly.

peril, danger, exposure, hazard, insecurity, jeopardy, liability, menace, pitfall, risk, snare. ANT.—immunity, protection, safety, security.

perimeter, ambit, border, boundary, circuit, circumference, compass, edge, periphery. ANT.—center, core, heart, hub, middle.

period, age, circuit, cycle, date, duration, epoch, era, interim, interval, limit, season, span, spell, tempo, term, time.

perish, cease, decay, decease, depart, die, expire, pass away, succumb, vanish. ANT.—exist, flourish, live, survive, thrive.

permanent, abiding, changeless, constant, durable, enduring, established, everlasting, fixed, indelible, indestructible, invariant, lasting, perpetual, persistent, stable, unalterable, unchangeable, unchanging. ANT.—ephemeral, mutable, temporary, transitory, vacillating, variable.

permeate, drench, imbue, impregnate, infiltrate, infuse, ingrain, penetrate, pervade, saturate, soak, steep.

permission, allowance, approval, authority, authorization, confirmation, consent, dispensation, enfranchisement, grace, leave, liberty, license, permit, sanction, tolerance, toleration, verification. ANT.—denial, opposition, prohibition, refusal, veto.

permit, admit, allow, approve, authorize, empower, endorse, give, grant, let, recognize, sanction, suffer, tolerate, yield; charter, law, license, pass, passport, patent, permission, warrant. ANT.—bar, forbid, inhibit, oppose, restrain; ban, embargo, inhibition, injunction, restriction.

perpendicular, erect, plumb, straight, upright, upstanding, vertical. ANT.—horizontal, level, oblique, slanting.

perpetrate, accomplish, do, commit, enact, execute, inflict, perform. ANT.—fail, miscarry, ignore, neglect.

perpetual, ceaseless, continual, constant, deathless, endless, enduring, eternal, everlasting, immortal, incessant, infinite, interminable, lasting, permanent, timeless, unceasing, undying, uninterrupted. ANT.—ephemeral, evanescent, finite, fleeting, temporal.

perplex, annoy, baffle, bewilder, complicate, confound, confuse, disconcert, disorganize, dumfound, entangle, fluster, mislead, muddle, mystify, puzzle, snarl, trouble, worry. ANT.—clarify, explain, illumine, inform, instruct.

perplexing, bewildering, complex, complicated, compound, confusing, difficult, intricate, involved, mystifying, puzzling. ANT.—clear, lucid, manifest, obvious, plain, simple.

persecute, abuse, afflict, aggrieve, annoy, badger, bother, castigate, gall, harass, harry, hound, maltreat, oppress, pester, plague, punish, rile, scourge, tease, torment, torture, vex, victimize, worry. ANT.—aid, assist, comfort, gladden, nurture, support.

persevere, abide, continue, endure, last, persist, prevail, pursue, remain, survive, sustain. ANT.—cease, desist, surrender, vacillate, waver.

perseverance, assiduity, constancy, determination, diligence, grit, industry, persistence, persistency, pertinacity, pluck, resolution, steadfastness, tenacity. ANT.—cessation, idleness, inertia, laziness, procrastination, sloth.

persist, see persevere.

persistence, see perseverance.

persistent, constant, determined, enduring, firm, fixed, immovable, indefatigable, lasting, persevering, resolute, steadfast, steady, tenacious; contumacious, dogged, headstrong, importunate, insistent, obstinate, pertinacious, perverse, stubborn. ANT.—dawdling, doubtful, hesitant, unsure, vacillating, wavering; humble, pliable, reasonable, submissive, yielding.

personality, being, character, disposition, identify, individuality, nature, oneself, self, style, temper, temperament; celebrity, cynosure, notable, star.

perspicuity, clarity, clearness, discrimination, distinctness, explicitness, intelligibility, lucidity, preciseness. ANT.—confusion, mystification, obscurity, perplexity, vagueness.

persuade, allure, arouse, cajole, coax, convince, entice, exhort, incite, induce, influence, lead, lure, move, prevail upon, prompt, provoke, urge, win over. ANT.—deter, dissuade, divert, hinder, repress, restrain.

persuasion, allegiance, belief, conviction, creed, faith, religion; enticement, incitement, inducement, influence, suasion.

pertain, appertain, apply, belong (to), concern, refer (to), relate (to).

pertinacious, constant, contumacious, determined, dogged, firm, headstrong, immovable, inflexible, intractable, obdurate, obstinate, persistent, resolute, stubborn, tenacious, unyielding. ANT.—compliant, docile, flexible, submissive, yielding.

pertinent, applicable, appropriate, apropos, apt, fit, fitting, germane, material, proper, relating, relevant, suited. ANT.—alien, extraneous, foreign, improper, irrelevant, unrelated.

perturb, agitate, aggravate, annoy, bother, discommode, disquiet, harass, heckle, irk, irritate, perplex, pester, plague, vex, worry. ANT.—assist, calm, delight, help, please.

pervade, diffuse, extend, fill, imbue, impregnate, infiltrate, overspread, penetrate, permeate, run through, saturate, spread.

perverse, cantankerous, contrary, contumacious, disobedient, dogged, forward, fractious, intractable, irascible, obstinate, peevish, petulant, resolute, splenetic, stubborn, ungovernable, unyielding; perverted, sinful, wayward, wicked. ANT.—agreeable, docile, manageable, obliging, tractable; angelic, saintly, virtuous.

perversion, abasement, abuse, corruption, debasement, degradation, depravity, desecration, falsification, humiliation, maltreatment, misuse, outrage, profanation, reviling, vitiation, wickedness. ANT.—elevation, enhancement, improvement, respect, veneration.

pessimistic, blue, cynical, depressed, desolate, despairing, despondent, doleful, downcast, foreboding, forlorn, gloomy, glum, hopeless, melancholy, misanthropic, rueful, spiritless. ANT.—bright, enthusiastic, hopeful, optimistic, trusting.

pester, annoy, badger, bait, bother, chafe, disturb, fret, harass, harry, heckle, inconvenience, irk, irritate, molest, plague, provoke, tease, torment, trouble, vex. ANT.—accommodate, comfort, delight, gratify, soothe, support.

petition, appeal, application, entreaty, invocation, plea, prayer, proposal, request, requisition, suit, solicitation, supplication.

petrify, calcify, deaden, fossilize, harden, lapidify, mineralize, ossify, solidify; amaze, astonish, benumb, frighten, paralyze, shock, stun, stupefy.

petty, childish, frivolous, insignificant, negligible, nugatory, paltry, puny, shallow, slight, small, trifling, trivial, unimportant, weak, worthless. ANT.—important, momentous, serious, significant, vital.

petulant, acrimonious, choleric, cranky, cross, crusty, fretful, ill-humored, ill-natured, ill-tempered, irascible, irritable, peevish, querulous, snappish, sullen, surly, testy, touchy, unamiable, waspish. ANT.—affable, congenial, good-natured, pleasant, temperate.

philanthropic, altruistic, beneficent, benevolent, charitable, compassionate, generous, gracious, humanitarian, liberal, magnanimous, munificent. ANT.—antisocial, cruel, egotistical, merciless, selfish.

phlegmatic, cold, dispassionate, impassive, inexcitable, passionless, stoical, stolid, unemotional, unfeeling. ANT.—ardent, demonstrative, enthusiastic, lively, passionate.

phobia, aversion, avoidance, disgust, dislike, distaste, fear, hatred, resentment. ANT.—attraction, endurance, liking, love, tolerance.

phraseology, diction, expression, idiom, language, locution, manner, phrasing, speech, style, usage, vocabulary, wording.

physical, anatomical, bodily, carnal, corporal, corporeal, material, mortal, natural, palpable, real, sensible, somatic, tangible, visible. ANT.—abstract, immaterial, incorporeal, spiritual, unreal.

pick, acquire, choose, cull, elect, gather, opt, prefer, select, single, take. ANT.—decline, refuse, reject.

picture, advertisement, appearance, blueprint, cartoon, cinema, design, draft, drawing, effigy, engraving, etching, facsimile, figure, film, illustration, image, landscape, likeness, lithograph, outline, pageant, painting, panorama, photo, photograph, portrait, portrayal, print, representation, scene, sketch,

spectacle, tableau, tracing, view; delineate, depict, draw, represent, sketch.

piece, amount, bit, chunk, fraction, fragment, hunk, morsel, part, portion, scrap, section, segment, shred; combine, patch, repair, unite. ANT.—all, entirety, sum, total, whole.

pigment, brilliance, color, coloration, coloring, complexion, dye, hue, intensity, oil paint, paint, shade, stain, taint, tincture, tinge, tint, wash.

pinnacle, acme, apex, chief, climax, crest, crown, culmination, head, peak, summit, top, zenith. ANT.—base, bottom, depths, foot, foundation, nadir.

pious, blessed, consecrated, devotional, devout, divine, godly, hallowed, holy, prayerful, pure, religious, reverent, sacred, saintly, sanctified, seraphic, spiritual, unworldly.

blasphemous, evil, irreverent, profane, sacrilegious, wicked.

pitch, cast, chuck, fling, heave, hurl, launch, propel, sling, throw, thrust, toss; decline, slant, slope. ANT.—catch, grab, receive.

pitiful, clement, compassionate, lenient, merciful, tender, tenderhearted, sympathetic; abject, contemptible, despicable, vile, wretched; cheerless, doleful, lamentable, miserable, mournful, piteous, sad, sorrowful, tearful. ANT.—dignified, exalted, grand, joyful, noble, sublime.

pity, charity, clemency, commiseration, compassion, condol-

ence, empathy, kindness, mercy,
philanthropy, sympathy, tenderness. ANT.—brutality, cruelty,
inhumanity, ruthlessness, vengeance.

place, allocate, allot, arrange, assign, deposit, dispose, distribute,
group, install, invest, locate,
plant, put, set, store, stow; abode,
dwelling, home, residence; area,
locality, point, position, post, region, site, situation, spot, station. ANT.—disarrange, disturb,
empty, remove, unsettle.

placid, calm, composed, dispassionate, equable, gentle, imperturbable, pacific, peaceful, quiet,
serene, still, tranquil, undisturbed, unmoved, unruffled.
ANT.—agitated, disturbed, excited, stormy, turbulent, wild.

plague, see persecute.

plain, even, flat, level, smoothe;
apparent, clear, distinct, evident,
exposed, lucid, manifest, obvious, palpable, perceptible, rec-
ognizable, unmistakable, visible;
candid, definite, explicit, frank,
open, simple, sincère, unpretentious; absolute, unqualified.
ANT.—broken, rough, uneven;
abstruse, ambiguous, cloudy,
enigmatical, obscure, puzzling;
adorned, embellished, feigned,
insincere, pretentious; qualified.

plan, chart, contrive, create, delineate, design, devise, invent, map,
plot, prepare, scheme, shape; intent, mean, purpose; depict,
draw, illustrate, outline, sketch;
arrangement, blueprint, chart,

contrivance, delineation, design,
device, diagram, draft, drawing,
map, method, model, outline,
plot, policy, program, project,
proposal, proposition, prospectus, sketch, view.

plant, complex, establishment,
factory, foundry, mill, shop;
bush, flower, herb, organism,
shoot, shrub, sprout, vegetable;
establish, locate, place, put, set,
settle; bed, implant, pot, sow.

plastic, ductile, flexible, formable,
formative, impressible, malleable, pliant, resilient; artificial,
counterfeit, fabricated, false,
simulated. ANT.—brittle, hard,
rigid, stiff; authentic, genuine,
real.

plausible, acceptable, believable,
credible, defensible, feasible,
justifiable, likely, possible, practical, probable, reasonable, specious. ANT.—implausible,
impossible, incredible, unlikely,
visionary.

play, amusement, diversion, enjoyment, entertainment, fun,
game, pastime, pleasure, recreation, relaxation, sport; caper,
frisk, frolic, gambol, revel, romp,
skip, sport, stake, toy, wager;
execute, perform, work; act, impersonate, personate, pretend;
finger, pedal, pipe, sound, strum,
thrum; dissemble, feign, imagine, pretend, simulate; drama
piece, musical, theatrical; compete, engage, participate, rival.

plead, appeal, ask, beg, beseech,
crave, entreat, implore, petition,

press, request, solicit, supplicate, urge; advocate, argue, attest, claim, contend, declare, defend, indicate, maintain, proclaim, profess, pronounce, state, swear.

pleasant, acceptable, agreeable, amiable, attractive, charming, comforting, cordial, delightful, engaging, enjoyable, gratifying, honeyed, mellifluous, melodious, pleasing, pleasurable, suitable, welcome, winning. ANT.—disagreeable, hateful, obnoxious, offensive, painful, repellent, repulsive.

pleasing, see pleasant.

pleasure, amusement, bliss, comfort, contentment, delight, diversion, ease, ecstasy, enjoyment, entertainment, felicity, exhilaration, gladness, gratification, happiness, indulgence, light-heartedness, joy, rapture, satisfaction. ANT.—affliction, distress, grief, hopelessness, misery, suffering.

pledge, affirmation, agreement, assertion, assurance, commitment, contract, covenant, declaration, engagement, guarantee, oath, pact, promise, security, token, troth, vow, word; candidate; affirm, agree, bind, commit, declare, deposit, engage, guarantee, hypothecate, obligate, promise, swear, vouch, vow, wage. ANT.—break faith, deceive, deny, renounce.

plentiful, abundant, ample, bounteous, bountiful, copious, inexhaustible, lavish, liberal, luxurious, plenteous, profuse, replete, rich, teeming, unsparing. ANT.—deficient, drained, impoverished, scanty, scarce, stripped.

pliable, adaptable, adjustable, compliant, docile, ductile, elastic, flexible, limber, manageable, pliant, resilient, supple, tractable, wavering, yielding. ANT.—brittle, intractable, rigid, stiff, unyielding.

plot, artifice, cabal, conspiracy, design, development, intrigue, machination, plan, progress, scheme, stratagem, trick, unfolding; chart, diagram, draft, graph, outline, sketch; contrive, frame, plan, scheme; area, land, lot, parcel.

plump, buxom, chubby, corpulent, fleshy, paunchy, portly, pudgy, puffy, rotund, round, stout, swollen, thickset. ANT.—emaciated, gaunt, lean, slender, slim.

poignant, affecting, heart-rending, moving, pitiable, sad, tender, touching; acute, biting, penetrating, piercing, pungent, trenchant. ANT.—painless, pleasant; blunt, dull, insipid, numb, obtuse.

point, aim, designate, direct, indicate, level, punctuate, sharpen, show; acme, apex, characteristic, end, gist, goal, intent, juncture, location, meaning, object, peak, place, position, promontory, prong, purpose, significance, summit, trait.

pointed, acute, biting, caustic, cutting, keen, knifelike, penetrating, piercing, razor-edged, sarcastic, severe, sharp, spiked, stinging, trenchant. ANT.—bland, blunt, dull, gentle, unsharpened.

poise, balance, equilibrium, equipoise, gravity; class, composure, culture, dignity, self-possession, serenity, stateliness.

poisonous, corrupt, deadly, deleterious, destructive, evil, fatal, malignant, morbid, noisome, noxious, pestilential, toxic, venomous, virulent. ANT.—curative, harmless, healthful, invigorating, nourishing, wholesome.

policy, contract, course, handling, management, method, order, outline, plan, plank, platform, procedure, strategy, system, tactic.

polish, art, breeding, courtesy, culture, elegance, finish, glaze, gloss, glossiness, grace, luster, politeness, refinement, skill, smoothness, suavity, tact, training; brighten, burnish, civilize, discipline, refine, refinish, rub, shine, smooth, wax. ANT.—baseness, crudity, harshness, lowliness, roughness; debase, dull, mar, roughen, ruin.

polite, accomplished, attentive, civil, considerate, cordial, courteous, cultivated, decorous, diplomatic, genteel, mannerly, polished, refined, tactful, urbane, well-bred, well-mannered. ANT.—abusive, coarse, discourteous, impudent, offensive, rude.

pollute, adulterate, befoul, contaminate, corrupt, defile, demoralize, infect, pervert, poison, soil, sully, taint, vitiate. ANT.—clean, disinfect, purge, purify, sanitize.

pomp, boasting, display, flourish, glory, grandeur, magnificence, ostentation, pageantry, parade, show, splendor, vaunting. ANT.—humility, modesty, plainness, shabbiness, simplicity, tawdriness.

pompous, august, dignified, grand, high, imposing, lofty, magnificent, majestic, noble, spectacular, stately, sublime; arrogant, boastful, domineering, egotistical, flaunting, haughty, inflated, ostentatious, pretentious, swaggering. ANT.—banal, common, humble, lowly, ordinary; bashful, demure, modest, reserved, submissive.

ponder, calculate, cogitate, contemplate, deliberate, devise, examine, investigate, meditate, muse, reflect, ruminate, scrutinize, study, weigh. ANT.—forget, ignore, neglect, overlook.

ponderous, burdensome, cumbersome, heavy, massive, unwieldy, weighty; dull, gloomy, grave, spiritless; important, momentous, serious, significant. ANT.—airy, fluffy, light; animated, brisk, buoyant, volatile; insignificant, petty, trivial, unimportant.

poor, destitute, impecunious, impoverished, indigent, insolvent, needy, penniless, poverty-stricken, substandard, underprivileged; bad, defective, deficient, inferior, insignificant, mediocre, miserable, shabby, unfavorable. ANT.—affluent, opulent, rich, solvent, wealthy; ample, commendable, excellent, favorable, superior.

popular, common, current, familiar, general, lay, ordinary, plebeian, prevailing, prevalent, public, universal; admired, approved, desired, favorite, liked. ANT.—esoteric, exclusive, restricted; disliked, disreputable, shunned, unpopular.

pornographic, coarse, corrupt, debauched, depraved, dirty, disgusting, filthy, gross, immoral, indecent, lascivious, lecherous, lewd, obscene, prurient, smutty. ANT.—chaste, decent, modest, pure, refined.

port, anchorage, bay, berth, cove, dock, door, entrance, gateway, harbor, haven, inlet, portal, shelter; bearing, carriage, deportment, demeanor, manner, mien, presence.

portion, allotment, consignment, cutting, dividend, division, fraction, fragment, measure, morsel, parcel, part, piece, quota, ration, section, segment, share, slice, subdivision. ANT.—aggregation, entirety, mass, sum, total.

portray, act, characterize, copy, delineate, depict, describe, draw, figure, impersonate, paint, picture, represent, reproduce, reveal, show, sketch.

position, bearings, environment, ground, locality, location, place, post, seat, site, situation, spot, station; caste, condition, place, rank, standing, status; berth, employment, incumbency, job, occupation, office, post, profession, situation; attitude, belief, judgment, opinion, view; bearing, carriage, pose, posture.

positive, absolute, affirmative, assertive, assured, certain, concrete, decided, definite, dogmatic, emphatic, firm, fixed, incontrovertible, indubitable, inevitable, resolute, secure, sure, uncompromising, undeniable, unmistakable, unquestionable. ANT.—ambiguous, doubtful, dubious, hazy, questionable, uncertain.

possess, appropriate, control, dominate, have, hold, keep, obtain, occupy, own, reserve, retain, seize, take. ANT.—abandon, lack, lose, need, renounce, surrender.

possessions, assets, belongings, capital, commodities, effects, equity, estate, goods, holdings, investments, lands, legacy, merchandise, property, resources, stock, wares, wealth.

possibility, chance, contingency, event, feasibility, happening, hope, incident, occasion, occurrence, opening, opportunity, outside chance, plausibility, potentiality. ANT.—disadvantage, impossibility, hindrance, obstacle.

possible, achievable, attainable, conceivable, contingent, credible, feasible, liable, likely, obtainable, performable, plausible, potential, practical, probable. ANT.—foolish, impossible, inconceivable, unattainable, unreasonable.

postpone, adjourn, defer, delay, discontinue, interrupt, pigeonhole, procrastinate, protract, remand, retard, shelve, stall, stay, suspend, table, waive. ANT.—accelerate, continue, maintain, persevere, persist, proceed.

potent, capable, cogent, compelling, effective, efficacious, enduring, firm, forceful, forcible, great, hardy, influential, intense, irresistible, mighty, overpowering, powerful, puissant, robust, staunch, strong, sturdy, vigorous, virile. ANT.—delicate, enervated, fragile, impotent, weak.

pound, batter, beat, buffet, clout, club, crush, dash, drum, flail, hammer, hit, knock, pelt, pulverize, pummel, punch, smite, strike, thrash, thump, whack; palpitate, pulsate, pulse, throb.

poverty, dearth, deficiency, destitution, distress, exigency, inadequacy, indigence, necessity, need, pauperism, penury, privation, scarcity, want. ANT.—abundance, affluence, opulence, riches, wealth.

power, ability, capability, capacity, competence, efficacy, efficiency, endowment, potency, skill, talent; energy, force, might, stamina, strength, vigor; authority, command, control, dominion, government, influence, jurisdiction, mastery, predominance, preponderance, sway, sovereignty, superiority, supremacy. ANT.—impotence, inability, ineptitude; debility, infirmity, weakness; servitude, subjection, subservience.

powerful, see potent.

practical, balanced, down-to-earth, effective, feasible, functional, operative, pragmatic, rational, realistic, reasonable, sensible, sound, unromantic, useful, utilitarian, workable. ANT.—foolish, idealistic, imperceptible, impractical, outlandish, useless.

practice, application, custom, drill, exercise, fashion, habit, manner, method, mode, recitation, rehearsal, repetition, system, training, usage, use; clients, patients.

praise, acclaim, admire, applaud, approve, boost, commend, compliment, endorse, exalt, extol, flatter, glorify, laud, magnify, recommend, sanction. ANT.—admonish, berate, condemn, impugn, reproach, upbraid.

precarious, critical, dangerous, deadly, hazardous, insecure, menacing, perilous, risky, threatening, treacherous, unsafe, unstable; doubtful, dubious, unassured, uncertain. ANT.—protected, safe, secure, stable; assured, certain, unquestionable.

precept, adage, belief, canon, code, commandment, direction, creed, doctrine, dogma, injunction, instruction, law, mandate, maxim, regulation, rule, teaching, tenet.

precious, beloved, costly, darling, dear, esteemed, excellent, expensive, exquisite, high-priced, inestimable, invaluable, priceless, profitable, select, superior, superlative, unequaled, useful, valuable, worthy. ANT.—cheap, insignificant, trifling, valueless, worthless.

precipitate, accelerate, hasten, quicken, speed; abrupt, hasty, headlong, impetuous, rash, sudden. ANT.—check, delay, moderate, preclude, retard, slow; deliberate, intentional, reflective, thoughtful.

precise, accurate, correct, definite, distinct, exact, meticulous, punctilious, rigorous, scrupulous, strict, unequivocal; ceremonious, formal, prim, prudish, rigid, stiff. ANT.—ambiguous, fallacious, inexact, negligent, slipshod; casual, informal, loose, relaxed.

predicament, bind, corner, crisis, difficulty, dilemma, fix, mess, muddle, perplexity, pinch, plight, puzzle, quandary, scrape, situation, strait. ANT.—comfort, ease, security, solace, tranquility.

prediction, augury, divination, foreboding, forecast, foretelling, fortunetelling, horoscope, omen, presage, prognosis, prognostication, prophecy.

predominant, cardinal, chief, controlling, distinguished, dominant, essential, first, foremost, highest, leading, main, notable, paramount, preponderant, prevailing, prevalent, principal, reigning, ruling, sovereign, supreme. ANT.—insignificant, minor, obscure, subordinate, subsidiary.

preface, beginning, foreword, introduction, overture, preamble, prelude, prologue. ANT.—addendum, afterword, conclusion, ending, epilogue.

preference, alternative, choice, decision, election, favorite, option, pick, selection.

prejudice, animosity, antipathy, apartheid, aversion, bias, contempt, detriment, dislike, enmity, intolerance, objection, partiality, pique, preconception, predilection, prejudgment, prepossession, repugnance, revulsion, unfairness. ANT.—approval, benevolence, kindness, regard, respect, tolerance.

premature, anticipatory, early, green, hasty, immature, incomplete, precipitate, precocious, rash, raw, sudden, unanticipated, unexpected, unfinished, unprepared, unripe, unseasonable, untimely. ANT.—anticipated, completed, expected, fully developed, matured, tardy.

premeditated, calculated, contemplated, deliberate, designed, intended, intentional, planned, plotted, prearranged, predetermined, studied, voluntary. ANT.—accidental, casual, fortuitous, spontaneous, unforeseen.

premise, assumption, basis, criterion, evidence, foundation, groundwork, justification, postulate, presumption, presupposition, principle, proof, proposition, reason. ANT.—derivative, superstructure, trimming.

premium, appreciation, award, bonus, boon, bounty, enhancement, favor, gift, gratuity, present, prize, recompense, remuneration; best, choicest, highest quality, top grade. ANT.—inferior, low grade, poor, third rate.

preoccupied, absorbed, abstracted, distracted, engrossed, inattentive, musing, oblivious, unobservant. ANT.—attentive, watchful.

prepare, adjust, adapt, anticipate, arm, arrange, concoct, cook, develop, devise, equip, fit, fix, foresee, form, furnish, outfit, plan, predispose, prime, provide, qualify, ready, settle. ANT.—forget, ignore, neglect, overlook.

prerogative, authority, birthright, claim, grant, immunity, liberty, license, perquisite, privilege, right. ANT.—duty, injustice, limitation, obligation, violation.

present, advance, assign, award, bestow, confer, deliver, endow, exhibit, extend, give, grant, introduce, offer, proffer, propose, sacrifice, show, tender; boon, donation, gift, grant, gratuity; instant, now, today. ANT.—accept, receive, reject, spurn, take.

preserve, conserve, defend, guard, hold, keep, maintain, protect, rescue, safeguard, save, secure, shield, spare, support, sustain, uphold. ANT.—abandon, abolish, abrogate, destroy, forego, waste.

pressing, absorbing, compelling, constraining, critical, crucial, crying, distressing, exigent, impelling, imperative, important, importunate, insistent, necessary, serious, urgent, vital. ANT.—insignificant, meaningless, petty, superficial, trivial.

pressure, burden, compression, encumbrance, force, stress, tension, thrust, weight; affliction, coercion, compulsion, constraint, exigency, hurry, obligation, persuasion, stress, urgency. ANT.—relief, release; assistance, ease, encouragement, leniency, relaxation.

prestige, ascendancy, authority, credit, effect, fame, glory, honor, influence, power, rank, renown, repute, supremacy, weight. ANT.—impotence, insignificance, weakness, unimportance.

presume, assume, believe, conclude, conjecture, consider, guess, hypothesize, imagine, posit, presuppose, regard, speculate, suppose, surmise, theorize, think. ANT.—ascertain, confirm, demonstrate, manifest, prove.

pretense, affectation, affection, cloak, deceit, disguise, dissimulation, evasion, excuse, fabrication, falsification, garb, mask, pomposity, pretension, pretext, prevarication, ruse, semblance, sham, show, simulation, subterfuge, trickery, wile. ANT.—candor, frankness, honesty, sincerity, truth, veracity.

pretty, see handsome.

prevalent, accepted, catholic, common, comprehensive, controlling, familiar, frequent, general, ordinary, popular, predominant, prevailing, sweeping, ubiquitous, universal, usual, widespread, world-wide. ANT.—exceptional, extraordinary, infrequent, isolated, sporadic.

prevent, avert, block, check, foil, forestall, halt, hinder, impede, inhibit, interrupt, obstruct, obviate, preclude, prohibit, repress, stop, thwart. ANT.—allow, assist, expedite, further, promote, stimulate.

previous, aforesaid, antecedent, anterior, earlier, foregoing, former, preceding, prefatory, preliminary, preparatory, prior. ANT.—ensuing, latter, pursuant, subsequent, succeeding.

pride, arrogance, conceit, egoism, egotism, haughtiness, loftiness, pomposity, pretension, self-esteem; self-glorification, self-love, self-respect, superciliousness, vanity. ANT.—humility, meekness, modesty, reserve, self-effacement.

primary, basic, beginning, chief, earliest, elementary, first, fundamental, initial, leading, main, opening, original, prime, primeval, primitive, principal, pristine; chief, foremost. ANT.—following, hindmost, last, latest; inferior, least, secondary, subordinate.

primeval, first, initial, original, primary, primordial, pristine; creative, fresh, inventive, new, novel. ANT.—derivative, subsequent, terminal; banal, trite.

primitive, aboriginal, ancient, antiquated, archaic, early, old, primary, primeval, primordial, pristine; barbaric, crude, first, fundamental, rudimentary, simple, uncivilized, untaught. ANT.—civilized, complex, modern, polished, sophisticated.

primordial, see primeval.

principal, cardinal, chief, dominant, essential, first, foremost, greatest, highest, leading, main, paramount, predominant, preeminent, prime, supreme; chief, commander, director, executive, head, leader, master. ANT.—accessory, auxiliary, inferior, minor, negligible, unimportant; attendant, follower, pupil, subordinate.

principle, axiom, base, canon, doctrine, formula, foundation, ground, guide, law, maxim, method, order, policy, precept, reason, regulation, rule, statute, system, teaching, theorem; belief, conviction, faith; integrity, rectitude, uprightness.

prior, see previous.

private, clandestine, concealed, covert, hidden, latent, secluded, secret, sequestered, surreptitious, unknown, unrevealed; individual, personal. ANT.—disclosed, exposed, known, open, public.

privation, see poverty.

privilege, advantage, benefit, exemption, favor, franchise, freedom, immunity, liberty, license, perquisite, prerogative, right, sanction; chance, event, occasion, opportunity. ANT.—deprivation, disallowance, inhibition, limitation, prohibition, restriction.

prize, accolade, advantage, award, bonus, booty, bounty, citation, compensation, honor, inducement, laurel, possession, premium, privilege, recompense, remuneration, requital, reward, spoil. ANT.—charge, earnings, forfeiture, penalty, punishment.

problem, conundrum, difficulty, dilemma, enigma, intricacy, mystery, obstacle, perplexity, plight, puzzle, quandary, query, riddle. ANT.—answer, certainty, clarification, explanation, solution.

procedure, arrangement, course, custom, fashion, form, formula, habit, manner, method, mode, order, plan, practice, proceed-ing, process, routine, rule, style, system, technique, way.

proceed, advance, continue, forge ahead, improve, move, progress, rise, thrive. ANT.—recede, regress, retire, retreat, withdraw.

proceeds, crop, fruit, earnings, gain, gross, harvest, income, net, produce, product, profits, reaping, receipts, result, return, store, yield. ANT.—costs, expenses, outlay.

proclaim, advertise, affirm, announce, assert, aver, broadcast, circulate, declare, divulge, express, make known, profess, promulgate, protest, publish, reveal, state, tell, voice. ANT.—camouflage, conceal, mask, repress, suppress.

procrastinate, adjourn, dally, dawdle, defer, delay, extend, loiter, postpone, prolong, protract, retard, stall, suspend, tarry. ANT.—accelerate, hasten, hurry, persevere, quicken.

produce, aftermath, consequence, crop, effect, fruit, gain, goods, harvest, outcome, outgrowth, proceeds, product, profit, realization, reaping, result, return, store, yield; bear, breed, conceive, generate, hatch, procreate, propagate, sire, yield; fabricate, make, manufacture, supply; bring forward, exhibit, present, show; accomplish, author, cause, create, institute, issue, originate.

production, authoring, bearing, creation, erection, generation, harvest, making, origination, output, performance, procreation, product, project, rendering, work, yield.

profess, see proclaim.

proficient, able, accomplished, adept, adroit, agile, clever, competent, cunning, deft, dexterous, expert, gifted, ingenious, masterful, practiced, skilled, skillful, talented, versed. ANT.—bungling, incapable, incompetent, inept, maladroit, unskilled.

profit, advantage, benefit, earnings, emolument, gain, improvement, interest, proceeds, receipts, remuneration, return, returns, service, use. ANT.—destruction, detriment, failure, loss, ruin.

profligate, see corrupt.

profound, abstruse, abysmal, consummate, deep, erudite, heartfelt, heavy, intense, mysterious, penetrating, recondite, scholarly, serious, solemn. ANT.—frivolous, shallow, superficial, trivial, unenlightened, unlearned.

profuse, abundant, copious, excessive, extravagant, exuberant, immoderate, improvident, lavish, liberal, luxuriant, overflowing, plentiful, prodigal, redundant, superfluous, wasteful. ANT.—barren, deficient, inadequate, meager, scanty.

progress, advance, advancement, attainment, betterment, development, growth, headway, improvement, increase, locomotion, movement, proficiency, progression; advance, improve, move onward, press on, proceed, rise, thrive. ANT.—deferment, delay, moratorium, regression, suspension; backtrack, regress, resign, retard, retreat.

prohibit, ban, block, check, circumscribe, debar, deny, exclude, forbid, hinder, inhibit, interdict, preclude, prevent, proscribe, refuse, restrain, restrict, taboo, veto, withhold. ANT.—allow, empower, endorse, license, permit, sanction.

project, contrivance, design, device, idea, outline, plan, plot, procedure, projection, scheme, undertaking, working draft.

prolific, bountiful, breeding, fecund, fertile, fruitful, luxuriant, plenteous, productive, propagating, rich, swarming, teeming. ANT.—barren, sterile, unfruitful, unproductive.

prolong, amplify, augment, continue, elongate, extend, increase, lengthen, protract, stretch, sustain. ANT.—condense, curtail, shorten, shrink.

prominent, celebrated, conspicuous, distinguished, eminent, famous, illustrious, influential, leading, noteworthy, outstanding, popular, remarkable, salient, renowned, well-known; convex, extended, jutting, projecting, protruding. ANT.—common, humble, obscure, ordinary, unknown; concave, depressed, flat, level, sunken.

promise, affirmation, agreement, assurance, bestowal, betrothal, commitment, consent, contract, covenant, engagement, fulfillment, guarantee, insurance, oath, obligation, pact, pledge, swearing, troth, undertaking, vow.

promote, advance, aggrandize, aid, assist, contribute, cultivate, dignify, elevate, encourage, endow, exalt, facilitate, forward, foster, further, help, push, raise, urge. ANT.—degrade, discourage, hinder, impair, impede, obstruct.

prompt, arouse, cause, evoke, incite, induce, inspire, make, occasion, originate, provoke; active, alert, direct, early, immediate, instant, keen, precise, punctual, quick, ready, swift, timely, vigilant. ANT.—dilatory, late, overdue, slow, tardy.

promulgate, see proclaim.

proof, affidavit, attestation, confirmation, corroboration, credentials, data, demonstration, evidence, facts, reasons, substantiation, test, testimony, verification, warrant, witness. ANT.—aberrancy, failure, fallacy, invalidity, misconception, untruth.

propagate, beget, breed, create, develop, diffuse, disseminate, engender, father, generate, grow, increase, multiply, originate, procreate, produce, publish, raise, reproduce, sire, spread, teach. ANT.—annihilate, destroy, exterminate, extinguish, kill, ravage.

propel, actuate, agitate, drive, force, impel, induce, instigate,

move, persuade, push, start, thrust, urge. ANT.—delay, discourage, drag, halt, hinder, stop.

propensity, aim, aptitude, bent, bias, drift, flair, gift, inclination, knack, leaning, penchant, predilection, predisposition, prejudice, proclivity, proneness, tendency, trend. ANT.—antipathy, aversion, deviation, disinclination, dislike.

proper, appropriate, befitting, conventional, correct, decent, fair, fit, formal, just, legitimate, meet, pertinent, respectable, right, seemly, suitable; individual, peculiar, special. ANT.—improper, inaccurate, objectionable, unfit, unsuitable.

property, assets, belongings, capital, commodities, effects, equity, estate, goods, holdings, lands, merchandise, plot, possessions, premises, resources, stock, wares, wealth; attribute, characteristic, peculiarity, quality, trait.

propitious, auspicious, encouraging, favorable, fortunate, kindly, hopeful, lucky, opportune, promising.

proportion, balance, composure, dimension, equilibrium, equivalence, poise, relationship, share, stability, steadiness, symmetry. ANT.—fall, imbalance, inequality, instability, unsteadiness.

proposal, offer, overture, presentation, proposition, recommendation, suggestion, tender; design, idea, intention, outline, plan, program, prospectus, scheme. ANT.—acceptance, refusal, rejection, withdrawal.

proposition, see proposal.

proprietor, heritor, holder, keeper, landlady, landlord, master, owner, possessor, proprietary, title holder. ANT.—leaseholder, renter, resident, servant, tenant.

propriety, appropriateness, aptness, conventionality, correctness, decency, decorum, dignity, fitness, righteousness. ANT.—impropriety, misconduct, unfitness, unseemliness.

prosper, achieve, advance, be fortunate, bloom, blossom, flourish, flower, gain, increase, prevail, rise, succeed, thrive, win. ANT.—fail, lose, miscarry, miss, perish.

prosperous, affluent, flourishing, luxurious, moneyed, opulent, rich, sumptuous, wealthy, well-off, well-to-do. ANT.—destitute, indigent, needy, poor, poverty-stricken.

protect, see preserve.

protection, bulwark, camouflage, covering, fence, refuge, safeguard, screen, shelter, shield; assurance, certainty, defense, guard, invulnerability, reassurance, security, stability, strength. ANT.—exposure, insecurity, fragility, frailty, weakness.

protest, challenge, clamor, demonstration, difference, disagreement, dissent, dissentience, mass meeting, moratorium, noncompliance, nonconformity, objec-

tion, opposition, recusancy, rejection, remonstrance, tumult, turmoil, variance. ANT.—acceptance, agreement, assent, compliance, peace, recognition.

protract, continue, defer, delay, distend, distort, elongate, expand, extend, lengthen, postpone, procrastinate, prolong, spread, strain, stretch. ANT.—abridge, condense, curtail, hasten, reduce, shorten.

proud, arrogant, dignified, disdainful, exalted, haughty, imperious, lofty, lordly, majestic, overbearing, stately, supercilious, vain. ANT.—ashamed, humble, lowly, meek, modest.

prove, confirm, corroborate, demonstrate, establish, justify, manifest, show, substantiate, test, try, verify. ANT.—contradict, deny, disprove, expose, refute.

proverb, adage, aphorism, apothegm, axiom, bromide, byword, dictum, epigram, maxim, moral, motto, platitude, precept, saying, teaching, tenet, theorem, truism.

provide, afford, arm, cater, contribute, endow, equip, fit, fit out, furnish, give, produce, purvey, replenish, stock, store, supply, yield. ANT.—denude, deprive, divest, remove, strip, withhold.

provident, careful, cautious, discreet, economical, foresighted, frugal, prudent, saving, sparing, thoughtful, thrifty, wise. ANT.—extravagant, lavish, prodigal, profuse, wasteful.

provision, accumulation, arrangement, emergency equipment, fund, hoard, outline, plan, preparation, procurement, reserve, stock, store, supply; prerequisite, requirement, stipulation, terms.

provoke, see disturb.

proximate, adjacent, adjoining, beside, bordering, close, contiguous, handy, near, neighboring, nigh; approaching, imminent, impending. ANT.—distant, far, remote, removed.

prudent, careful, cautious, circumspect, discerning, discreet, judicious, reasonable, sensible, sound, vigilant, wary, watchful, wise. ANT.—absurd, foolish, impetuous, rash, reckless, stupid, unaware.

prying, curious, inquisitive, interfering, meddling, nosy, peeping, peering, searching, seeking, snoopy, spying. ANT.—aloof, incurious, indifferent, nonchalant, uncaring, unconcerned.

pseudo, bogus, counterfeit, fake, false, imitation, mock, phony, quasi, sham, simulated, spurious. ANT.—genuine, honest, real, sound, true.

public, complimentary, free, gratis, known, open, unrestricted. ANT.—charged, costly, personal, private, restricted.

publish, announce, broadcast, circulate, communicate, declare, disclose, disseminate, divulge, impart, issue, post, print, proclaim, promulgate, publicize, reveal, utter.

pull, drag, draw, haul, lift, stretch, tow, tug; extract, pluck, remove, take out, unsheathe; allure, attract, entice, induce, lure, persuade.

pulse, beat, oscillation, palpitation, throb, vibration.

punctual, dependable, early, exact, meticulous, particular, precise, prompt, punctilious, ready, scrupulous, strict, timely. ANT.—careless, desultory, dilatory, late, tardy.

punish, afflict, castigate, chasten, chastise, correct, discipline, fine, flog, imprison, inflict, pummel, scold, strike. ANT.—acquit, exonerate, forgive, free, pardon, reward.

puny, decrepit, delicate, diminutive, dwarfish, enervated, exhausted, faint, feeble, frail, impaired, inferior, infirm, languid, powerless, small, stunted, undeveloped, weak. ANT.—mighty, robust, strong, sturdy, vigorous.

purchase, see obtain.

pure, clean, clear, genuine, immaculate, perfect, spotless, stainless, unadulterated, unblemished, unmixed, untainted; chaste, guiltless, holy, incorrupt, innocent, modest, undefiled, virginal, virtuous; absolute, bare, sheer. ANT.—adulterated, foul, polluted, rotten, tainted; corrupt, defiled, licentious, immodest, obscene.

purge, see eliminate.

purify, chasten, clarify, clean, cleanse, clear, correct, deodorize, disinfect, filter, fumigate, mop, purge, refine, revise, scrub, sweep, wash. ANT.—debase, dirty, pollute, stain, tarnish, vitiate.

purpose, aim, design, determination, end, goal, inclination, intent, intention, object, objective, resolve, view. ANT.—accident, chance, fate, hazard.

pursue, chase, follow, hound, hunt, persist, seek, shadow, track, trail. ANT.—abandon, elude, flee, ignore, stop.

push, butt, compel, crowd, drive, elbow, force, impel, jostle, nudge, press, propel, shove, thrust; hasten, expedite, promote, urge. ANT.—drag, halt, pull, retreat; discourage, ignore, oppose.

put, assign, deposit, establish, imbed, insert, install, lay, locate, lodge, place, plant, settle. ANT.—displace, misplace, oust, remove, transfer.

putrid, contaminated, corrupt, decayed, disgusting, polluted, purulent, rotten. ANT.—clean, fragrant, pure, wholesome, uncontaminated.

puzzle, complexity, conundrum, enigma, intricacy, labyrinth, maze, mystery, perplexity, problem, riddle; baffle, bewilder, confound, confuse, disconcert, entangle, mystify, perplex. ANT.—answer, key, solution; clarify, elucidate, explain, reveal, solve, unravel.

Q

quack, charlatan, cheat, counterfeiter, deceiver, faker, imposter, phony, pretender, swindler.

quaint, anomalous, antique, curious, droll, eccentric, fanciful, odd, old-fashioned, peculiar, queer, strange, unique, unusual, whimsical. ANT.—common, familiar, fashionable, regular, usual.

quake, flutter, quail, quiver, shake, shiver, shudder, totter, tremble, vibrate; earthquake, temblor.

qualified, able, adequate, capable, clever, competent, efficacious, efficient, eligible, experienced, fitted, skillful, tempered. ANT.—incapable, ineffectual, inept, unfit, unqualified.

quality, attribute, character, characteristic, condition, distinction, feature, nature, peculiarity, property, qualification, trait; caliber, grade, rank, status, value.

quantity, abundance, amount, bulk, capacity, extent, mass, measure, multitude, number, pile, portion, sum, volume.

quarrel, affray, altercation, argument, bickering, brawl, clash, contention, disagreement, dispute, dissension, feud, fray, fuse, row, spat, squabble, strife, tiff, wrangle. ANT.—agreement, armistice, harmony, peace, silence.

quaver, see quake.

queer, see quaint.

query, ask, challenge, dispute, doubt, examine, inquire, interrogate, probe, quest, question, quiz, search, seek. ANT.—answer, reply, respond, retort, state.

quest, adventure, crusade, enterprise, examination, expedition, exploration, inquiry, inspection, interrogation, investigation, journey, pursuit, research, scrutiny, search, seeking, survey, trek.

question, see query.

quick, brisk, expeditious, fast, fleet, hasty, immediate, instantaneous, lively, precipitate, prompt, rapid, speedy, swift; excitable, impatient, impetuous, irascible, mercurial, rash, sharp, testy, touchy; active, acute, alert, clever, discerning, keen, ready, sensitive, sharp, shrewd, vigorous. ANT.—slow, sluggish; apathetic, drowsy, languid, lazy, listless; dull, insipid, obtuse, vapid.

quicken, see hurry.

quiescent, abeyant, calm, dormant, hidden, inactive, latent, motionless, peaceful, placid, quiet, resting, secret, serene, smooth, still, tranquil, undeveloped, undisturbed, unruffled. ANT.—active, dynamic, manifest, spirited, stirring, vivacious.

quiet, hushed, motionless, muffled, mute, pacific, peaceful, placid, quiescent, secluded, serene, soundless, still, tranquil, undisturbed; calm, contented, gentle, meek, mild, passive, patient, silent; allay, alleviate, appease, assuage, calm, compose, cool, gratify, lull, moderate, pacify, placate, please, quell, relax, relieve, restrain, smooth, soothe, still, tranquilize. ANT.—loud, noisy, strident; agitated, excited, impatient, perturbed; arouse, excite, incense, inflame, provoke.

quiet, abandon, cease, depart, desert, desist, discontinue, forsake, leave, stop; give up, relinquish, resign, surrender, withdraw, yield. ANT.—continue, endure, keep, persevere, remain, retain, stay.

quiver, see quake.

quiz, see query.

quotation, blurb, citation, citing, excerpt, extract, passage, quote, recitation, reference, repetition, selection; estimate, price, rate.

R

race, ancestry, breed, clan, cultural group, family, folk, lineage, mankind, nation, nationality, people, stock, strain, tribe.

racket, see noise.

radiant, beaming, bright, brilliant, dazzling, effulgent, glittering, glorious, glowing, grand, luminous, lustrous, magnificent, resplendent, shimmering, shining, sparkling, splendid. ANT.—cloudy, dark, dim, dull, obscure.

radiate, brighten, broadcast, circulate, diffuse, disperse, disseminate, emanate, emit, gleam, glitter, illumine, propagate, shed, shine, spread, transmit. ANT.—absorb, concentrate, converge, gather.

radical, complete, entire, total, thorough; basic, congenital, constitutional, essential, fundamental, inborn, ingrained, inherent, inherited, innate, intrinsic, native, natural, organic, original; communistic, excessive, extreme, fanatical, insurgent, leftist, liberal, militant, progressive, revolutionary, ultra, uncompromising, violent. ANT.—incomplete, partial; extraneous, extrinsic, nonessential, superficial; casual, conservative, moderate, stable, traditional.

rage, anger, animosity, choler, exasperation, explosion, frenzy, fury, hysterics, indignation, ire, irritation, outburst, passion, petulance, storm, tantrum, temper, uproar, vehemence, wrath; boil (over), foam, fume, rail at, rant, rave, roar, scold, scream, seethe, splutter, yell. ANT.—conciliation, forbearance, patience, peace, self-control, tranquility; appease, calm, lull, placate, quiet, soothe.

raise, elevate, erect, exalt, heave, heighten, hoist, honor, lift, uplift; breed, cultivate, grow, produce, rear; collect, gather, levy, muster; advance, aggrandize, amplify, augment, boost, increase, intensify, magnify. ANT.—abase, degrade, depreciate, destroy, lower, reduce.

ramble, deviate, digress, drift, meander, range, roam, rove, saunter, straggle, stray, stroll, traipse, wander.

rancor, see malice.

rank, column, file, line, order, range, row, series, string, tier; class, division, grade, order; degree, position, seniority, standing, station; dignity, distinction, eminence, reputation.

rapid, see quick.

rapture, bliss, delight, ecstasy, enchantment, exultation, felicity, gladness, happiness, joy, passion, transport. ANT.—depression, grief, melancholy, misery, pain, suffering.

rare, infrequent, occasional; odd, peculiar, strange, unusual; choice, exceptional, extraordinary, incomparable, precious, remarkable, scarce, singular, uncommon, unique, unparalleled, unprecedented. ANT.—frequent, habitual, incessant, recurring; common, normal, ordinary, regular, typical; cheap, worthless.

rash, see impetuous.

rate, appraise, assess, calculate, determine, estimate, evaluate, measure, price, rank, value; succeed, triumph; comparison, degree, fixed amount, measure, percentage, proportion, quota, ratio, relationship, standard.

ration, see portion.

rational, deductive, discriminating, intelligent, judicious, logical, prudent, reasonable, sagacious, sensible, wise; conscious, lucid, sane, sober, sound. ANT.—absurd, foolish, inconsistent, ridiculous, stupid; insane, irrational, unconscious.

ravage, see devastate.

ravenous, see hungry.

raw, callow, coarse, crude, green, harsh, ill-prepared, immature, inexperienced, rough, rude, undisciplined, unfinished, unpolished, unprepared, unrefined, unripe. ANT.—adult, courteous, mature, polished, ripe, seasoned, well-prepared.

raze, annihilate, demolish, destroy, devastate, dismantle, efface, eradicate, exterminate, extinguish, level, obliterate, overthrow, ravage, ruin, topple, wreck. ANT.—build, construct, erect, raise, repair, restore.

reach, extend to, span, stretch, touch; accomplish, achieve, arrive at, attain, earn, gain, get to, join, overtake. ANT.—bungle, fail, fall short, leave, miss.

react, act, answer, reciprocate, rejoin, reply, respond; be affected, be involved, be moved, feel. ANT.—disregard, ignore, overlook; be insensitive to.

read, apprehend, browse, comprehend, decipher, discern, glance over, grasp, interpret, learn, perceive, peruse, scan, skim, study, translate, understand, unravel.

ready, active, available, complete, consummate, disposed, equipped, finished, fit, mature, mellow, prepared, prompt, ripe, season-able, suitable, willing; concoct, condition, equip, fit, furnish, make ready, order, predispose, prepare. ANT.—immature, unavailable, undeveloped, unready.

real, see genuine.

reality, actuality, authenticity, entity, existence, realness, substance, tangibility, truth, verity. ANT.—fantasy, fiction, imagination, nonentity.

realization, accomplishment, achievement, attainment, completion, performance; appreciation, awareness, comprehension, perception, understanding. ANT.—defeat, failure; blindness, disregard, ignorance.

realm, area, department, district, domain, estate, farm, kingdom, land, province, region, sphere, territory, vicinity.

reap, accumulate, acquire, collect, cut, earn, gain, garner, gather, glean, harvest, hoard, obtain, pick, win. ANT.—lose, plant, seed, sow.

rear, bring up, elevate, foster, lift, nurture, raise, support, train; build, erect.

reason, account, aim, argument, basis, cause, design, end, foundation, ground, motive, object, purpose, sake, view; intelligence, intuition, judgment, mind, rationality, sense, understanding; analyze, argue, conclude, contend, debate, deduce, deliberate, discuss, establish, infer, judge, question, reflect, speculate, study, trace. ANT.—bewilder, confuse, fabricate, guess.

reasonable, see rational.

rebellion, coup, disorder, disturbance, insurrection, mutiny, outbreak, overthrow, revolt, revolution, riot, sedition, tumult, upheaval, uprising. ANT.—conciliation, law, order, peace, submission.

rebellious, contumacious, defiant, disobedient, insubordinate, intractable, mutinous, pugnacious, recalcitrant, refractory, undutiful, unmanageable, unruly. ANT.—docile, dutiful, manageable, obedient, subservient, tractable.

rebuke, accuse, admonish, berate, censure, chide, condemn, criticize, implicate, punish, reprimand, reproach, reprove, scold, upbraid. ANT.—approve, exonerate, laud, praise, reward.

recall, recollect, remember, remind, reminisce, review, revive; annul, disqualify, revoke; reassemble, reconvene, summon. ANT.—forget, ignore, overlook; reestablish, restore; disperse, separate, terminate.

recede, abate, decline, ebb, fade, lessen, regress, retire, retreat, revert, shrink from, withdraw. ANT.—advance, approach, gain, increase, near, rise.

receive, accept, acquire, catch, gain, get, obtain, take, win; admit, shelter; entertain, welcome. ANT.—bequeath, donate, give, return; evict, expel, oust; deny, refuse, reject.

recent, contemporary, foregoing, fresh, late, latter, modern, new, newfangled, novel, original, preceding, retiring, streamlined, young. ANT.—ancient, antiquated, archaic, obsolete, oldfashioned.

recite, address, convey, declaim, delineate, deliver, describe, detail, discourse, enumerate, explain, impart, mention, narrate, quote, read, recapitulate, recount, rehearse, relate, repeat, report, state, tell.

reckless, careless, daring, foolhardy, heedless, impetuous, imprudent, precipitate, rash, wild. ANT.—cautious, circumspect, prudent, wary.

recognize, accede, accept, acknowledge, admit, apprehend, concede, confess, distinguish, identify, know, perceive, realize, recollect, remember. ANT.—forget, ignore, overlook, renounce, repudiate.

recommend, advise, allude, counsel, hint, imply, insinuate, intimate, offer, prescribe, propose, refer, suggest, urge; acclaim, advocate, applaud, approve, commend, endorse, extol, praise, sanction. ANT.—demand, dictate, insist; condemn, denigrate, disapprove.

reconcile, accommodate, adapt, adjust, arrange, conciliate, conform, correct, harmonize, mediate, mitigate, pacify, placate, rectify, regulate, reunite, settle. ANT.—alienate, annoy, bother, divide, irritate, separate.

record, account, archive, chronicle, docket, document, inventory, memorandum, note, register, registry, report, schedule; inscription, mark, memorial, trace, vestige; achievement, career, experience, history; catalogue, enroll, enter, file, list, note, register, report, tape.

recover, cure, heal, mend, rally, recuperate, revive; recapture, recoup, redeem, regain, renew, renovate, repossess, restore, retrieve, salvage. ANT.—perish, regress, relapse, wane, weaken; forfeit, lose, mislay.

recreation, amusement, diversion, entertainment, frolic, fun, game, pastime, play, refreshment, relaxation, relief, sport. ANT.— drudgery, labor, task, toil, work.

rectify, adjust, amend, correct, fix, improve, mend, purify, refine, reform, remedy, repair, revise, right. ANT.—adulterate, debase, falsify, ruin, spoil.

recuperate, see recover.

redeem, atone, deliver, emancipate, expiate, extricate, free, liberate, propitiate, ransom, recoup, recover, regain, repair, repurchase, rescue, retrieve, save. ANT.—abandon, forfeit, ignore, neglect, overlook, shun.

reduce, abate, abbreviate, abridge, assuage, condense, contract, curtail, decimate, decrease, degrade, diminish, impoverish, lessen, lower, moderate, modify, shorten, subdue, suppress, thin, weaken. ANT.—amplify, enlarge, increase, magnify, strengthen.

redundant, copious, diffuse, excessive, extra, profuse, prolix, repetitious, verbose, wordy. ANT.—concise, laconic, succinct, terse.

refer, advert, allude, appeal, apply, ascribe, attribute, belong, cite, commit, concern, connect, consign, consult, deliver, include, involve, pertain, point, quote, regard, relate, submit, suggest.

refinement, breeding, civilization, clarification, cultivation, culture, delicacy, education, elegance, enlightenment, finesse, poise, polish, purification, purity. ANT.—barbarism, coarseness, crudity, rusticity, vulgarity.

reflect, cogitate, concentrate, consider, contemplate, deliberate, meditate, muse, ponder, reason, ruminate, speculate, study, think, weigh; copy, echo, imitate, mirror, reproduce; rebound, revert.

reform, amend, better, correct, freshen, improve, mend, reconstruct, rectify, redress, renew, renovate, reorganize, repair, restore, revise, right, transmute. ANT.—aggravate, corrupt, damage, impair, ruin, vitiate.

refrain, abstain, avoid, check, curb, desist, forebear, restrain, withhold; burden, chorus, undersong. ANT.—continue, indulge, persevere, persist.

refresh, air, animate, brace, cheer, enliven, freshen, invigorate, renew, renovate, rest, restore, revive, stimulate. ANT.—bore, exhaust, fatigue, tire, weary.

refuge, asylum, fortress, harbor, haven, hideaway, protection, retreat, sanctuary, seclusion, shelter, stronghold. ANT.—danger, exposure, hazard, jeopardy, pitfall, risk.

refuse, decline, deny, disavow, disown, negate, protest, rebuff, reject, renounce, repel, repudiate, spurn, veto, withhold; dross, garbage, junk, litter, rubbish, rubble, scoria, sweepings, trash, waste. ANT.—accept, consent, grant, present, sanction, welcome; assets, resources, valuables.

refute, confound, confute, controvert, disprove, expose, falsify, invalidate, overthrow, parry, rebut, repel, stultify. ANT.—assist, defend, encourage, sanction, strengthen, uphold.

regal, courtly, dignified, imperial, kingly, lordly, magnificent, majestic, monarchial, noble, princely, queenly, royal, sovereign, splendid, stately, sublime. ANT.—common, ignoble, lowly, ordinary, plebeian, servile.

regard, attention, concern, consideration, notice, observation; reference, relation, respect; affection, esteem, estimation, liking; honor, value; contemplate, notice, observe, view, watch; believe, hold, imagine, reckon, suppose, think. ANT.—avoidance, neglect; antipathy,

disgust; deride, insult, mock; forget, ignore, neglect, omit, overlook.

register, admit, chronicle, declare, enroll, enter, establish, express, fix, indicate, insert, list, note, record, save, table; annal, archive, catalogue, list, roll, roster, schedule.

region, area, belt, climate, district, domain, locale, locality, location, neighborhood, place, quarter, realm, sector, site, spot, station, territory, vicinity, zone.

regression, backsliding, deterioration, ebb, recession, recidivism, retrogression, return, reversion, withdrawal. ANT.—advancement, headway, progress, progression.

regret, bitterness, compunction, contrition, disappointment, grief, heartache, lamentation, penitence, qualm, remorse, repentance, repining, self-reproach, sorrow, vexation, worry; bewail, deplore, lament, repent, repine, rue, sorrow. ANT.—contentment, impenitence, induration, obduracy, satisfaction, tranquility; celebrate, cheer, enjoy, exult, rejoice.

regular, consistent, conventional, customary, homogeneous, homologous, invariable, methodical, natural, normal, orderly, ordinary, periodic, punctual, steady, symmetrical, systematic, uniform, unvaried, usual. ANT.—anomalous, erratic, inconsistent, infrequent, rare, strange, unusual.

regulate, adapt, adjust, allocate, arrange, classify, control, correct, direct, fix, govern, legislate, organize, readjust, reconcile, rectify, rule, systematize. ANT.—confuse, disarrange, disorganize, entangle, jumble, sunder.

rehabilitate, overhaul, reawaken, rebuild, reconstitute, reconstruct, recreate, reestablish, refinish, refresh, reinstate, reinvigorate, renew, renovate, repair, replenish, restore, revamp, revive.

reinforce, augment, buttress, energize, fortify, invigorate, pillar, strengthen, support. ANT.—detract, weaken.

reject, decline, deny, discard, dismiss, eject, eliminate, exclude, rebuff, refuse, renounce, repudiate, spurn, veto, withhold. ANT.—accept, admit, choose, select, welcome.

relate, describe, detail, narrate, recite, recount, rehearse, report, state, tell; apply, associate, compare, connect, correlate, link, parallel, pertain, refer.

relation, alliance, bearing, connection, correlation, correspondence, likeness, reference, relationship, relevancy, similarity; affinity, bond, family connection, filiation, kindred, kinship, link, sibling, tie, union.

relationship, see relation.

relative, appositive, cognate, comparative, conditional, contingent, definite, dependent, germane, particular, pertinent, referable, relevant, respecting, special; connection, kin, relation.

relaxation, abatement, amusement, comfort, diversion, ease, leisure, loosening, mitigation, peacefulness, reclining, recreation, relief, repose, respite, rest, slackening, tranquility. ANT.—drudgery, exertion, labor, striving, struggle, toil.

release, deliver, discharge, emancipate, free, liberate, set free; absolution, acquittal, deliverance, discharge, dispensation, emancipation, exoneration, freedom, liberation, relinquishment, surrender. ANT.—confine, imprison, oppress; restriction, subjugation.

relent, abdicate, accede, acquiesce, capitulate, cede, comply, defer, quit, relinquish, resign, submit, succumb, surrender; abate, bend, bow, relax, soften, subside, yield. ANT.—assert, persevere, persist, strive, struggle; harden, stiffen.

relentless, fierce, hard, implacable, inexorable, inflexible, obdurate, pitiless, rigid, rigorous, ruthless, strict, stringent, unyielding, vindictive. ANT.—compassionate, gentle, lenient, merciful.

relevant, see pertinent.

reliable, certain, conscientious, constant, definite, dependable, faithful, firm, positive, reputable, responsible, safe, secure, solid, stable, staunch, steadfast, sterling, strong, sure, tried, true, trustworthy, unimpeachable. ANT.—dangerous, dubious, insecure, questionable, undependable, unreliable.

relief, aid, alleviation, assistance, backing, comfort, ease, help, mitigation, palliation, succor, support. ANT.—aggravation, agitation, distress.

relieve, abate, aid, allay, alleviate, assist, assuage, calm, comfort, disburden, disentangle, ease, extricate, facilitate, free, lighten, mitigate, pacify, redress, remedy, solace, soothe. ANT.—disturb, irritate, trouble, vex.

religious, believing, canonical, devout, divine, ecclesiastical, ethical, god-fearing, godly, holy, ministerial, moral, pietistic, pious, reverent, sacred, sanctimonious, spiritual, theological; careful, methodical, scrupulous, thorough. ANT.—atheistic, freethinking, immoral, impious, profane, secular; careless, indifferent, negligent, slovenly.

relinquish, abandon, abdicate, abjure, acquiesce, capitulate, cede, deny, desert, discard, dismiss, forego, forsake, quit, reject, renounce, resign, revoke, sacrifice, spare, submit, surrender, vacate, yield. ANT.—conquer, keep, perpetuate, persist, pursue, retain.

relish, appetizer, seasoning, spice; appreciation, enjoyment, gratification, gusto, inclination, par-

tiality, preference, satisfaction, zest. ANT.—disfavor, distaste.

reluctant, averse, backward, demurring, disinclined, doubtful, hesitant, indisposed, loathe, opposed, slow, tardy, unready, unwilling. ANT.—amenable, disposed, eager, enthusiastic, ready, willing.

rely, bank, confide, count, depend, lean, trust. ANT.—distrust, doubt.

remain, abide, continue, dwell, endure, inhabit, last, reside, rest, stay, survive. ANT.—depart, dissipate, go, leave, terminate.

remainder, balance, dregs, excess, leavings, leftovers, remains, remnant, residue, residuum, rest, surplus.

remark, comment, mention, note, observation, point, saying, statement, utterance; assert, declare, express, maintain, mention, observe, relate, say, speak, talk, tell, utter.

remarkable, arresting, awesome, commanding, distinguished, exceptional, exciting, extraordinary, great, impressive, memorable, moving, notable, peculiar, prominent, rare, special, stirring, striking, wonderful, uncommon, unusual. ANT.—common, inconspicuous, normal, regular, unimpressive, usual.

remedy, antidote, bracer, cure, help, medicant, medication, nostrum, panacea, redress, relief, reparation, restorative; ameliorate, amend, better, correct, cure, fix, heal, improve, mend, rectify, redress, reform, relieve, renew, repair, restore. ANT.—burden, hindrance, impediment, ruination; aggravate, intensify, neglect, worsen.

remember, memorize, recall, recollect, remind, reminisce, retain, retrace, review. ANT.—disregard, forget, obliterate, overlook, repress, suppress.

remembrance, commemoration, keepsake, memento, memoir, memorial, memory, recollection, reminiscence, reminder, souvenir, token, trophy. ANT.—forgetfulness, nirvana, oblivion.

remit, absolve, alleviate, defer, discontinue, excuse, exempt, forgive, mitigate, moderate, overlook, pardon, postpone, relax, release, relinquish, restore, soften; compensate, make payment, pay, reimburse, remunerate. ANT.—avenge, bind, control, dominate, restrict, suppress; deceive, swindle, victimize.

remorse, see regret.

remorseless, see inhuman.

remote, alien, distant, far, faraway, foreign, inaccessible, indirect, removed, secluded, unconnected, unrelated. ANT.—adjacent, close, near, proximate, related.

remove, depart, dislodge, displace, evacuate, leave, migrate, move, separate, shift, transfer, transport, vacate; discharge, dismiss, eject, evict, oust, unseat; eliminate, extract, pull, uproot, wrench; destroy, kill. ANT.—dwell, place, remain; establish, maintain; imbed, plant, root; preserve.

renew, continue, reestablish, refresh, regenerate, reiterate, renovate, repeat, replace, replenish, restore, resume, resuscitate, revive. ANT.—deplete, diminish, enfeeble, exhaust.

renounce, abandon, abdicate, desert, drop, forego, forsake, quit, relinquish, resign, sacrifice, secede, surrender; deny, disavow, disclaim, disown, recant, reject, repudiate, retract, revoke. ANT.—maintain, persevere, persist, remain; acknowledge, assert, claim.

renovate, see rehabilitate.

renowned, see eminent.

repair, amend, correct, darn, fix, mend, patch, rectify, refit, remedy, remodel, renew, renovate, replace, restore. ANT.—damage, destroy, mar, neglect, ruin.

repeal, abolish, abrogate, annul, cancel, invalidate, nullify, quash, recall, rescind, revoke, veto. ANT.—continue, keep, maintain, renew, validate.

repeat, duplicate, echo, iterate, quote, recapitulate, recite, recur, rehearse, reiterate, relate, reproduce, tell.

repentance, compunction, contrition, penitence, regret, regretfulness, remorse, self-disgust, self-reproach, sorrow. ANT.—

callousness, complacency, impenitence, recusancy, shamelessness.

replace, reconstitute, reconstruct, refund, rehabilitate, reinstate, repay, restore, return, substitute, succeed, supersede, supplant. ANT.—alter, change, diversify, modify, transform.

replicate, see duplicate.

reply, acknowledge, answer, counter, echo, react, rejoin, respond, retort; answer, rejoinder, repartee, response, retort. ANT.—ask, disregard, ignore, question; examination, inquiry, question, summoning.

report, advertise, announce, broadcast, chronicle, communicate, declare, describe, detail, disclose, herald, impart, inform, mention, notify, proclaim, promulgate, publish, recite, relate, specify, state, tell; account, announcement, chronicle, communication, description, dispatch, hearsay, intelligence, message, narration, narrative, news, publication, recital, record, statement, story, tidings. ANT.—conceal, delete, mask, screen, veil; concealment, evasion, deletion, reserve, secrecy, suppression.

repose, calm, calmness, comfort, ease, hush, leisure, peace, quiescence, quiet, quietude, relaxation, respite, rest, serenity, silence, stillness, tranquility. ANT.—activity, disturbance, noise, tumult, turmoil.

represent, delineate, depict, describe, draw, imitate, impersonate, paint, personate, picture, portray, show, sketch, symbolize, typify.

repress, bridle, check, choke, constrain, curb, dull, hinder, inhibit, overpower, quell, restrain, silence, smother, still, stop, subdue, suppress. ANT.—advance, assist, encourage, exhilarate, invigorate, stimulate.

reprimand, admonish, berate, blame, censure, chide, lecture, punish, rebuke, reprehend, reproach, reprove, revile, scold, upbraid, vilify, vituperate. ANT.—approve, commend, forgive, laud, praise, reward.

reproach, see blame.

reproduction, casting, copy, duplicate, exemplar, facsimile, imitation, print, replica, representation, tracing, transcript; generation, procreation, propagation. ANT.—archetype, original, pattern, prototype; infertility, sterility.

repugnant, abhorrent, adverse, antagonistic, contrary, disagreeable, disgusting, distasteful, hostile, invidious, obnoxious, offensive, opposed, refractory, repellent, revolting, unbearable. ANT.—agreeable, appealing, conciliatory, harmonious, pleasant.

repulsive, abhorrent, abominable, detestable, disgusting, gross, gruesome, hideous, homely, horrible, horrid, nauseating, obnoxious, odious, offensive, repellent, repugnant, revolting, ugly, uncomely. ANT.—alluring, captivating, enticing, inviting, pleasing.

reputation, acceptability, character, class, credit, dependability, description, esteem, honor, kind, name, nature, prestige, reliability, repute, respectability, sort, standing, trustworthiness; eminence, notoriety, prominence.

repute, see reputation.

request, appeal, apply, ask, beg, beseech, bid, entreat, implore, importune, invite, petition, plead, pray, seek, solicit, sue, summon, supplicate.

requirement, behest, bidding, call, charge, claim, command, decree, demand, essential, exigency, injunction, mandate, necessity, need, pinch, requisite, requisition, urgency, want.

requisite, basic, binding, compelling, compulsory, crucial, essential, expedient, fundamental, imperative, important, indispensable, intrinsic, mandatory, necessary, needed, obligatory, required, urgent, vital. ANT.—accidental, expendable, extrinsic, nonessential, optional.

rescue, deliver, disenthrall, extricate, free, liberate, preserve, ransom, recapture, reclaim, recover, redeem, release, retrieve, save. ANT.—abandon, bind, enslave, hinder, incarcerate.

research, analysis, examination, experimentation, exploration, inquiry, interrogation, investigation, observation, query, quest, question, scrutiny, study, testing.

resemblance, affinity, agreement, analogy, correspondence, facsimile, likeness, match, purity, semblance, similarity, simile, similitude. ANT.—contrast, deviation, dissimilarity, distinction, inconsistency, variance.

resentment, acerbity, anger, animosity, annoyance, bitterness, displeasure, exasperation, grudge, huff, indignation, ire, irritation, perturbation, pique, rancor, rankling, umbrage. ANT.—affection, concord, geniality, good humor, happiness, harmony.

reserved, aloof, bashful, cautious, demure, detached, diffident, distant, formal, modest, restrained, reticent, retiring, shy, taciturn, timorous, undemonstrative, wary; booked, preserved, saved. ANT.—affable, blatant, expansive, uninhibited; unreserved.

residue, see remainder.

resign, abandon, abdicate, abjure, cede, eschew, forego, quit, relinquish, renounce, retract, surrender, vacate, waive, withdraw, yield. ANT.—accept, receive, remain, retain, stay.

resilient, buoyant, elastic, flexible, spirited, springy, supple. ANT.—inflexible, stiff, tense, unbending.

resist, attack, check, confront, contest, counteract, defy, frustrate, hinder, impede, impugn, neutralize, obstruct, oppose, thwart, withstand. ANT.—acquiesce, assist, collaborate, comply, defer, submit, yield.

resolution, constancy, courage, decision, determination, devotion, firmness, fortitude, persistence, resolve, stamina, steadfastness, zeal. ANT.—caprice, hesitation, indecision, uncertainty, vacillation.

resolve, adjudicate, choose, close, conclude, decide, decree, determine, elect, end, fix, propose, purpose, settle, terminate. ANT.—hesitate, procrastinate, vacillate, waver.

respect, admiration, consideration, deference, esteem, fealty, honor, recognition, regard, reverence, veneration; admire, appreciate, consider, heed, honor, note, notice, prize, regard, revere, reverence, treasure, uphold, value, venerate. ANT.—contempt, disdain, irreverence, scorn; abuse, blame, censure, deride, despise.

respectable, adequate, becoming, comely, decent, decorous, estimable, honorable, mediocre, moderate, presentable, proper, seemly, suitable, tolerable, upright, virtuous, worthy. ANT.—dishonorable, improper, indecent, reprehensible, scandalous, unworthy.

resplendent, see radiant.

respond, see reply.

response, see reply.

responsible, accountable, amenable, answerable, liable, obligatory, subject; dependable, reliable, trustworthy. ANT.—arbitrary, exempt, free, immune, unbound; careless, irresponsible, lax, negligent, unreliable.

restful, calm, comfortable, cozy, easy, mild, peaceful, placid, quiet, relaxing, reposeful, serene, soothing, still, tranquil, untroubled. ANT.—alarming, annoying, disconcerting, disturbing, upsetting.

restless, agitated, anxious, changeable, disquieted, disturbed, fidgety, fitful, irresolute, nervous, sleepless, uneasy, unsettled, worried; active, moving, roving, transient, wandering. ANT.—calm, composed, placid, tranquil, unperturbed.

restore, see rehabilitate.

restrain, see repress.

restrict, bind, bridle, check, confine, constrain, curb, fence, hinder, impede, inhibit, limit, obstruct, repress, restrain, stop, suppress. ANT.—enlarge, expand, extend, free, release.

result, conclusion, consequence, determination, effect, end, eventuality, fruit, issue, outcome, product, resolution, resolve, termination, upshot; accrue, arise, come, eventuate, flow, follow, issue, originate, proceed, resolve, spring.

retain, detain, employ, engage, hire, hold, keep, maintain, preserve, reserve, secure, withhold.

ANT.—discard, dismiss, jettison, relinquish, surrender.

retaliate, avenge, match, punish, reciprocate, repay, requite, retort, return, vindicate. ANT.—forget, forgive, ignore, pardon.

retard, arrest, check, clog, delay, detain, hamper, hinder, impede, interrupt, postpone, stay. ANT.—accelerate, advance, hasten, speed.

retire, see relinquish.

retort, see reply.

retract, abjure, abnegate, abrogate, annul, cancel, deny, disclaim, disown, nullify, recall, recant, renounce, reverse, revoke. ANT.—affirm, confirm, endorse, ratify, uphold.

retrogress, backslide, decline, degenerate, deteriorate, regress, relapse, retreat, retrograde, revert. ANT.—advance, develop, improve, proceed, progress.

return, reappear, recur, retreat, revert; reciprocate, repay, replace, reply, requite, restore. ANT.—appropriate, retain, take.

reveal, announce, betray, confess, disclose, divulge, explain, expose, express, impart, inform, open, publish, show, uncover, unfold, unmask, unveil. ANT.—conceal, deceive, disguise, mask, secrete.

revenge, avenging, implacability, malevolence, reprisal, requital, retaliation, retribution, vengeance, vindictiveness. ANT.—forgiveness, mercy, pardon, reconciliation, remission.

reverence, admiration, adoration, approbation, awe, deference, dignity, esteem, fame, glory, homage, honor, praise, regard, renown, respect, veneration, worship. ANT.—contempt, derision, execration, dishonor, irreverence, mockery.

reverse, alter, convert, invert, modify, shift, transpose, turn about; overthrow, overturn, subvert, upset; annul, cancel, countermand, invalidate, nullify, repeal, rescind, retract, revoke, undo.

revert, go back, recur, repeat, retreat, return, reverse. ANT.—advance, go forward, proceed.

review, consider, examine, inspect, reconsider, rehearse, retrace, survey; analyze, correct, criticize, edit, judge, revise; commentary, criticism, critique, examination, inspection, reconsideration, reflection, retrospection, revision, study, survey; digest, journal, periodical; abstract, outline, summary, synopsis.

revision, see review.

revive, animate, awaken, freshen, improve, invigorate, reanimate, recall, refresh, reinforce, renew, renovate, repair, reproduce, resuscitate, revivify, rouse. ANT.—decay, decline, fade, perish, waste, wither.

revoke, see repeal.

revolting, see repulsive.

revolution, anarchy, *coup d'état,* disorder, foment, insubordina-

tion, insurrection, mutiny, overthrow, rebellion, revolt, tumult,
uprising; gyration, revolving, rotation, spin, swirl, twirl.

revolve, circle, circulate, eddy, gyrate, orbit, roll, rotate, spin, turn,
twirl, wheel, whirl; brood over,
consider, ponder, ruminate,
study.

reward, acknowledgment, amends,
award, bonus, bounty, compensation, gain, gratuity, indemnity,
payment, premium, prize, recompense, recoupment, redress,
remuneration, requital, retribution, return, satisfaction. ANT.—
assessment, charge, deprivation,
divestment, forfeiture, levy, sei-
zure.

rhythm, accent, beat, cadence, lilt,
measure, meter, periodicity, pulsation, regularity, swing, tempo.

rich, ample, bountiful, costly, elegant, exorbitant, expensive,
generous, luscious, luxurious,
opulent, resplendent, splendid,
sumptuous, superb, valuable;
abundant, exuberant, fecund,
fertile, fruitful, lush, luxuriant,
plentiful, profuse, prolific; intense, strong, vivid; affluent,
moneyed, prosperous, wealthy,
well-to-do. ANT.—drab, plain,
unadorned; barren, sterile, unfruitful, unproductive; faint,
powerless, unsubstantial, weak;
destitute, impoverished, indigent, penniless, poor.

riddle, see mystery.

ridicule, banter, contempt, derision, disdain, disparagement,
gibe, irony, jeering, mockery,
persiflage, raillery, sarcasm, satire, scorn, sneering. ANT.—approval, commendation, honor,
praise, respect.

ridiculous, absurd, bizarre, comic,
droll, farcical, foolish, funny, hilarious, inconsistent, irrational,
laughable, ludicrous, nonsensical, odd, preposterous, self-contradictory, silly, unreasonable.
ANT.—conventional, rational,
reasonable, sensible, wise.

right, ethical, fair, honest, just,
lawful, legitimate, reasonable,
rightful; accurate, correct, true,
valid; appropriate, proper, suitable; direct, erect, straight, upright; authority, exemption,
immunity, liberty, license, prerogative, privilege; equity, honesty, integrity, justice, morality,
propriety, rectitude, uprightness,
virtue. ANT.—dishonest, illegitimate, unethical, unreasonable;
false, inaccurate, invalid; improper, inappropriate, unsuitable; crooked, devious, dishonest,
twisted; encroachment, injustice,
violation, wrong; dishonesty,
immorality, inequity, injustice,
vice.

righteous, chaste, commendable,
conscientious, decent, equitable,
ethical, good, honorable, just,
pure, right, scrupulous, virtuous,
worthy; devout, godly, pious, religious, saintly. ANT.—amoral,
corrupt, immoral, licentious,
unethical; impious, irreligious.

rigid, austere, exacting, harsh, precise, relentless, rigorous, scru-

pulous, severe, stern, stony, strict, stringent, unyielding; inelastic, inflexible, petrified, stiff, unbending. ANT.—compassionate, considerate, forbearing, indulgent, lenient, tolerant; elastic, flexible, limber, mobile, pliant.

rigorous, austere, blunt, coarse, cruel, exacting, grating, gruff, hard, harsh, inflexible, jarring, oppressive, rigid, rough, severe, stern, stiff, strict, stringent, uncompromising, unfeeling. ANT.—easy, easygoing, lax, lenient, mild, soft, tender.

rim, border, brim, brink, brow, curb, edge, fringe, hem, limit, lip, margin, outskirts, terminus, top, verge. ANT.—center, core, interior, middle.

ring, arena, band, chime, circle, clangor, clique, confederation, coterie, faction, gang, hoop, resonance, reverberation; chime, circle, clang, encircle, enclose, girdle, jingle, knell, peal, resound, surround, tinkle, toll.

riot, altercation, commotion, fray, insurgence, melee, pandemonium, protest, rebellion, row, strife, tumult, turmoil, uprising. ANT.—order, peace, quiet, regularity, tranquility.

rip, burst, cleave, cut, disunite, lacerate, rend, rive, separate, sever, shear, shred, slash, slit, split, sunder, tear. ANT.—join, mend, unite.

ripe, complete, consummate, developed, finished, full-grown, mature, matured, mellow, per-

fect, ready, ripened, seasonable, seasoned. ANT.—budding, green, immature, undeveloped, unfit, unseasoned.

rise, arise, ascend, begin, climb, commence, grow, increase, mount, originate, proceed, progress, prosper, scale, soar, spring, start, thrive, tower. ANT.—decline, descend, fall, recede, sink, tumble.

risk, danger, hazard, imperilment, jeopardy, peril; chance, gamble, opportunity, prospect, uncertainty, venture; endanger, expose, hazard, jeopardize, venture. ANT.—defense, immunity, protection, safety; certainty, guarantee; defend, insure, protect, secure, shield.

risky, chancy, critical, dangerous, hazardous, insecure, jeopardous, menacing, perilous, precarious, threatening, uncertain, unsafe. ANT.—certain, protected, safe, sure.

rite, ceremony, custom, duty, formality, liturgy, observance, ordinance, parade, pomp, protocol, ritual, sacrament, service, solemnity.

ritual, see rite.

rival, adversary, antagonist, combatant, competitor, contestant, disputant, emulator, enemy, foe, opponent; antagonize, attack, battle, challenge, combat, compete, conflict, confront, contend, contest, dispute, emulate, fight, oppose, struggle, wrestle. ANT.—advocate, ally, assistant, helper, partner, patron, supporter; assist, champion, cooperate, encourage, support, uphold.

roam, deviate, digress, err, gallivant, hike, meander, prowl, ramble, range, rove, saunter, straggle, stray, stroll, traipse, traverse, wander. ANT.—halt, lodge, settle, stay.

rob, appropriate, burglarize, cheat, defraud, embezzle, fleece, forge, loot, pilfer, pillage, plunder, purloin, rifle, sack, steal, strip.

robber, bandit, burglar, despoiler, forager, forger, marauder, gallager, pirate, plunderer, poacher, raider, rustler, swindler, thief.

robust, brawny, hale, hardy, healthy, muscular, powerful, sound, strapping, strong, sturdy, tough, vigorous, well. ANT.—debilitated, feeble, flabby, frail, sickly, weak.

rock, boulder, cliff, crag, gravel, jewel, pebble, promontory, reef, slab, stone; defense, foundation, support; agitate, convulse, jiggle, jolt, oscillate, roll, shake, shove, sway, swing, tremble, vibrate.

role, acting, character, characterization, function, impersonation, part, performance, presentation, task.

roll, catalogue, document, inventory, list, register, rota, schedule, scroll; bind, enfold, flatten, fluctuate, level, press, resound, reverberate, revolve, rotate, rumble, smooth, swathe, tumble,

turn, undulate, wallow, wheel, whirl.

romantic, charming, chimerical, chivalrous, courtly, dreamy, enchanting, extravagant, fanciful, fantastic, fictitious, ideal, idealistic, imaginary, imaginative, improbable, picturesque, poetic, sentimental. ANT.—definite, practical, pragmatic, realistic, solid.

roomy, ample, broad, capacious, commodious, extensive, grand, immense, large, spacious, vast, wide. ANT.—condensed, cramped, inconsiderable, little, small, tiny.

root, base, basis, bottom, foundation, groundwork, substructure, support, underpinning; cause, motive, reason; etymon, radical, radix, stem.

rot, corrode, decay, decline, decompose, decrease, degenerate, disintegrate, dwindle, ebb, fade, putrefy, spoil, wane, waste, weaken, wither. ANT.—bloom, flourish, grow, thrive.

rotate, circle, circulate, eddy, gyrate, invert, loop, revolve, roll, spin, swirl, swivel, turn, twirl, twist, wheel, whirl.

rough, bumpy, craggy, irregular, jagged, rugged, scabrous, scraggy, scratchy, serrated, uneven; approximate, coarse, cursory, imperfect, incomplete, unfinished, unpolished, unrefined; hard, harsh, severe, stormy, tempestuous, violent; austere, blunt, burly, crude, gruff,

impolite, indecent, rude, uncivil.
ANT.—even, level, sleek,
smooth; complete, finished, polished, refined, thorough; gentle,
mild, placid; courteous, cultivated, polite.

round, annular, circular, cylindrical, discoid, globular, orbed, or-
bicular, rotund, spherical;
bulging, convex, protuberant;
arched, bowed, coiled, curled,
looped.

rouse, agitate, animate, arouse,
awaken, excite, inflame, inspire,
inspirit, motivate, provoke, raise,
revive, stimulate, urge, whet.
ANT.—calm, lull, pacify, tranquilize.

route, avenue, beat, channel, circuit, course, detour, digression,
divergence, meandering, passage, path, rambling, road,
rounds, street, thoroughfare,
track, trail, walk, way.

routine, course, custom, cycle,
fashion, habit, method, practice,
round, system, usage, use; conventional, customary, habitual,
methodical.

royal, august, courtly, dignified,
elevated, grand, high, honorable, imperial, kingly, lofty,
lordly, majestic, monarchial, noble, princely, regal, reigning, resplendent, ruling, sovereign,
stately, sublime, superior, supreme, worthy. ANT.—low,
plebeian, proletarian, servile,
unadorned.

rude, abusive, arrogant, blunt,
boorish, brash, brazen, brusque,

churlish, crass, crusty, discourteous, disrespectful, gross, gruff,
impertinent, impolite, impudent,
insolent, insulting, obstreperous,
rough, saucy, surly, uncouth,
ungracious, vulgar; barbarous,
coarse, crude, ignorant, ill-bred,
illiterate, inelegant, primitive,
raw, rough, savage, uncivilized,
uncouth, unpolished, unrefined,
untaught; harsh, inclement,
rough, stormy, turbulent, violent; approximate, guessed, unprecise.   ANT.—affable,
considerate, engaging, genial,
tactful; chivalrous, civilized,
courtly, cultured, genteel, refined; gentle, peaceful, placid,
tranquil; exact, precise.

rugged, arduous, brawny, broken,
corrugated, craggy, difficult,
furrowed, harsh, husky, irregular, jagged, rough, scabrous,
scratchy, uneven. ANT.—delicate, even, feeble, gentle, level,
refined.

ruin, see destroy.

rule, axiom, canon, criterion, edict,
formula, guide, law, maxim,
method, norm, order, precept,
prescript, principle, propriety,
regulation, ruling, standard, statute, system; administration, authority, control, direction,
domination, dominion, dynasty,
empire, government, jurisdiction, mastery, regency, regime,
reign, sovereignty, sway; command, control, dictate, direct,
dominate, domineer, govern, influence, manage, prevail, regu-

late, restrain, superintend, sway.
ANT.—accident, chance, hazard, irregularity; anarchy, chaos, disorder, disorganization, servility; abandon, follow, forsake, submit, yield.

rupture, break, burst, cleave, crack, crush, demolish, destroy, disjoin, fracture, gash, infringe, pound, puncture, rack, rend, rive, sever, shatter, slash, slice, smash, split, squeeze, sunder, tear. ANT.—join, mend, renew, repair, restore.

rural, agrarian, agrestic, agricultural, agronomic, backwoods, bucolic, country, countrified, farm, nonurban, pastoral, ranch, rustic, suburban. ANT.—commercial, industrial, urban, urbane.

rush, accelerate, bolt, bustle, dash, expedite, fly, gallop, hasten, hurry, precipitate, press, quicken, scurry, scuttle, speed, sprint, tear, zoom; activity, demand, haste, hurry. ANT.—delay, detain, hinder, procrastinate, tarry.

rustic, agrestic, agricultural, country, pastoral, rural; coarse, homely, inelegant, plain, simple; boorish, bucolic, countrified, rough, rude, uncouth, unpolished, unsophisticated; artless, unaffected. ANT.—commercial, industrial, urban; cultured, elegant, polished, refined, urbane; artificial, insincere, pretentious, unnatural.

rut, channel, crevice, furrow, groove, hollow, track, trench;

course, custom, habit, practice, procedure, routine; rote, tedium.

ruthless, barbarous, bestial, brutal, brutish, coarse, cruel, ferocious, gross, harsh, implacable, inhuman, malevolent, merciless, pitiless, rancorous, relentless, remorseless, rough, rude, savage, tyrannical, unforgiving, unkind, vengeful, vindictive. ANT.—benevolent, charitable, compassionate, humane, merciful, sympathetic.

S

sack, demolish, despoil, devastate, loot, pillage, plunder, ravage, ruin, strip, waste; bag, pack, package, pocket.

sacred, blessed, consecrated, devout, divine, hallowed, holy, inviolable, pious, religious, sacrosanct, sanctified, saintly, spiritual, venerable. ANT.—blasphemous, evil, profane, sacrilegious, temporal, worldly.

sacrifice, abnegation, atonement, giving up, immolation, libation, loss, oblation, offering, self-denial, surrender, tribute; destroy, forfeit, forgo, give up, immolate, lose, offer, relinquish, renounce, surrender, yield.

sad, cheerless, dejected, depressed, despondent, disconsolate, dismal, doleful, downcast, funereal, gloomy, lugubrious, melancholy, mournful, pathetic, piteous, plaintive, somber, sorrowful, unhappy, woeful.

ANT.—blithe, cheerful, elated, happy, joyful.

safe, certain, dependable, harmless, immune, impregnable, intact, invulnerable, protected, reliable, secure, snug, sure, trustworthy, unharmed, unscathed. ANT.—endangered, hazardous, insecure, perilous, unsafe.

safeguard, bulwark, fence, palladium, protection, refuge, shelter, shield; convoy, defense, escort, guard, guardian, security.

safety, asylum, custody, escape, harbor, haven, preservation, protection, refuge, sanctuary, security, shelter, surety; exemption, immunity. ANT.—danger, hazard, jeopardy, peril, risk.

sag, bend, crumple, decline, droop, incline, lean, list, settle, sink, slant, slope, stoop, strain, sway, tend, tilt, waver, weaken. ANT.—ascend, climb, mount, rise, straighten.

sage, intellectual, philosopher, professor, pundit, savant, scholar. ANT.—dolt, dunce, fool, idiot, lunatic.

salary, allowance, commission, compensation, earnings, fee, pay, payment, recompense, redress, reimbursement, remuneration, settlement, stipend, wages.

salient, clear, conspicuous, distinguished, impressive, manifest, marked, notable, noticeable, obvious, outstanding, prominent, significant, striking, visible. ANT.—hidden, inconspicuous, insignificant, minor, obscure, unimportant.

salubrious, see healthy.

same, alike, analogous, corresponding, duplicate, equal, equivalent, identical, indistinguishable, invariable, isomeric, like, matching, twin, uniform. ANT.—contrary, different, disparate, distinct, opposed.

sample, case, cutting, example, exemplification, illustration, instance, model, part, pattern, prototype, representation, slice, specimen; check, examine, experiment, inspect, judge, smell, taste, test, try.

sanction, allowance, approbation, approval, assent, authority, authorization, commendation, consent, endorsement, permission, permit, praise, privilege, ratification, support; allow, approve, authorize, confirm, endorse, favor, let, permit, promote, ratify, suffer, support, sustain, tolerate. ANT.—censure, denunciation, objection, prohibition, stricture; ban, exclude, forbid, prevent, refuse, veto.

sanctuary, see safety.

sane, healthy, lucid, normal, rational, reasonable, self-possessed, sensible, sober, sound, sound-minded, steady, wholesome. ANT.—delirious, demented, insane, irrational, maniacal.

sap, debilitate, deplete, drain, enervate, enfeeble, exhaust, impair, impoverish, mine, subvert, tunnel, undermine, unsettle, weaken.

sarcastic, acrimonious, biting, bitter, caustic, cutting, derisive, hostile, ironic, mocking, sardonic, satirical, scornful, sneering, taunting. ANT.—affable, agreeable, amiable, courteous, gracious, respectful.

sate, cloy, content, fill, fill up, glut, gorge, gratify, pervade, please, quench, satiate, satisfy, saturate, slake, stuff. ANT.—deplete, drain, empty, exhaust, frustrate.

satire, abuse, banter, burlesque, derision, invective, irony, lampoon, mockery, parody, quip, raillery, ridicule, sarcasm, twist, wit.

satisfaction, comfort, content, contentment, delight, fulfillment, gladness, gratification, happiness, joy, pleasure, relief, serenity; amends, atonement; recompense, reimbursement, reparation. ANT.—despair, discontent, dissatisfaction, misery, sadness.

satisfactory, acceptable, adequate, ample, enough, fitting, gratifying, pleasing, satisfying, sufficient, suitable. ANT.—deficient, inadequate, insufficient, lacking, scanty.

satisfy, appease, cheer, comfort, compensate, content, gladden, gratify, please, remunerate, satiate; indemnify, repay; accomplish, complete, do, fill, fulfill, meet requirements, perform, qualify, suffice. ANT.—annoy, displease, fail to do, frustrate, neglect.

saturate, diffuse, drench, drown, fill, flood, immerse, impregnate, infiltrate, overfill, penetrate, permeate, pervade, run through, soak, steep, wet. ANT.—dehydrate, desiccate, dry, wipe.

savage, see ruthless.

save, accumulate, amass, collect, store; conserve, defend, deliver, economize, extricate, free, guard, hoard, keep, liberate, maintain, preserve, prevent, protect, redeem, rescue, reserve, safeguard, secure, shield, spare, uphold. ANT.—spend, waste; abandon, condemn, desert, impair, injure, leave.

savory, see delicious.

say, affirm, allege, articulate, assert, cite, declare, express, mention, pronounce, recite, rehearse, speak, state, talk, tell, utter.

saying, adage, affirmation, aphorism, apothegm, assertion, byword, citation, declaration, dictum, maxim, motto, pronunciation, proverb, quotation, remark, saw, statement, utterance.

scalding, blazing, blistering, burning, hot, red-hot, scorching, searing, torrid; ardent, fervent, fiery, flaming, passionate; peppery, pungent, spicy. ANT.—cold, freezing, frigid, frozen; apathetic, indifferent, phlegmatic, unconcerned; bland, dull, tasteless.

scan, audit, browse, consider, examine, inspect, investigate, regard, scrutinize, skim, survey, thumb over.

scandal, see disgrace.

scandalize, abuse, asperse, backbite, defame, detract, disgrace, disparage, libel, malign, offend, revile, shock, slander, traduce, vilify. ANT.—applaud, eulogize, honor, praise, respect.

scandalous, despicable, discreditable, disgraceful, disgusting, dishonorable, disreputable, flagrant, gross, hellish, ignominious, infamous, infernal, outrageous, shameful. ANT.—admirable, creditable, esteemed, honorable, respectable.

scanty, bare, few, inadequate, insufficient, lacking, limited, little, meager, narrow, pinched, ragged, scarce, scrimpy, skimpy, small, sparse, thin. ANT.—abundant, ample, plentiful, profuse, sufficient.

scarce, deficient, expensive, infrequent, isolated, limited, occasional, precious, rare, scanty, sparse, uncommon, unique, unplentiful. ANT.—cheap, customary, frequent, numerous, profuse.

scare, alarm, astound, cow, daunt, dismay, frighten, horrify, intimidate, petrify, shock, startle, terrify, terrorize, threaten. ANT.—calm, compose, encourage, inspirit, pacify, soothe.

scared, afraid, alarmed, apprehensive, fainthearted, fearful, frightened, nervous, petrified, startled, timorous, trembling, upset, worried. ANT.—assured, bold, composed, confident, self-assured.

scatter, see disperse.

scene, display, exhibition, pageant, panorama, representation, scenery, setting, show, sight, spectacle, tableau, view.

scent, aroma, bouquet, essence, fragrance, fume, incense, odor, perfume, redolence, smell, stench, stink, sweetness.

scheme, arrangement, cabal, conspiracy, design, intrigue, machination, method, plan, plot, procedure, project, stratagem, system; chart, diagram, draft, graph, outline, sketch; conspire, contrive, delineate, design, devise, engineer, frame, intend, invent, map, outline, plan, plot, prepare, project, shape, sketch.

scholar, apprentice, disciple, learner, novice, pupil, student; intellectual, philomath, sage, savant. ANT.—dolt, dunce, fool, ignoramus, numskull, simpleton.

scholarly, see learned, pedantic.

scholarship, see knowledge.

scoff, deride, fleer, flout, gibe, jeer, mock, rail, ridicule, scorn, sneer, taunt, twit. ANT.—applaud, approve, commend, laud, praise.

scold, see reprimand.

scope, amount, area, compass, degree, expanse, extent, field, length, magnitude, measure, purview, range, reach, room, size, space, span, stretch, sweep, width.

scorch, blaze, brand, burn, char, incinerate, kindle, parch, roast, scald, sear, shrivel, singe.

ANT.—douse, extinguish, quench, snuff out, stifle.

scorn, see contempt, disdain.

scrap, apportionment, bit, crumb, fragment, moiety, morsel, part, particle, piece, portion, section, segment, share; trash, waste material; brawl, fight, quarrel, squabble.

screen, camouflage, cloak, conceal, cover, defend, examine, guard, hide, inspect, protect, separate, shield, sift, sort, winnow.

scrub, clean, cleanse, purify, rub, scour, wash. ANT.—dirty, pollute, soil, stain, smirch.

scrupulous, see honest, just.

scrutinize, analyze, appraise, criticize, evaluate, examine, inspect, investigate, observe, probe, review, scan, search, stare, study, view. ANT.—disregard, ignore, neglect, overlook, slight.

search, examination, exploration, hunting, inquiry, investigation, pursuit, quest, research, seeking out; examine, explore, ferret out, hunt, investigate, look for, probe, ransack, rummage, scour, scrutinize, seek, shadow, track down, trail. ANT.—abandonment, cession, resignation, withdrawal; forgo, quit, relinquish, waive, vacate.

searching, see inquisitive.

season, age, complete, develop, mature, perfect, ripen; acclimate, accustom, harden, inure; flavor, spice.

seclusion, alienation, aloofness, apartness, concealment, insulation, isolation, loneliness, privacy, quarantine, quiet, refuge, remoteness, retirement, retreat, segregation, separation, sequestration, solitude, tranquility, withdrawal. ANT.—association, communion, connection, exposure, union.

secondary, see inferior.

secret, see clandestine.

secrete, see disguise, mask.

section, component, division, fragment, part, piece, portion, segment, share, slice, subdivision; country, district, division, domain, locality, province, realm, region, sector, territory, vicinity, zone.

secular, see lay, mundane.

secure, adjusted, assured, bound, certain, confident, definite, fastened, firm, fixed, immovable, indemnified, indubitable, inevitable, positive, safe, stable, sure, tight, undeniable, unharmed, unquestionable; accomplish, achieve, acquire, attain, earn, gain, get, grasp, obtain, possess, procure, realize, receive, win; assure, ensure, guarantee; defend, guard, protect, shield; adjust, bind, fasten, moor, settle, tighten. ANT.—doubtful, dubious, indefinite, questionable, uncertain; abandon, fail, forsake, relinquish; deny, disaffirm, disclaim, renounce; desert, leave, quit, relinquish, withdraw; detach, loosen, release, unfasten.

security, see refuge, safeguard.

sedate, calm, composed, demure, dignified, earnest, grave, imperturbable, proper, serene, serious, sober, solemn, staid. ANT.—excitable, flighty, frivolous, lively, mercurial.

see, behold, contemplate, descry, detect, discern, distinguish, espy, examine, gaze, grasp, heed, inspect, mark, mind, note, notice, observe, perceive, recognize, regard, scan, scrutinize, spy, stare, survey, understand, view, watch, witness; accompany, attend, escort; consult, discuss, interview, visit.

seek, see search.

seeming, apparent, external, ostensible, pretending, specious, superficial. ANT.—certain, definite, real, specific, true.

segment, allotment, apportionment, compartment, component, department, division, element, fraction, fragment, ingredient, moiety, parcel, part, piece, portion, scrap, section, share. ANT.—aggregate, entirety, sum, total, whole.

seize, see hinder, restrain.

select, adopt, appoint, choose, cull, decide, designate, elect, nominate, opt, pick, prefer, single out, specify. ANT.—eliminate, rebuff, refuse, reject.

selection, adoption, alternative, appropriation, choice, determination, election, favorite, option, pick, preference, reservation; assortment, collection.

self-contradictory, see irrational.

self-denial, see abstinence.

selfish, covetous, egoistic, egotistical, grasping, greedy, illiberal, mercenary, miserly, narrow, narrow-minded, parsimonious, rapacious, self-centered, self-indulgent, self-seeking, stingy, uncharitable, ungenerous. ANT.—altruistic, charitable, generous, liberal, magnanimous, philanthropic.

send, carry, cast, consign, convey, delegate, deliver, discharge, dispatch, drive, emit, fling, forward, hurl, impel, project, propel, ship, sling, throw, toss, transfer, transmit. ANT.—get, hold, keep, receive, retain.

senile, aged, ancient, decrepit, doddering, elderly, enfeebled, feeble, infirm, old, superannuated. ANT.—alert, strong, young, youthful, vigorous.

senior, advanced, chief, dean, elder, older, superior.

sensation, consciousness, excitement, feeling, passion, perception, response, sense, sensibility, sentiment. ANT.—apathy, insensibility, lethargy, narcosis, stupor.

sense, apprehension, connotation, consciousness, discernment, drift, explanation, feeling, gist, implication, import, insight, intent, interpretation, judgment, meaning, notion, opinion, purport, purpose, reason, sagacity, sensation, sensibility, sentiment, significance, signification, understanding, view, wisdom.

senseless, absurd, brainless, dense, dull, dumb, fatuous, foolish, idiotic, insensible, nonsensical, obtuse, ridiculous, silly, stupid, unconscious, unwise, witless. ANT.—alert, brilliant, clever, discerning, perceptive.

sensibility, awareness, consciousness, delicacy, discernment, emotion, feeling, impressibility, insight, sensation, sense, sensitiveness, subtlety, susceptibility, sympathetic response, sympathy, taste. ANT.—anesthesia, coldness, detachment, indifference, insensitivity, nonchalance.

sensible, apprehensible, perceptible; alive, attentive, awake, aware, cognizant, comprehending, conscious, informed, perceiving, sentient; capable, careful, discreet, intelligent, judicious, keen, prudent, rational, reasonable, sagacious, sage, sharp, shrewd, sober, sound, thoughtful, wise. ANT.—foolish, half-witted, inattentive, insensitive, unaware.

sensitive, alert, aware, conscious, delicate, impressionable, liable, painful, perceptive, predisposed, prone, responsive, sentient, subject, susceptible, sore, tender; irritable, high-strung, nervous, tense. ANT.—heartless, indifferent, obdurate, unconscious, unfeeling; calm, placid, relaxed, serene, tranquil.

sensual, arousing, carnal, debauched, dissolute, earthy, fleshly, intemperate, lascivious, lecherous, lewd, licentious, orgiastic, pleasure-loving, salacious, self-indulgent, sensory, sensuous, sybaritic, unspiritual, voluptuous, wanton. ANT.—ascetic, chaste, moderate, self-controlled, spiritual, temperate.

sentence, see condemn.

sentiment, sensation; affection, emotion, feeling, passion, sensibility, sympathy, tenderness; impression, judgment, notion, opinion, perception, remark, thought; maxim, saying, toast.

sentimental, dreamy, effusive, emotional, fanciful, gushing, idealistic, imaginative, languishing, maudlin, mushy, mawkish, overemotional, poetic, romantic, sappy, tender, unrealistic, visionary. ANT.—factual, literal, matter-of-fact, pragmatic, realistic.

separate, detach, disconnect, disjoin, dissociate, dissolve, disunite, divide, isolate, part, rend, segregate, sequester, sever, sunder, withdraw; alone, apart, disjoined, distinct, disunited, divergent, independent, parted, private, radial, unconnected, unique. ANT.—assemble, attach, combine, fuse, intertwine; associated, connected, joined, mixed, united.

separation, alienation, disconnection, disengagement, disjunction, dissolution, disunion, division, divorce, insulation, isolation, loneliness, partition, quarantine, retirement, rupture, seclusion, segregation, sequestration, severance, solitude, withdrawal. ANT.—association, communion, connection, relationship, union.

sequence, arrangement, chain, following, graduation, order, progression, series, string, succession, train; consequence, result, sequel.

serene, see quiescent, quiet.

serenity, see peace, repose.

series, see sequence.

serious, great, important, momentous, weighty; austere, deep, earnest, grave, profound, sedate, sober, solemn, somber, staid, thoughtful; alarming, critical, dangerous, risky. ANT.—flippant, insignificant, small, trifling, trivial; informal, reassuring, relaxed, safe.

serve, advance, aid, answer, assist, attend, benefit, content, contribute, distribute, forward, give, help, promote, requite, satisfy, succor, suffice, supply, support, treat, uphold, wait on. ANT.—attack, combat, impede, oppose, rival.

service, advantage, assistance, avail, behalf, benefit, co-operation, favor, gain, good, help, interest, profit, use, utility; ceremony, ritual, rite, worship; business, duty, employment, function, labor, ministry, office.

serviceable, advantageous, applicable, beneficial, conducive, contributive, favorable, good, helpful, important, practical, profitable, salutary, usable, useful, valuable, wholesome. ANT.—deleterious, detrimental, impractical, ineffective, useless.

servile, see contemptible, ignoble.

set, adjust, anchor, appoint, arrange, deposit, dispose, establish, expose, fix, lay, locate, mount, place, plant, predetermine, put, regulate, settle, situate, stand, station; coagulate, congeal, harden, jell, solidify, thicken; established, firm, fixed, formal, immovable, located, placed, positive; arrangement, association, attitude, circle, class, club, cluster, collection, company, coterie, group, party, position, posture, series.

settle, adjudicate, close, conclude, confirm, decide, determine, dispose, end, reconcile, resolve, terminate; drop, fall, sink, subside; calm, pacify, quiet, tranquilize; colonize, domesticate, people; establish, fix, locate, place, put, set, station; adjust, arbitrate, regulate, stabilize, straighten. ANT.—doubt, hesitate, suspend, vacillate, waver; anger, antagonize, roil, stir; destroy, disestablish, raze, ruin, unsettle; confuse, disarrange, disorganize, disrupt, entangle.

settlement, close, completion, conclusion, end, finale, issue, termination; decision, deduction, inference, judgment; colonization, colony, community, establishment; adjustment, compensation, pay, recompense, reimbursement, remuneration, reward; agreement, arrangement, compact, contract, covenant, pledge, understanding.

sever, see divide, separate.

several, different, distinct, divers, diverse, manifold, many, numerous, quite a few, separate, sundry, unlike, various. ANT.—one, none.

severe, acute, arduous, austere, despotic, distressing, domineering, drastic, exacting, extreme, forbidding, grim, hard, harsh, inflexible, intense, obdurate, oppressive, relentless, rigid, rigorous, sharp, stern, stiff, strict, stringent, uncompromising, unmitigated, unrelenting, unyielding, violent; plain, simple, unadorned. ANT.—compassionate, courteous, gentle, lenient, placid; beautified, decorated, embellished.

sew, baste, bind, fasten, fix, mend, patch, piece, refit, repair, restore, seam, stitch, tack, tailor. ANT.—deface, destroy, hurt, rend, ruin.

shabby, see inferior, poor.

shade, brilliance, color, complexion, dye, hue, paint, pigment, saturation, stain, tincture, tinge, tint; shadow, umbrage; cloud, darken, dim, eclipse, obscure. ANT.—achromatism, paleness, transparency; brighten, illuminate, manifest, reveal.

shake, agitate, convulse, discourage, dishearten, dissuade, flutter, intimidate, jar, joggle, jolt,

jounce, oscillate, quake, quiver, rock, shiver, shudder, sway, totter, tremble, trill, vibrate, wave, waver.

shallow, cursory, exterior, flimsy, frivolous, imperfect, inconsiderable, senseless, silly, simple, slight, stupid, superficial, trifling, trivial. ANT.—bottomless, complete, deep, intelligent, profound, thorough, unfathomable.

sham, affect, assume, dissimulate, feign, imitate, personate, pretend, simulate; counterfeit, deceit, delusion, dissimulation, fake, fakery, fraud, humbug, imitation, mockery, pretense, pretext, ruse, stratagem, trick, wile. ANT.—disclose, expose, reveal, unmask, unveil; actuality, fact, reality, substance, truth.

shame, abash, degrade, discomfit, discredit, dishonor, embarrass, humiliate, mortify; abashment, chagrin, discomfiture, embarrassment, humiliation, mortification, remorse; baseness, contempt, disfavor, disgrace, dishonor, disrepute, ignominy, infamy, odium, opprobrium, reproach, scandal. ANT.—encourage, glorify, honor, respect, uphold; contentment, impenitence, satisfaction, serenity, tranquility; dignity, glory, honor, praise, respect.

shameful, see scandalous.

shape, appearance, aspect, build, cast, configuration, conformation, construction, contour, cut, figure, form, frame, guise, image, mold, outline, pattern; arrange, cast, combine, compose, constitute, construct, create, develop, devise, direct, discipline, fashion, forge, form, frame, invent, make, make up, model, mold, organize, produce, regulate, sketch. ANT.—contortion, deformity, distortion, malformation, mutilation; destroy, disfigure, distort, injure, mar, wreck.

shapeless, amorphic, amorphous, deformed, disfigured, formless, irregular, misshapen, unshapely, unsymmetrical. ANT.—proportionate, proportioned, shapely, symmetrical, well-formed.

share, allotment, bit, contingent, dividend, division, dole, dose, fraction, fragment, helping, parcel, part, percentage, piece, portion, quota, ration, section, segment; administer, allot, apportion, appropriate, assign, deal, dispense, distribute, divide, experience, parcel, partake, participate in, partition, portion. ANT.—bulk, entirety, sum, totality, whole; aggregate, amass, combine, unite, withhold.

shared, see mutual.

sharp, acute, honed, keen, pointed, razor-edged, sharpened; acrid, barbed, biting, bitter, cutting, peppery, piquant, pungent, sour, spicy, stinging; excruciating, penetrating, piercing, severe, shrill; astute, brilliant, clever, cunning, discerning, incisive, intelligent, quick, sagacious, shrewd, wily, wise, witty; abrupt, harsh, precipitous, rough, rugged, steep. ANT.—blunt, dull, pointless, unsharpened; bland, tasteless, unsavory; delicate, faint, low, melodious, mild, soft; dull-witted, inept, insipid, stupid, vapid; even, flat, gradual, level, smooth.

shatter, see break.

shattered, broken, collapsed, crushed, demolished, destroyed, flattened, fractured, hurt, interrupted, mutilated, reduced, ruptured, separated, slivered, smashed, splintered, wrecked. ANT.—intact, integral, repaired, sound, united.

shelter, asylum, harbor, haven, refuge, retreat, sanctuary; cover, defense, lee, protection, safety, screen, security, shield; cloak, clothe, conceal, cover, curtain, defend, disguise, ensconce, envelop, guard, harbor, hide, house, mask, preserve, protect, safeguard, screen, secure, shield, shroud, veil. ANT.—danger, exposure, hazard, jeopardy, menace, threat; endanger, expose, ignore, neglect, uncover.

shield, avert, forbid, repel; also see shelter.

shift, displace, exchange, remove, substitute; adapt, adjust, alter, change, convert, moderate, modify, transfigure, transform, vary; move, stir, turn, veer. ANT.—keep, retain; continue, establish, preserve, stabilize; cease, halt, rest, stop.

shifting, see fickle.

shine, beam, blaze, dazzle, flare, flash, glare, gleam, glimmer, glisten, glitter, glow, irradiate, radiate, scintillate, shimmer, sparkle, twinkle; excel, surpass; buff, burnish, polish, wax.

shining, see magnificent, radiant.

ship, consign, convey, dispatch, forward, remit, route, send, transmit, transport; deport, dismiss, send away.

shock, alarm, amaze, appall, astonish, astound, disconcert, dumfound, embarrass, flabbergast, frighten, horrify, offend, startle, stun, surprise, terrify, terrorize. ANT.—calm, console, mitigate, pacify, prepare, soothe.

shocking, see horrible.

shoot, cast, catapult, dart, discharge, eject, emit, expel, fire, hit, hurl, propel; kill, wound; bloom, bud, germinate, sprout; branch, channel, chute, offshoot, scion, sprout, sucker, trough, twig.

shore, bank, beach, border, brink, coast, margin, seacoast, seaside, strand; brace, buttress, prop, stabilize, support.

short, compact, diminutive, little, low, slight, small, tiny; abbreviated, abridged, abrupt, brief, compendious, compressed, concise, condensed, laconic, pithy, precise, succinct, summary, terse; deficient, inadequate, insufficient, lacking, limited, scanty; abrupt, curt, uncivil. ANT.—colossal, enormous, gigantic, ti-

tanic, towering; diffuse, jumbled, redundant, repetitive, wordy; abundant, adequate, excessive, profuse, sufficient; civil, courteous, gracious, patient, polite.

shortcoming, see defect, imperfection.

shorten, see contract, diminish.

shout, acclaim, bellow, call out, clamor, cry, cry out, ejaculate, exclaim, howl, roar, scream, screech, shriek, vociferate, yell, yelp. ANT.—intimate, murmur, mutter, suggest, whisper.

shove, butt, crowd, drive, elbow, force, impel, jostle, press, propel, push, ram, shoulder, thrust. ANT.—drag, halt, pull, stop.

show, array, demonstration, display, entertainment, exhibition, exposition, exposure, flourish, ostentation, pageantry, parade, performance, production, spectacle, splendor, splurge; appearance, semblance; pretense, puppetry, sham, simulation, speciousness; disclose, display, exhibit, expose, indicate, parade, present, reveal, unfold; demonstrate, evidence, explain, manifest, prove, verify; conduct, direct, guide, usher; inform, instruct, teach.

showy, affected, artificial, ceremonious, dramatic, flashy, gaudy, glaring, histrionic, melodramatic, ornate, pompous, theatrical, tinseled. ANT.—genuine, humble, modest, subdued, unaffected.

shred, bit, fragment, frazzle, jot, mite, particle, rag, scrap, smidgen, speck, strip, tatter; lacerate, rend, rip, slice, slit, split, strip, tear, wound. ANT.—aggregate, bulk, mass, quantity, volume; heal, join, mend, repair, restore, unite.

shrewd, artful, clandestine, covert, crafty, cunning, foxy, furtive, guileful, insidious, sly, stealthy, surreptitious, tricky, underhand, wily; acute, alert, astute, careful, circumspect, clever, discerning, ingenious, intelligent, knowing, mindful, observant, perspicacious, prudent, reflective, sagacious, sapient, sharp. ANT.—candid, frank, genuine, open, sincere; dense, frivolous, ignorant, impetuous, undiscerning.

shrill, see keen, severe.

shrink, balk, contract, cringe, decline, decrease, deflate, diminish, droop, dwindle, fail, flinch, languish, lessen, quail, recoil, shrivel, waste, weaken, wilt, wince, withdraw, wither. ANT.—expand, grow, rejuvenate, renew, revive.

shun, see avoid, escape.

shut, close, lock, seal; debar, exclude, preclude; confine, immure, imprison, incarcerate; complete, conclude, end, finish, terminate. ANT.—open, unbar, unlock; clear, free, liberate, release; begin, commence, initiate, start.

shy, see modest, reserved.

sick, ailing, confined, diseased, ill, impaired, indisposed, infirm, invalid, morbid, sickly, unhealthy, unwell. ANT.—hale, hardy, healthy, robust, vigorous

sift, analyze, discuss, evaluate, examine, investigate, probe, screen, scrutinize, separate, sort, winnow; bolt, colander, filter, grade, screen, size, sort, strain.

sign, augury, badge, emblem, gesture, identification, indication, manifestation, mark, note, notice, omen, portent, presage, proof, representation, signal, suggestion, symbol, symptom, token.

signal, alarm, cue, gesture, indicator, mark, message, sign, warning; conspicuous, famous, important, memorable, momentous, outstanding, prominent, remarkable, salient, striking.

significance, consequence, effect, force, implication, import, importance, meaning, point, purpose, relevance, substance, weight.

significant, critical, emphatic, expressive, grave, important, indicative, meaningful, momentous, notable, outstanding, prominent, remarkable, serious, suggestive, telling, vital, weighty, worthy. ANT.—inconsequential, insignificant, petty, shallow, trivial.

signify, denote, designate, disclose, express, imply, import, indicate, intimate, manifest, mean, purport, reveal, show, specify, suggest. ANT.—conceal, cover, hide, obscure, withhold.

silent, calm, hushed, mute, noiseless, peaceful, placid, quiescent, quiet, reserved, reticent, secretive, still, taciturn, tight-lipped, tranquil, uncommunicative. ANT.—clamorous, communicative, loquacious, noisy, raucous, voluble.

silhouette, configuration, conformation, contour, delineation, figure, form, outline, profile, shape.

silly, see irrational, preposterous, ridiculous.

similar, akin, alike, allied, analogous, comparable, correlative, correspondent, corresponding, facsimile, homogeneous, like, parallel, reciprocal, related, resembling. ANT.—alien, different, dissimilar, divergent, opposed, unlike.

similarity, affinity, analogy, association, comparison, concordance, conformity, correlation, correspondence, harmony, homogeneity, likeness, parallelism, parity, relation, resemblance, semblance, simile, similitude. ANT.—difference, disparity, distinction, divergence, variance.

simple, apparent, easy, effortless, elementary, facile, mere, obvious, pure, simplistic, single, unblended, uncompounded, unmixed; homely, humble, modest, plain, unadorned; artless, frank, naive, natural, open, unaffected, unpretentious, unsophisticated; asinine, credulous, foolish, gullible, ignorant, oafish, silly. ANT.—complicated, complex, difficult, intricate; decorated, embellished, opulent, ornate; contrived, deceptive, pretentious, sophisticated; discerning, intelligent, judicious, sagacious, wise.

simulate, see mimic.

simultaneous, accompanying, coeval, coincident, concomitant, concurrent, contemporaneous, synchronal, synchronous. ANT.—foregoing, following, preceding, prior, subsequent.

sin, see evil, offense.

sincere, candid, conscientious, direct, earnest, frank, genuine, guileless, heartfelt, honest, ingenuous, open, straightforward, true, trustworthy, truthful, unaffected, undisguised, unfeigned, unreserved, upright, veracious. ANT.—deceitful, deceptive, evasive, false, hypocritical, untrustworthy.

sincerity, see honesty.

sinewy, able-bodied, active, athletic, brawny, burly, energetic, firm, hardy, husky, manly, mighty, muscular, powerful, robust, stalwart, steely, strapping, strong, sturdy, tough, vigorous, virile, wiry. ANT.—delicate, emaciated, feeble, puny, weak.

sinful, see bad, corrupt, immoral.

sing, carol, chant, chirp, croon, hum, hymn, intone, lilt, trill, troll, vocalize, warble, yodel.

singe, see scorch.

single, celibate, distinctive, elemental, individual, isolated, marked, one, only, particular, pure, separate, simple, singular, sole, solitary, special, specific, unaccompanied, unique, unmixed, unwed. ANT.—associated, common, general, multiple, ordinary, universal.

singular, see eccentric, extraordinary, rare.

sinister, adverse, corrupt, deleterious, dire, disastrous, dishonest, evil, foreboding, harmful, hostile, malefic, mischievous, ominous, pernicious, perverse, threatening, unfavorable, unlucky. ANT.—auspicious, expedient, favorable, opportune, propitious.

sink, collapse, decline, decrease, descend, diminish, drop, fall, slump, subside; droop, extend downward, hang; be submerged, engulf, go down, immerse, touch bottom. ANT.—arise, ascend, climb, mount, surge; come up, float, rise, stay afloat, swim.

site, district, locality, locus, place, position, region, section, situation, spot, station.

situation, case, circumstance, condition, exigency, plight, predicament, state, status; employment, environment, job, location, place, position, post, setting, site, spot, station, surroundings, whereabouts.

size, amplitude, area, bigness, bulk, capacity, dimensions, enormity, expanse, extent, greatness, immensity, largeness, magnitude, measurement, mass, quantity, scope, space, vastness, volume.

skeleton, frame, shell, structure; also see outline.

skeptic, agnostic, apostate, cynic, deist, detractor, dissenter, doubter, free-thinker, idolator, infidel, nihilist, questioner, schismatic, unbeliever. ANT.—believer, devotee, disciple, evangelist, worshiper.

skepticism, agnosticism, cynicism, disbelief, distrust, doubt, doubting, hesitation, incredulity, infidelity, misgiving, mistrust, questioning, suspicion, wavering. ANT.—belief, certainty, conviction, faith, reliance, trust.

sketch, see outline.

skill, cunning, ingenuity, knack; also see dexterity, facility.

skillful, able, accomplished, adept, adroit, apt, capable, clever, competent, cunning, deft, dexterous, efficient, expert, handy, ingenious, masterful, practiced, proficient, ready, skilled, talented, trained, versed. ANT.—awkward, blundering, clumsy, inept, inexperienced.

skin, bark, coat, covering, cuticle, derma, dermis, epidermis, hide, husk, integument, lamina, lining, parchment, peel, pelt, plating, rind, surface, tegument, veneer.

skip, drop, miss, neglect; also see eliminate, exclude, ignore.

slack, disengaged, free, indefinite, lax, limp, loose, relaxed, slow, stagnant, unbound, unfastened, untied, vague; backward, careless, dilatory, dissolute, heedless, indifferent, negligent, remiss, tardy, unrestrained, wanton. ANT.—drawn, engaged, fast, taut, tied; alert, careful, disciplined, dutiful, restrained.

slander, see libel, scandalize.

slant, bent, bias, disposition, inclination, leaning, partiality, penchant, predilection, predisposition, prejudice, proclivity, proneness, propensity, tendency, turn; acclivity, angle, declivity, divergence, grade, list, obliquity, slope, tilt; lean, slope, tilt, tip, slope.

slavery, serfdom, thralldom, vassalage; also see captivity.

slaughter, see kill, massacre.

sleazy, feeble, flabby, flaccid, flimsy, fragile, limp, poor, tenuous, thin, trashy, weak, worthless. ANT.—excellent, fine, firm, forceful, strong.

sleek, glossy, lustrous, oily, polished, satiny, shiny, silky, slick, smooth, velvety. ANT.—coarse, dry, dull, harsh, rough.

sleep, catnap, coma, doze, dozing, drowse, hibernation, lethargy, nap, nod, repose, rest, siesta, slumber, snooze, somnolism, stupor, trance.

slender, feeble, flimsy, gaunt, lank, lean, meager, narrow, rare, scanty, scrawny, skinny, slight, slim, spare, tenuous, thin, trivial. ANT.—broad, bulky, fat, strong, thick, wide.

slide, glide, skate, skid, skim, skip, slip, slither; chute, incline, ramp.

slight, disregard, ignore, neglect, omit, overlook, skip; also see slender.

sling, cast, dangle, hang, heave, hoist, hurl, impel, pitch, propel, shove, suspend, throw, toss.

slip, blunder, boner, error, fallacy, fault, fluff, inaccuracy, indiscretion, lapse, misstep, mistake. ANT.—accuracy, perfection, precision, truth.

slope, see slant.

slothful, see lazy.

slow, crawling, creeping, dawdling, deliberate, dull, gradual, laggard, languid, leisurely, lingering, loitering, moderate, slack, torpid, unready; apathetic, dilatory, idle, indolent, lazy, lethargic, negligent, phlegmatic, procrastinating, sleepy, sluggish, tired; belated, delayed, overdue. ANT.—quick, rapid, speedy, swift; conscientious, enthusiastic, industrious, lively, zealous; prompt, punctilious, punctual, timely.

sluggish, see slow.

slumber, see sleep.

sly, artful, astute, calculating, clandestine, covert, crafty, cunning, deceitful, designing, foxy, furtive, guileful, insidious, knowing, mischievous, nimble, scheming, shifty, shrewd, stealthy, subtle, surreptitious, traitorous, tricky, underhand, wary, wily. ANT.—artless, candid, frank, genuine, open, sincere.

small, diminutive, feeble, inconsiderable, insignificant, little, microscopic, miniature, minute, petty, puny, pygmy, scanty, slender, slight, tiny, trivial, ungenerous, weak, wee, young. ANT.—enormous, generous, huge, immense, powerful.

smart, adroit, apt, clever, dexterous, quick, quick-witted, skillful, talented, witty; acute, alert, bright, intelligent, keen, sharp, shrewd; chic, dapper, modish, stylish. ANT.—awkward, bungling, clumsy, slow; dense, dull, stupid, unintelligent; dowdy, frowzy, shabby.

smash, see rupture.

smell, see odor.

smooth, even, flat, flush, level, plane; glossy, polished, silky, sleek, slick; diplomatic, glib, suave, unruffled, urbane; calm, mild, still, tranquil. ANT.—craggy, jagged, rocky, uneven; hairy, rough, rugged; blunt, rash, rude, tactless; agitated, inflamed, furious, stormy, violent.

snag, see obstacle.

snare, ambush, apprehend, arrest, capture, catch, clutch, grasp, grip, lure, net, seize, trap; artifice, deception, decoy, hoax, lure, pitfall, ruse, stratagem, trap, trick, wile. ANT.—free, liberate, release, unchain, unshackle; fact, fidelity, genuineness, honesty, truth.

sneer, fleer, scoff; also see mock.

snub, abash, crush, cut, discomfit, disdain, disregard, humble, humiliate, ignore, neglect, rebuke. ANT.—comfort, honor, love, regard, respect.

snug, compact, constricted, contracted, firm, narrow, neat, stretched, taut, tense, tight, trim; close, comfortable, cozy, warm. ANT.—lax, loose, open, relaxed, slack; cold, detached, distant, removed, uncomfortable.

soar, circle, dart, flit, float, flutter, fly, glide, hover, mount, remain aloft, sail, swoop, wing. ANT.—descend, fall, plummet, sink, topple.

sober, abstemious, austere, calm, dispassionate, earnest, grave, moderate, quiet, reasonable, sedate, serious, solemn, staid, steady, temperate, unintoxicated, unruffled. ANT.—boisterous, dissipated, drunk, excited, immoderate, joyful, overwrought.

social, affable, communicative, outgoing; also see hospitable, pleasant.

soft, amenable, bland, compassionate, downy, elastic, flaccid, flexible, fluffy, gentle, impressible, indulgent, lenient, malleable, meek, mellow, merciful, mild, pliable, pliant, silky, smooth, spongy, subdued, supple, tender, tolerant, tractable, yielding. ANT.—brittle, cruel, domineering, insensible, selfpossessed, unyielding.

soften, abate, allay, alleviate, diminish, dissolve, extenuate, lessen, melt, mitigate, moderate, relax, relieve, solace, soothe, tenderize, thaw, weaken. ANT.—aggravate, agitate, augment, increase, irritate, lengthen.

soil, continent, country, earth, field, ground, land, plain, region, tract; blemish, blight; also see defile.

solace, see console.

sole, alone, deserted, desolate, isolated, lonely, secluded, unaided; individual, lone, one, only, remaining, single, solitary. ANT.—accompanied, attended, surrounded; collective, multiple, public, social.

solemn, august, awe-inspiring, ceremonious, consequential, formal, imposing, impressive, majestic, momentous, precise, regular, reverential, ritualistic; austere, earnest, grave, grim, heavy, intense, reserved, sedate, serious, sober, somber, staid, stern, thoughtful. ANT.—informal, insignificant, ordinary, transitory, uneventful; animated, cheerful, frivolous, giddy, lively.

solid, compact, dense, firm, hard, rigid, sound, stable, substantial, unyielding. ANT.—liquid, porous, vaporous, vulnerable, weak.

solitary, see sole.

solitude, alienation, asylum, concealment, isolation, loneliness, privacy, quiet, refuge, retirement, retreat, seclusion, silence, stillness. ANT.—clamor, exposure, notoriety, publicity, tumult.

solve, decipher, discover, elucidate, explain, interpret, resolve, unfold, untangle. ANT.—complicate, involve, tangle.

somatic, bodily, carnal, corporal, corporeal, fleshly, human, material, natural, organic, physical, substantial, tangible, unspiritual. ANT.—ethereal, mental, spiritual.

somber, bleak, dull, funereal; also see dismal.

soon, beforehand, before long, early, quickly, shortly. ANT.—late, overdue, slow, tardy.

soothe, allay, alleviate, assuage, calm, cheer, comfort, compose, console, ease, encourage, gladden, lull, mollify, pacify, please, relieve, solace, sympathize, tranquilize. ANT.—afflict, annoy, antagonize, distress, vex.

soothing, docile, relaxed, soft; also see gentle, peaceful.

sophisticated, astute, blase, cultivated, cultured, experienced, knowledgeable, polished, refined, wise, worldly. ANT.—artless, crude, immature, ingenuous, naive.

sorcery, see magic.

sordid, base, debased, depraved, dirty, foul, loathsome, obscene, odious, revolting, squalid, vicious, vile, vulgar, wicked; abject, contemptible, degraded, despicable, ignoble, low, mean, worthless, wretched. ANT.—attractive, charming, decent, laudable; distinguished, eminent, honorable, noble, upright.

sorrow, affliction, anguish, contrition, distress, grief, heartache, lamentation, misery, misfortune, mourning, penitence, regret, remorse, sadness, trial, tribulation, woe. ANT.—comfort, delight, happiness, joy, solace.

sorrowful, see gloomy, melancholy.

sort, category, character, class, description, kind, nature, species, strain, type, variety.

sound, binding, cogent, durable, effective, efficacious, faithful, genuine, hale, healthy, intact, legal, logical, powerful, reliable, satisfactory, solvent, stable, strong, substantial, unimpaired, valid, vigorous, weighty; din, noise, note, tone. ANT.—counterfeit, defective, impaired, spurious, void; hush, quiet, stillness.

sour, acid, acrid, acrimonious, astringent, bitter, complaining, curdled, embittered, glum, grouchy, morose, peevish, querulous, rancid, sharp, spoiled, sullen, tart, vinegary. ANT.—amiable, cheerful, cordial, kindly, sugary, sweet.

source, agent, cause, determinant, incentive, inducement, motive, origin, principle, reason; beginning, birth, commencement, cradle, derivation, foundation, fountain, inception, incipience, origin, primogenitor, rise, root, spring, start, wellspring. ANT.—consequence, effect, result; harvest, issue, outcome, product, termination.

souvenir, see memorial.

spacious, see roomy.

spare, rescue, safeguard; also see preserve.

sparkle, see glare.

speak, announce, articulate, chatter, communicate, converse, debate, declaim, declare, discourse, discuss, express, proclaim, pronounce, report, say, talk, tell, utter, vocalize, voice.

special, choice, definite, determinate, distinctive, exceptional, exclusive, extraordinary, individual, particular, peculiar, proper, rare, restricted, singular, specific, uncommon, unique, unusual. ANT.—broad, commonplace, ecumenical, prevalent, universal.

specific, categorical, characteristic, concrete, definite, especial, exact, explicit, express, individual, limited, particular, peculiar, precise, special. ANT.—general, generic, indefinite, uncertain, vague.

specify, appoint, call, choose, denominate, designate, entitle, individualize, mention, name, particularize, select, single out, stipulate. ANT.—discard, generalize, hint, miscall, misname, reject.

specimen, instance, unit; see also example.

speck, crumb, smidgen; see also particle.

spectacle, parade, representation, scene, splurge; see also display.

speculate, apprehend, assume, believe, conjecture, consider, contemplate, deduce, guess, imagine, meditate, muse, ponder, presume, reflect, suppose, surmise, think, weigh. ANT.—ascertain, conclude, demonstrate, prove, substantiate.

speech, articulation, chatter, communication, diction, discourse, enunciation, lecture, locution, oration, pronunciation, report; see also conversation; language.

speed, facilitate, forward, further, promote, rush, urge; see also hasten.

spend, consume, deplete, disburse, dispense, dissipate, exhaust, expend, liquidate, pay, scatter, squander, use, waste. ANT.—cache, collect, conserve, hoard, pocket, retain.

sphere, ball, circle, compass, department, domain, globe, orb, province, realm, scope, spheroid.

spirit, apparition, ghost, phantom, specter, vision; animation, courage, energy, enthusiasm, fervor, fortitude, life, liveliness, verve, vigor, vitality, vivacity, zeal; intent, meaning; disposition, feeling, mood, nature, temper; essence, psyche, soul, substance.

spiritual, divine, ecclesiastical, ethereal, ghostly, holy, immaterial, incorporeal, pure, refined, religious, sacred, supernatural, unearthly, unworldly. ANT.—carnal, corporeal, material, physical, secular, worldly.

spite, see malice.

spiteful, antagonistic, disagreeable, hostile, ill-natured, malevolent, malicious, malign, mean, rancorous, surly, ugly, vengeful, venomous, vicious, vindictive. ANT.—forgiving, friendly, generous, helpful, merciful.

splendid, brilliant, bright, dazzling, effulgent, eminent, excellent, glorious, gorgeous, grand, illustrious, magnificent, radiant, refulgent, resplendent, shining, showy, sumptuous, superb. ANT.—drab, dull, humble, mediocre, unimpressive.

splendor, brilliance, radiance; see also luster.

split, rive, sever, shred, wound. see also rip; sever.

spoil, decay, decompose, disintegrate, putrefy, rot, waste; corrupt, damage, debase, destroy, disfigure, harm, impair, injure, mar, pervert, ruin, vitiate; booty, loot, plunder. ANT.—flourish, grow, increase, luxuriate, thrive; enhance, improve, mend, perfect, repair.

spoken, announced, expressed, oral, unwritten, uttered, verbal, vocal, voiced. ANT.—documentary, nonverbal, recorded, written.

sponsor, advertiser, advocate, backer, champion, helper, patron, protector, subscriber, supporter, surety; godparent.

spontaneous, automatic, casual, extemporaneous, impulsive, instinctive, involuntary, offhand, unbidden, unconscious, unforced, unintentional, unwilling. ANT.—deliberate, designed, intended, premeditated, rehearsed.

sport, contest, match, merriment; caper, frolic, gamble, play, revel, romp, stake, toy, wager; display, exhibit, wear; see also recreation.

spread, circulate, diffuse, dispense, disperse, disseminate, distribute, exhibit, expand, extend, open, promulgate, propagate, publish, radiate, scatter, sow, stretch, strew, unfold, unroll, unseal. ANT.—collect, conceal, condense, suppress, tighten.

sprightly, agile, animated, blithe, brisk, buoyant, cheerful, debonair, effervescent, elated, hopeful, jocund, lively, quick, spirited, sportive, vivacious. ANT.—dejected, depressed, despondent, gloomy, pessimistic.

spring, birth, cradle, derivation, foundation. see also beginning.

sprout, bud, burgeon, develop, germinate, grow, shoot. ANT.—decrease, shrink, wither.

spry, active, agile, alacritous, alert, blithe, brisk, flexible, frisky, lively, nimble, quick, spirited, sprightly, supple, vivacious. ANT.—feeble, inactive, lethargic, sluggish, torpid.

spur, cause, incitement, principle, purpose, reason; see also incentive.

squabble, see quarrel.

squalid, dirty, filthy, foul, grimy, muddy, soiled, sordid, unclean; base, contemptible, despicable, low, mean, miserable, pitiful, poor, shabby, unkempt, wretched. ANT.—clean, immaculate, pure, spotless; appealing, attractive, comfortable, inviting, presentable.

squander, abuse, consume, corrode, dissipate, drain, exhaust, expend, lavish, misspend, misuse, scatter, spend, splurge, waste. ANT.—economize, hoard, invest, preserve, retain.

squeamish, see particular.

stability, composure, steadiness; see also balance.

stable, balanced, constant, determined, durable, enduring, equable, established, firm, fixed, immovable, immutable, lasting, permanent, regular, resolute, secure, settled, solid, staunch, steadfast, steady, unwavering. ANT.—erratic, fluctuating, mercurial, mutable, vacillating.

staid, dignified, earnest, grave, reserved, sedate, serious, sober, solemn, steady, stuffy, unimaginative. ANT.—boisterous, flighty, frivolous, impulsive, volatile.

stain, befoul, blemish, blight, blot, defile, discolor, disgrace, dishonor, mark, soil, spot, sully, taint, tarnish; color, dye, tinge, tint. ANT.—cleanse, decorate, honor, purify; blanch, bleach, whiten.

stale, see insipid.

stand, abide, bear, continue, endure, hold, last, persist, prevail, remain, suffer, survive, sustain, tolerate; discontinue, halt, hold, pause, remain, rest, stay, stop. ANT.—falter, succumb, surrender, weaken, yield; advance, continue, develop, grow, progress, run.

standard, gauge, touchstone; see also criterion.

start, see commence; origin.

startle, alarm, amaze, astonish, astound, bewilder, confound, daze, disconcert, dumbfound, flabbergast, overwhelm, petrify, shock, stun, surprise, unsettle. ANT.—caution, forewarn, prepare, signal, warn.

starving, craving, dying, longing, weakening; see also hungry.

state, claim, explain, express, propound, recount, say, specify, utter; see also assert; recite; situation.

stately, courtly, lordly, monarchial, princely, regal, royal, ruling, sovereign, supreme; see also majestic.

statement, acknowledgment, affirmation, allegation, announcement, assertion, declaration, dictum, mention, profession, proposition, report, specification, thesis.

status, caste, circumstance, condition, distinction, footing, grade, place, position, rank, reputation, situation, standing, state, station.

statute, act, decree, edict, injunction, law, order, ordinance, regulation, ruling.

staunch, reliable, trusty. see also loyal.

stay, abide, delay, halt, linger, lodge, pause, persist, remain, sojourn, stand, tarry, visit, wait; arrest, check, hinder, impede, obstruct, restrain, retard. ANT.—dart, hasten, leave, progress, scurry; assist, encourage, facilitate, promote, sustain.

steady, inflexible, unswerving, unyielding; see also stable.

steal, pillage, plagiarize, snitch, swipe; see also embezzle; rob.

steep, abrupt, angular, craggy, hilly, perpendicular, precipitous, rugged, sharp, sheer, sudden, vertical. ANT.—flat, gradual, horizontal, level, smooth.

steer, control, escort, supervise; see also guide.

stench, fetidness, fetor, stink. see also odor.

sterile, arid, barren, childless, fallow, fruitless, impotent, infecund, infertile, unfruitful, unproductive, unprolific, worthless; antiseptic, decontaminated, pure, sanitary, sterilized. ANT.—fecund, fertile, fruitful, generative, prolific, proliferous; contaminated, infectious, noxious, unhygienic, unsanitary.

stern, see severe.

stiff, firm, hard, hardened, inflexible, petrified, rigid, solid, tense, unbending; see also severe.

stigma, brand, defect, disfigurement, imprint, mark, scar, stain, trace, vestige.

still, hushed, inaudible, inert, motionless, mum, mute, noiseless, quiet, quiescent, soundless, stagnant, stationary, undisturbed, unruffled; calm, gentle, meek, mild, passive, peaceful, patient, placid, silent, tranquil; besides, but, furthermore, however, yet. ANT.—clamorous, disturbed, loud, piercing, stirring, tumultuous; aggressive, dynamic, hostile, impassive, perturbed.

stilted, affected, bombastic, fustian, grandiose, grandiloquent, high-flown, high-sounding, magniloquent, pompous, pretentious, swelling, turgid. ANT.—candid, honest, humble, reserved, shy, simple.

stimulate, animate, arouse, awaken, disquiet, energize, excite, impel, incite, instigate, invigorate, irritate, kindle, pique, provoke, rouse, stir up, urge. ANT.—calm, deaden, pacify, quell, tranquilize.

stimulus, arousal, encouragement, goad, stimulant; see also incentive.

stingy, see greedy; miserly.

stir, beat, mix; impel, persuade; see also move.

stock, accumulation, fund, goods, hoard, inventory, merchandise, produce, provision, reserve, store, wares; calves, cattle, cows, herd, steers; fill, fill up, furnish, replenish, store, supply.

stoical, assiduous, forbearing, indulgent, uncomplaining; see also patient.

stone, boulder, crag, flint, gem, granite, gravel, jewel, marble, pebble, quartz, rock, rubble, shale.

stop, see cease; halt; hinder; interrupt.

store, see heap.

storm, agitation, commotion, cyclone, disturbance, fury, hurricane, outbreak, paroxysm, rage, tornado, tumult, turbulence, turmoil, upheaval, violence, whirlwind; assail, assault, attack, blow, boil, bombard, fume, hail, rage, rain, rant, snow, whirlwind. ANT.—calm, peace, placidity, repose, serenity, tranquility; assuage, ease, lull, pacify, soothe.

stormy, agitated, angry, blustery, excitable, frenzied, furious, gusty, inclement, passionate, raging, raving, roaring, rough, tempestuous, turbulent, violent, windy. ANT.—calm, clear, composed, gentle, peaceful, tranquil.

story, account, allegory, anecdote, apologue, burlesque, chronicle, epic, fable, fantasy, fiction, history, legend, memoir, myth, narration, narrative, novel, parable, report, romance, saga, satire, tale, yarn; canard, fabrication, falsehood.

stout, paunchy, pudgy, stocky, thickset; see also fat; obese.

straight, direct, erect, even, level, perpendicular, rectilinear, right, unbent, undeviating, unswerving, upright, vertical; candid, fair, honest, honorable, just, regular, reliable, trustworthy, upright. ANT.—bent, circuitous, crooked, distorted, swerving, twisted; deceptive, devious, dishonest, fraudulent, unreliable.

strain, breed, extraction, lineage, pedigree, race, stock; kind, sort, variety; effort, endeavor, overexertion, struggle; melody, tune; manner, style; anxiety, burden, mental tension, pressure, stress.

strange, abnormal, alien, anomalous, bewildering, bizarre, curious, dissociated, eccentric, exotic, extraordinary, fantastic, foreign, grotesque, inapplicable, incredible, irregular, irrelevant, misplaced, mysterious, nondescript, odd, peculiar, remote, singular, stupefying, surprising, unaccustomed, uncommon, unfamiliar, unrelated, unusual. ANT.—conventional, familiar, ordinary, prevailing, regular, typical.

stranger, alien, drifter, foreigner, immigrant, interloper, intruder, newcomer, outsider, squatter, visitor. ANT.—acquaintance, associate, companion, friend, neighbor, peer.

stratagem, artifice, cabal, conspiracy, design, device, finesse, intrigue, logistics, machination, maneuver, plan, plot, ruse, scheme, strategy, tactics, trick.

stray, err, go astray, traipse, wander; see also deviate; ramble.

stream, spout, spurt; abound, be copious. see also emanate; flow.

strength, durability, fortitude, intensity, lustiness, stamina, sturdiness, toughness; see also power.

strengthen, confirm, corroborate, substantiate, sustain, verify; brace, buttress, fortify, harden, invigorate, reinforce, rejuvenate, steel; augment, enlarge, extend, heighten, intensify, sharpen.

stress, burden, compulsion, exigency, force, press, pressure, strain, tension, urgency; accent, emphasis, importance, significance, weight.

stretch, distort, spread, strain. see also distend; extend.

strict, accurate, exact, precise, stern, rough, rugged; see also severe.

strike, hurt, knock, pummel, smite. see also hit.

striking, affecting, august, grandiose, majestic, over-powering, splendid; see also impressive.

stripped, defenseless, unprotected; see also naked.

strive, see endeavor.

strong, athletic, concentrated, durable, enduring, forcible, fortified, hale, impregnable, resistant, resolute, solid, strenuous, tough; see also mighty; sinewy.

struggle, brawl, feud, fray, quarrel, row, scuffle, skirmish; see also combat; conflict.

stubborn, adamant, contumacious, determined, dogged, headstrong, immovable, inflexible, intractable, mulish, obdurate, obstinate, pertinacious, recalcitrant, refractory, uncompromising, ungovernable, unyielding. ANT.—amenable, compliant, reasonable, submissive, tractable, yielding.

student, apprentice, disciple, learner, novice, observer, pupil, scholar.

study, cogitate, examine, investigate, scrutinize, weigh; see also contemplate.

stumble, fall, pitch, slide, slip, sprawl, tilt, topple, trip, tumble. ANT.—arise, ascend, mount, soar.

stun, amaze, astonish, disconcert, dumbfound, flabbergast, surprise; see also shock.

stupid, asinine, brainless, crass, dense, dull, dumb, feeble-minded, foolish, inane, inept, moronic, obtuse, senseless, vapid, witless. ANT.—clever, discerning, perspicacious, saga, wise.

stupor, apathy, coma, daze, drowsiness, inertness, insensibility, languor, lethargy, narcosis, numbness, stupefaction, torpor, unconsciousness. ANT.—activity, consciousness, liveliness, sensibility, vivacity.

sturdy, see mighty; sinewy; strong.

suave, adroit, affable, amiable, courteous, cultured, debonair, gallant, genteel, glib, gracious, pleasing, polished, polite, smooth, sophisticated, tactful, urbane, well-bred. ANT.—brusque, crude, displeasing, inept, rude.

subdue, beat, conquer, control, crush, defeat, humble, master, moderate, overcome, quell, restrain, rout, soften, subjugate, suppress, surmount, tame, temper, vanquish. ANT.—awaken, enrage, incite, rouse, stimulate.

subject, citizen, dependent, inferior, liegeman, subordinate, vassal; argument, case, material, matter, point, problem, question, substance, theme, thesis, thought, topic.

sublime, elevated, glorious, lofty, raised, supreme; see also majestic.

submerge, see immerse.

submit, abdicate, abide, accede, acquiesce, bear, bend, capitulate, cede, defer, obey, quit, relent, resign, succumb, suffer, surrender, yield; offer, present, propose, suggest. ANT.—defy, obstruct, resist, struggle, withstand; deny, refuse, reject, retain, withhold.

subordinate, ancillary, dependent, inferior, insignificant, junior, minor, paltry, secondary, subject, subservient, subsidiary, unimportant; control, subdue, subjugate. ANT.—chief, dominant, excellent, leading, superior; dignify, elevate, glorify, promote, revere.

subsequent, after, consequent, ensuing, following, later, next, posterior, succeeding, successive. ANT.—antecedent, anterior, earlier, preceding, prior.

subside, descend, drop, fall, sink; droop, extend downward, hang; see also collapse; decline.

substance, see material; moment.

substantiate, see confirm.

substitution, alternation, exchange, replacement, variety. see also change; modification.

subtract, deduct, remove, take away, withhold; see also decrease; lessen.

subvert, demolish, depress, destroy, extinguish, invert, overthrow, overturn, overwhelm, pervert, reverse, supplant, topple, upset. ANT.—conserve, establish, perpetuate, preserve, sustain.

succeed, achieve, accomplish, attain, conquer, defeat, flourish, gain, prevail, prosper, surmount, thrive, triumph, vanquish, win; ensue, follow, replace, supersede, supervene, supplant. ANT.— blunder, fail, lose, miscarry, miss; anticipate, herald, introduce, precede, preface.

succession, continuation, progression; see also sequence.

succinct, compendious, curt; see also concise.

sudden, abrupt, immediate, instantaneous, unexpected; see also hasty; rapid.

suffer, bear, endure, experience, feel, stand, sustain; admit, allow, indulge, let, permit, submit, tolerate; ache, agonize, undergo. ANT.—avoid, resist, surrender; deny, disallow, prohibit, refuse; heal, rally, overcome, recover, revive.

suffering, see distress; pain.

sufficient, abundant, adequate, ample, commensurate, enough, fitting, plenty, proper, satisfactory, satisfying, suitable. ANT.— deficient, inadequate, insufficient, lacking, scant.

suggest, advise, allude to, counsel, hint, imply, infer, insinuate, intimate, offer, propose, recommend, submit.

suggestion, admonition, advice, allusion, caution, counsel, exhortation, hint, idea, implication, indication, innuendo, insinuation, intimation, proposal, recommendation, thought, warning; design, layout, outline, plan, project, scheme, strategy.

suit, accommodate, adapt, adjust, alter, conform, fit, revise; fill, gratify, please, satisfy. ANT.— misapply, misfit; annoy, disturb, vex.

suitable, acceptable, accordant, adapted, agreeable, applicable, appropriate, becoming, conformable, congruous, consonant, eligible, expedient, fitting, gratifying, just, meet, pertinent, proper, relevant. ANT.—disagreeable, improper, incongruous, irrelevant, obnoxious, reprehensible.

sullen, churlish, crabbed, cross, dismal, dour, fretful, gloomy, glum, moody, morose, sour, stubborn, sulky, surly. ANT.— amiable, cheerful, genial, jovial, sociable.

sum, aggregate, amount, bulk, collection, entirety, entity, everything, gross, lump, total, totality, unity, value, whole, worth. ANT.—fraction, ingredient, part, portion.

summary, abstract, analysis, condensation, core, digest, epitome, outline, recapitulation, reduction, report, resumé, survey, syllabus, synopsis.

summit, apex, cap, crest, crown, culmination, head, height, peak, pinnacle, tip, top, vertex, zenith. ANT.—base, bottom, foot, foundation, nadir.

sunny, bright, brilliant, clear, cloudless, dazzling, fair, gleaming, shining, shiny, splendid, sunlit. ANT.—cloudy, dark, dull, foul, overcast.

superficial, cursory, desultory, exterior, external, flimsy, frivolous, hasty, ignorant, imperfect, outward, shallow, short-sighted, slight, surface, unenlightened. ANT.—careful, deep, deliberate, learned, profound, thorough.

superfluous, abounding, exaggerated, excessive, exorbitant, extra, extravagant, extreme, inexhaustible, inordinate, lavish, lush, luxuriant, needless, overmuch, profuse, redundant, spare, superabundant, unnecessary, useless. ANT.—inadequate, insufficient, scanty, scarce.

superior, above, better, distinguished, excellent, finer, greater, higher, major, preferred, sovereign, supreme, unsurpassed, upper. ANT.—below, deficient, inferior, minor, substandard.

supernatural, ghostly, metaphysical, mysterious, mystic, spectral, spiritual, superhuman, unearthly; see also miraculous.

supervise, command, dominate, manage, superintend; see also regulate.

supple, see elastic.

supplicate, adjure, importune, request; see also beg.

supply, fund, reserve; endow, fit out, produce; see also hoard; furnish.

support, base, basis, bolster, brace, buttress, foundation, fulcrum, groundwork, prop, shore, stanchion, stay; advocacy, aid, assistance, backing, comfort, contribution, encouragement, favor, help, patronage, succor; livelihood, living, maintenance, subsistence, sustenance; confirmation, evidence; advance, advocate, aid, assist, back, bear, bolster, brace, carry, contribute, defend, encourage, expedite, foster, further, help, hold, keep, maintain, preserve, prop, shore, sustain, uphold, verify. ANT.—apex, cupola, peak, pinnacle, summit; blockage, discouragement, hindrance, impediment, injury, opposition; abandonment, betrayal, denial, desertion; delusion, fantasy, illusion; check, cripple, destroy, encumber, frustrate, obstruct, undermine.

supporter, advocate, defender, devotee, pillar, sustainer, upholder, votary; see also follower.

suppose, conjecture, deduce, speculate, surmise; see also imagine.

suppress, lower, moderate; see also lessen.

supremacy, domination, predominance, sovereignty, transcendence; see also mastery.

supreme, best, cardinal, chief, dominant, essential, final, first, foremost, greatest, highest, leading, main, paramount, peerless, predominant, principal, transcendent, ultimate. ANT.—auxiliary, inferior, subordinate, subsidiary, supplemental.

sure, assured, indubitable, inevitable, secure, undeniable, unquestionable; see also definite.

surplus, see excess.

surprise, curiosity, marvel, miracle, phenomenon, oddity, prodigy, rarity, sensation, spectacle; admiration, amazement, astonishment, awe, bewilderment, curiosity, incredulity, perplexity, shock, stupefaction, wonder, wonderment; alarm, amaze, astonish, astound, bewilder, confound, dazzle, disconcert, dumbfound, flabbergast, overwhelm, shock, startle, stun. ANT.—familiarity, habit, routine, triviality; anticipation, apathy, expectation, indifference, tranquility; admonish, caution, forewarn, prepare, warn.

surrender, acquiesce, capitulate, resign, sacrifice, submit; see also relinquish.

surround, bound, confine, enclose, fence, limit; see also encircle, encompass.

surveillance, charge, control, management, superintendence; see also inspection.

suspect, disbelieve, dispute, distrust, doubt, mistrust, query, question, waver; assume, guess, imagine, presume, speculate, suppose, theorize. ANT.—believe, confide in, rely on, trust; ascertain, discern, know.

suspend, adjourn, cease, defer, delay, desist, discontinue, interrupt, postpone, stay; append, balance, dangle, hang, hitch, poise, sling, swing. ANT.—accelerate, continue, expedite, persist, proceed, support.

suspicion, incredulity, scruple, skepticism, suspense, unbelief; see also distrust.

sustain, advocate, back, bear, brace, further; see also encourage, help, preserve.

swallow, absorb, accept, assimilate, bear, believe, bolt, consume, devour, endure, engulf, envelop, imbibe, stomach, tolerate; recant, retract, suppress, withdraw. ANT.—discharge, doubt, emit, expel, reject; affirm, confirm, uphold.

swarthy, brown, dark, dusky, sable, tawny. ANT.—bright, fair, light.

sway, impel, incite, stir; see also influence.

swear, affirm, declare, protest, state; see also maintain.

sweep, brush, clean, clear, graze, mop, rake, remove, touch, traverse, whisk; amplitude, bend, compass, contour, curve, extent, range, reach, scope, stretch, swing.

sweet, engaging, gentle, honeyed, mellifluous, melodious, saccharine, sugary, winning; see also luscious.

swell, amplify, bulge, dilate, distend, expand, heave, increase, inflate, intensify, protrude, puff, rise, tumefy; bulge, crescendo, curve, elevation, intensity, power, protuberance, swelling. ANT.—compress, contract, diminish, shrink, shrivel; decline, depression, flatness, reduction, shrinkage.

swift, see fast.

swindle, cheat, chicanery, guile, imposture; bilk, dupe, fool, gull, hoax, hoodwink, victimize; see also deceit; deceive.

symbol, character, figure, mark, representative, sign, token, type.

symmetry, agreement, arrangement, balance, centrality, conformity, equality, equilibrium, equivalence, evenness, finish, form, harmony, order, proportion, regularity, shapeliness. ANT.—disagreement, disparity, distortion, imbalance, irregularity.

sympathetic, forbearing, kindly, tender, thoughtful; see also humane.

sympathize, gladden, soothe; see also comfort.

sympathy, accord, affinity, agreement, alliance, concord, condolence, congeniality, consolation, empathy, harmony, warmth. see also compassion. ANT.—antipathy, harshness, indifference, insensitivity, malevolence.

symptom, characteristic, diagnostic, evidence, feature, indication, mark, property, token, trace, trait, vestige.

synthetic, artificial, ersatz, fake, feigned, fictitious, phony, unreal; see also counterfeit.

system, network, operation, organization, policy, program; see also method.

T

tact, adroitness, dexterity, diplomacy, discretion, discrimination, finesse, knack, perception, perspicacity, poise, savoir-faire, skill, subtlety.

tactful, discreet, discriminating, judicious, politic; see also diplomatic.

take, catch, clasp, clutch, grasp, grip, procure, seize; appropriate, arrogate, capture, confiscate, ensnare, steal, usurp; apprehend, deprehend; necessitate, need, require; adopt, assume, choose, select; bear, endure, stand, tolerate; attract, captivate, charm, delight, interest; accept, obtain, receive.

tale, account, anecdote, chronicle, history, narration, narrative, report, yarn; see also fiction.

talent, cleverness, endowment, genius; see also ability, faculty.

talented, bright, sharp, smart, quick, quick-witted, witty; see also skillful.

talk, chatter, gossip, lecture, report; blab, chat, comment, gossip, harangue, jabber, mutter, plead, prattle, preach, rant, speak, spout, tattle; see also conversation; discourse, speak.

talkative, chatty, communicative, glib, voluble; see also garrulous.

tall, see high.

tame, domestic, domesticated, gentle, obedient, subdued, timid; boring, dull, flat, insipid, tedious, vapid; see also docile.

tamper, alter, discommode, inconvenience, interrupt, intervene, mix in, monkey, trouble; see also interfere.

tangible, palpable, sensible; see also corporeal.

tangle, complicate, confuse, ensnare, entrap, hinder, interfere, intertwine, involve, jumble, muddle, snare, spoil; dilemma, disorder, embarrassment, muddle, perplexity, puzzle, quandary, snarl.

tardy, detained, lax, overdue, retarded, slack; see also late.

tarnish, befoul, besmirch, blemish, blight, blot, defame, defile, discolor, disgrace, dishonor, smudge, soil, spot, stain, sully, taint. ANT.—brighten, cleanse, defend, honor, restore.

tart, see bitter.

task, assignment, burden, business, charge, chore, duty, function, job, labor, mission, office, pursuit, stint, toil, work, undertaking.

taste, flavor, gusto, piquancy, relish, savor, tang, zest; acumen, appreciation, discernment, discrimination, disposition, inclination, judgment, liking, predilection, refinement, sensibility, susceptibility. ANT.—antipathy, disinclination, indelicacy, rudeness, vulgarity.

taut, bound up, constricted, firm, fixed, snug, stretched, tight, unbending, unyielding. ANT.—lax, loose, relaxed, shaky, slack.

tax, assessment, charge, custom, dues, duty, exaction, excise, fine, impost, levy, obligation, rate, tariff, toll, tribute; burden, demand, strain, task. ANT.—gift, grant, present, remuneration, reward; comfort, ease, relaxation, rest.

teach, advise, coach, direct, educate, enlighten, explain, expound, guide, imbue, inculcate, indoctrinate, inform, instill, instruct, interpret, lecture, nurture, prepare, school, train, tutor. ANT.—follow, imbibe, learn, misguide, misinform.

tear, cleave, disunite, rive, sever, shed, sunder, wound; see also rip.

tease, aggravate, badger, bother, disturb, harry, nag; see also harass.

tedious, boring, burdensome, dilatory, dreary, drowsy, dull, fatiguing, humdrum, irksome, monotonous, slow, sluggish, soporific, tardy, tiresome, uninteresting, wearisome. ANT.—animating, exhilarating, fascinating, inspiring, refreshing.

teeming, abounding, abundant, ample, bountiful, copious, overflowing, plenteous, plentiful, profuse, prolific, replete, rich, rife. ANT.—deficient, inadequate, meager, scant, scarce.

tell, describe, narrate, recite, recount, rehearse, relate, report; assert, communicate, declare, discuss, express, mention, publish, say, speak, state, utter; announce, betray, confess, disclose, divulge, reveal; discern, discover, distinguish, recognize; acquaint, apprise, explain, impart, inform, instruct, notify; direct, order, request.

temper, anger, animosity, choler, fury, indignation, ire, irritation, petulance, rage, resentment, wrath; composition, disposition, humor, mood, nature, quality, structure, type; anneal, assuage, change, moderate, modify, mollify, qualify, soften, soothe. ANT.—composure, conciliation, patience, peace, repose; agitate, harden, intensify, strengthen, toughen.

temperament, constitution, disposition, humor, makeup, mood, nature, personality, propensity, spirit, temper.

temperate, abstemious, abstinent, frugal, mild, moderate, reasonable, self-restrained, sober, unruffled. ANT.—excessive, immoderate, impetuous, tempestuous, uncontrolled.

temporal, earthly, ephemeral, fleeting, laic, lay, mundane, profane, secular, temporary, transient, transitory, worldly. ANT.—ecclesiastical, eternal, everlasting, religious, spiritual.

temporary, brief, changeable, cyclical, ephemeral, evanescent, fleeting, impermanent, momentary, passing, provisional, shifting, short, summary, transient, transitory. ANT.—abiding, durable, endless, permanent, perpetual, timeless.

tempt, allure, bait, captivate, charm, coax, court, decoy, entice, fascinate, incite, induce, inveigle, lure, rouse, seduce, test, try. ANT.—discourage, disenchant, nauseate, repel, repulse.

tend, accompany, attend, escort, guard, keep, manage, nurse, protect, serve, watch; gravitate, incline, lean, point, verge on.

tendency, aim, aptness, bent, bias, direction, disposition, drift, inclination, learning, mood, predisposition, proclivity, proneness, propensity, susceptibility, tone, trend, turn. ANT.—apathy, aversion, deviation, disinclination, opposition.

tender, benevolent, delicate, loving, merciful, responsive, sympathetic, warm; feeble, fragile, immature, weak, young; advance, extend, offer, present, proffer, propose, suggest, volunteer; see also mild.

tenet, belief, conviction, creed, doctrine, dogma, position, precept, principle, system, teaching, view.

tense, firm, rigid, stiff, strained, taut, tight; anxious, distraught, edgy, high-strung, nervous, overwrought, restless, troubled. ANT.—lax, limp, loose, slack; calm, placid, relaxed, tranquil, unruffled.

tentative, experimental, makeshift, probationary, provisional, temporary. ANT.—conclusive, decisive, definitive, final, permanent.

term, boundary, course, cycle, duration, interval, limit, period, phase, span, time; condition, stipulation; expression, name, nomenclature, phrase, terminology, word.

terminate, abolish, achieve, cease, close, complete, conclude, end, expire, finish, perfect, stop. ANT.—begin, commence, inaugurate, initiate, start.

terrible, alarming, appalling, awful, dire, dreadful, fearful, frightful, gruesome, hideous, horrible, horrid, severe, shocking, terrifying. ANT.—appealing, attractive, captivating, happy, pleasing.

terrify, see frighten.

territory, area, boundary, country, district, division, domain, dominion, land, place, province, quarter, region, section, township.

terror, see fear.

terse, brief, compact, compendious, concise, condensed, crisp, incisive, laconic, neat, pithy, sententious, short, succinct, summary, trenchant. ANT.—profuse, rambling, redundant, verbose, wordy.

test, assay, examine, experiment, inspect, prove, scrutinize, substantiate, try, verify; criterion, demonstration, essay, examination, proof, standard, trial.

testimony, affidavit, attestation, certification, confirmation, credentials, declaration, deposition, evidence, indication, proof, warrant, witness.

text, book, handbook, manual, manuscript, matter, passage, publication, quotation, sentence, stanza, subject, textbook, theme, topic, verse, volume, wording, writing.

texture, character, coarseness, composition, constitution, disposition, feel, fiber, firmness, flexibility, grain, makeup, nap, organization, rigidity, roughness, smoothness, structure, tissue.

thankful, appreciative, beholden, contented, grateful, gratified, pleased, satisfied. ANT.—critical, discontented, dissatisfied, faultfinding, thankless.

thaw, deliquesce, dissolve, flow, liquate, liquefy, melt, run. ANT.—chill, congeal, freeze, petrify, solidify.

theft, burglary, depredation, embezzlement, fraud, holdup, larceny, misappropriation, pillage, piracy, plagiarism, plunder, rapine, robbery, spoliation, swindle.

theme, composition, description, discourse, dissertation, essay, idea, motive, narrative, proposition, report, statement, subject, tenor, text, thesis, topic, trend, writing.

theoretical, analytical, formal, ideal, scholastic; see also learned.

theory, assumption, attribution, doctrine, guess, opinion, perception, plea, presupposition, speculation, surmise, thesis, viewpoint; see also hypothesis.

therefore, accordingly, consequently, for, hence, since, so, then, thence, wherefore.

thesis, affirmation, argument, composition, dictum, dissertation, doctrine, essay, position, proposition, report, study, theme.

thick, abundant, close, compact, compressed, condensed, crowded, dense, impenetrable, multitudinous, numerous, packed, populous, profuse, solid, swarming; coagulated, curdled, gelatinous, glutinous, gummy, heavy, miry, muddy, opaque, ropy, solidified, viscid, viscous; cloudy, dull, indistinct, turbid; doltish, dull, ignorant, obtuse, stolid, stupid; coarse, crass, gross; broad, chunky, dumpy, squat, thickset. ANT.—barren, inadequate, scattered, spacious, sparse; clear, diaphanous, gaseous, limpid, rarified, transparent; clear, distinct; acute, bright, intelligent, perceptive; genteel, polite, refined; fragile, frail, slender, thin.

thin, diaphanous, diluted, fine, gauzy, gossamer, rare, scanty, scrawny, skeletal, threadlike, wasted; see also gaunt, slender.

think, conceive, imagine, picture, recall, recollect, remember; cogitate, contemplate, deliberate, determine, examine, meditate, muse, ponder, reason, reflect, ruminate, speculate, study; apprehend, believe, conjecture, consider, deem, esteem, guess, hold, judge, opine, presume, reckon, regard, suppose, surmise; devise, intend, mean, plan, propose.

thorough, absolute, accurate, complete, concluded, consummate, ended, entire, exact, exhaustive, finished, full, painstaking, perfect, plenary, radical, scrupulous, sweeping, thoroughgoing, total, unbroken, undivided, unmitigated. ANT.—deficient, incomplete, perfunctory, sketchy, superficial.

thought, cerebration, cogitation, conception, consideration, contemplation, deliberation, fancy, idea, imagination, impression, judgment, lucubration, meditation, memory, notion, opinion, perception, recollection, reflection, regard, retrospection, sentiment, speculation, view. ANT.—emptiness, fatuity, inanity, vacancy, vacuity.

thoughtful, attentive, careful, cautious, charitable, concerned, considerate, empathic, heedful, kind, provident, prudent, sympathetic; cogitative, contemplative, engrossed, introspective, meditative, pensive, philosophic, rapt, reflective, speculative, studious. ANT.—careless, heedless, indifferent, negligent, thoughtless; fatuous, idiotic, inane, obtuse, vacuous.

thoughtless, desultory, heedless, imprudent, inaccurate, inattentive, neglectful, reckless, unconcerned. see also inconsiderate, lax.

threatening, see imminent.

thrift, conservation, economy, frugality, parsimony, providence, prudence, saving. ANT.—extravagance, prodigality, shiftlessness, waste.

thrill, excitement, flutter, sensation, shock, tingling, tremor; affect, agitate, electrify, inspire, move, penetrate, rouse, stimulate, stir, strike, tingle, touch, tremble, vibrate.

thrive, advance, bloom, flourish, grow, improve, increase, luxuriate, prosper, succeed. ANT.— decline, fail, fall, lose.

throb, beat, oscillate, palpitate, pulsate, pulse, vibrate; beating, palpitation, pulsation, vibration.

throng, aggregation, assemblage, assembly, bevy, concourse, crowd, crush, gang, horde, host, legion, masses, mob, multitude, populace, press, rabble, swarm.

throw, cast, chuck, drive, fling, hurl, impel, launch, pitch, project, propel, sling, thrust, toss. ANT.—catch, draw, haul, hold, retain.

thrust, cast, crowd, drive, extend, fling, force, impel, jostle, penetrate, pierce, press, propel, push, shove, stab, tilt; hasten, promote, urge; explosion, force, impact, pressure, propulsion, push. ANT.—drag, falter, halt, retreat; impede, obstruct, oppose; debility, powerlessness, weakness.

thwart, see frustrate.

tidy, clean, clear, methodical, neat, nice, orderly, precise, shipshape, snug, spruce, systematic, trim. ANT.—deranged, disheveled, littered, slovenly, unkempt.

tie, affinity, alliance, association, band, bond, brace, conjunction, connection, cord, coupling, ligament, ligature, link, relationship, rope, security, strap, string, tackle, union, yoke; attach, bind, confine, connect, constrain, engage, fasten, fetter, hitch, join, link, moor, obligate, restrain, restrict, secure, shackle, tether, unite. ANT.—detachment, disunion, isolation, separation, sunderance; detach, free, loosen, unbind, separate.

tight, close, compact, contracted, narrow, tense; penny-pinching; see also taut; greedy, miserly.

time, age, course, cycle, date, duration, eon, epoch, era, interim, interval, measure, period, season, sequence, span, spell, stage, succession, tempo, term, while; adjust, measure, regulate, set.

timely, appropriate, convenient, exact, opportune, precise, prompt, proper, propitious, providential, punctual, ready, seasonable, suitable, well-timed. ANT.—dilatory, inexpedient, inopportune, tardy, untimely.

timid, abashed, afraid, bashful, coy, daunted, diffident, embarrassed, faltering, fearful, hesitant, humble, irresolute, modest, recoiling, scared, shamefaced, sheepish, shy, skulking, spiritless, terrified, timorous, unspirited, vacillating, wavering. ANT.—adventurous, courageous, dauntless, determined, gregarious, intrepid.

tiny, insignificant, trivial, wee; see also small.

tire, bore, drain, exhaust, fatigue, harass, irk, jade, overtax, overwork, pall, prostrate, strain,

tucker, wear out, weary, worry.
ANT.—amuse, energize, invigorate, refresh, restore.

tired, collapsing, drained, drooping, drowsy, exhausted, faint, fatigued, haggard, jaded, spent, wasted, weary, wearied, worn. ANT.—active, energetic, fresh, invigorated, lively.

title, appellation, caption, cognomen, denomination, designation, epithet, heading, inscription, name; birthright, claim, due, honor, ownership, possession, prerogative, privilege, right.

toil, achievement, business, drudgery, effort, employment, grind, labor, occupation, opus, pains, performance, production, task, travail, work. ANT.—leisure, recreation, relaxation, repose, rest.

token, badge, emblem, evidence, index, manifestation, mark, memorial, note, symbol, trait; see also souvenir.

tolerant, enduring, fair, forbearing, lenient, liberal, open-minded, patient, receptive, understanding. ANT.—bigoted, discriminatory, intolerant, prejudiced, unyielding.

tolerate, allow, authorize, concede, let, license, sanction, permit; abide, bear, brook, endure, persevere, prevail, stand, stomach, sustain, swallow, undergo. ANT.—bar, forbid, hinder, inhibit, veto; avoid, evade, falter, succumb, surrender, yield.

toll, see tax.

tongue, cant, lingo, slang; see also language.

too, additionally, also, as well, besides, further, furthermore, in addition, likewise, moreover, similarly.

tool, agent, apparatus, appliance, device, equipment, implement, instrument, means, mechanism, medium, utensil, vehicle. ANT.—hindrance, impediment, obstacle, obstruction.

top, acme, apex, chief, crest, crown, culmination, head, peak, pinnacle, summit, surface, tip, vertex, zenith. ANT.—base, bottom, foot, foundation, nadir.

topic, affair, argument, issue, material, matter, motion, point, problem, proposition, question, resolution, subject, text, theme, theorem, thesis.

torment, abuse, ache, agony, anguish, cruelty, distress, excruciation, malady, martyrdom, misery, pain, persecution, rack, suffering, throe, torture, woe, wretchedness; afflict, aggravate, annoy, badger, bait, bother, distress, disturb, grill, gull, harass, harry, hurt, irritate, mistrust, nag, oppress, pain, pester, plague, provoke, rack, tantalize, taunt, tease, torture, trouble, vex. ANT.—comfort, ease, mitigation, relief, solace; console, help, mollify, please, relieve, soothe.

torrid, hot-blooded, scalding, scorching, sweltering, warm; see also hot, passionate.

torture, see torment.

toss, see throw.

total, see sum; thorough.

touch, affect, allude, brush, concern, feel, finger, glance, graze, handle, hint, impress, melt, mollify, pat, regard, soften, strike, stroke, tap; dash, feeling, infusion, palpability, sensation, sprinkling, tangency, taste, tinge, trace.

touching, affecting, heart-rending, impressive, pitiable, sad; adjacent, adjunct, bordering, tangent; see also impressive; poignant; tender.

touchy, choleric, fiery, hasty, snappish; see also irritable.

tough, adhesive, coherent, fibrous, firm, hardened, hardy, seasoned, stalwart, strong, sturdy, tenacious, wiry; difficult, formidable, hard, intricate, laborious, puzzling, rigorous, troublesome, trying; boisterous, bullying, callous, fierce, incorrigible, intractable, obdurate, obstinate, raging, savage, stubborn, turbulent, unmanageable, unyielding, vicious. ANT.—defenseless, delicate, fragile, puny, vulnerable, weak; easy, effortless, elementary, facile, simple; amenable, compliant, deferential, docile, passive, tractable, yielding.

tour, see journey.

tow, see draw, pull.

towering, see lofty.

toy, caper, frisk, frolic, gamble, gambol, play, revel, romp, sport, wager; bauble, game, pastime, plaything, trinket; little, miniature, small.

trace, mark, scar, stain, stigma, tinge; characteristic, clue, evidence, feature, fragment, impression, indication, memorial, property, record, sign, symptom, trait, vestige. ANT.—deletion, effacement, extinction, nonexistence, obliteration.

track, see pursue.

tractable, acquiescent, adaptable, amenable, compliant, deferential, docile, dutiful, governable, manageable, obedient, pliant, submissive, willing, yielding. ANT.—insubordinate, intractable, obstinate, rebellious, stubborn.

trade, barter, business, calling, commerce, contract, dealing, employment, enterprise, exchange, job, livelihood, metier, occupation, position, profession, pursuit, sales, speculation, traffic, transaction, undertaking, vocation, work; art, craft, handicraft; bargain, barter, buy, deal, exchange, patronize, purchase, sell, shop, swap.

traffic, see business; trade.

trail, course, footprint, mark, path, scent, trace, track; chase, climb, crawl, creep, drag, draw, follow, grow, hunt, persist, pull, straggle, track. ANT.—abandon, elude, escape, evade, withdraw.

train, chain, line, procession, retinue, sequel, sequence, series, staff, string, succession, suite; accustom, aim, bend, coach, direct, discipline, drill, educate, enlighten, exercise, guide, habituate, imbue, implant, inculcate, indoctrinate, inform, infuse, innure, instruct, lead, practice, prepare, prime, rear, school, teach.

training, background, coaching, cultivation, development, direction, discipline, drilling, education, exercise, foundation, groundwork, guidance, instruction, learning, nurture, practice, preparation, schooling, study, tutelage.

trait, attribute, characteristic, distinction, earmark, feature, habit, mannerism, mark, nature, peculiarity, property, quality, style, tone, trademark.

traitorous, apostate, disloyal, faithless, false, insidious, mutinous, perfidious, rebellious, recreant, renegade, seditious, treacherous, treasonable. ANT.— constant, devoted, faithful, loyal, steadfast.

tramp, beggar, bum, derelict, hobo, indigent, landloper, nomad, rover, vagabond, vagrant, wanderer; harlot, prostitute.

tranquil, dispassionate, dulcet, imperturbable, sedative, softened, solacing, stifled, unstirred, whispering; see also peaceful, placid, quiet.

tranquility, calmness, hush, quiescence, quietude, rest, serenity; see also peace.

transact, accomplish, achieve, buy, carry on, conclude, conduct, dispatch, enact, execute, exercise, manage, negotiate, operate, perform, perpetrate, sell, settle, treat, work.

transaction, act, action, activity, affair, business, deal, deed, disposal, doing, event, execution, matter, negotiation, occurrence, performance, proceeding, purchase, sale, step, undertaking.

transfer, carry, dispatch, relegate, send, shift, transmit, transplant, transport; assign, confer, convey, dispense, give, grant, impart, sell.

transform, shift, vary, veer; see also convert.

transgression, breach, crime, delinquency, encroachment, error, fault, infraction, infringement, iniquity, injustice, invasion, misbehavior, misdeed, misdemeanor, offense, sin, slip, trespass, vice, violation, wrong. ANT.—benevolence, goodness, honor, innocence, virtue.

transient, flitting, flying, fugitive, short-lived, temporal, vanishing, volatile; see also temporary.

translate, explicate, transform, transmute. see also interpret.

transmit, broadcast, communicate, confer, convey, disclose, dispatch, divulge, forward, impart, inform, notify, pass on, relate, relay, reveal, send, tell, transfer. ANT.—conceal, hide, mask, secrete, shroud, withhold.

transparent, crystalline, thin; guileless, manifest, open, patent; see also lucid.

transport, bring, cart, haul, relocate, transplant; see also convey.

trap, ambush, artifice, bait, blind, intrigue, lure, maneuver, net, noose, pit, pitfall, plot, ruse, snare, stratagem, trick, wile; ambush, deceive, decoy, dupe, ensnare, entrap, fool, lure, mislead, outwit, seduce, swindle, victimize.

trash, debris, dregs, dross, garbage, junk, leavings, litter, rags, refuse, riffraff, rubbish, rubble, scourings, slag, sweepings, trumpery, waste. ANT.—advantages, benefits, goods, perquisites, valuables.

travel, drive, fly, go, journey, move, ramble, roam, rove, sail, tour, walk, wander; circuit, course, cruise, excursion, exodus, expedition, journey, march, migration, peregrination, pilgrimage, ramble, ride, sojourn, tour, trip, wandering.

treacherous, base, deceitful, disloyal, evil, faithless, false, foul, ignominious, inglorious, malevolent, malicious, malign, perfidious, rancorous, recreant, traitorous, treasonable, unfaithful, unreliable, venomous, vile. ANT.—dependable, faithful, honest, reliable, trustworthy.

treason, betrayal, cabal, collusion, conspiracy, deception, dishonesty, disloyalty, intrigue, machination, plot, revolution, sedition, subversion, treachery.

treasure, appreciate, cherish, foster, guard, hold dear, love, nurture, prize, sustain, value. ANT.—abandon, detest, disregard, loathe, reject.

treat, arrange, employ, handle, manage, manipulate, operate, use, utilize; administer, assist, attend, care for, doctor, heal, minister to, nurse, prescribe; amuse, divert, entertain, indulge, satisfy; comment, criticize, discuss, explain, interpret, negotiate, review. ANT.—disarrange, disorder, mismanage, spoil, waste; ignore, neglect, overlook; annoy, bore, irritate, offend, vex; befuddle, cloud, confuse, mystify, perplex.

treaty, agreement, alliance, arrangement, bargain, compact, concordat, covenant, negotiation, pact, protocol, settlement.

tremble, agitate, flutter, jar, jolt, oscillate, pulsate, quail, quake, quaver, quiver, rock, shake, shiver, shudder, sway, teeter, totter, vibrate, waver, wobble.

tremendous, alarming, amazing, appalling, astounding, awesome, colossal, enormous, gigantic, great, huge, immense, monstrous, monumental, prodigious, startling, stupendous, vast. ANT.—insignificant, miniature, tiny, trivial, unimportant.

trespass, encroach, infringe, interfere, interlope, intrude, invade, meddle, penetrate, poach, transgress, violate. ANT.—abandon, evacuate, guard, protect, relinquish, vacate.

trial, analysis, examination, experiment, proof, test; attempt, effort, endeavor, exertion; adversity, affliction, difficulty, hardship, misery, misfortune, ordeal, suffering, tribulation, trouble; arraignment, case, cross-examination, hearing, lawsuit, litigation, prosecution.

tribulation, adversity, affliction, agony, anguish, distress, grief, hardship, misery, oppression, sorrow, suffering, trial, trouble, woe, wretchedness. ANT.—consolation, delight, elation, joy, peace.

trick, antic, artifice, caper, cheat, deceit, deception, device, fraud, guile, hoax, humbug, illusion, imposture, maneuver, ploy, ruse, stratagem, stunt, subterfuge, swindle, wile. ANT.—candor, honesty, justness, openness, sincerity.

tricky, foxy, guileful, insidious, stealthy, subtle; see also covert, shrewd.

trim, clean-cut, compact, harmonious, precise, streamlined, symmetrical; bedeck, embellish, gild; clip, cut, lop, prune, scissor, shave, shear, snip; see also spruce, tidy; embellish.

trip, see journey, travel.

trite, banal, bromidic, common, driveling, dull, hackneyed, humdrum, monotonous, obvious, ordinary, prosaic, shopworn, stale, stereotyped, tedious, uninspiring, uninteresting, wearisome. ANT.—bracing, effectual, novel, original, rousing.

triumph, achievement, ascendancy, celebration, conquest, exultation, gain, joy, jubilation, mastery, ovation, prize, routing, success, trophy, victory; celebrate, exult, flourish, glory, master, prevail, rejoice, succeed, surpass, thrive, win. ANT.—adversity, defeat, downfall, failure, subjugation; default, fail, flounder, lose, quit, succumb.

trivial, beggarly, diminutive, dribbling, frivolous, inappreciable, inconsiderable, insignificant, little, meager, minute, paltry, petty, scanty, small, trifling, unessential, unimportant, useless, valueless, worthless. ANT.—paramount, precious, significant, valuable, vital, weighty.

troop, army, band, company, crowd, group, herd, host, legion, multitude, party, squad, throng, unit.

trophy, award, citation, crown, cup, honor, laurel, loving cup, medal, memento, memorial, palm, prize, reward, token, wreath.

trouble, afflict, agitate, annoy, bother, concern, distract, distress, disturb, inconvenience, irk, irritate, molest, perturb, pester, plague, tease, upset, vex, worry; affliction, ailment, bind, crisis, difficulty, distress, effort, grief, hardship, illness, ordeal, pain, sorrow, woe; annoyance, bother, embarrassment, irritation, torment, worry; disorder, disturbance, hindrance, predicament, plight, problem; care, drudgery, effort, exertion, grind, labor, toil; altercation, argument, controversy, dispute, feud, fight, hostility, wrangle. ANT.—accommodate, console, gratify, please, soothe; delight, ecstasy, happiness, joy, pleasure; comfort, gratification, peace, quietude, repose, satisfaction, security, solace, tranquility.

troublesome, afflictive, annoying, bothersome, burdensome, damaging, difficult, distressing, disturbing, galling, harassing, irksome, tedious, trying, upsetting, wearisome. ANT.—comfortable, facile, gratifying, manageable, smooth.

true, absolute, accurate, actual, authentic, correct, definite, exact, factual, genuine, legal, legitimate, positive, precise, real, uncontradictable, valid, veracious, veritable; constant, dependable, faithful, honest, honorable, incorrupt, just, loyal, reliable, righteous, scrupulous, sincere, steadfast, straight, trustworthy, upright. ANT.—erroneous, false, fictional, imaginary, inaccurate, invalid, mythical; deceitful, disloyal, fickle, perfidious, treacherous.

trunk, body, bole, box, casing, chest, coffer, column, compartment, portmanteau, proboscis, shaft, snout, stalk, stem, stock, thorax, torso.

trust, assurance, belief, certainty, certitude, confidence, conviction, credence, credit, depend-ence, faith, reassurance, reliance, security; corporation, estate, holding, institution, monopoly; bank, believe, commit, confide, count on, credit, depend upon, entrust, esteem, expect, hope, intrust, presume, rely on. ANT.—disbelief, incredibility, misgiving, skepticism, suspicion; assail, disbelieve, discredit, impugn, suspect.

trustworthy, certain, constant, dependable, faithful, honest, honorable, loyal, reliable, safe, secure, sincere, steadfast, steady, sure, tried, true, truthful, upright, veracious. ANT.—deceitful, perfidious, sneaking, traitorous, underhand, unfaithful.

truth, accuracy, actuality, authenticity, candor, constancy, correctness, exactness, fact, fidelity, honesty, honor, ingenuousness, rectitude, rightness, sincerity, truthfulness, uprightness, veracity, verisimilitude, verity. ANT.—deception, duplicity, evasion, fabrication, falsehood, hypocrisy.

truthful, candid, frank, honest, just, open, reliable, sincere, true, trustworthy, veracious; accurate, correct, exact, factual, legitimate, verifiable. ANT.—deceitful, misleading, sly, venal; fictitious, inaccurate, incorrect, inexact.

try, aim, aspire, attempt, design, endeavor, essay, exert, intend, labor, mean, risk, seek, strive, struggle, tackle, undertake, venture; afflict, test, torment, trouble; adjudicate, adjudge, assay, decide, examine, hear, investigate, judge, probe. ANT.—abandon, decline, ignore, neglect, omit; comfort, console, ease, solace, support; cover, defer, hide, postpone, procrastinate.

trying, aggravating, annoying, bothersome, disquieting, distressing, disturbing, galling, irksome, irritating, perturbing, provoking, troublesome, upsetting, vexatious; arduous, backbreaking, burdensome, demanding, difficult, hard, laborious, painful, strenuous, tedious. ANT.—accommodating, encouraging, gratifying, pleasing, soothing; easy, facile, inconsiderable, manageable, paltry, simple.

tug, drag, draw, haul, labor, lug, pull, strive, struggle, tow, wrench, yank; effort, haul, jerk, pull, rending, strain, towboat, uprooting.

tumble, derange, disarrange, dishevel, disturb, fall, heave, pitch, plunge, roll, rumple, sprawl, stumble, topple, toss, trip, wallow.

tumult, disarray, hubbub, jumble, stir; see also chaos, commotion, disorder.

tune, accord, air, harmony, lyric, melody, song, strain, unison.

turbulent, agitated, blustery, brawling, disturbed, gusty, inclement, insurgent, obstreperous, restless, riotous, roaring, rough, stormy, tempestuous, tumultuous, violent, wild, windy. ANT.—calm, orderly, peaceful, placid, tranquil.

turmoil, disarray, hubbub, jumble, stir, tumult. see also chaos, commotion, disorder.

turn, circle, circulate, gyrate, invert, loop, oscillate, pivot, reel, revolve, rotate, spin, swing, swivel, twirl, twist, wheel, whirl; alter, change, convert, invert, transform, transmute, vary; avert, avoid, deflect, deviate, divert, dodge, sidetrack, swerve, veer; cycle, gyration, pirouette, revolution, rotation; bend, curve, hook, twist; climax, crisis, juncture, shift.

twist, bend, bow, coil, complicate, contort, convolve, crook, curve, deflect, distort, encircle, gnarl, incline, knot, lean, pervert, rotate, screw, squirm, turn, twine, wind, wreathe, wrench, wring, writhe.

type, emblem, figure, letter, mark, sign, symbol; assortment, breed, cast, category, character, class, description, genus, kind, nature, sort, species, stamp, variety; example, exemplar, form, model, mold, pattern, representation, sample.

typical, accustomed, average, common, conventional, customary, figurative, habitual, ideal, illustrative, indicative, middling, modal, model, normal, ordinary, plain, regular, representative, symbolic, usual. ANT.—aberrant, atypical, deviant, distinctive, rare.

tyrannous, authoritative, dictatorial, domineering, imperious, oppressive. see also despotic.

tyrant, autocrat, despot, dictator, inquisitor, martinet, oppressor, persecutor, slavedriver.

U

ugly, deformed, hideous, homely, horrible, offensive, repellent, repulsive, revolting, uncomely, unsightly; bullying, corrupt, disagreeable, disorderly, ill-natured, pugnacious, quarrelsome, rough, rude, spiteful, surly, threatening, tough, vicious, vile. ANT.—beautiful, captivating, dazzling, exquisite, magnificent; agreeable, charming, gentle, inviting, loving, pleasant.

ultimate, absolute, concluding, decisive, eventual, extreme, farthest, final, hindmost, last, latest, maximum, terminal, utmost. ANT.—beginning, first, initial, opening, preliminary, primary.

umpire, arbiter, arbitrator, assessor, censor, compromiser, inspector, judge, mediator, moderator, negotiator, peacemaker, propitiator, referee, settler.

unadulterated, see clean, clear, immaculate.

unanimity, accord, agreement, apposition, compatibility, concert, concord, concordance, conform-ity, congruence, correspondence, harmony, unity. ANT.—disagreement, discord, dissonance, division, variance.

unassuming, compliant, lowly, plain, simple, submissive; see also modest.

unbecoming, gauche, improper, inappropriate, indecent, indecorous, inept, maladroit, unbefitting, unfit, unseemly, unsuitable. ANT.—appropriate, becoming, fitting, proper, suitable.

unbeliever, see heretic.

unbiased, equitable, fair, honest, impartial, judicial, just, neutral, objective, reasonable, unimpassioned, unjaundiced, unprejudiced. ANT.—biased, partial, prejudiced, slanted, unfair.

uncertain, ambiguous, dim, doubtful, dubious, equivocal, hazy, indefinite, indistinct, insecure, irresolute, obscure, precarious, questionable, unclear, undecided, undetermined, unsettled, unstable, unsure, vacillating, vague. ANT.—certain, definite, explicit, lucid, precise, specific.

uncertainty, see distrust; doubt.

uncivilized, barbarian, crude, discourteous, heathenish, ignorant, low, remorseless, ruthless, uncultured, unenlightened, unrelenting. see also barbarous; cruel.

unclad, see naked.

unclean, abominable, beastly, dirty, fetid, filthy, foul, grimy, impure, nasty, obscene, offensive, repulsive, slimy, smutty, soiled, sooty, squalid, unwashed, vile. ANT.—chaste, clean, immaculate, impeccable, pure.

uncommon, different, exceptional, exotic, extraordinary, infrequent, noteworthy, occasional, odd, rare, remarkable, scarce, singular, strange, unconventional, unique, unusual, unwonted. ANT.—conventional, customary, expected, typical, usual.

uncompromising, confirmed, contumacious, determined, dogged, firm, fixed, headstrong, immovable, inflexible, intractable, intransigent, narrow, obdurate, obstinate, orthodox, pertinacious, rigid, stiff, strict, stubborn, tough, unyielding. ANT.—adaptable, amenable, compliant, flexible, submissive, yielding.

unconcern, see indifference.

unconditional, absolute, carte blanche, certain, complete, definite, entire, full, genuine, positive, thorough, unequivocal, unlimited, unqualified, unrestricted, whole. ANT.—conditional, contingent, limited, partial, qualified.

uncouth, awkward, clumsy, coarse, crass, crude, gawky, graceless, harsh, ill-prepared, raw, rough, rude, rustic, unfinished, ungainly, ungraceful, unpolished, unrefined, vulgar. ANT.—cultivated, elegant, graceful, refined, symmetrical.

uncover, betray, divulge, impart; see also open.

under, below, beneath, following, inferior, subject to, subordinate, underneath. ANT.—above. over, superior.

undergo, feel, encounter, experience, sustain; see also tolerate.

understand, accept, appreciate, experience, gather, hear, interpret, learn, realize, recognize; see also comprehend.

understanding, accordance, agreement, concord, concurrence, harmony, unison; bargain, compact, contract, covenant, pact, stipulation; comprehension, discernment, grasp, insight, intellect, intelligence, knowledge, perception, perspicacity, rationality, reason, reasoning, sapience, wisdom. ANT.—contention, disagreement, discord, dissension, variance, wrangling; fatuity, foolishness, imbecility, incapacity, stupidity.

undertaking, action, attempt, business, effort, endeavor, engagement, enterprise, essay, experiment, performance, project, task, trial, venture, work. ANT.—inertia, laziness, negligence, passivity, shiftlessness.

undisguised, genuine, open, real, true, unadulterated, uncovered; see also sincere.

undivided, intact, integral, unimpaired; see also complete.

undying, see eternal.

unearthly, metaphysical, spiritual, superhuman; see also miraculous.

uneasy, afraid, alarmed, anxious, apprehensive, disturbed, fearful, fidgety, fretful, frightened, harried, irritable, nervous, peevish, petulant, restless, shaky, troubled, uncomfortable, unquiet, wakeful, worried. ANT.—calm, content, peaceful, serene, undismayed.

uneducated, uninformed, unlettered, unschooled; see also ignorant.

unemployed, idle, inactive, inert, jobless, loafing, out of work, unoccupied. ANT.—active, busy, employed, industrious, occupied.

unequal, disparate, ill-matched, inequitable, irregular, lop-sided, odd, one-sided, unbalanced, uneven, unfair, unlike, unparallel. ANT.—balanced, coequal, even, matched, uniform.

uneven, intermittent, irregular, jagged, notched, rough, rugged, spasmodic, unequal, variable. ANT.—even, matched, regular, smooth.

unexpected, amazing, astonishing, immediate, instantaneous, rapid, surprising, unforeseen; see also hasty.

unfair, biased, dishonest, disingenuous, hypocritical, inequitable, one-sided, partial, prejudiced, slanted, unethical, unjust. ANT.—ethical, fair, honest, just, unbiased.

unfavorable, counteractive, disastrous, unlucky; see also hostile.

unfeeling, apathetic, callous, cold, cruel, hard, harsh, inconsiderate, insensate, insensible, merciless, numb, pitiless, rigorous, senseless, severe, stony, unkind, unsympathetic ANT.—compassionate, empathic, merciful, responsive, sympathetic.

unfit, improper, inappropriate, incapable, incompetent, inexpert, objectionable, unconditioned, unhealthy, unqualified, unsuitable. ANT.—capable, competent, fit, skilled, suitable.

unfold, elaborate, evolve, mature; see also expand.

unfortunate, afflicted, burdened, calamitous, desolate, disastrous, doomed, ill-fated, ill-starred, inexpedient, inopportune, miserable, overwhelmed, ruined, troubled, unhappy, unlucky, unsuccessful, unpropitious, untimely, wretched. ANT.—advantageous, beneficial, fortunate, opportune, propitious.

unhappy, calamitous, dejected, despondent, disconsolate, dismal, distressed, dolorous, gloomy, grievous, heartsick, miserable, mournful, sad, sorrowful, troubled, unfortunate, woeful, wretched. ANT.—contented, delighted, exhilarated, gratified, peaceful, satisfied.

uniform, agreeable, agreeing, alike, comformable, consistent, constant, customary, equable, equal, even, harmonious, homogenous, homologous, methodical, natural, normal, orderly, ordinary, periodical, proportionate, regular, stable, steady, symmetrical, systematic, unchanging, undeviating, undiversified, unvaried, unvarying. ANT.—amorphous, disordered, distorted, diversified, erratic, irregular, unsystematic.

unify, ally, amalgamate, blend, combine, concentrate, conjoin, connect, consolidate, entwine, join, merge, mix, organize, rally, solidify, strengthen, unite. ANT.—disperse, disrupt, divide, separate, split.

unimportant, commonplace, immaterial, incidental, inconsequential, inferior, irrelevant, mediocre, nugatory, ordinary, picayune, poor, slight; see also trivial.

uninformed, see ignorant.

unintelligible, cloudy, dim, dusky, indistinct, vague; see also mysterious.

uninteresting, burdensome, dreary, sluggish; see also monotonous.

union, amalgamation, annexation, attachment, blending, combination, commixture, concurrence, conjunction, connection, consolidation, coupling, fusion, incorporation, joining, junction, meeting, merging, mingling, solidarity, symbiosis, unification, uniting; affinity, agreement, concord, cooperation, harmony, unanimity, unison, unity; alliance, association, coalition, concert, confederacy, federation, league, marriage, organization. ANT.—

disconnection, dispersion, division, separation; clash, conflict, disagreement, discordance, rebellion; dissociation, divorce, segregation, schism.

unique, choice, different, distinctive, exceptional, individual, matchless, novel, one, only, original, peculiar, rare, remarkable, single, singular, sole, solitary, uncommon, unequaled, unlike, unmatched, unparalleled, unprecedented, unrivaled, unusual. ANT.—commonplace, conventional, familiar, ordinary, prevailing.

unite, affiliate, ally, amalgamate, annex, associate, attach, blend, coalesce, combine, concur, confederate, conjoin, connect, consolidate, cooperate, couple, embody, embrace, entwine, fuse, join, link, meet, merge, mingle, mix, solidify, strengthen, unify. ANT.—disconnect, divide, part, separate, sever.

unity, agreement, concert, concord, constancy, continuity, harmony, oneness, singleness, solidarity, unification, uniformity, union. ANT.—discord, dissimilarity, diversity, multiplicity, variety.

universal, all, all-embracing, boundless, catholic, complete, comprehensive, cosmic, cosmopolitan, ecumenical, entire, exhaustive, generic, pandemic, prevailing, sweeping, total, unlimited, whole, world-wide. ANT.—distinctive, individual, partial, singular, unique.

universe, cosmos, creation, earth, firmament, galaxy, heavens, macrocosm, nature, world.

unlawful, see illegal.

unlike, divergent, incongruous, miscellaneous, sundry, variant; see also contrary, different.

unlimited, limitless, unconfined, unconstrained, undefined, unrestrained, unrestricted; see also infinite.

unlocked, ajar, disengaged, exposed, open, unclosed, unlatched; accessible, clear, free, passable, unobstructed. ANT.—closed, locked, sealed, shut; barred, blocked, impassable, inaccessible, obstructed, unobtainable.

unmistakable, see obvious.

unpretentious, candid, frank, modest, open, plain, simple, sincere, unobtrusive, unostentatious, unpretending. ANT.—deceitful, false, hypocritical, ostentatious, pompous.

unqualified, absolute, certain, conclusive, downright, indisputable, outright, positive, unconditional, unquestionable, unrestricted, utter; inappropriate, incapable, incompetent, ineligible, inept, inexperienced, unfit, unprepared. ANT.—conditional, contingent, dependent, qualified, questionable, uncertain; capable, competent, eligible, experienced, qualified.

unreasonable, absurd, fatuous, foolish, illogical, implausible, inconsistent, irrational, ludicrous, mindless, nonsensical, preposterous, ridiculous, self-contradictory, senseless, silly, stupid, untenable. ANT.—consistent, judicious, rational, reasonable, sensible, wise.

unrestricted, accessible, accorded, allowable, available, clear, exposed, free, open, passable, permitted, public, sanctioned, unobstructed, welcoming. ANT.—denied, forbidden, private, prohibited, refused.

unruly, disobedient, fractious, headstrong, lawless, mutinous, obstreperous, rebellious, recalcitrant, refractory, stubborn, ungovernable, violent, wanton, willful. ANT.—docile, law-abiding, manageable, obedient, tractable.

unsafe, critical, dangerous, hazardous, imperiled, insecure, menacing, perilous, precarious, risky, threatening, treacherous, unreliable, unstable. ANT.—firm, harmless, protected, safe, secure.

unscrupulous, dishonorable, reckless, ruthless, unconscientious, unprincipled, unrestrained; see also dishonest.

unseemly, boorish, brutish, clownish, depraved, disgraceful, disorderly, dissolute, dowdy, gross, ill-advised, immoral, improper, imprudent, inappropriate, indecorous, inept, inexpedient, inopportune, objectionable, rowdy, slovenly, unbecoming, unfit, ungraceful, unkempt, unpolished,

unsightly, unsuitable, vulgar, worthless. ANT.—commendable, cultivated, fitting, polished, proper, suave.

unselfish, see generous.

unsettled, adrift, apprehensive, changeable, fickle, inconstant, nervous, perturbed, restless, stirred, troubled, unhinged, unnerved, unstable, unsteady, vacillating, wavering; uninhabited, wild; outstanding, owing, unpaid; foul, muddy, roily, turbid. ANT.—calm, certain, constant, peaceful, secure; inhabited, settled; cleared, paid, solvent; clarified, immaculate, pure, sparkling, untainted.

unskilled, awkward, clumsy, ignorant, ill-qualified, incompetent, inept, inexperienced, maladroit, rusty, unfit, unpracticed. ANT.—accomplished, competent, efficient, expert, trained.

unsophisticated, artless, candid, frank, fresh, genuine, guileless, ignorant, ingenuous, innocent, naive, natural, open, pure, real, simple, true, unaffected, undesigning, unspoiled, unstudied, unvitiated. ANT.—experienced, guileful, hard, initiated, sophisticated, worldly.

unstable, see fickle.

unswerving, fast, inflexible, solid, unyielding; see also stable.

unusual, aberrant, abnormal, anomalous, atypical, awesome, capricious, curious, devious, distinguished, eccentric, exceptional, extraordinary, incredible, irregular, odd, rare, strange, uncommon, unique, unnatural, unparalleled, variable. ANT.—common, normal, ordinary, regular, usual.

unyielding, see unswerving.

upbraid, blame, lecture, reprehend, vituperate; see also rebuke.

uphold, see maintain.

upright, direct, right, undeviating, unswerving; erect, standing, straight, unbent, vertical; conscientious, ethical, fair, faithful, honest, honorable, incorruptible, just, moral, scrupulous, square, straightforward, true, trustworthy, virtuous. ANT.—deviating, indirect, swerving; bent, horizontal, prone; corruptible, crooked, dishonest, fraudulent, immoral, lax.

upset, disturb, haunt, inconvenience, perplex, worry; see also pester.

urbane, considerate, well-mannered; see also polite.

urge, appetite, aspiration, hungering, lust; induce, prevail upon, win over; see also desire; persuade.

urgency, importance, need, seriousness; see also emergency.

urgent, absorbing, breathless, chief, cogent, compelling, critical, crucial, demanded, essential, exigent, grave, impelling, imperative, important, importunate, insistent, instant, momentous, necessary, pressing, principal, required, salient, serious, vital, weighty. ANT.—common, insignificant, petty, trivial, unessential, uneventful.

use, apply, avail, employ, exploit, handle, manage, manipulate, operate, ply, utilize, wield; exercise, exert, practice, work; consume, exhaust, expend; accustom, familiarize, habituate, inure; application, employment, service, utilization; necessity, need; advantage, usefulness; method, technique, usage; see also habit.

useful, advantageous, applicable, beneficial, gainful, good, helpful, practical, pragmatic, profitable, remunerative, salutary, serviceable, suitable, utilitarian, valuable, wholesome. ANT.—deleterious, destructive, detrimental, harmful, noxious.

usefulness, adaptability, advantage, application, convenience, helpfulness, practicality, utility, versatility; see also merit.

useless, abortive, empty, fruitless, futile, idle, inadequate, ineffective, ineffectual, pointless, unavailing, unproductive, unserviceable, vain, valueless, vapid, worthless. ANT.—beneficial, effective, potent, profitable, valuable.

usual, accustomed, common, commonplace, conventional, current, customary, everyday, expected, familiar, frequent, general, habitual, normal, ordinary, prevailing, prevalent, pro-

saic, recognized, regular, stereotyped. ANT.—abnormal, exceptional, extraordinary, rare, unconventional.

utensil, apparatus, appliance, device, equipment, implement, instrument, medium, tool, vehicle, ware.

utility, adequacy, advantage, avail, benefit, convenience, efficacy, efficiency, expediency, favor, productiveness, profit, service, serviceableness, usefulness, utilitarianism, value, worth. ANT.—disadvantage, futility, inefficacy, uselessness, worthlessness.

utilize, adopt, apply, appropriate, avail, employ, exercise, exert, exploit, occupy, practice, use. ANT.—discard, discharge, expel, refuse, reject.

utmost, absolute, chief, extreme, farthest, greatest, highest, last, main, maximum, most, ultimate, unqualified, uttermost. ANT.—closest, least, merest, minimum, nearest.

utopian, chimerical, exemplary, fabulous, fancied, fantastic, faultless, ideal, illusory, imaginary, perfect, supreme, unreal, visionary. ANT.—actual, faulty, imperfect, substantial, tangible, visible.

utter, complete, entire, finished, full, perfect, thorough, total, whole; consummate, excellent, ideal, pure, superlative, supreme; absolute, downright, sheer, unconditional, unquali-

fied, unrestricted, wholehearted;
acclaim, air, announce, articulate, assert, claim, declare, disclose, divulge, emit, enunciate,
express, inform, proclaim, pronounce, speak, talk, tell, vocalize,
voice, whisper. ANT.—imperfect, incomplete, lacking, partial, unfinished; inferior, lesser,
negligible, poor; conditional,
limited, qualified, restricted;
conceal, cover, hide, mask,
withhold.

V

vacant, abandoned, bare, barren,
blank, depleted, deserted, empty,
hollow, idle, tenantless, unfilled,
uninhabited, unoccupied, unten-
anted, unused, vacuous, void;
dreaming, empty-headed, foolish, inane, silly, thoughtless.
ANT.—filled, full, inhabited,
occupied, overflowing; cogitative, contemplative, meditative,
reflective, thoughtful, wise.

vacate, abandon, abdicate, abjure,
depart, desert, empty, evacuate,
forsake, leave, quit, relinquish,
resign, surrender, waive. ANT.—
assume, maintain, remain, stay,
support.

vacillate, change, oscillate, undulate, vary; see also hesitate.

vacillation, changeableness, faltering, fluctuation, hesitation, inconstancy, indecision,
irresolution, oscillation, reeling,
rocking, swaying, uncertainty,
unsteadiness, wavering. ANT.—

certainty, constancy, dependability, firmness.

vagrant, beggar, bum, hobo, idler,
loafer, rambler, rogue, rover,
straggler, tramp, truant, vagabond, wanderer; changeable, digressive, discursive, divergent,
erratic, fickle, fluctuating,
homeless, idle, inconstant, irresolute, itinerant, nomadic, peri-
patetic, ranging, roaming, roving,
straying, traveling, unsettled,
unstable, unsteady, wandering.
ANT.—gentleman, laborer,
toiler, worker, workman; anchored, established, fixed,
rooted, stable.

vague, cryptic, dark, doubtful, dubious, enigmatic, formless, imprecise, mysterious, nebulous,
questionable, unsure, visionary;
see also indefinite.

vain, abortive, bootless, delusive,
empty, fleeting, frivolous, fruitless, futile, hollow, idle, ineffective, ineffectual, nugatory,
pointless, shadowy, trifling, trivial, unavailing, unprofitable, unsatisfactory, useless, valueless,
vapid, visionary, worthless; arrogant, conceited, egotistical, inflated, ostentatious, proud,
showy, vainglorious. ANT.—
advantageous, effective, potent,
profitable, valuable; demure,
genuine, humble, meek, modest,
unpretentious.

valiant, adventurous, assertive,
audacious, bold, brave, chivalrous, courageous, daring, dauntless, fearless, gallant, heroic,

indomitable, intrepid, magnanimous, manly, plucky, puissant, spirited, strong-willed, unafraid, undismayed, unflinching, unshrinking, valorous, venturesome, vigorous. ANT.— cowardly, craven, fearful, timid, timorous, weak.

valid, accurate, actual, authentic, binding, cogent, conclusive, convincing, definite, effective, efficacious, efficient, factual, forceful, genuine, legal, legitimate, logical, operative, powerful, real, solid, sound, strong, substantial, sufficient, telling, tested, true, weighty. ANT.— counterfeit, erroneous, fallacious, invalid, spurious.

valor, chivalry, manliness, prowess, spiritedness; see also courage.

valuable, costly, expensive, high-priced, rare; dear, esteemed, precious, worthy; profitable, serviceable, useful. ANT.—cheap, common, unmarketable; abhorred, disliked, disrespectable, worthless; profitless, useless.

value, appreciate, cherish, esteem, hold dear, prize, treasure; appraise, assess, compute, estimate, figure, rate; advantage, appreciation, consideration, esteem, estimation, excellence, importance, merit, price, profit, quality, significance, usefulness, utility, valuation, virtue, worth, worthiness. ANT.—abandon, despise, ignore, neglect, overlook, reject; inexpedience, inutility, unfitness, uselessness, worthlessness.

vandalism, barbarism, burning, damage, destruction, looting, piracy, spoliation, wasting, wrecking. ANT.—care, preservation, protection, repair, replacement.

vanish, cease, depart, die, disappear, dissolve, evaporate, fade, go away, sink. ANT.—appear, emerge, reappear.

vanity, affectation, arrogance, conceit, conceitedness, display, egotism, ostentation, pretension, self-applause, self-glorification, selfishness, self-laudation, self-love, show, vainglory. ANT.— bashfulness, diffidence, humility, modesty, unobtrusiveness.

vanquish, beat, outwit, suppress; see also conquer.

vapid, banal, bland, commonplace, dry, dull, feeble, flat, hackneyed, inane, insipid, lifeless, prosaic, spiritless, tasteless, trite, uninteresting. ANT.— bright, fresh, original, pungent, stimulating, striking.

vapor, breath, cloud, condensation, effluvium, emanation, exhalation, fog, fume, gas, haze, mist, smoke, smog, spray, steam.

variable, see fickle.

variation, aberration, alteration, change, contrariety, contrast, departure, deviation, difference, disagreement, discord, discrepancy, disparity, dissent, dissidence, dissimilarity, dissimilitude, distinction, diversity, fluctuation, heterogeneity, incongruity, inconsistency, innovation, modification, mutation, noncomformity, oscillation, variety, vicissitude. ANT.—agreement, congruity, homogeneity, permanence, stability, uniformity.

variety, change, difference, dissimilarity, diversification, diversity, heterogeneity, medley, miscellany, mixture, multifariousness, variance; array, assortment, brand, breed, category, class, division, family, genus, grade, kind, race, rank, sort, species, stock, strain, subspecies, tribe, type. ANT.—homogeneity, likeness, monotony, sameness, uniformity, unity.

various, assorted, different, disparate, divergent, divers, diverse, manifold, many, miscellaneous, numerous, several, sundry. ANT.—alike, congruous, identical, same, uniform.

vary, exchange, substitute; shift, transfigure, veer; see also modify.

vast, ample, big, capacious, extensive, great, large; see also colossal.

vault, see jump.

vehement, ardent, burning, eager, enthusiastic, excitable, fervent, fervid, fiery, glowing, hot, impetuous, intense, irascible, passionate. ANT.—apathetic, calm, cool, indifferent, lukewarm.

veil, cloak, clothe, curtain, envelop, guard; see also conceal.

velocity, alacrity, celerity, impetus, pace, quickness, rapidity, speed, swiftness.

venerable, adored, aged, ancient, antiquated, antique, archaic, elderly, erudite, esteemed, honored, old, patriarchal, respected, revered, superannuated, timeworn, venerated, worshipped. ANT.—callow, immature, inexperienced, modern, new.

venerate, admire, adore, appreciate, approve, cherish, esteem, honor, regard, respect, revere, worship. ANT.—abhor, despise, dislike, loathe, scorn.

vengeance, reparation, reprisal, requital, spitefulness; see also revenge.

venom, acerbity, bitterness, contempt, enmity, gall, hate, malevolence, malice, malignity poison, rancor, resentment, virulence. ANT.—benevolence, charity, fellowship, love, warmheartedness.

vent, belch, breathe, discharge, eject, emanate, emit, expel, explode, shoot, spurt, ventilate; airhole, crenel, emission, escape, hole, inlet, loophole, mouth, nostril, opening, orifice, outlet, overflow, passage, plug, spiracle, spout, tap, valve.

ventilate, aerate, air, circulate air, cool, explain, express, fan, freshen, open, oxygenate, purify, refresh, vent.

venture, adventure, attempt, business, chance, dare, enterprise, experiment, gamble, hazard, investment, peril, project, risk, speculation, stake, trial, undertaking, work; advance, assay, attempt, bet, brave, dare, experiment, gamble, grope, hazard, invest, risk, speculate, try, wager.

veracity, accuracy, candor, credibility, exactitude, fidelity, frankness, honesty, probity, reality, sincerity, truth, truthfulness. ANT.—chicanery, deception, duplicity, falsehood, misrepresentation.

verbal, announced, communicated, expressed, lingual, literal, nuncupative, oral, sounded, spoken, told, unwritten, uttered, vocal, voiced. ANT.—documentary, printed, unspoken, written.

verbose, chattering, chatty, fluent, garrulous, long-winded, loquacious, redundant, talkative, verbal, wordy. ANT.—concise, laconic, silent, stammering, taciturn, uncommunicative.

verdict, adjudication, arbitrament, conclusion, decision, decree, determination, finding, judgment, result.

verge, border, boundary, brim, brink, confine, edge, end, extreme, limit, lip, margin, rim, skirt. ANT.—body, bulk, center, inside.

verification, affirmation, attestation, authentication, confirmation, corroboration, demonstration, evidence, proof, recognition, support, testimony.

ANT.—contradiction, denial, failure, fallacy, invalidity.

verify, acknowledge, affirm, approve, assure, attest, authenticate, certify, corroborate, confirm, determine, establish, fix, prove, ratify, sanction, settle, strengthen, substantiate, validate. ANT.—contradict, deny, disprove, invalidate, repudiate.

versed, acquainted, aware, cognizant, conversant, familiar, intimate, knowing, proficient, skilled. ANT.—unaware, unfamiliar, unknowing.

versatile, adaptable, apt, changeable, many-sided, movable, ready, variable. ANT.—awkward, limited, unadaptable, unchanging.

vertical, erect, perpendicular, plumb, standing, straight, upright. ANT.—flat, horizontal, inclined, oblique, prone, supine.

vestige, mark, remainder, remains, remnant, residue, scrap, sign, trace.

vex, aggravate, embitter, inflame; see also irritate.

vibrate, agitate, flicker, fluctuate, flutter, jar, jolt, oscillate, pulsate, quake, quaver, quiver, rock, shake, shiver, shudder, sway, swing, totter, tremble, undulate, wave, waver.

vice, blemish, blot, carnality, debauchery, defect, excess, fault, impropriety, impurity, iniquity, offense, perversity, sin, transgression, ungodliness; see also evil.

vicinity, district, domain, environment, environs, locality, neighborhood, realm, region, sector, territory; adjacency, nearness, proximity. ANT.—outskirts; distance, remoteness.

vicious, bad, base, corrupt, debased, degenerate, demoralized, depraved, destructive, evil, harmful, hurtful, malignant, obnoxious, pernicious, profligate, reprehensible, sinful, unruly, vile, virulent, wicked. ANT.—admirable, exemplary, honorable, noble, upright, virtuous.

victim, dupe, gull, martyr, prey, puppet, quarry, sacrifice, scapegoat, sufferer, wretch. ANT.—culprit, evil-doer, felon, swindler.

victor, champion, conqueror, hero, master, vanquisher, winner. ANT.—failure, loser, underdog, vanquished, victim.

victory, achievement, ascendancy, conquest, defeating, mastery, overcoming, subjugation, success, superiority, supremacy, triumph, win, winning. ANT.—collapse, defeat, failure, frustration, overthrow.

view, aim, belief, conception, examination, glance, glimpse, goal, impression, inspection, judgment, look, object, observation, opinion, outlook, panorama, perspective, picture, prospect, range, regard, scene, sight, survey, theory, vision, vista; behold, consider, discern, examine, eye, gaze, glance, inspect, look, observe, regard, scan, scrutinize, see, stare, survey, watch, witness. ANT.—avert, disregard, ignore, miss, overlook, sidetrack.

viewpoint, angle, aspect, attitude, disposition, light, outlook, perspective, pose, position, posture, slant, stand, standpoint.

vigilant, alert, attentive, careful, cautious, circumspect, guarded, heedful, observant, wakeful, wary, watchful, wide-awake. ANT.—careless, foolhardy, negligent, rash, reckless.

vigor, endurance, energy, force, fortitude, hardihood, health, liveliness, lustiness, spirit, strength, verge, virility, vitality, well-being, zeal. ANT.—exhaustion, languor, lassitude, listlessness.

vigorous, active, animated, blithe, brisk, energetic, flourishing, forceful, frolicsome, healthy, lively, lusty, powerful, robust, spirited, sprightly, strenuous, strong, virile, vital, vivacious. ANT.—debilitated, feeble, frail, inactive, lethargic.

vile, abject, base, brutish, cheap, contemptible, debased, depraved, despicable, disgusting, evil, foul, gross, ignoble, impure, iniquitous, loathsome, low, mean, obscene, odious, repulsive, revolting, sinful, sordid, ugly, vicious, vulgar, wicked, worthless, wretched. ANT.—attractive, decent, elevated, honorable, laudable, valuable.

vilify, abuse, asperse, ill-use, revile, scandalize; see also malign.

villainous, bad, base, evil, unsound, unwholesome; see also deleterious, iniquitous.

vindicate, advocate, assert, avenge, defend, excuse, maintain, support, uphold; see also exonerate.

vindictive, avenging, grudgeful, implacable, malevolent, malicious, rancorous, resentful, unforgiving, vengeful. ANT.—conciliatory, excusing, forgiving, placable.

violate, break, disobey, disregard, encroach, infringe, invade, transgress; debauch, defile, deflower, desecrate, dishonor, outrage, pollute, profane, rape, ravish.

violence, assault, fury, intensity, outrage, vehemence, violation, wildness; see also force.

violent, angry, convulsive, fierce, fiery, frantic, frenzied, fuming, furious, hysterical, obstreperous, passionate, raging, rampant, raving, riotous, savage, turbulent, ungovernable, uproarious, vehement, wild; acute, extreme, forceful, great, intense, mighty, potent, powerful, severe, strong. ANT.—composed, kind, pacific, peaceful, tranquil, unruffled; feeble, insignificant, mild, moderate, weak.

virgin, chaste, clean, immaculate, innocent, modest, pure, spotless, stainless, unadulterated, unblemished, undefiled, unsullied, untainted, virginal; first, fresh, genuine, natural, new, original, undisturbed, untamed, untouched. ANT.—corrupt, defiled, shameless; foul, poisoned, polluted, soiled.

virile, hardy, lusty, vigorous; see also masculine.

virtue, chastity, decency, goodness, honesty, honor, impeccability, innocence, integrity, morality, probity, prudence, purity, rectitude, sanctity, temperance, uprightness, virginity; effectiveness, efficacy, force, fortitude, power, strength; distinction, excellence, merit, superiority, value, worth. ANT.—corruption, depravity, dishonor, vileness, wickedness; debility, enervation, infirmity, weakness; deficiency, inferiority, inutility, uselessness, worthlessness.

virtuous, decent, honorable, just, right, scrupulous; see also chaste, ethical.

visible, see evident, fair, manifest.

vision, apparition, appearance, chimera, conception, daydream, discernment, dream, fancy, ghost, hallucination, hope, illusion, image, manifestation, mirage, perception, phantasm, phantom, prophecy, revelation, shadow, sight, specter. ANT.—actuality, blindness, corporality, fact, substantiality, verity.

visionary, chimerical, delusory, dreamy, fancied, fanciful, ideal, illusory, imaginary, imaginative, romantic, unreal, utopian. ANT.—actual, material, real, substantial.

vital, alive, animate, existing, living; basic, cardinal, essential, fundamental, important, indispensable, necessary, paramount, requisite, urgent. ANT.—dead, inanimate, lifeless; dispensable, excessive, insignificant, trivial, unimportant.

vitality, being, existence, life; animation, ardor, buoyancy, energy, intensity, liveliness, spirit, spunk, verve, vigor, vim, vivacity. ANT.—death, demise, extinction; apathy, lassitude, lethargy, passivity, torpor.

vitiate, abase, adulterate, alloy, annul, contaminate, corrupt, damage, debase, defile, degrade, deprave, depress, deteriorate, humiliate, impair, infect, injure, lower, nullify, pervert, poison, pollute, ruin, spoil, void. ANT.—clean, enhance, improve, purify, revive, vitalize.

vivid, animated, bright, brilliant, clear, expressive, fresh, graphic, intense, lifelike, lively, lucid, pictorial, picturesque, realistic, sprightly, striking, strong, telling, vibrant. ANT.—cloudy, dreary, dull, vague, weak.

vocal, announced, articulate, communicated, expressed, expressive, fluent, musical, oral, spoken, sung, uttered, verbal, vocalized, voiced, voluble. ANT.—printed, quiet, silent, unspoken, written.

vocation, art, business, calling, commerce, employment, engagement, enterprise, field, job, lifework, mission, occupation, office, position, profession, pursuit, role, situation, trade, trading, undertaking, work. ANT.—avocation, diversion, entertainment, hobby, pastime.

voice, accent, articulation, call, cry, enunciation, expression, intonation, noise, pronunciation, sound, speech, tongue, utterance, vocalization; choice, election, suffrage, vote; announce, assert, cry, declaim, declare, express, say, sound, speak, talk, tell, utter.

void, blank, lacking; see also empty.

volatile, airy, buoyant, changeable, effervescent, evaporable, fleeting, gaseous, inconstant, irresolute, light, resilient, vacillating, vaporous, vapory, wavering, weak; active, animated, blithe, cheerful, elated, jocund, lively, playful, vivacious. ANT.—durable, heavy, massive, soluble, weighty; dejected, despondent, hopeless, melancholy, sad.

volition, choice, decision, determination, election, intention, resolution, resolve, selection, will. ANT.—coercion, compulsion, force, persuasion, pressure.

volume, capability, power, talent; amount, extent, mass, size; book, edition, printed document, publication; see also capacity.

voluntary, deliberate, elective, free, intentional, self-determining, uncoerced, unforced, volitional, willful, willing. ANT.—compulsory, enforced, forced, instinctive, involuntary, mandatory, required.

volunteer, come forward, enlist, extend, sacrifice, submit oneself; see also offer.

vouch, affirm, assert, attest, avow, certify, confirm, declare, depose, guarantee, support, swear, testify, uphold, warrant. ANT.—abnegate, controvert, deny, disavow, repudiate.

vow, oath, pledge, promise; affirm, assert, certify, consecrate, dedicate, devote, pledge, promise, swear.

vulgar, abusive, base, brutish, cheap, coarse, common, crass, disgusting, general, gross, ignorant, ill-bred, indecent, inelegant, low, obscene, odious, offensive, plebeian, popular, profane, ribald, rough, rowdy, rude, tawdry, uncouth, uncultured, unpolished, unrefined. ANT.—aristocratic, charming, cultured, elegant, polished, refined.

vulnerable, assailable, defenseless, exposed, unprotected, unsafe; see also insecure.

W

wager, bet, chance, gage, gamble, hazard, play, punt, risk, sport, stake; betting, gambling, risk, speculation.

wages, compensation, earnings, fee, income, pay, payment, recompense, remuneration, salary, stipend. ANT.—donation, gift, gratuity.

wait, abide, bide, delay, linger, remain, rest, stay, tarry; await, expect, watch; attend, minister, serve. ANT.—act, depart, hasten, leave, proceed; disregard, neglect, reject; hamper, hinder, impede, oppose.

waive, see renounce.

wake, activate, animate, arouse, awake, awaken, call, enkindle, excite, kindle, prod, revive, rouse, stimulate, stir, wake.

wallow, flounder, grovel, immerse, revel, roll, toss, welter.

wander, deviate, digress, diverge, drift, err, journey, meander, peregrinate, ramble, range, roam, rove, saunter, straggle, stray, stroll, tour, traipse, travel, traverse. ANT.—halt, pause, remain, settle, stay.

want, aspire, covet, crave, desire, long for, wish; be destitute, lack, need, require, suffer privation; dearth, deficiency, depletion, destitution, exigency, inadequacy, indigence, insufficiency, lack, necessity, need, neediness, pauperism, penury, poverty, privation, scarcity, starvation. ANT.—abhor, detest, dislike; enjoy, have, own, possess; abundance, affluence, opulence, riches, wealth.

ward, care, charge, custody, dependent, guardianship, minor, protection; district, division, precinct, quarter, section; defend, guard, keep, parry, protect, safeguard, watch.

warfare, armed struggle, battle, combat, conflict, contest, fighting, hostilities, military operations, mobilization. ANT.—accord, armistice, harmony, peace, truce.

wariness, see heed.

warlike, see hostile.

warm, affable, affectionate, ardent, compassionate, cordial, earnest, empathic, enthusiastic, fervent, friendly, genial, gracious, heartfelt, hearty, loving, responsive, sincere, sociable, sympathetic, tender, warm-hearted; feverish, flushed, heated, lukewarm, melting, mild, sunny, temperate, tepid; comfortable, cozy, secure, sheltered, snug; chafe, foment, heat, incite, melt, thaw. ANT.—aloof, cold, detached, diffident, taciturn; cold, cool, freezing, frosty, icy; disturbed, exposed, insecure, uncomfortable, uneasy; calm, chill, freeze, soothe, temper.

warn, admonish, caution, counsel, forebode, forewarn, signal, summon; see also notify.

warning, admonition, advice, alarm, augury, caution, indication, information, notice, omen, portent, prediction, premonition, sign, signal, summons, threat.

wary, attentive, alert, awake, aware, careful, cautious, circumspect, discreet, guarded, heedful, mindful, observant, provident, scrupulous, thoughtful, vigilant, watchful. ANT.—foolhardy, impulsive, negligent, precipitate, rash.

wash, bathe, clean, cleanse, douse, immerse, launder, lave, rinse, scour, scrub, soak, soap, wet, wipe. ANT.—dirty, foul, soil, stain.

waste, abandoned, bare, bleak, deserted, desolate, discarded, empty, forlorn, forsaken, futile, lonely, pointless, solitary, uninhabited, useless, wild, worthless; abuse, consume, dissipate, exhaust, lavish, misapply, misspend, misuse, scatter, spend, squander, wear out; decay, diminish, dwindle, pine, wither; corrode, damage, despoil, destroy, devastate, pillage, plunder, ravage, ruin, sack, strip. ANT.—attended, cultivated, fertile, inhabited, productive; hoard, preserve, redeem, retain, save; grow, prosper, thrive, triumph; defend, guard, harbor, protect, shield.

wasteful, careless, destructive, dissipated, extravagant, improvident, lavish, prodigal, profligate, profuse, reckless, ruinous, squandering, thriftless, unthrifty, wild. ANT.—conservative, economical, hoarding, mercenary, thrifty.

watch, attend, behold, contemplate, descry, discern, distinguish, espy, follow, glimpse, guard, inspect, mark, mind, notice, observe, perceive, regard, scan, scrutinize, see, view, wait, witness.

watchful, alert, attentive, careful, cautious, circumspect, guarded, heedful, observant, prudent, vigilant, wakeful, wary, watchful, wide-awake. ANT.—careless, inattentive, lax, neglectful, oblivious.

water, bathe, deluge, dilute, douse, drench, flood, immerse, irrigate, moisten, soak, sprinkle, steep, wash, wet. ANT.—dehydrate, drain, dry, parch, sear.

wave, billow, breaker, ripple, roller, surge, swell, undulation; beckon, flap, flutter, oscillate, shake, signal, stir, sway, swing.

waver, boggle, deliberate, dilly-dally, equivocate, falter, flicker, fluctuate, flutter, hesitate, oscillate, quiver, reel, shake, totter, tremble, twitch, vacillate, vibrate.

wavering, see fickle.

way, allay, approach, artery, avenue, channel, course, driveway, entrance, gateway, highway, lane, pass, passage, path, pathway, road, roadway, route, street, thoroughfare, track, trail, walk; design, fashion, form, habit, manner, means, method, mode, plan, practice, procedure, process, style, system.

weak, bending, delicate, faint, fragile, frail, pliant, soft, tender, yielding; debilitated, decrepit, enervated, exhausted, feeble, flaccid, impotent, infirm, nervous, shaky, wasted, worn; illogical, inadequate, ineffective, ineffectual, lame, poor, vague; assailable, defenseless, exposed, helpless, powerless, unguarded, unsubstantial, vulnerable. ANT.—rigid, strong, unyielding; animated, healthy, robust, vigorous; cogent, effective, efficacious, persuasive, potent; defended, protected, safe, secure, unthreatened.

weaken, attenuate, cramp, cripple, debilitate, devitalize, dilute, diminish, enervate, enfeeble, exhaust, impair, incapacitate, reduce, relax, sap, thin, undermine. ANT.—brace, energize, fortify, invigorate, strengthen.

weakness, see disability.

wealth, abundance, affluence, assets, capital, fortune, luxury, means, money, opulence, plenty, possessions, prosperity, riches, resources, securities, stock, substance, treasure. ANT.—indigence, need, poverty, privation, want.

wear, abrade, bear, carry, consume, diminish, display, endure, erode, impair, use, waste; service, use, utilization.

weariness, annoyance, disgust, ennui, exhaustion, faintness, fatigue, languor, lassitude, lethargy, prostration, tedium, tiredness. ANT.—alertness, amusement, energy, strength, vim.

weary, bored, exhausted, faint, fatigued, jaded, spent, tired, wearied, worn; anger, annoy, bore, bother, deject, depress, discourage, disgust, dishearten, dispirit, displease, distress, enfeeble, exhaust, fatigue, grieve, irk, irritate, jade, overburden, overtax, pain, prostrate, sadden, strain, tire, vex. ANT.—animated, fresh, invigorated, refreshed, rested; arouse, brace, energize, enliven, revive, strengthen.

weather, bear, bleach, discolor, disintegrate, dry, endure, expand, fade, overcome, resist, rot, shrink, split, stand, sustain, tan, toughen.

weave, braid, compose, construct, crochet, design, fabricate, form, imagine, intertwine, knit, lace, mat, twist.

wedding, see marriage.

weigh, consider, examine, heed, study; see also ponder.

weight, ballast, burden, contents, density, gravity, heaviness, load, mass, tonnage; pressure; authority, consequence, domination, emphasis, import, importance, influence, moment, power, seriousness, significance, stress, sway, value. ANT.—airiness, buoyancy, levity, lightness; insignificance, pettiness, smallness, triviality, worthlessness.

weird, curious, eerie, ghostly, mysterious, odd, peculiar, spooky, strange, supernatural, uncanny, unearthly, wild. ANT.—common, normal, ordinary, regular, usual.

welcome, accept, address, admit, embrace, entertain, greet, hail, hug, receive, recognize, salute, shelter, take in. ANT.—discharge, ignore, reject, snub, turn away.

well, adequately, admirably, competently, expertly, extremely, favorably, satisfactorily, strongly, suitably; see also healthy.

well-being, contentment, delight, felicity, fortune, gladness, happiness, health, pleasure, prosperity, satisfaction, serenity, welfare, wholeness. ANT.—depression, distress, illness, suffering, trouble.

well-bred, see polite.

well-known, see distinguished.

wheel, bicycle, circle, disk, roller; eddy, gyrate, pirouette, revolve, roll, rotate, spin, swirl, transport, turn, twist, veer, whirl, wind.

whim, caprice, dream, fancy, fantasy, humor, idea, impulse, inclination, notion, quirk, tendency, vagary, vision, whimsy.

whimsical, curious, droll, peculiar, quaint; see also eccentric.

whole, absolute, all, complete, entire, full, inclusive, intact integral, inviolate, perfect, plenary, total, unabridged, unbroken, undivided, unimpaired; hale, healed, healthy, sound, well. ANT.—defective, fragmentary, imperfect, incomplete, partial; diseased, feeble, impaired, infirm, sickly.

wholesome, beneficial, nourishing, nutritive; hearty, robust, strong; see also healthy; whole.

wicked, atrocious, base, corrupt, criminal, deleterious, disorderly, disreputable, dissolute, erring, evil, fiendish, foul, gross, hellish, immoral, impure, infamous, iniquitous, irreligious, malevolent, murderous, nefarious, noxious, pernicious, scandalous, shameful, sinful, unrighteous, unsound, vicious, vile, villainous, wayward, wrong. ANT.—admirable, commendable, honorable, moral, noble, praiseworthy, virtuous.

wide, all-inclusive, blanket, broad, comprehensive, expanded, extensive, general, large, sweeping, universal, vast. ANT.—confined, hampered, limited, narrow, restricted.

wild, undomesticated, untamed; rough, uncultivated; impetuous, irregular, turbulent, wayward; extravagant, foolish, giddy; boisterous. see also barbarous, fierce; desolate; reckless; stormy.

will, choice, conviction, decision, desire, determination, inclination, intent, intention, mind, preference, purpose, resolution, volition, willingness, wish. ANT.—coercion, compulsion, doubt, indecision, wavering.

willful, see intentional.

win, see gain, succeed.

wind, air, blast, breeze, current, cyclone, draft, flurry, flutter, gale, gust, hurricane, squall, storm, tempest, typhoon, zephyr; coil, fold, twine, twist, wreathe; bend, crook, curve, deviate, meander, sinuate, snake, zigzag.

winding, bending, coiling, crooked, curving, devious, involuted, meandering, sinuous, turning, twining, twisting, writhing. ANT.—direct, plain, straight.

wisdom, acumen, astuteness, comprehension, depth, discernment, discretion, discrimination, enlightenment, erudition, farsightedness, foresight, insight, intelligence, judgment, knowledge, learning, perspicacity, prudence, reason, reasoning, sagacity, sense, understanding. ANT.—absurdity, fatuity, foolishness, ignorance, imprudence, misjudgment.

wise, advisable, alert, astute, calculating, deep, discerning, discreet, enlightened, erudite, foresighted, informed, intelligent, judicious, penetrating, profound, prudent, rational, sagacious, sage, sane, sensible, shrewd, smart, sound.

wish, appetite, aspiration, bid, craving, desire, hungering, longing, lust, need, petition, plea, request, urge, yearning; covet, crave, desire, hanker, hope, hunger, long, pine, thirst, want, yearn.

wit, comprehension, intellect, intelligence, mind, perception, perspicacity, reason, sagacity, sense, understanding; banter, burlesque, cleverness, drollery, facetiousness, fun, humor, irony, jest, jocularity, playfulness, raillery, sarcasm, satire, witticism; comedian, humorist, joker, wag. ANT.—dullness, stupidity; gloom, gravity, melancholy, pessimism, solemnity; cynic, misanthrope, pessimist.

witchcraft, bewitchment, black art, black magic, charm, conjuration, conjuring, demonology, divination, enchantment, incantation, legerdemain, magic, necromancy, sorcery, spell, voodooism, witchery, wizardry.

withdraw, abandon, abjure, abstract, deduct, depart, desert, dissociate, disengage, draw, forsake, give up, go, leave, part, quit, recall, recant, relinquish, remove, renounce, retire, retract, retreat, revoke, secede, separate, sequester, shrink, vacate, wean. ANT.—abide, introduce, remain, return, stay, tarry.

wither, decay, decline, deteriorate, droop, dry up, fail, languish, shrink, shrivel, sink, waste, weaken, wilt, wizen, wrinkle. ANT.—bloom, invigorate, refresh, rejuvenate, revive.

withhold, abstain, check, conceal, deny, desist, detain, forbear, hide, hinder, keep, refrain, refuse, reserve, restrain, retain, suppress. ANT.—accord, concede, grant, indulge, persist, yield.

withstand, bar, combat, confront, contradict, counteract, defy, endure, face, hinder, hold out, obstruct, resist, thwart. ANT.—acquiesce, consent, submit, succumb, yield.

witness, attestation, confirmation, declaration, evidence, proof, testimony; attestor, beholder, bystander, corroborator, deponent, eyewitness, observer, onlooker, spectator, testifier, watcher; attest, bear witness, confirm, corroborate, mark, note, observe, see, testify, vouch, watch.

witty, droll, facetious, funny; see also clever.

wizardry, see witchcraft.

woe, see disaster; misery.

womanly, compassionate, gentle, ladylike, maidenly, modest, protective. see also feminine.

wonder, curiosity, marvel, miracle, oddity, phenomenon, portent, prodigy, rarity, sight, sign, spectacle; admiration, amazement, astonishment, awe, bewilderment, confusion, curiosity, fascination, perplexity, stupefaction, surprise, wonderment; admire, doubt, gape, marvel, ponder, query, stare. ANT.—commonness, familiarity, triviality; anticipation, apathy, expectation, indifference, stolidity; abhor, disregard, ignore, ridicule, scorn.

wordy, diffuse, digressive, long-winded, loquacious, prolix, rambling, redundant, talkative, verbose, voluble. ANT.—brief, concise, succinct, summary, terse.

work, accomplishment, achievement, action, business, calling, deed, drudgery, duty, effort, employment, exertion, function, job, labor, occupation, office, opus, performance, production, profession, pursuit, task, toil, travail; accomplish, achieve, act, control, do, form, function, labor, manage, operate, make, mold, react, serve, slave, strive, struggle, sweat, toil. ANT.— ease, idleness, leisure, recreation, relaxation; abandon, ignore, malfunction, mismanage, quit, rest.

working, see industrious; operative.

worldly, carnal, corporeal, earthly, irreligious, materialistic, mundane, opportunistic, practical, secular, sensual, temporal, terrestrial, ungodly. ANT.—exalted, incorporeal, intellectual, refined, spiritual.

worn, exhausted, faint, fatigued, jaded, shabby, spent, threadbare, tired, used, wasted, wearied, weary. ANT.—fresh, invigorated, new, rested, unused.

worry, agitation, anxiety, apprehension, care, concern, disquiet, doubt, fear, trouble, uneasiness; annoy, bother, disturb, gall, gnaw, harass, harry, haze, irritate, pain, persecute, pester, plague, tease, torment, torture, trouble, vex; fret, fume, fuss, grieve. ANT.—contentment, ease, peace, satisfaction, serenity; aid, comfort, please, soothe, support; enjoy, rejoice, relax, rest, unbend.

worship, honor, respect; see also idolize; reverence.

worth, advantage, benefit, estimation, price, usefulness, utility; see also merit.

worthless, barren, bootless, inane, insignificant, meritless, pointless, poor, profitless, unimportant, unproductive; see also futile.

worthy, charitable, creditable, decent, dependable, deserving, dutiful, exemplary, fit, good, honorable, incorrupt, incorruptible, meritorious, model, moral, noble, pure, reliable, reputable, righteous, suitable, trustworthy, virtuous, worthy. ANT.—corrupt, dishonorable, iniquitous, reprehensible, vicious, villainous.

wound, affront, dishonor, insult; disfigure, gash, scrape; see also abuse; hurt.

wrangle, affray, bickering, spat, squabble; see also dispute.

wrap, bundle, cloak, clothe, conceal, cover, curtain, disguise, enclose, enfold, envelop, furl, guard, hide, lap, mask, muffle, package, protect, roll, screen, shield, shroud, swathe, veil, wind; blanket, cape, cloak, coat, coverlet, overcoat, shawl. ANT.—bare, divulge, expose, open, reveal, unfold.

wrath, choler, irritation, petulance, provocation, tantrum; see also indignation.

wreck, annihilate, break, damage, demolish, destroy, devastate, eradicate, exterminate, extinguish, injure, obliterate, ravage, raze, ruin, shatter, smash; accident, crash, desolation, destruction, junk, litter, loss, perdition, shreds, smash, wreckage. ANT.—conserve, construct, establish, preserve, repair; gain, improvement, recovery, renewal, restoration.

wretched, see miserable.

write, compose, correspond, draft, draw, formulate, inscribe, pen, record, scrawl, scribble, sign, transcribe.

writer, author, biographer, calligrapher, composer, contributor, correspondent, creator, editor, essayist, father, inventor, journalist, maker, novelist, originator, playwright, poet, reporter, scribe, stenographer.

writing, calligraphy, composition, document, handwriting, inscription, manuscript, penmanship.

wrong, amiss, askew, awry, erroneous, fallacious, false, faulty, imprecise, inaccurate, incorrect, inexact, mistaken, untrue; improper, inappropriate, unsuitable; aberrant, abusive, bad, base, corrupt, criminal, cruel, evil, hurtful, immoral, indecent, iniquitous, injurious, malevolent, reprehensible, sinful, wicked. ANT.—accurate, correct, exact, precise, right; appropriate, becoming, fitting, proper, suitable; blameless, decent, ethical, honest, noble, virtuous.

X

xanthic, dusky, fulvous, saffron, swarthy, tawny, yellow, yellowish.

xerox, copy, ditto, duplicate, recreate, reproduce.

x-ray, radiant energy, radiation, radioactivity, radiograph, radium emanation, Roentgen ray.

xylography, woodcutting, woodengraving.

Y

yard, backyard, corral, court, courtyard, enclosure, garden, playground, terrace.

yardstick, criterion, gauge, measure, rule, ruler, standard, test, touchstone.

yearning, see wish.

yell, bawl, bellow, cry, howl, roar, scream, screech, shout, shriek, shrill, squall, squeal, vociferate, whoop, yelp.

yet, additionally, although, besides, but, despite, further, furthermore, hitherto, however, nevertheless, notwithstanding, now, still, though.

yield, crop, fruit, harvest, proceeds, produce, product, reaping, result, store; bear, breed, generate, impart, produce, supply; allow, bestow, concede, confer, grant, permit, sanction, tolerate; abdicate, accede, acquiesce, capitulate, cede, defer, quit, relent, relinquish, resign, submit, succumb, surrender, waive. ANT.—deny, forbid, oppose, prevent, refuse; assert, master, overcome, overpower, strive, struggle.

young, active, adolescent, blooming, budding, childish, childlike, fresh, green, growing, immature, inexperienced, juvenile, pubescent, puerile, strong, vibrant, vigorous, youthful.

ANT.—aged, ancient, elderly, experienced, mature, withered.

youthful, see young.

Z

zeal, activity, ardor, courage, dedication, determination, devotion, eagerness, energy, enthusiasm, excitement, fanaticism, fervency, fervor, inclination, industry, inspiration, intensity, intentness, involvement, passion, perseverance, vehemence, vigilance, warmth, willingness. ANT.—apathy, detachment, ennui, indifference, nonchalance.

zealot, adherent, bigot, devotee, dogmatist, dreamer, enthusiast, fanatic, martyr, opinionist, partisan, patriot, visionary. ANT.—dawdler, idler, shirker, slacker.

zealous, alert, animated, assiduous, brisk, bustling, diligent, fervid, fiery, hustling, indefatigable, passionate, resolute, sedulous, steadfast, vivacious. see also eager.

zenith, acme, apex, apogee, cap, climax, consummation, crest, crown, culmination, eminence, height, maximum, peak, pinnacle, pitch, summit, top. ANT.—base, bottom, floor, foundation, nadir.

zero, blank, cipher, naught, nil, nobody, nonentity, nothing, nullity, unreality, unsubstantiality. ANT.—corporeality, existence, matter, object, substance.

zest, ardor, delight, desire, energy, enhancement, enjoyment, enthusiasm, exhilaration, gusto, passion, pleasure, relish, spirit; flavor, piquancy, pungency, savor, savoriness, sharpness, tang, taste.

zigzag, askew, awry, bent, crinkled, crooked, curved, devious, diagonal, erratic, fluctuating, forked, inclined, indirect, jagged, meandering, oblique, oscillating, rambling, serrated, sinuous, sloping, spiral, straggling, transverse, twisted, undulatory, vibratory, waggling, wry. ANT.—direct, even, rectilinear, straight, unbent.

zone, area, band, belt, circuit, climate, commune, district, dominion, enclosure, ground, latitude, locality, location, locus, meridian, precinct, quarter, region, section, sector, segment, site, terrain, territory, tract, ward.

<u>NOTES</u>

<u>NOTES</u>

NOTES

NOTES

NOTES

NOTES

NOTES